David Power Conyngham

Sherman's March Through the South

David Power Conyngham

Sherman's March Through the South

ISBN/EAN: 9783744759069

Printed in Europe, USA, Canada, Australia, Japan

Cover: Foto ©ninafisch / pixelio.de

More available books at **www.hansebooks.com**

SHERMAN'S

MARCH THROUGH THE SOUTH.

WITH

Sketches and Incidents of the Campaign.

BY

CAPT. DAVID P. CONYNGHAM.

NEW YORK:
SHELDON AND COMPANY.
1865.

Entered, according to Act of Congress, in the year 1865, by
DAVID P. CONYNGHAM,
In the Clerk's Office of the District Court of the Southern District of New York.

STEREOTYPED AT THE
BOSTON STEREOTYPE FOUNDRY,
No. 4 Spring Lane.

TO

JAMES GORDON BENNETT, ESQ.,

EDITOR NEW YORK HERALD.

DEAR SIR:

My connection with the Herald, as a member of that large and energetic corps of War Correspondents which you established at the commencement of the Rebellion, has afforded me the opportunity of collecting the valuable historical materials which are laid before the public in the following pages. With feelings of pride and pleasure, I avail myself of your kind permission to dedicate this work to one who is justly esteemed the NESTOR OF JOURNALISM IN THIS COUNTRY.

Respectfully,

Your ob't serv't,

THE AUTHOR.

NEW YORK, *Sept.* 10, 1865.

INTRODUCTION.

The Campaign of GENERAL SHERMAN in the West and South, which is treated of in the following pages, will be accorded a place in history as the most important of the entire war. While the brilliant achievements of the armies of the Potomac and the James around Richmond contributed materially to the final success of the national cause, the military operations inaugurated at Chattanooga, and brought to a triumphant end in South Carolina, comprised a vital part of the grand plan for the suppression of the rebellion — a plan conceived in consummate wisdom, and executed with a boldness and precision wholly unprecedented in military history. We know of no single instance of two great armies, a thousand miles apart, acting in such perfect concert, with a view to attain one end, and accomplishing the purpose so completely, as did the army of the Potomac and the army of the West. The abandonment of Richmond, the surrender of Lee's army, and the subsequent inevitable submission of General Johnston were the results of their combined operations.

It might almost be said that while the left wing of the national army under Grant was threatening Petersburg and Richmond, the right wing, under Sherman, was sweeping round on the flanks of the rebellion, and enclosing it in a net from which escape was impossible.

At the time when Sherman was known to be on his venturesome march to the sea, it was a matter of speculation in the public mind as to whether the capture of Richmond would fall to his lot, or that of the general who was besieging it. It was subsequently proved by the result, and admitted by the southern generals, that Sherman's bold move through Georgia and the Carolinas cut off all chance of the rebellion being maintained longer. It is not assigning undue importance, then, to "Sherman's March through the South," to say that it was the most decisive campaign of the war.

The author of the following pages, having acted in the capacity of army correspondent of the NEW YORK HERALD with the army of the Potomac during the latter part of the campaign which ended at Mine Run; joined General Sherman's army at Chattanooga in March, 1864, and served all through his brilliant campaigns, as volunteer aid-de-camp and war correspondent.

The instructions of the HERALD to its army correspondents were brief, but comprehensive. They were simply these: To obtain the most accurate information by personal observation, and forward it with the utmost despatch, regardless of expense, labor, or danger. Guided by these concise instructions,—with his horse, his revolver, his field-glass, his note-book, blanket, and haversack,—the army correspondent of the NEW YORK HERALD started forth to share the vicissitudes and hardships of the camp, the fatigues of the march, and the perils of the battle-field, to contribute his narrative to the history of the great war.

It was thus that the materials for the present work were collected. The writer was an eye-witness of all the battles, and most of the incidents, described; and he may claim for the work, at least, the merit of strict fidelity to truth. As it is no part of his design to give a partial view of anything that transpired during the eventful period over which the story runs, he has chronicled the facts as they occurred, without detraction or exaggeration, believing this to be the duty of the historian.

The condition of the southern people, and the workings of the now extinct institution of slavery, were but little understood in the north before the late war called so many of its citizen-soldiers to the south. As frequent opportunities of obtaining information upon these subjects necessarily came within the reach of the writer, several faithful, and, he trusts, not uninteresting, pictures of social relations in the Southern States will be found in this volume.

DAVID P. CONYNGHAM.

NEW YORK, September 10, 1865.

CONTENTS.

CHAPTER I.

En Route to General Grant's Army of the West. — Scenes and Stories in Louisville. — Romantic History of "Stud Reynolds." — Colonel Scully. — The Defences of Nashville. 11

CHAPTER II.

Sketch of Tennessee. — Lookout Mountain. — The Battle of Chickamauga. — The Camp Breakfast. — The dead Captain. — His blighted Love. 20

CHAPTER III.

Opening of the Campaign of 1864. — Disposition of the Armies. — Awful Condition of the People in Tennessee. — Battle of Rocky Face Ridge. . . . 28

CHAPTER IV.

Headquarters of the Generals. — Sufferings of the Wounded. — The Enemy's Position at Resaca. 40

CHAPTER V.

Sketches of our Generals. — Personnel of Sherman, Thomas, Schofield, Hooker, McPherson, Logan, and Geary. 48

CHAPTER VI.

Battle of Resaca. — What it cost to take two Guns. — Terrible Scenes on the Battle-field. — Our Losses. 56

CHAPTER VII.

The Pursuit. — Our Army cross the River on Pontoons and Bridges. — Capture of a Rebel Courier. — A good Trick of General Thomas. — Splendid Achievement of General Sweeny. — Storming the Heights at Snake Creek. — Deeds of individual Valor. — Sherman and the Lone Widow. — A Coup d'Œil from Buena Vista. — Description of the Country. — Troubles of the Correspondents. — Personal Anecdotes of Sherman. 66

CHAPTER VIII.

A Carnival in the Camps. — Racing and Hunting Parties. — Stragglers and Marauders. — Excesses of our Troops. — Murder of Rebel Officers. — Capriciousness of the Southern Ladies. — Mrs. Major Dash and Mrs. Captain Smart. — Condition of the Poor Whites. — Incidents and Anecdotes. — Whites and Blacks, ... 78

CHAPTER IX.

Scenes in Camp. — Stories by the Fireside. — How an Illinois Man sold a Horse. — The Double-ender Gun. — Misery of the People. — The Hiding-place in the Thicket, and the dead Girl. 90

CHAPTER X.

Assaults and Skirmishes near Dallas and Allatoona. — Wood's Division storming the Hill. — Cleburne's Rebel Division drive them back. — Gallant Attack of General T. W. Sweeny. — Kenesaw Mountain. — General Frank P. Blair arrives. — Personal Risks of our Generals. — Sherman shelling a Skulker. — Attack on a Train, and its Consequences. 99

CHAPTER XI.

Kenesaw Mountain. — Sherman commands a Battery. — Death of Bishop Polk. — The March through the Mountain Passes. — Sherman's steam Scout. — A friendly Visit, and its Consequences, ... 111

CHAPTER XII.

A Chapter of Fighting. — Johnston addresses false Words to his Men. — A Disappointment to the Rebels. — Battle of Culp's Farm. — Death of General Harker. — Hibernian Anecdote. 120

CHAPTER XIII.

Kenesaw. — Crossing the Chattahoochee. — Sherman outwits and outflanks Johnson. — First Sight of Atlanta. — Cruelty of the Slave Dealers. — The Story of the Negro Ostin. 141

CHAPTER XIV.

Our Cavalry at Work. — Hood replaces Johnston. — Their Tactics compared. — The Battle of Peach-tree Creek. — Atlanta surrounded. 154

CHAPTER XV.

Battle of the 22d July. — Death of General McPherson. — His Life and Services. — Scenes among the Dead and Wounded. 167

CHAPTER XVI.

Unsuccessful Cavalry Raids of McCook and Stoneman.—Change of Commanders.—Howard's Appointment and Hooker's Resignation.—The Battle of Proctor's Creek. 181

CHAPTER XVII.

Shelling Atlanta.—A Scout's Experience of Hanging.—The Lady Major. . 192

CHAPTER XVIII.

The Siege continued.—Sharpshooters fraternizing.—A Military Game of Chess between Sherman and Hood.—Sherman wins the Game, and Atlanta too.—Cavalry Raids of Kilpatrick and Wheeler.—The decisive Battle of Jonesboro'.—Atlanta occupied by our Troops. 198

CHAPTER XIX.

Atlanta ours.—Sherman's Entrance.—Feeling of the Citizens.—Sketch of the City.—Buried alive in a Bomb Proof.—The Citizens sent north and south.—An inhuman Fiend. 213

CHAPTER XX.

A new Campaign.—Battle of Allatoona.—Sherman signalling from Kenesaw Mountain.—Who planned the Campaign and March through Georgia, Sherman or Grant?—The Conflagration of Atlanta. 227

CHAPTER XXI.

The March to the Sea commences.—How the Army supplied itself.—Sherman among his Men.—Sack of Madison.—Negro Auxiliaries.—Farm-yard and Plantation Scenes. 239

CHAPTER XXII.

The Army in Milledgeville.—Flight of the Government and Legislature.—A mock Session in the Capitol.—Our Cavalry Movements.—The Jew and the General.—The Way Sherman's Army lived on the Country. . . . 253

CHAPTER XXIII.

Howell Cobb's fast Mare.—Joe, the Forager.—Contrabands.—Capture of Fort McAllister. 270

CHAPTER XXIV.

Evacuation of Savannah.—Surrender to General Geary.—His just and conciliatory Government.—Description of the City. 289

CHAPTER XXV.

The March into South Carolina. — Bummers. — Shooting Bloodhounds. — The Pets of the Army. 300

CHAPTER XXVI.

Description and Appearance of South Carolina. — Visit to Woodlands. . . 318

CHAPTER XXVII.

Description of Columbia. — The City on Fire. — Dreadful Scenes in the Streets. — Who is responsible. — Sufferings of the Planters' Families. 329

CHAPTER XXVIII.

Cheraw. — Crossing the Pedee. — Kilpatrick's Fight with Wade Hampton. — Fayetteville. — Communication with the Seaboard. 350

CHAPTER XXIX.

The Battles of Averysboro' and Bentonville. — News of Lee's Surrender. — Interview between Sherman and Johnston. — Homeward Bound. . . . 360

APPENDIX.

I. SKETCH OF THE LIFE OF GENERAL SHERMAN. 367

II. ORGANIZATION OF GENERAL SHERMAN'S STAFF AND ARMY. . . 382

III. THE SURRENDER AND PAROLE OF GENERAL JOHNSTON'S ARMY. . 384

IV. GENERAL SHERMAN'S TESTIMONY BEFORE THE COMMITTEE ON THE WAR. 394

V. SPEECH OF GENERAL SHERMAN AT ST. LOUIS. 427

GENERAL SHERMAN'S

MARCH THROUGH THE SOUTH.

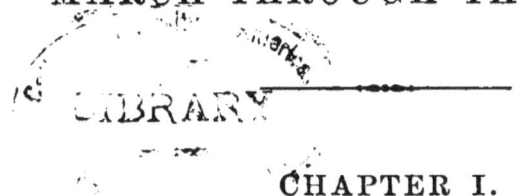

CHAPTER I.

EN ROUTE TO GENERAL GRANT'S ARMY OF THE WEST.—SCENES AND STORIES IN LOUISVILLE.—ROMANTIC HISTORY OF "STUD REYNOLDS."—COLONEL SCULLY.—THE DEFENCES OF NASHVILLE.

IN the spring of 1864 I started to join General Grant's army in the West, which then lay cantoned around Huntsville, Chattanooga, and Knoxville. My connection with the army was that of a war correspondent — a position which I had previously filled with the grand army of the Potomac.

Arriving at Louisville, the military system of passports began to stare me in the face; but having a letter from General Burnside to General Schofield, then in command at Knoxville, I was proof against the repeated and inexorable demand of "Your pass, sir."

At Louisville I put up at the Gault House, and, of course, was shown the very spot where General Jeff C. Davis (not the rebel Jeff, but the Union general) shot General Nelson. This was a very prolific subject for the guests. As a *dernier ressort* I have always found it on the table. It appeared to be part and parcel of the dessert, and led to strong debates, some justifying and some censuring the act. One thing was certain — that Nelson, though a thorough soldier and stanch Union man, was a blustering, insolent naval martinet. At Stone River he performed the most heroic acts of valor and savage acts of cruelty. His bravery is respected; but he atoned for his insolence by his life.

The hotel was pretty full of officers; some, who were on duty in the city, gayly strutting about in all the pomp of power; others, less demonstrative, were hastening to the front to join their commands, for the spring campaign was expected soon to open. Vast preparations in the way of hurrying supplies to the front were being made, and all officers were ordered to join their commands at once.

General Grant had just been appointed lieutenant general and commander-in-chief of the armies of the United States, and General Sherman had been appointed his successor as commander of the division of the Mississippi. Officers lolled around, some smoking their cigars, some enjoying the fragrance of a meerschaum; but with all the war was a prolific subject, and grave battles and guerilla adventures were discussed and related.

"They counted Sherman crazy," said a little fiery captain with an ugly scar on his face, "because he could see farther than others. He said that it would take two hundred thousand men to crush out the war in the south-west; but I ask you who was right?" continued the captain, taking his cigar from his mouth, and looking around him to see if any one questioned his assertion.

"And didn't he come up in time by a rapid march from the Mississippi to relieve Chattanooga, and make Longstreet clear out from Knoxville?" said another officer, approvingly.

"I tell you what, gentlemen," said a gay, handsome-looking young colonel. "Only for Governor Johnson we would not have much to fight for here; for when Buell thought to evacuate Nashville, Andy Johnson insisted on retaining it; and after Buell had drawn off his troops, he still retained it with what available militia he could muster. I command his body-guard, the 10th Tennessee; and I tell you, the rage and despair of the governor at the idea of evacuating Nashville was a caution to rebels. 'Colonel Scully,' he said, 'While we have one man left we must hold Nashville.'"

"And old Andy did it, too," said a long Tennesseean captain, who wore a slouched hat, long boots with pants stuck inside them, and had altogether the negligent air of a man ready and willing to carry on war on his own account, as well as Uncle Sam's.

I have remarked that the Kentuckian and Tennesseean troops and officers have been superior skirmishers and scouts, while they possess a strong repugnance to regular drill and discipline. This is partly owing to their training at the beginning of the war, and how much each man depended on self-reliance and pluck. When the gallows was the reward of loyalty in Tennessee, each man lived in fear of his neighbor, and slept with his bowie knife and revolver under his head. Brother's hand was raised against brother's, and the rebels, while in the ascendancy, used their power with merciless cruelty, while the Union men retaliated, exacting blood for blood. Thus was Tennessee converted into one vast battle ground, not only by contending armies, but also by private factions and individuals.

Every county, town, and almost every hamlet has been the scene of some fierce struggle, bloody drama, or savage murder. Towns and villages were laid waste, homesteads desolated, nothing remaining but blackened ruins and red graves to tell their bloody history.

Fire-eating politicians, and ranting preachers, whose mission was not from above, "fired the southern heart" of the poor white trash with a fanaticism that made them savagely thirst for the blood of their nearest neighbor.

Despite such terrors, despite death, there were found brave, uncompromising men, whose creed was the union of their country, and whose faith in the right never faltered, though hunted down by Vigilance Committees and bloodthirsty guerrillas. Though they saw their friends dangle from some tree, their homes in ruins, their families poor wandering outcasts, or perhaps laid in some bloody grave, still they never yielded to seduction or force. "God and their Country," was their motto.

Never has a nobler heroism been displayed, nor a truer national devotion, than by the faithful people of East Tennessee.

It was worthy the days of William Tell. History will speak of them with admiration; romance and poetry will couple their names with the deeds of heroes, and unborn generations will crown their praise.

"I tell you what, colonel," said the tall, gaunt captain, "Andy Johnson is a trump!" and the captain struck the table with his clinched hand by way of emphasis. "I know him well, — I hail from near Greenville, and was raised just beside him, — his firmness and determination to all the small-souled, blue-blasted Secesh around. Only for him we could scarcely maintain the unequal contest, when the devils were hanging and butchering men, women, and children. But didn't we pay them, eh, colonel?" and he addressed himself to a middle-aged man with sharp features and quick eye, who sat beside him.

The colonel was dressed as if he had thrown on his clothes in a hurry, and had not had time to button them. As he wore no insignia of rank, we were rather incredulous whether he addressed him so in joke or according to rank.

As the colonel replied only with a nod of acquiescence, I asked, —

"You don't mean to say, friend, that they killed women and children?"

"Don't I, though," and he squirted a volume of tobacco juice across me. "Reckon, stranger, you were never up in Tennessee, about our 'ere part."

"Never," I replied.

"Well, if business let you, go there, and jist ask the people there, and in the few gibbets you'll see the Secesh receipt for making rebels; that's all. At Knoxville they hung poor old Harman and his boy, and dragged Haun from his young wife and babe. Scarcely a day passed but some one was strangled amidst the curses and jeers of as drunken a set of ruffians as ever graced hell.

"In Jefferson County, Colonel Leadbetter, who was a southern Yankee, a Maine man, and as unprincipled a ruffian as ever butchered a helpless prisoner, hung Fry and Henry from the limb of a tree so close to the track that the passengers could kick and strike them, which they did even while the breath was in them.

"I had a taste of their mercy myself. I was in that dirty jail up in Knoxville, and was thrown into an iron cage, with vermin and filth for my companions, because I shot the leader of a cut-throat gang who attacked my house. I had too many friends to hang me; so they sent me with another batch off for Tuscaloosa, with the intention of killing us on the way. Beyond Athens they stopped the train, and ordered us out into the woods to rest; we knew what that rest meant, I tell you. As soon as we got out, I called out, 'Boys, they are going to shoot us; let us fight, and not die like dogs.' I struck the man near me, seized his musket, shot down another, and in the confusion darted through the woods.

"That little band fought like devils; but they were all killed except myself and three others. We escaped, Heaven knows how.

"I had my revenge. A few months since we captured a body of guerrillas near Cumberland Gap; and among them I recognized my former captors. Well, I forgot to turn over that eleven men."

"I reckon, cap, you gave them close quarters."

"As close as you, col; and that was too close for their friends to find them."

"Mercy," I exclaimed, "you didn't murder them!"

"Well, I gave them in charge to the sergeant, who was one of those that escaped with me. He says they escaped; any way, they were never seen afterwards; Stud Reynolds always forgets to bring in his prisoners."

"Who is this Stud Reynolds?" I asked; "short as I have been in this region I have heard much of his daring exploits."

"I guess you look upon him as a regular raw head and bloody bones," said the captain, nodding at the little colonel.

"I have heard much of his cruelty and desperation; he must have suffered terribly to be such a bloodthirsty persecutor of the rebels."

"Guess he has," said the captain, standing up and laying his hand upon my shoulder, as he shot a squirt of juice over my head. "Look you here, stranger."

I looked into his face. There was a savage earnestness in the compressed lips and glaring eyes that almost made me quail.

"Look here;" and he tightened his grasp like a vice.

"Tell me, stranger, if you had a kind wife and fair daughter, wouldn't you love them?"

"Certainly."

"It's but human natur. Well! Stud Reynolds had a wife, a good woman; he had a daughter, as fair and gentle a girl as ever blessed a parent's care. Stud loved them; that was nat'ral; wasn't it? Because Stud was a Union man, he had to sleep out in the woods, little dreaming that the foul fiends would injure his innocent ones.

"One night a pack of those hell-hounds came to his house. The leader of that gang was a rejected suitor of Miss Reynolds. He asked the girl that night to elope with him, or he would hunt down her father like a coon, and bring dishonor and shame upon herself. Her reply was, 'You are a bad man. I could never love you; besides, I am the promised wife of another.'

"Brave, noble girl! The devils tore her out of the house; and because her mother clung to her to save her, a devil — a fiend of hell — shot her through the breast, and then hurried the insensible girl, with her mother's hot blood spattered over her, into the woods.

"The father returned home to find his house burned down, the body of his wife in ashes, and his outraged daughter a maniac."

While the captain was speaking, the colonel clapped his hands to his face, and wept.

"That man"—and he pointed to the colonel—"is Stud Reynolds, and I was to be the husband of that girl. Do you wonder, then, what we do?"

"O, it is fearful."

"Yes, it is; but who began it? We have dogged and tracked every one of these fiends. We have made their lives a hell, and their death a torture. I have tied the arch devil himself to a tree, and lit slow fagots around him, while the men made a target of his body, at long range, and a bonfire of his house. It was the death of a dog, and such he got."

So that quaint little man beside me was the notorious Stud Reynolds — the Jibberryssee of Tennessee, whose name was a terror to guerrillas, — who stealthily stole on them in their houses and in their camps, and whose knife pierced their hearts as they slept around the watch-fire.

No doubt his provocation was great.

A few weeks afterwards I met him in Knoxville. He was just after capturing the infamous guerrilla Captain Reynolds. I was paying a visit to Governor Johnson. I think it was at Horace Maynard's house. Colonel Reynolds, or, as he is more familiarly called, Stud, came in to report progress.

"So, colonel," said the governor, "you have captured Reynolds?"

"I reckon so, governor. He is caged."

"Well, colonel, it is not true, after all, that you never take a prisoner, as is said of you."

"Couldn't help it, governor;" and Stud held down his head, as if ashamed of this act of clemency. "I'll tell you how it was. You see, I knew where they were, and that they had their horses tied near a shanty, where they were having a big time of it, with a barrel of rotgut, and a dance with the girls. I surrounded the horses, knowing that they would run for them. As soon as they got the alarm, they rushed for the horses, and bang we slapped into them, turning up their heels. Captain Reynolds, the cowardly skunk, hid behind a log, where some of my men took him prisoner; and as they did not wish to shoot him, and a crowd had collected, I thought it was as well to cage him. I assure you it wasn't my fault, governor;" and Stud looked as if such an unusual act of mercy was a reproach on him.

"Well, well; colonel, it is well to get rid of these cutthroat guerrilla scoundrels; but it is not right nor soldierly to shoot a prisoner, no matter how great the provocation."

Stud looked a little abashed; but I could plainly see that he did not coincide with the governor.

2 *

"And are such acts of barbarous cruelty and savage retaliation committed here?" I asked of Colonel Scully, as we steamed next day for Nashville.

"Undoubtedly, sir. I have often heard of Stud Reynolds's story; but scenes as bad are every day being enacted under my own eyes, and we are powerless to prevent them. The country is infested with guerrilla bands, who keep out of the reach of our troops, but then murder and pillage all before them. We sometimes make fearful retaliations, and I am afraid the innocent too often suffer with the guilty. Lately, my major's father, a Dr. Moore, was savagely butchered in his house by these ruffians. The major took out a squad of men to scour the country for them. They shot several men against whom they had information. I am afraid guilty parties themselves too often give information against loyal men, and some are too apt to act upon it."

"Then you think innocent men are often shot down by their own party?"

"I fear so."

"It is a sad state of things when society is so disruptured."

"We have no society here. At the inception of the rebellion, the Union and Secesh parties were nearly balanced in Eastern Tennessee. The Secesh party took the initiative, and shot down their Union neighbors in order to intimidate the rest. A reign of terror followed, in comparison to which the Bastile, and all the horrors of the French revolution, were mild. The Union party soon recovered themselves, and retaliated with a vengeance, imbittered by former sufferings."

"What do you think of slavery in Tennessee, colonel?"

"It is already dead, sir. Nothing can galvanize its corpse. It was a deadly disease. I came down here with pretty strong slavery proclivities, until I saw its workings, its debasing nature even on the whites themselves. I now abhor it as a damnable institution. Only a few weeks since, a case occurred in the street where I lived that sickened me with slavery. A lady had a slave, a pretty mulatto woman, of about thirty years. This woman had a smart, intelligent child, of about eight years. The mistress had sold the boy to a trader from Alabama, though her own blood and the blood of a distinguished senator flowed in that boy's veins. Chloe wept, and besought the mistress not to separate them, — to keep both or sell both. It was no use. At night Chloe and the boy were missing, and, on searching an outhouse, were found dead, with both their throats cut. Such are the blessed effects of slavery."

The colonel kindly invited me to his quarters in Nashville. This gave me an opportunity of inspecting all the forts and works around the city.

The colonel's regiment, 10th Tennessee, was a splendid body of troops, and nearly one thousand strong. I have often seen them drilled and reviewed, and I am not surprised that Governor Johnson felt so proud of his fine-looking body-guard.

The chief works about Nashville are Fort Gillem, called after General Gillem (it was designed and garrisoned by my friend Colonel Scully; it has embrasures for seven field-pieces and six light guns); Fort Morton, called after Brigadier General Morton, who was killed at Petersburg, mounts thirty guns, commanding the Franklin and Hillsboro' pikes; Fort Negly, after Major General Negly, who, at one time, commanded the post of Nashville; Fort Cassina, on College Hill; Fort Houston, after Mr. Russell Houston, a thorough Union man. He owned the site, and some rebel, taunting him, said, —

"See what your friends are doing — tearing down your house to build a fort!"

"Let them. If the Confederacy succeed, I don't want the house; if the Federals win, they will build me a better one."

Another work was Fort Andrew Johnson, on Capitol Hill, so called in honor of the governor, now President Johnson. In addition to these, there were several redoubts, batteries, and minor forts, making Nashville a strongly fortified city. So Hood found it when he rashly butted up his troops against it. In a few days I left for Chattanooga. The road along was guarded by posts and strong stockades, and appeared flanked by broken locomotives, wagons, and cars, the joint work of guerrillas and frequent railroad accidents.

CHAPTER II.

SKETCH OF TENNESSEE.—LOOKOUT MOUNTAIN.—THE BATTLE OF CHICKAMAUGA.—THE CAMP BREAKFAST.—THE DEAD CAPTAIN.—HIS BLIGHTED LOVE.

THE State of Tennessee was first settled by a party of adventurers from North Carolina, who built a fort at Loudon, in 1757, to protect themselves from the Indians, different tribes of whom occupied the fertile region of country along the Tennessee and Holston Rivers, extending back as far as the mountain borders of Carolina. Of these the Cherokees were the most powerful and numerous tribe. Our border states, such as Kentucky and Tennessee, were harassed by the Indian tribes, and the settlers embroiled in continual and bloody struggles with their savage neighbors.

The first colony at Fort Loudon were soon expelled, or butchered by their merciless foes. Despite all this, the forest gave way to the axe of the sturdy pioneer, and hamlets and towns soon dotted the landscape.

In 1796 Tennessee was admitted into the Union as a state. Several of her children figured in the war of independence, and she played a very honorable part in the war of 1812.

The landscape and scenery of Tennessee are magnificently grand, and need but be known to entitle her to the privilege of being called "The Switzerland of America." The Cumberland Hills rise to an elevation of almost two thousand feet. Their appearance forms a striking feature in the beauty of the landscape, their shaggy sides bristling with forest trees, while the granite and marble peaks and cliffs glitter in the sunshine like sparkling diamonds.

In the valleys below, the mighty Tennessee River winds its

way through fertile plains, through rich plantations, through wild forests, and bold, towering rocks, from its source in Virginia, cradled among the Alleghanies ; through the State of Tennessee, among the Cumberland Mountains; through the cotton plantations of Alabama; through the rich fields of Kentucky, until it rests in the bosom of the mighty Mississippi at Paducah.

Tennessee has rich mineral products, such as coal, iron, copper, and even gold; and at no very distant day she is destined to become one of the leading states of the Union. She cannot help it.

With a salubrious climate, a soil of unbounded fertility, immense water power, great, though undeveloped, mineral resources, — such is her inevitable destiny

From the summit of Lookout Mountain what a magnificent panoramic view is presented ! Beneath your feet lies the scattered and rather dirty little town of Chattanooga, a place almost unknown before, but rendered memorable now. As far as the eye can reach, flows the magnificent Tennessee, with its wooded banks, its bold, rocky cliffs. Stately and grandly it winds in serpentine bends, sparkling, as we now see it, beneath the rays of a bright sun.

A rich valley, miles in length, open to your view, bounded by Mission Ridge, with its woody crest, recalling some proud recollections of victory, and Chickamauga, with its dark record of defeat and disaster.

From this point I could trace the path and dark ravines through which Cross's regiment of East Tennesseans crawled down the mountain to give way to a rebel gun which was placed on the very crest of the towering rock, looking down with its brazen throat on the devoted town, camps, and intrenchments of the Federal lines.

The battle of Chickamauga, though one of the most desperate struggles of the western campaign, was one of the most disastrous. For three long days, against heavy odds, the Federal troops fought with dogged desperation. At length, overpowered and defeated, they fell back to Chattanooga, where they strongly intrenched themselves. The defeat might have been disastrous, had not the cool courage and military genius of one man saved the army, perhaps the nation. That man was General Thomas. The same imperturbable leader cleared the road for Sherman's sweeping raid; for had Hood captured Nashville, Sherman's raid would avail nothing. Thomas very quietly laid his plans, and caught the impulsive Hood in his meshes.

The battle of Chickamauga was fought between a creek of that name and Pea Vine Creek, and about eight miles west of Ringgold. The battle-field extended about ten miles. I have been informed by a spectator, who had been through most of our great battles, that on that terrible Sunday night, September 20, 1862, the field presented one of the most fearful, ghastly sights of all war's sad pictures.

"On the morning of the 18th," said my friend, who was an *attaché* of the press, "I had a hurried breakfast with some officers of McCook's staff. We could distinctly hear the picket firing with a scattered artillery fire. It was evident that the battle had commenced. Aids were riding to and fro, and columns of troops were slowly and steadily advancing to the front. A young, bright-eyed, fair-haired captain, named Stenton, looked after them, sighed, and remarked, 'Do you know, but it makes me feel bad when I see all these brave fellows advancing in proud, serried lines, and then — what a mass of crushed and torn humanity they will be before night!' 'Pshaw! Stenton,' said a dashing young major, 'don't be scaring us with such gloomy pictures; the dose is bad enough, man, without making us taste it beforehand.'

"'Stenton appears gloomy,' said another; 'I guess his ladylove has jilted him. Cheer up, Stenton, old boy!'

"'Well, I confess,' replied Stenton, affecting a laugh, 'I feel somehow depressed. I suppose, gentlemen, I need not say to you, who know me so well, that it is not fear.'

"'Certainly not, old boy! But here comes the general; let us get ready to mount.'

"On Sunday night," continued my friend, "I rode over a

part of the battle-field. The pale moonbeams glittered on the ghastly faces of the dead, with their glassy eyeballs turned towards the heavens, and their frames distorted into every conceivable posture. The ground was piled with dead, dying, and wounded — men and horses. Small arms were strewn around; broken artillery carriages and caissons made up the desolating picture. I was passing near a creek when my horse shied at some bodies that blocked up the stream. I pressed him over, but he still snorted, and refused to advance. I heard a feeble voice call to me from among the mangled pile of dead and wounded. 'Mr. ——, take me out of this,' groaned the voice. I removed two or three bodies from a young officer; his dress and hair were so covered with dirt and puddle that at first I did not recognize him.

"I dragged him out, and laid him on the bank, and gave him a drink from a flask of brandy which I carried.

"This revived him. He opened his eyes and looked at me. 'Mr. ——,' says he, 'I am dying.' As soon as he spoke I recognized my young friend, Captain Stenton.

"'Stenton,' I exclaimed, 'my dear friend, I fear you are; but what's to be done? The troops are retreating; we can't remain here.' 'I know that; leave me here; but take these and send them as directed;' and he pulled two letters and a locket from his breast. 'Send these letters; one is for my dear mother, the other is for one I loved with a hopeful, boyish love; but it was but a dream! For their sakes I would like to live; but then, my country called me, and I gladly resign my life for her sake.'

"He pressed the blood-dyed locket to his lips, and remained silent for some time. I lifted his head; he was breathing heavily, a bullet having passed right through his lungs. He opened his eyes and murmured, 'Won't you send them? and bury me with this locket on my breast. How I loved her, and my dear mother! Tell them so. I knew I'd fall to-day; something told me so; so I had these letters written beforehand.' Again he tried to raise himself, and said, 'I hear the noise of artillery and troops passing: who are they?'

"'Ours retreating.'

"'Too bad, too bad: and for this we died! Go, my friend, and leave me.'

"'I do not like to leave you behind me: do you think you could bear being removed?'

"'I'd sooner, I'd sooner: then I'd be buried with this on my breast; and he pressed the locket to his lips.'

"Wagons, ambulances, caissons, and artillery were by this time hurrying by in mad confusion. I tried to stop the ambulances; but they were all full, and the drivers too excited to stop. At length a caisson stuck in the heavy road. By bribes and entreaties I induced the driver to take poor Stenton on the box. I tenderly placed him on it, wraping my poncho around him, and made two of the men sit beside him to keep him steady. I then mounted and rode after them.

"As we approached the main road the confusion was intense, — drivers swearing, ambulances and wagons striking against one another, officers and men hurrying to the rear. To heighten this confusion an occasional shell burst near us, and there was a general cry that the rebels were pursuing. It was one of those scenes common to the retreat of a discomfited army. Beside the narrow road I noticed a dead horse, with his feet ground off by the wheels of the passing wagons. An officer's uniform between his feet drew my attention. I dismounted, and found the legs of a man beside the horse's, crushed and broken from the same cause.

"I succeeded in pulling him out; but he was dead. As I could find no wounds upon him, he must have been caught by his fallen horse, whose head was knocked off by a round shot, and smothered and crushed to death. I at once recognized him: it was the young major of the morning. After laying his body beside a tree, I mounted and rode after my friend. When I came up I found that the men had left the box, scared by the shells, and the driver was swearing and whipping his jaded horses for bare life. The captain was dead: his head hung over the box, and was crushed against the wheel. His light golden hair hung down, clotted with gore oozing from his dripping wounds and crushed head.

"He was dead. I could do nothing for him. I laid his body, with the locket over his heart, to rest beside many a brother officer who had fallen upon that bloody field.

"I sent the letters to that dear mother, who wept for her faired-haired young soldier boy, and to that loved young heart whose warm impulses and cherished hopes were so rudely blighted."

This was the story my friend told me of Chattanooga, as we sat together on Lookout Mountain and viewed with our glasses the surrounding country, which appeared torn, and gutted, and ridged by contending armies.

"Where we sit now," said my friend, "is near two thousand feet high; and yonder is Missionary Ridge, from where the rebels dated their despatches while besieging Chattanooga; it is one thousand feet high. As you see, Chattanooga is in a deep basin, completely surrounded by hills and the Tennessee River. From this point, in a clear atmosphere, you can see the mountains of four states, though the Blue Ridge of North Carolina and the mountains of Alabama are near sixty miles away. The ascent from Chattanooga is by a winding road that twines round the hill to its highest point, one mile to the rear of Lookout Point. On the summit of the hill is a pleasant little village called Summertown, a favorite resort for invalids, who there seek shelter from the intense heat and malarious effects of the low grounds.

"This pile of rocks, where we sit, and which looks something like an old *Cromlech* or Druid's altar, so often found in England and Ireland, is Lookout Point. It is a glorious spot, as much from its locality as its memories. And when bronze statues will have lost the story that made them historic, and history itself will have become almost merged into fable, that mountain will stand forth as a monument of the heroism of the men that could climb such a hill in the face of plunging round shot and bullets, and the iron hosts that crowned them.

"Men will say that there were giants in those days; and so there were, if not in body, at least in invincible courage. If I had my will to affix a name to this mountain, I would rebaptize it. I would call this rough-jointed pile of rocks Hooker's Point; and as for the valley beneath us, where General Geary rallied his troops for the final charge, I would call that Geary's Valley. Neither title would be inappropriate.

"It was a glorious victory for Hooker. Fresh from the army of the Potomac, he had a new field to operate in, new victories to gain and a late disaster to retrieve, and nobly did he succeed. We have heard of Hooker's battle in the clouds. It is true that a dense fog obscured the plains and valley, and that the ringing minie bullet and plunging shot of the rebel batteries came whistling and hurtling through dense fogs and obscure clouds that shut out the mountain top from our view.

"I will tell you about Chattanooga. The rebels at once saw its advantage as a grand strategic point, and consequently one of their earliest military movements was to occupy and fortify it.

"For two years they stoutly held it as a pivot for their depredatory army which radiated to Tennessee, Georgia, and Alabama. At length they were forced to give it up to Rosecrans, with his army of the Cumberland, which entered Chattanooga on the 7th September, 1863.

"Bragg, finding himself outnumbered and outmanœuvred, was forced to evacuate. The army of the Cumberland was reënforced by the 11th and 12th corps, under Major General Hooker, which, afterwards consolidated, formed the 20th corps.

"Hooker's first appearance on the western battle-ground was by a night attack on Brown's Ferry, two miles from Chattanooga, in which he was remarkably successful.

"He followed this up by driving the enemy from Raccoon Mountain and Lookout Valley, which gave us the initiative, and might be put down as a set-off against Chickamauga. We soon obtained possession of the railroad between Chattanooga and Bridgeport, secured our supplies, and only needed the possession of Lookout Mountain and Mission Ridge to give us a secure base to commence the campaign of 1864.

"I have said that this point should be called after Hooker. I also state that Missionary Ridge should be called Sherman's

Ridge; for there, with his brave 15th corps, with which, wearied, exhausted, and prostrated, as it was, with a march of several hundred miles, he met the repeated assaults of the enemy, and finally overcame them. I say it should be called 'Sherman's Ridge.'

"The battle of Ringgold concluded the campaign of 1863."

CHAPTER III.

OPENING OF THE CAMPAIGN OF 1864.—DISPOSITION OF THE ARMIES.—AWFUL CONDITION OF THE PEOPLE IN TENNESSEE.—BATTLE OF ROCKY FACE RIDGE.

FROM the vast preparations making on all sides, it was evident that the campaign of 1864 would be the most vigorous and desperate of the war. General Easton, Sherman's quartermaster general, was stationed at Nashville, superintending the shipment of stores and supplies for the army. Sherman himself had taken up his quarters there, and seemed to infuse his restless energy into all his officials.

Stores were rapidly pushed forward to Knoxville, Chattanooga, and other points. There were similar indications of a grand campaign in the army of the Potomac, and it was evident on all sides that a fierce struggle was impending both in Virginia and Northern Georgia.

The following were the relative positions of the contending armies at the opening of the campaign : The rebels held Tunnel Hill and Dalton, with cavalry confronting Cleveland, Ringgold, Huntsville, and Decatur, also the Virginia line of railroad beyond Bull's Gap, while the Federal posts occupied Knoxville, Loudon, Athens, Cleveland, Ringgold, Bridgeport, and Huntsville.

Sherman himself estimated the rebel army, comprising Hardee's, Hood's, and Polk's corps of infantry and artillery, at about fifty thousand, with Wheeler's cavalry at ten thousand,—total sixty thousand,—while he set down his own force as follows : —

SHERMAN'S FORCES.

Army of the Cumberland, Major Gen. Thomas com'g.

Infantry 54,568
Artillery 2,377
Cavalry 3,828

Total 60,733
Guns 130

Army of the Tennessee, Major Gen. McPherson com'g.

Infantry 22,437
Artillery 1,404
Cavalry 624

Total 24,465
Guns 96

Army of the Ohio, Major Gen. Schofield com'g.

Infantry 11,183
Artillery 676
Cavalry 1,697

Total 13,559
Guns 28

Grand total 98.797
Total guns 254

On the morning of May 6, these armies were grouped as follows: that of the Cumberland, near Ringgold; that of the Tennessee, near Gordon's Mills, on the Chickamauga; and that of the Ohio, near Red Clay, north of Dalton, on the Georgian line.

Sherman had lately issued an order that the railroads should be used exclusively for military purposes, thus depriving thousands, who were living on government rations, of support. He believed the safety and support of his army paramount to all other considerations. He had a long campaign before him, a long and uncertain line of communications to guard from a vigilant enemy. "Let the citizens go south, or to the rear; I cannot leave my army at the mercy of every raiding party; the campaign must open with thirty days' surplus rations at Chattanooga." This was Sherman's logic. And good logic it was for the safety of his army, but fatal, in their terrible starving condition to the unfortunate sufferers of East Tennessee.

A hegira of poor, forlorn refugees then commenced, followed by human sufferings that might appall the angels. The distress and starvation were terrible throughout Tennessee, and many who had stood the fiery ordeal of battle now succumbed to the pale spectre of starvation.

The 1st of May was appointed for one grand simultaneous movement of the army under the following commanders: The army of the Tennessee, under Major General J. B. McPherson, comprising the 15th and parts of the 16th and 17th corps, then stationed in and around Huntsville, Alabama; the army of the Cumberland, under Major General Thomas, comprising the 14th and 20th corps, and stationed around Chattanooga, Tunnel Hill, and Dalton; and the army of the Ohio, under Major General Schofield, comprising the 4th and 23d corps, stationed at Knoxville, Strawberry Plains, and Bull's Gap.

General Kilpatrick had assumed command of the cavalry division of the army of the Cumberland, stationed at Ringgold, with General Stoneman in command of the cavalry corps in Kentucky.

Georgia, like Tennessee, being the theatre of some of the most stirring events of the late rebellion, has attracted the attention of the world by the fierce nature of the conflict that has desolated her cities and homesteads, and converted her fertile fields into one vast cemetery. Now, when that strife is over, and we are cultivating a better and more amicable acquaintance, it is well that the people of the North should know something of her resources and capabilities.

The State of Georgia lies between thirty and thirty-five degrees north latitude, and eighty-one and eighty-four degrees west longitude, and covers an area of about sixty-three thousand square miles, or over forty millions of acres.

Its soil and climate are varied, the latter changing from the cool breeze and salubrious air of its northern frontier, bordering on Tennessee and Carolina, to the torrid, fever-producing climate that prevails along the swamps and bayous towards the southern coast, bordering on the Savannah and South Carolina.

In like manner her soil varies, in quality, from the rich alluvial land and rice plantations along the Savannah and Alatamaha Rivers, to the red, rich, loamy lands, producing cotton, tobacco, and grain, of the middle portion, and the poorer, but more hilly, picturesque, and healthy regions bordering on Tennessee and North Carolina.

It has some very fine navigable rivers, such as the Savannah, the Alatamaha, the Chattahoochee, and several others, which we shall have occasion to notice more fully. These rivers are, for the most part, of a clay-red color, owing to the nature of the soil, and the shores of the lower rivers are abundantly inhabited by alligators, snakes, and other reptiles.

Georgia was one of the original "thirteen states of the Union," and was colonized by General Oglethorpe in 1773, and was thenceforth continually at war with the Spaniards or Indians. Savannah was an important position during the revolutionary war, and was captured by the British in 1778. Only as late as 1838, the great Cherokee country came into the possession of the whites.

On the whole, Georgia possesses unrivalled sources of wealth and power, and is destined for a glorious future of material wealth and political power.

In the first week in May a simultaneous movement of the armies of the Potomac, under General Meade, and the armies of the West, under General Sherman, took place. While the former were engaged in the bloody conflicts of the Wilderness, the latter were repulsing Johnston and his army from Dalton, Rocky Face Ridge, and Resaca.

On the 1st of May General Sherman removed his headquarters to Chattanooga, and a general movement commenced for the purpose of concentrating around Ringgold. On the 3d, McPherson's army was quietly conveyed by rail from Huntsville to Chattanooga.

We now held the principal gaps of Taylor's Ridge, while Johnson's division of the 14th corps lay at the eastern mouth of Ringgold Gap, threatening Tunnel Hill.

Howard had occupied Cleveland with the 4th corps, and was now marching towards Tunnel Hill, followed by the 23d corps.

On the night of the 7th these corps bivouacked in a valley about two miles from Tunnel Hill and four from Dalton.

On the 4th General Sherman broke up his headquarters at Chattanooga, and moved to Ringgold, announcing that he intended making the campaign without a tent, and by a general order cutting down baggage and transportation to the lowest possible figure. The whole army was now in motion, the campaign was fairly inaugurated. Howard and Palmer were closing on Tunnel Hill, forcing back the enemy to Buzzard Roost. Hooker was moving through Hickajack and Gordon Gaps. McPherson was bringing up the rear with his lines extending from Gordon's Mills to Villanow.

The enemy made but slight resistance on Taylor's Ridge, through which the Tunnel passes. Our columns were moving through the valleys on their flank, threatening to cut them off from Dalton and Resaca. They fell back to the strong position along the Rocky Face Ridge.

We now held Tunnel Hill, and had trains running right up to the troops with supplies. On the morning of the 8th the whole army lay in front of the Mountain, McPherson with the 15th corps, and Dodge's division, 16th corps, on the right; Hooker next, Palmer's 14th corps next, Howard on the left centre, and Schofield on the extreme left. General Elliot's cavalry was occupied covering our flanks and keeping open communication. Stoneman's cavalry had not yet come up, while Kilpatrick was feeling the enemy's outposts along Dogwood Valley.

Rocky Face Ridge, which the rebels defended with such dogged pertinacity, is a long, abrupt continuation of the Chattoogata range of mountains, running in a south-westerly direction from Dalton to Rome. It is about fifteen hundred feet high, and so precipitous in places that the rocks present a smooth, perpendicular front from twenty to fifty feet high, thus forming a natural and impregnable fortification. Its top and sides are sparsely covered with trees and brushwood.

An immense gorge, called Buzzard Roost Gap, opens through the mountain. Through this run the common road, the Chattanooga and Atlanta Railroad, also Mill Creek Stream. The rebels dammed the gorge, forming a large reservoir of water some sixteen feet deep, with which they boasted that they could drown our army beneath them. They strengthened this strong natural position by artificial works of the most formidable kind. All the heights around bristled with cannon, and were dotted with rifle-pits. To the right of this gorge is Buzzard Roost, being about eighteen hundred feet high, and almost inaccessible from its rugged nature. During the five days we lay in front of this mountain, flocks of buzzards hovered over it, scared by the roar and din of battle beneath, yet wheeling round and round like birds of ill omen. On the whole, the entire position is perhaps one of the strongest an army could occupy. As I have stated, Howard's and Schofield's columns had moved from Catoosa Springs, east of Taylor's Ridge, and on the evening of the 7th reached the foot of Rocky Face Ridge. Stanley's division pressed up the valley to Buzzard Roost Gap in order to connect with the 14th corps, with Schofield's corps extended towards the eastern point of the ridge.

The enemy skirmished briskly with our advance during the afternoon of the 7th. We were endeavoring to take up our position to assault the enemy on the following day, if practicable, or at least to draw their attention from McPherson's movement on their flank. On the night of the 7th, General Harker conceived the bold design of dragging a section of artillery to the crest of the hill on the enemy's flank, which he had gained by his assault in the evening. In this movement he was supported by McClean's brigade of General Judah's division, 23d corps. The horses were unhitched from the guns, ropes were tied to them, and hundreds of volunteers rushed to the willing task. Pioneers cleared the timber and brushwood, and levelled the rocks in their advance. So steep was the ascent that the men had to grasp the projecting cliffs and roots with one hand, while they hauled with the other. All this time our skirmishers and sharpshooters were keeping up a brisk fire on the enemy, in order to draw their attention from the movement. After much toil we succeeded in gaining the crest and getting the guns into position, much to the surprise of the enemy next morning.

I have seldom witnessed so splendid a panoramic view as that seen from the summit of Rocky Face Ridge. The men had cleared away the forest timber and brushwood, and had piled up barricades of the loose rocks. The rebel works commanding Buzzard Roost Gap, and the ridge of the hill, were but a few hundred yards from our pickets. Night had now set in, the din and roar of battle had ceased, except the occasional whirring of a minie bullet fired by the pickets, and the boom of a gun bidding the enemy "good night." A thick fog rose up from the valleys, obscuring the mountains; but through this sparkled the glare of innumerable camp fires from the valleys, looking like so many huge fireflies glowing beneath us, or the flickering lamps of a city seen from a distance. The metallic sound of the rifle, the whir and the crash of shot and shell, and the whizzing hum of the minie had ceased. The encouraging shouts and cheers of battle, the death groan of the dying and wounded, had sunk into repose and given place to the solemn stillness of night. We had broken the tender branches from the trees, and placed them over the sharp rocks for our beds, sure to select the safe side of some projecting cliff or stately pine. As we lay down, I could hear the tramp of our sentries marching up and down, the men as they conversed in a hushed tone, some recounting the events of the day; others in solemn groups joined in prayer, while from some obscure nook a regular devil-may-care fellow hurled a defiant song at the enemy. The latter quietly lay behind their works, apparently heedless of our proximity. The moon floated over our heads, its silvery light struggling to pierce that hazy mist. There, on our rough beds, on that mountain top, some fifteen hundred feet high, we slept as soundly as if pillowed on a couch of eider down. Our wearied frames forgot all in the sweet oblivion of sleep.

The thick haze of the morning was clearing away, the sentries still marching on their beats, and the men standing beside their guns, as I awoke. The sun was rising along the eastern horizon, with its fiery beams trying to pierce the thick fog. The fog gradually cleared away, revealing the densely wooded valleys extending far away in the distance, the numerous hills, and mountains with their towering peaks and shaggy sides. The expiring camp fires and the tents of the enemy lay, as it were, at our feet. We could almost look into their intrenchments, and count their numbers as they deployed beneath us.

We had a bird's eye view of Dalton, Resaca, and several other towns and villages, while numerous streams sparkled with the morning beams like polished mirrors. This might be a very pleasing sight for us if we were mere tourists; but the grim cannons, and the lines of troops with their glittering bayonets beside us, reminded us that our mission was not one of peace and refinement. To impress us more forcibly, the noise of the booming cannon and the whirring bullet soon rang upon our ears, heralding in another day of slaughter.

It is strange how soldiers will joke even under the most trying circumstances. As we were not allowed to light fires in order to conceal our position from the enemy, the men had nothing but hard tack for their supper, and some, more fortunate than others, had water in their canteens. A man of the 125th Ohio, an amateur preacher, had some of his comrades collected around him in solemn conclave; and with hushed breath he was exhorting them to repentance, drawing their attention to their comrades who had fallen that day, telling them that such might be their own fate to-morrow.

"Arrah, in sure, what are ye whishpering about?" said an Irish soldier, coming up to the group.

"Praying, Paddy, praying; trying to get to heaven," replied one of them.

"And will that take ye's there?"

"Certainly," said a wag; "what better preparations can we make than praying and fasting?"

"Devil a doubt of it; sure ye's fifteen hundred feet nearer heaven now than ye were in the morning, any way, and I think a good many of us will die pretty high up in the world to-morrow, please God," was Paddy's reply.

A sharpshooter had taken down several of the enemy by the

following plan. He lay behind a barricade of rock, through which he had an opening for his gun. He dressed up a stick with an old coat and hat, and would occasionally raise this over the barricade, when the rebels were sure to pop at it, and then raise up their heads to see the result, thus offering targets to the sharpshooter, which he seldom missed.

As I lay upon my branch couch, I was continually disturbed by the low, piteous moans of a wounded man. The moon was shining bright, and the troops lay around us buried in sleep. I knew it was not safe to walk through the lines at night for fear of getting shot as a spy; however, I could not resist that suffering appeal. I got up, picked my way through the prostrate lines until I came to the edge of a cliff. The moan seemed to proceed from a gorge beneath me. Grasping tree branches and roots, I jumped from rock to rock until I landed on a kind of platform. There I found a soldier lying on his face with a huge rock across his feet. The poor fellow was nearly speechless. I rolled off the stone, which had caused him much suffering. I then turned him on his back, placed his knapsack under his head, and gave him a drink from his canteen. This relieved him very much; and I learned that in the assault of the evening he was shot through the breast, and lay down on this platform, when the rebels hurled down large rocks upon them, one of which fell on him. I stanched the wound in his breast, and on examination I found that his leg was badly fractured. I remained some time with him, listening to the poor fellow's little stories about his mother and his home, and how he should like to see them again; and should he die, would not I write to them, and tell mother that "I died a soldier and a Christian," said the brave lad, for he was a mere boy. Next day he died under the scalpel knife, and I wrote to his mother that her noble boy died "a soldier and a Christian."

The previous evening, while riding near the field hospital of the 105th Ohio, a shell, thrown from the rebel guns on the hill, burst among the patients, killing some of them. It is hard enough to see strong men stricken down in battle, but there is something harrowing in seeing poor helpless wounded wretches killed, as it were, twice.

ROCKY FACE RIDGE.   37

General Sherman had ordered that a heavy demonstration should be made all along the enemy's lines on the morning of the 8th of May. Schofield, on the extreme left, moved cautiously down the eastern side of the mountain, in order to draw the enemy's attention from Geary's attack on Mill Creek. The whole of Newton's division, of the 4th corps, had ascended the ridge during the night to support Harker. About 10 o'clock, Schofield ordered the 23d corps to wheel round and move in line of battle along the valley which separates the ridge from a parallel range. The corps moved in echelon; General Judah's division extended in double line of battle, connecting with Harker's brigade on the ridge. General Cox's division moved along the slope and crest of a hill on the left, the front being protected by heavy lines of skirmishers. The rebels having fallen back, General Judah had made arrangements to assault. This movement was contingent upon the coöperation of Harker's troops on the top of the hill, but his advance was retarded by the desperate nature of the resistance he encountered, which rendered him barely able to hold his own. The ridge rose cliff over cliff, as it receded towards the enemy's lines, so that Harker's advance was a continuation of desperate assaults. The roll of musketry from the hill top rang incessantly for over an hour, the enemy contesting every inch, every tree and rock, with deadly obstinacy.

As he approached the gorge, a wall of rocks, bristling with guns and bayonets, vomiting forth a continuous volcano of lead and fire, checked him, compelling him to raise barricades to protect his lines.

Connecting with Harker's right, but extending down Dogwood Valley, west of the ridge, Generals Stanley and Woods, of the 4th corps, made repeated assaults upon the ridge, which were met by a fierce fire from behind every cliff and rock.

Huge rocks were even rolled from the top of the ridge, which came down plunging from crag to crag, crashing and tearing among the trees, and sweeping through the advancing lines.

Later in the day Croft's brigade, of Stanley's division, supported by Mitchel's and Morgan's brigades, of Davis's division,

14th corps, succeeded in driving the enemy from a strong position in front of Buzzard Roost.

Hooker's corps, while on the right of Palmer's 14th corps, was hotly engaged all the afternoon. Ross's brigade, supported by Colonel Woods' brigade, of Butterfield's division, participated in the assault on Buzzard Roost.

Meantime Geary's division had moved to the right, in order to attempt the passage of Mill Creek Gap, and thus flank Dalton, which was only about three miles distant. Colonel Ireland's brigade had been detached to support Kilpatrick in covering McPherson's flanking column, leaving only Colonel Jones's and Candie's brigades to execute the order.

Mill Creek Gap is accessible by a road winding from Hall's Mill through a depression in the mountain. It was a formidable position, strongly defended.

About 3 o'clock in the afternoon, Candie's brigade in advance, supported by Jones's, moved up the sides of the mountain, under cover of a fire from Knapp's Pennsylvania battery. The enemy stubbornly resisted all the time, but were steadily driven back to the crest of the hill. In this gallant charge of Geary's division, through a dense wood, up a steep ascent, scrambling through rocks and tangled underbrush, many a brave fellow fell. It was the dashing game and heroic achievement of Lookout Mountain again.

Near the crest of the hill a palisade of abrupt cliffs checked their advance. Behind these lay lines of rebel troops. Against this our men made five consecutive assaults. Officers and men struggled up, one by one, and grappled with the enemy in a hand-to-hand conflict. Some succeeded in reaching the plateau. Some were hurled over, dragging the enemy in their death embrace, and in their fall displacing rocks, which crushed and tore through the toiling, surging ranks.

At length they gained a landing. Alas! it availed them little; for a volley of canister from a covered line of fortifications on their flank soon cleared the rocky stage. Again was the charge repeated: again were their lines swept down. Sergeant Hamilton, of a New Jersey regiment, and only ten men, defiantly held their position until another column filled up the place of those who had fallen. General Geary, not having troops enough to attack the batteries, and seeing the impossibility of keeping the ridge, exposed to such an artillery fire, drew off his troops at 8 o'clock in the evening. His loss was — officers, three killed, fifteen wounded; privates, fifty killed and two hundred and fifty wounded.

Meantime McPherson and Kilpatrick's cavalry were swinging around on Dalton, threatening to cut the railroad between that point and Resaca.

This ended the heavy fighting around Rocky Face Ridge. It was evident that the enemy's position was too strong to be taken by assault, and that Sherman must resort to some strategic movement.

The 10th and 11th of May were spent in slight skirmishing and demonstrations to draw the enemy's attention from McPherson's flank movement, and give us a chance of following him up with supports.

CHAPTER IV.

HEADQUARTERS OF THE GENERALS.—SUFFERINGS OF THE WOUNDED.—THE ENEMY'S POSITION AT RESACA.

DURING the five or six days we lay in front of Rocky Face Ridge, the different corps and division commanders had their headquarters contiguous to their commands. Major General Howard, who commanded the 4th corps, had his unassuming quarters of fly tents in the rear of his command, and under fire of the enemy's long-range guns. Several shells fell quite near, creating some commotion in the camp, without disturbing Howard in the least. Howard had ridden out in front of his lines, when he got struck by a spent ball. Meantime Sherman called at his quarters, and being told that they expected the general in every moment, he sat down, when whir-r goes a shell; and another bursting quite near the quarters, some of Sherman's staff felt anxious about him, and suggested that it would be as well to go, as Howard was not likely to return soon.

Sherman, in his nervous, fidgety way, was walking about, and spying General Howard, he exclaimed, "Here comes Howard!" As the latter rode up, Sherman said, "I say, Howard, do you know but you are the politest man in the army?"

"Indeed, I wasn't aware of that, general."

"Well, it's so. Here I am, in your absence; and though you were not here to receive me, I have got the warmest reception I have experienced for a long time!"

"Why, general, you need not thank me for it, but General Johnston; his compliments were so overpowering that one of them came near killing me;" and he pointed to his pants torn by the bullet.

Thomas's headquarters comprised a most gorgeous outlay of

tents of all kinds; wall tents, Sibley tents, fly tents, octagon tents, and all kinds of tents. Every officer had a tent; almost every servant had a tent; while the adjutant general's tent was a sort of open rebellion against all restrictory orders. A kind of caravan, full of pigeon holes, and covered over with an immense fly, was one of its most peculiar features. Sherman, on the contrary, had but one old wall tent, and some three or four flies, for his quarters.

Whether it was that General Thomas felt sore at the contrast, or General Sherman did not like the example set by General Thomas, he could never let slip an opportunity to pass a joke at Thomas's expense.

He would frequently rein up his horse in front of Thomas's quarters, and ask, "Whose quarters are these?"

"General Thomas's, general," would be the reply.

"O, yes; Thomastown — Thomasville; a very pretty place, indeed; appears to be growing rapidly!" and he would chuckle and ride off.

One thing that has forcibly impressed me, in the many battle-fields I have been through — how heroically men undergo the most excruciating torture, almost without a murmur. A soldier thinks it an act of cowardice to cry or moan; and the suffering that wrings one or the other from his brave bosom must be fearful indeed.

"Won't you keep quiet? and don't be making a fool of yourself," I heard one wounded soldier say to another.

"O, dear me, I can't help it; my arm is torn off," was the reply.

"Your arm!" said the other, with contempt, "why, my leg and arm are torn off, and I am making no fuss about them."

It is in the hospital that a soldier's courage is tried. Men with the most fearful wounds will coolly ask, "Well, doctor, must you take it off?" alluding to some shattered limb.

"Well, I fear so, my fine fellow."

"Don't mind, doctor; go at it; the sooner it is over, the better. It's going in a good cause."

Piles of legs and arms would be strewn about the new subjects, many of whom would be earnestly discussing the merits of the battle, while waiting their turn to come under the surgeon's hands.

War hardens the hearts of men, and renders them insensible to the sufferings of others.

This is partly owing to the uncertainty of life, and to the fact that each man holds his life, as it were, in the palm of his hand; besides, a soldier thinks it weak to mourn a fallen comrade, no matter how dear. A painful instance of this came under my observation. A sergeant, a truly brave fellow, who had a brother deeply attached to him, was shot dead near me.

The brother stooped down over his fallen kinsman, and finding him dead, coolly emptied his cartridge-box into his own, remarking to me, "Poor James! wasn't he a brave soldier, captain?" and then moved on with his comrades.

The tract of country over which we now operated is extremely fertile, as well as picturesque.

There are some very rich valleys lying in the shelter of the Raccoon and Lookout Mountains.

The cultivated portions yield profitable returns of cereals and grasses.

The country evidently abounds in mineral resources. Bituminous coal is found in large quantities, also iron ore. There are traces, too, of gold and copper.

As the mineral resources of Georgia and Tennessee have never been developed, it is not well known to what extent they exist. This picturesque region was formerly the hunting-ground of the Cherokees, a remnant of which tribe still inhabits the country between the Holston River and the frontiers of Carolina.

The march of the 4th corps lay near Catoosa Springs, where they bivouacked for a night before their advance on Rocky Face Ridge.

These fine mineral springs are said to possess great healing powers, and were much resorted to by invalids for health, and the wealthy for pleasure. They were situated in an opening in the forest. The lands about were tastefully laid out in plots and walks, and a very fine hotel and several cottages afforded accommodation. Not far from this is a mound of loose stones, raised to the memory of a Cherokee chief, who, in the war of independence, saved the patriot army from a joint surprise of the English and Indians by deserting and swimming across the Chattahoochee River and apprising them of their danger.

The country was thinly inhabited, only small sections of land along the roads being cleared.

Flowers and shrubs of the most gorgeous kind appear indigenous to Georgia. Even at this early season the forests were blooming with them, making the air redolent with their rich odor. Where the flowers and shrubs were cultivated around the houses, it was pleasant to see the bees and humming-birds darting from one to another. It was peace in the midst of war.

General Sherman, finding the enemy's position too formidable to be taken by direct assault, now inaugurated his flanking tactics, which have earned him the sobriquet of "the great flanker." McPherson's movements would have rendered his victory decisive had his assaults in front succeeded, for he could have struck their broken ranks on the flank by wedging in between them and Resaca.

This having failed, Sherman's object now was to reënforce McPherson, at the same time leaving a sufficient force in the enemy's front to keep them in check and follow up their retreat. It was not practicable to make the flank movement on the left, as the mountain range extended back towards the Oostanaula River in broken ridges. The attempt would only bring the flanking party into other gorges like Buzzard Roost. About fifteen miles south of Buzzard Roost is a large gap or defile in the mountain, called Snake Creek Gap, and within about seven miles of Resaca.

This was the objective point aimed at by McPherson, and was the only available passage for Sherman's army. McPherson met little opposition from the enemy on his line of march. He observed the strictest silence, every man being instructed not to tell even their commands.

"To what corps do you belong?" I asked of some stragglers whom I met plodding along the road.

"Corps is it? Sure we belong to Sherman's army. Do you know old fighting Billy?"

"I asked you to what corps you belong."

"Cap, dear, it is too wet to tell you; don't you see the state we are in? and we in such a hurry to get up before night. Let us move on, Hugh."

On the 9th McPherson marched from Villanow through Snake Creek Gap, where they were opposed only by a small party, which were soon routed by the 9th Illinois mounted infantry, in which skirmish their commander, Lieutenant Colonel Philips, was severely wounded. General Dodge, commanding the 16th corps, led McPherson's advance, and by a rapid movement secured the Gap, while Logan, with his 15th corps, passed through.

McPherson's army defiled through the Gap, marched through Sugar Valley, and occupied, without opposition, a range of hills overlooking Resaca and commanding the railroad bridge across the Oostanaula. These hills were occupied by Logan and Dodge at 8 o'clock in the morning. Sherman's instructions to McPherson were imperative to take Resaca and destroy the railroad bridge.

McPherson, finding several good roads leading north and south, thus endangering his left flank, while he could find no safe road to advance his army on,—besides, the enemy seemed to be strongly intrenched, and in force around Resaca,—got discouraged, and rapidly fell back at night, under a pitiless storm, to the southern mouth of Snake Creek Gap.

This retrograde movement of McPherson's has been censured very much; for had he intrenched himself in his new position, he could keep Johnston's army at bay until he would be reënforced. Had he held this point, his force would have full command of the town and railroad, thus compelling Johnston to make a detour to the left in order to cross the river—a thing which he could not well do, through impracticable roads and pressed by a superior army.

A squad of the 9th Illinois remained after the troops as skirmishers; and so little was the opposition they met that they

SUFFERING OF THE TROOPS. 45

succeeded in tearing up some of the rails and cutting the telegraph wires, and then safely returned to camp next day.

Sherman had now decided to debouch, with the bulk of his army, through Snake Creek Gap, leaving Howard to keep the enemy in check and follow up their retreat. The rest of the army was to follow up the army of the Tennessee on the night of the 10th; but a fierce thunder and rain storm set in, thus retarding the movement. The 11th, too, was excessively wet, cold, and unpleasant.

Some of our troops who had marched from Ringgold to support McPherson suffered severely. Their blankets became so wet and heavy after the previous day and night's rain and mud they threw them away. They had no cover, neither would the green, saturated wood, light; so they had to suffer all night with cold and hunger, having but the poor shelter of the dripping pines.

"This is a comfortable bed," said a bright-eyed boy, who was stretched upon a pile of brush to keep him from the ground, while some of his comrades were vainly trying to light a fire beside him, their effort being rewarded with thick volumes of smoke.

"An' haven't you a nice mattress anyhow?"

"Yes; but the roof leaks dreadfully."

"Well, don't mind; there is one comfort; I guess a good many of us will have hospital accommodations to-morrow."

"Boys, let us get up a song; it will do us good," said another.

"No, let us have prayers, and thank the Lord for all his favors, though we have had no supper," said a cynic.

They compromised the matter by praying and singing together. In this light-hearted way did this grand army bear hardships and hunger that might dishearten the most patriotic.

The contest for Rocky Face Ridge had now subsided into a straggling fire, which we kept up to cover our flank movement. It was not, properly speaking, a battle, though in the days of the revolution, or the war of 1812, it might be dignified with that title.

We live in an age when thousands of men have been pitted against each other in the most deadly strife, when battle followed battle in rapid and painful succession, and when armies have been recuperated as fast as decimated. Personal as well as political animosities imbittered the combat. One party fought for the great principles of free government and national unity; the others, many, no doubt, under the mistaken notion that they were fighting for their liberty, their homes, and their altars. Both sides fought gallantly; one with frenzied desperation, the other with a firm purpose and resolute perseverance. Their ministers prayed loudly, and called on God to smite the opposing hosts and protect the right.

In such a struggle, excited by religious and political fanatics and fire-eaters, no wonder that the result was one of the bloodiest wars that stain the pages of history. Before it, the wars of the Roses, of Charlemagne, and even of Napoleon himself, pale into insignificance.

It is true, this was considered no battle, though our total loss would number near one thousand, and our lines extended nearly twenty miles. Hooker's corps, the 20th, was now close up to McPherson, and Palmer's corps, the 14th, and Newton's division of the 4th corps, Howard's, had followed, moving by the right flank; Schofield came next with his 23d corps.

On the night of the 12th and morning of the 13th General Johnston fell back from Rocky Face Ridge and Dalton with the main portion of his army, leaving a small force behind to check our advance.

Resaca was now threatened by Sherman's main army, which was massed in Snake Creek Gap and Sugar Valley, closing in on Johnston's rear. His present position was no longer tenable; so he concentrated all his force at Resaca, in order to meet Sherman's attack on his flank.

On the evening of the 13th sharp skirmishing ensued along the lines, the enemy resisting our attempt to take up our position. General Osterhaus with his division pushed forward, and occupied a hill on the right of the road overlooking Resaca.

We could plainly distinguish the enemy's lines and works.

Their wagons and ambulances lay packed right in view, while their huge trains were laboring up and down to the bridge. Captain De Grass, of the 15th corps, soon got his guns into position, and opened on them, driving them under shelter. The skirmishers along our front were keeping up a rattling fire.

General Kilpatrick had brilliantly skirmished all day in front of our advance, for the woods and hills were full of rebel sharpshooters. A bullet whizzed from every tree and crag, bringing down his brave men. On he passed, driving them back from point to point, until at length the dashing Kilpatrick fell, badly wounded through the thigh. Colonel Murray then assumed the command of his men, and vigorously continued the pursuit.

Herron's division, of Logan's corps, had a brisk engagement with the enemy, who disputed their advance into position. Kilpatrick was wounded near a cross road, where a board informs you that it is "three miles to Calhoun Ford." At this point Giles A. Smith, marching in double quick, moved to the right, while Morgan L. Smith deployed along the Calhoun road, on the right of the Resaca road. Herron connected with Osterhaus. This was the position of the 15th corps on the night of the 13th. The other corps had not yet taken up position.

CHAPTER V.

SKETCHES OF OUR GENERALS.—PERSONNEL OF SHERMAN, THOMAS, SCHOFIELD, HOOKER, McPHERSON, LOGAN, AND GEARY.

SHERMAN, attended by one staff officer and an orderly, had ridden up the valley to the front. He was anxious and nervous, as was evident from the fierce manner he pulled at his unlit cigar, and twitched that strange, coarse face of his.

His ride through the lines created no enthusiasm. His old 15th corps alone brightened up, and looked the better for his presence. They fully knew — "Old Billy."

Sherman was, at all times, too cold and undemonstrative for the men to love him. They had unbounded confidence in him, and believed whatever he did was right, and that is all. If sent on any expedition, no matter how hazardous or apparently useless, their only reply was, — " Well, boys, if Old Billy said so, it's all right."

McPherson by his noble bearing and dashing appearance, Hooker by his fine martial presence and princely air, Logan by his dashing, kind manner, might create enthusiasm among troops, but Sherman or Thomas never.

On the morning of this day, the following incident occurred.

Sherman was anxiously engaged maturing his plans the previous night. Next day, wearied and sleepy, he sat on a log, beside a shady tree, to rest himself, and soon fell asleep. He had but a single orderly with him; and few of the men, as they marched by, knew that he was Sherman.

"Is that a general?" asked one of the men.

"Yes," said the orderly.

"A pretty way we are commanded when our generals are lying drunk beside the road!" exclaimed the soldier, walking off in disgust.

"Stop, my man," said Sherman, jumping up; for Sherman sleeps with one eye and one ear, too, open, and heard him. "Stop, my man. I am not drunk. While you were sleeping last night, I was planning for you, sir; and now I was taking a nap. General Sherman never gets drunk, sir."

The soldier slunk away, and never minded a sleeping general again.

Sherman had ridden up to the front, and a council of generals was held at that little cross where the road branches for Resaca and Hilton. He alighted, walked up and down beside the group for some minutes, and then turning to them, exclaimed,—

"Johnston has evacuated Rocky Face and Dalton, and is fast massing around Resaca."

"So I understand," replied Logan; "I have heard so from prisoners captured by Kilpatrick's cavalry, and have sent an aid to you with the account."

"Ah, Kilpatrick, is he much wounded?"

"Rather badly, general; shot through the thigh."

"Ah, sorry for it; but, Logan, I have heard that news before you, and, of course, expected it. Johnston is too wily to let us get in behind him. Well, it was the only way of getting them out of that d—d place; but they will make a desperate stand here; it is a strong position. I know every inch of country here; you know I was a military professor down here at Marietta. Well, we must get them out of this too. McPherson, had you held this position when you first occupied it, they would find themselves in a nice trap."

"General," replied McPherson, "I found my flanks exposed, and open to them by good roads, whilst I had not a single road by which reënforcements could come up, if attacked; so I fell back to a stronger position."

"O, psha! It can't be helped now, though."

As I cannot repeat every word said at that council, I will only state that they decided on a vigorous attack on all points. McPherson was to guard the Oostanaula, and open on Resaca; if possible, throw a portion of his forces over it, and destroy the bridge.

Schofield was to support Howard, who was now thundering after Johnston, while Hooker, supported by Palmer, was to make a vigorous assault on the range of hills west of Resaca. This was a strong post, and, in fact, the key-stone of the rebel position.

While they are engaged in council, I will sketch them in detail.

Major General William Tecumseh Sherman is near six feet high; but his spare frame gives him the appearance of being over this. His face is rather sharp and angular, and covered with a short, grizzly beard, of a sandy color. His eyes are piercing, with something of a harsh, cruel expression about them. His manner of speaking is rapid and rather sarcastic. His hands are continually twisting about, and his features twitching, as if suffering from pain.

As a soldier, he has been wonderfully successful; he has had the wisdom to avail himself of the counsel of others, and to draw his own conclusions, and act energetically upon them. Though some of his movements savored of rashness, when calmly weighed, they showed the good judgment and military genius that conceived them.

Hooker assaulted the enemy at Pumpkin Vine Creek by his orders, and though pretty well used up, succeeded in developing the enemy's position, and drawing their attention from McPherson's attack on Dallas.

Again, the assault on Kennesaw, in which the noble Harker fell, might appear rash and uncalculating; but had it succeeded it would have split Johnston's army in two, and thus exposed it to wholesale destruction. I think he displayed more judgment in his march through Carolina, from the admirable manner in which he baffled and confounded the enemy, than in any other of his campaigns. In manner he is rather dictatorial, even to his generals. He gives his orders in a blunt, decisive fashion, without any courteous prefacing, and in such a way as to make it evident that they are to be obeyed.

When once he forms an opinion, he acts upon it with an unbending, uncompromising resolve.

He has little reserve in concealing his opinions of other officers; and, if displeasing to him, he handles them in a bold, caustic manner, keeping them in torture as long as possible.

When unbent, and enjoying the sociability of a convivial hour, he is rather agreeable; can laugh heartily, and contest the palm for joking with Father Abe himself.

I once heard an officer, who had just spent an hour with him, listening to his keen, comprehensive views of the war, and to some of his raciest tales and anecdotes, say, —

" Well, after all, Sherman's bark is worse than his bite."

On the whole, he is a cold, ascetic, nervous, irritable man, who commands admiration more for his brilliant qualifications as a general, than for any good or amiable traits he possesses as a man.

Major General Thomas is quite the reverse of Sherman, both in manner and appearance. He is tall, stout, with brawny frame and shoulders. His head is slightly bent forward, as if drooping with thought and care. His hair and beard, which he wears cut pretty short, are rather dark, and slightly sprinkled with gray. He is about fifty years of age, and looks his age fully.

He is very reserved; speaks little. His cold, phlegmatic features never wear a smile, or, if he smiles, "he smiles in such a sort as if he mocked himself, and scorned the spirit that could be moved to smile at anything."

As a general, Thomas is calm and cautious; does everything by rule; leaves nothing to chance. He makes his arrangements for a battle with caution and foresight, and is sure to have every column and division move with clock-work regularity, and strike at the proper time and place.

Nothing disturbs or unnerves him.

At Chickamauga, when our right and centre were crushed, and McCook's and Crittenden's forces were falling back in full retreat, shattered, broken, and routed, Thomas was as cool as if nothing was going wrong.

He was resolved to hold the left at all odds. The enemy massed their troops against him, and repeatedly assaulted him;

but he held that position all that long afternoon, despite the repeated assaults of Bragg, and the masses hurled against him, thus saving the army from what before seemed an irretrievable defeat.

Again, at Nashville, he was calmly making his preparations to meet Hood, while Schofield was slowly falling back, all the time holding Hood in check with only two corps, thus giving Thomas time to mature his plans. And when Hood lay down before Nashville to besiege it, the President, Grant, and the country were surprised and becoming disheartened because Thomas was not attacking him. Thomas heard all this, knew all this, but he followed his own inclination. The cry was loud against him. An order was issued to relieve him from command. All this did not move him until he had his arrangements made, and then he swept down upon Hood, crushing up his army, and totally destroying the rebel forces in the southwest.

Major General Schofield, commanding the department of the Ohio, is a middle-sized, stout man, of very pleasing appearance and address. His hair is rather short — his beard long and flowing.

He, too, is rather taciturn and retired, but possessed of a great deal of vigor and judgment.

His services as an officer have been rather brilliant. In Sherman's campaign, he commanded the 23d corps. This corps had been recently made up of raw, undisciplined material from Tennessee and Kentucky. Schofield soon remodelled it, so that it rendered as efficient service as any other corps during Sherman's Atlanta campaign. The masterly manner in which Schofield, with only two corps, the 4th and 23d, checked Hood's advance, as he fell back to Nashville, stamps him as one of the great generals of the day. His defeat of Hood, at Franklin, was the first crushing blow to his army, which was so admirably followed up at Nashville. These were followed by his subsequent military services and able administration of affairs in Carolina.

Major General Joe Hooker, the beau ideal of a gentleman

and a soldier, is of a noble, portly appearance, with fine features, and a complexion soft and clear as a woman's. He is kind and courteous to all, without compromising his dignity. He was beloved by his officers, almost adored by his men, who, on account of his well-established bravery, called him "fighting Joe."

His career of a soldier would have been a brilliant record of dashing exploits — of noble victories — had not Chancellorsville thrown its dark blot upon him. Well-informed persons attribute our disastrous failure there to Halleck's interference. Be this as it may, Hooker bears the odium.

There is no doubt there was a jealous clique bent on ruining him, even at the cost of the welfare and honor of their country; and they partly succeeded.

Hooker's services in the west were of the most brilliant nature. His charge at Lookout Mountain, where the roar and din of battle was high above the fogs and clouds in the valley; at Resaca, where he crushed in the centre of Johnston's army; at Pea Vine Creek, where with his single corps he charged the bulk of the rebel army; and before Atlanta, where he repulsed the mad assaults of two rebel corps, — will stand forth in history as some of the noblest exploits of the war.

Major General McPherson, commanding the army of the Tennessee, was a noble-looking man, of fine, dignified appearance. He was a courteous, refined gentleman, an educated general, and brave officer. His hair and whiskers were dark and flowing, his features well defined and expressive. He had fully the confidence of General Sherman, as a general, and took a distinguished part with him in all his great battles, until he fell on that fatal 22d of July, in front of Atlanta, in the thirty-sixth year of his age.

Major General O. O. Howard, then commanding the 4th corps, afterwards the army of the Tennessee, is a man of slight frame, and apparently delicate constitution, of a grave, pleasing demeanor, and of most affable and courteous manner. He has served all through the war, lost his right arm at Fair Oaks, under McClellan, commanded the 11th corps at the battles of

Chancellorsville and Gettysburg. He was then sent to the west, and when the 11th and 12th corps were consolidated into the 20th, he got command of the 4th corps. He is a man imbued with a deep spirit of religion, and a true sense of his great responsibility.

His religious example and precept had a most salutary effect on his troops. He might be justly called the Havelock of the army. He was indefatigable in the discharge of his duties, and attentive to the wants and wishes of his men.

As a soldier he has won a high reputation, both for his cool bearing in danger, and his judgment in the disposition of his troops. His military services with Sherman, all through Georgia and the Carolinas, have been remarkably brilliant and successful, and mainly contributed to the great results.

General John A. Logan, or, as he was more familiarly called, "Black Jack," is of middle stature, compact, well-knit frame. His face is regular, but almost bronze, showing unmistakable evidence of his Franco-Celtic lineage.

He has a glorious pair of dark eyes, that scintillate beneath his heavy brows, and dark hair. A heavy, curved mustache covers his well-formed mouth. Such is his appearance, and his fighting qualities are in accordance.

Logan and his 15th corps have been through almost every battle-field of the west; and wherever his banner floated, down went the enemy's. His military career is a full record of dashing heroism, from Shiloh's bloody field to Johnston's surrender in North Carolina.

Though Logan is a civilian general, despite the prejudices existing against such, his military genius could not be overlooked; so he rose to the command of the army of the Tennessee.

There are men who are soldiers by inspiration. Logan is one.

West Point may mould him, and instruct him in the rudiments of war; but it could not infuse into many the spirit and military genius of John A. Logan.

He, and Brevet Major General John Geary, who commanded

the second division of Hooker's corps, were strong evidences of this.

Geary, too, was a civilian general, and won fame and reputation upon field after field, — upon the bloody crest of Lookout Mountain, upon the rugged cliffs of Mill Creek, — though every action that many a trained West Point veteran should feel proud of. Of civilian soldiers, he and Logan stand amidst the foremost.

CHAPTER VI.

BATTLE OF RESACA.—WHAT IT COST TO TAKE TWO GUNS.—TERRIBLE SCENES ON THE BATTLE-FIELD.—OUR LOSSES.

RESACA is situated on a bend of the Oostanaula River, which curves towards the east. It is a small place, of little importance except what it has historically acquired from the great struggle enacted there. It is on the north bank, and a station of the Western and Atlantic Railroad, and about eighteen miles south of Dalton.

Across the peninsula formed by the bend of the river the rebels had thrown up a strong, continuous line of intrenchments, strengthened by fortifications. Both their flanks rested on the river, thus forming a kind of semicircle, with the river for its arc.

The Oostanaula River is formed by the junction of the Conesauga and Coosewattee, which meet in Cass County, and form a junction with the Etowah at Rome.

On the morning of the 14th the rebels held a strong position behind Camp Creek. At an early hour skirmishing opened on the right of our line, and soon extended along our front. Toward noon, Howard, who was pressing on the enemy's rear in their retreat from Dalton, succeeded in effecting a junction with Schofield. Our whole force was now in line. Howard occupied the extreme left, his flank resting on the railroad; Schofield joined his right; Hooker had wheeled from the right and fell in on Schofield's right; Palmer, next, with Logan and Wood, with two divisions of the 16th corps, on the extreme right.

Sherman had ordered a pontoon bridge to be thrown across the Oostanaula at Day's Ferry, in the direction of Calhoun.

Sweeny's division, of the 16th corps, was ordered to protect it. General Gerrard was ordered to advance his cavalry from Villanow across the Oostanaula, and, if possible, break the railroad between Calhoun and Kingston. General McPherson had crossed Camp Creek, and made a lodgment close on the enemy's flank.

On the afternoon of the 14th, General Schofield moved his column in line of battle, through a dense wood, with the intention of piercing the enemy's centre. General Judah, commanding the second division, advanced on the right, with General Cox supporting on the left. Judah moved his column rapidly over an open valley, then through a thick wood, until he reached an open space which divided him from the enemy. Owing to the slowness of his movements, or to the impracticable nature of the country, Cox's advance was not as forward as Judah's. As Judah deployed his column out of the woods, a valley of some five hundred yards in width separated him from the enemy. Judah, believing that Cox was advancing simultaneously with him, or thinking that the enemy were not in force on the other side, or acting from imperative orders, charged right across the valley, when one dense, continuous, withering fire opened from masked batteries and concealed lines on the other side. His first line was broken, and fell back on his second. This rallied under the fierce storm of shot and shell, and advanced, but was also broken. After repeated attempts to form his lines and rally, Judah was forced to fall back to the shelter of the woods and works in his rear. Owing to the abrupt, impracticable nature of the ground, he was not able to place his artillery in position to cover his advance. By this time the wood had been cleared away from the crest of the hill, and our artillery got into position. I was then acting aid and captain on General Judah's staff. My horse was lamed by a piece of rock, splintered by a round shot, striking him in the leg, and I was leading him to the rear, when I met Major, now Colonel Wherry, of Schofield's staff, riding in.

"Good God, Captain C," he exclaimed, "where is General Judah?"

"He is at the front, trying to rally his broken line," I replied.

"I want to see him; where are the rest of his aids?"

"Two of them are there near that rock;" and I pointed them out.

He rode over to them; they refused to go in, and he turned to me, exclaiming, "What will I do?"

"Well, major, my horse is lame; dismount an orderly, and I will go in."

He did so. I went in, accompanied by the brave, dashing Major Wherry. We succeeded in reaching Judah's position between the contending batteries, though shot and shell were all the time ploughing through the ranks, and mowing down the columns and trees around us. Judah persisted in keeping his position, but wished Hovey's Indiana division to come to his support, and requested me to lead it in. While riding out to do so, a rifle bullet glanced off a tree, and struck me in the breast. Fortunately, I had a book stuffed with papers inside my vest, which turned its course. It stunned me, however, and for a moment I lay senseless beside a tree. Having recovered myself, I rode forward, and brought in Hovey's division to Judah's support. For this act General Schofield warmly thanked me, and General Judah presented me with a most complimentary letter.*

It was evening. Cox's division had now become fully engaged. The battle had grown pretty hot on the left. Both Cox and Judah were so badly pressed that they could scarcely hold their position, had not General Stanley's division, of Howard's corps, come up to our support, swinging round on the left so as to extend his line toward Dalton. Stanley became fiercely engaged, and made a desperate resistance; but the enemy had

---

* CEDAR SPRINGS, GA., May 18, 1864.

CAPTAIN D. P. CONYNGHAM, Acting A. D. C.

Captain: — I cannot disrupt the associations that bind me to my personal staff, without thanking you for the many services you have rendered me. The gallant manner in which you have conveyed my orders, under a heavy fire, during the fearful ordeal to which my division was subjected on the 14th instant, not only commands my acknowledgment and admiration, but attests my long confirmed opinion that the Irish soldier is the nonpareil of a soldier.

With the best wishes of your chief for your future success and welfare,
I am truly yours,

J. H. JUDAH, *Brigadier General U. S. A.*

massed their troops in this position, and strove hard to turn our flank. Sherman, seeing the severe nature of the attack on this position, had ordered Hooker to move two of his divisions, that were in reserve, to support Howard and Schofield. Stanley's troops had made a splendid resistance; but wearied from a long march, and overpowered by numbers, were gradually losing ground, when Williams's division, of the 20th corps — a portion of the old 12th corps — had come to their support. They dashingly threw themselves to the front, beating back the enemy with fearful slaughter, and retaking a battery that had been wrested from Stanley's division.

While this stubborn conflict was raging on the left, McPherson was busily engaged on the right. He had thrown Logan's corps across the creek, and occupied the heights on the east bank of the stream, overlooking the town. This movement had not been accomplished without hard fighting. The rebel batteries along the heights poured a dreadful storm of shot and shell upon Logan's advance. McPherson, in order to neutralize this, had placed batteries on the heights on the west bank of the stream, annoying the rebel batteries, and thus giving a chance to Logan to charge across the stream, and take possession of the ridge of hills commanding the rebel position around Resaca. In this day's battle the enemy had been foiled in attempting to turn our left flank, and had lost some important positions on their own left. In fact, Logan had succeeded in turning it, and exposing Resaca, and also their line of escape across the river.

It was generally stated and believed that a portion of Polk's troops from Mobile had arrived in the course of the day, and were hastening up to Johnston's support.

The country around was a succession of mounds, or large hills. The rebel line of battle extended in one circuitous line around these. The crest and slopes of these hills were sheltered by forest trees, which concealed their batteries and fortifications, the underbrush giving shelter to their skirmishers and sharpshooters. During the night and early morning, Hooker had massed Geary's and Williams's divisions under cover of a strong hill on his front; Butterfield had not yet taken up position.

The rebels had now occupied a strong position; stronger, even, than on the former day, and the battle of the 15th threatened to be a desperate one. Their lines were now considerably depressed, but protected by strong works on the left flank, by a deep stream and marshy banks on the centre, and by the Oostanaula on the right. In this position Johnston had drawn up his troops in line of battle, scarcely three miles in extent; while our line, occupying the outer line of a semicircle, was much more extended. Hooker was ordered to assault and take the position in his front. It was a strong one, protected by natural and artificial impediments of the most formidable kind. Sherman had ordered it to be taken, and taken it must be. It was a lofty elevation of hills, covered with a dense growth of timber and brushwood. Every nook and corner was burrowed with rifle-pits and intrenchments. Hooker's line of battle advanced from the south-west, barely skimming the western base of the hill, and then crossed a deep valley in a more northerly direction, extending to a commanding elevation we had gained the previous day.

It was noon before Butterfield's division got into position. Hooker had now arranged his columns. Butterfield's division was deployed in columns by brigades. For some time, Hooker was at a loss to know which range was occupied by the enemy, and which to attack; but they soon discovered themselves by opening on us from the hill on the left of the road. Colonel Woods's brigade, of Butterfield's division, charged the enemy's position on the left, while General Ward's brigade charged that on the right, supported by Colonel Colburn's brigade. The column on the right advanced up the hill steadily, bravely, as if on parade, driving back the rebel sharpshooters and skirmishers to their works. Over the hill they swept; down the valley in double quick time; across it, raked by a withering fire from the rebel artillery; up the opposite hill towards its base, where they met a regular shower of shell and bullets; yet on they swept, plunged through the woods, striving desperately to gain its ascent. Colonel Colburn's brigade was now advancing to their relief, when a conflict of the most awful kind ensued for that hill. The rebels here unmasked several batteries, which staggered our columns for a moment by the shower of canister they poured into our lines. In the dense thickets, Colburn's men opened fire on Ward's brigade; but some officers rushed to the front, and corrected this mistake. Ward had now gained the hill, and charged on the works, but fell, wounded. Colonel Harrison now led on the brigade. Their general fallen, their ranks broken, the gallant fellows had to fall back to the shelter of another hill.

A correspondent relates the following incident: "As we were falling back, the rebels, thinking that we had been repulsed, cheered lustily. This stung the gallant color-bearer of the 127th Illinois, named Hess. Springing back to the embrasure, he floated the colors defiantly at the enemy. Brave fellow! his death atoned for his rashness. A rebel shot him through the heart. Other hands took up the flag with a similar fate."

Colonel Woods's brigade encountered but little resistance in its first advance; but on gaining the crest of the hill, he found the timber cleared away on the other side, thus exposing his lines to an open fire from the enemy. Large masses of troops had moved across the open fields between the Dalton road and the railroad, as if attempting a flank movement. This was but a feint to cover a real attack; for soon a whole division burst on Colonel Woods's front. They came charging up the clear slope in double quick, and with a fierce yell. Woods's men reserved their fire until they came right up to them, and then poured a deadly volley into the column. They faltered, rallied, charged; but the same deadly fire thinned their lines, and drove them back. Again the rebels rallied, and would have crushed Woods's columns, had not General Knipe's brigade just then come to their assistance. Knipe charged directly into the rebel columns at the point of the bayonet.

Though largely outnumbered, his gallant brigade returned volley for volley, and bravely maintained their position until their general fell wounded, when the column steadily fell back, bearing their general with them. They also brought back a number of prisoners, and the battle-flags of the 38th and 58th Alabama. Our batteries all along our front continued all day pouring the deadly storm of lead upon the enemy, in order to cover the charges of Hooker and Logan.

As night approached, Hooker reënforced his front, and renewed the charge, with the most brilliant results, driving back the rebels from their works, capturing four guns, a number of flags, and seven hundred prisoners.

The brunt of the battle fell upon Butterfield's and Williams's divisions, which fought splendidly.

Geary's division was but slightly engaged, being held in reserve.

No serious engagement took place all day at any other point of the line.

They all skirmished briskly with the enemy, in order to distract their attention from Hooker's assault.

The skirmishing in Logan's front, on the right, brought on a sharp engagement at that point.

Night had set in. The ground was strewn with the dead and wounded. Our men slept beside their arms, for the rebel lines were quite close to them. The living, the dying, and the dead slept beside one another. We could hear the stealthy tramp of moving troops, and the rumble of wagons.

There was much conjecture as to whether the enemy were retreating, or bringing forward supports and artillery to renew the conflict in the morning.

During the day's battle we had temporarily seized a rebel battery, but were unable to hold it; but succeeded in dragging two guns from the embrasure, and into a trench near the works. As we did so, the rebel batteries opened a converging fire on the spot, and compelled us to retreat; so the guns lay there between both lines, and neither side dare touch them. Some of our men organized a volunteer party to bring in the guns at night. They clubbed together in a little valley near the fort, and waited until everything was silent, except the mournful cry of the whippoorwill, the groans of the wounded, and the tramp of the sentry.

They then stole to the fort, tied ropes to the pieces, and were dragging them away, when the rebels jumped up and fired on

SAD SCENES ON THE BATTLE-FIELD. 63

them. The rebel batteries, having the range since the previous evening, swept across the little fort. Our pickets fired; our skirmishers fired; and soon our columns had sprung up, seized their arms, and opened a fierce volley through the dark woods; they did not know where, or for what. Our batteries, too, took up the horrid din, and the whole combined to make the night hideous with the unearthly shrieking and hissing of shells and bullets.

Covered by the confusion, the rebels commenced retreating; and ere morning dawned their main body had crossed the Oostanaula. After some time the firing ceased; the wearied troops again lay down beside their arms to repose.

On the following morning I went to see that point where our troops fought so desperately, and grappled in a hand-to-hand death conflict with the foe.

The work was a lunette, just on the crest of a hill, and well masked by some trees and brushwood around it.

This was thickly strewn with the dead and wounded. Inside and around the work rebel and Union officers and men lay piled together; some transfixed with bayonet wounds, their faces wearing that fierce, contorted look that marks those who have suffered agony. Others, who were shot dead, lay with their calm faces and glassy eyes turned to heaven. One might think they were but sleeping.

Others had their skulls crushed in by the end of a musket, while the owner of the musket lay stiff beside them, with the death grip tightened on the piece.

Clinging to one of the guns, with his hand on the spoke, and his body bent as if drawing it, lay a youth with the top of his head shot off. Another near him, his body cut in two, still clung to the ropes.

Can a rescued nation sufficiently revere the memories of such heroes?

Men writhing in pain, men stark and cold; broken caissons, rifles, and bayonets; bloody clothes and torn haversacks, with all the other debris of war's havoc, were the price we paid for these two old cannon.

A battle-field, when the carnage of the day is over; when the angry passions of men have subsided; when the death silence follows the din and roar of battle; when the victors have returned triumphant to their camps to celebrate their victory, regardless of the many comrades they have left behind; when the conquered sullenly fall back to a new position, awaiting to renew the struggle, — is a sad sight. It is hard to listen to the hushed groans and cries of the dying, and to witness the lacerated bodies of your fellow-soldiers strewn around, some with broken limbs, torn and mangled bodies, writhing in agony. How often has some poor fellow besought me to shoot him, and put him out of pain! It would be a mercy to do so, yet I dared not.

Piled up together in a ditch, near a battery which they supported with their lines, I found several rebel dead and wounded. I dragged some of the wounded out under the shelter of the trees.

The ghouls of the army were there before me; they had rifled the pockets of the dead and wounded indiscriminately.

I gave many a poor fellow a reviving drink, amidst silent prayers.

In one place I found a mere boy of about fifteen. His leg was shattered with a piece of shell. I placed his knapsack under his head. Poor child! what stories he told me of his mother, away down in Carolina; and his little sisters, how glad they would be, now that he was wounded, to see him home.

They never saw him home, for he went to the home where the weary are at rest.

I came up to the corpse of a rebel soldier, over whom a huge Kentuckian federal soldier was weeping.

"My man," I exclaimed, "why do you weep over him? Look at your comrades around you."

"True, sir," he replied, wiping his eyes; and pointing to a federal soldier near, he said, "There is my brother; this man shot him: I killed him in return. He was my bosom friend. I loved him as a father loves his child."

Next morning, as we were removing our wounded to hospital, I saw a group collected. I rode up, and found that they were some raw troops jeering and insulting rebel wounded. They belonged to Hovey's Indiana division. Veteran troops will never do this, but share their last drink and bite with them. I rated them pretty roundly, and ordered the cowardly sneaks to their regiments. After another battle or two, these very boys would feel indignant at such conduct.

I then helped the doctor to put them in ambulances. The poor fellows' gratitude well repaid me. One man's brain was protruding through his wound. We left him, thinking he could not live long. I went there the following evening, and found him still living.

Our loss in the battle of Resaca was pretty heavy. We had four generals wounded — Kilpatrick and Willech badly, Manson seriously, and Hooker slightly.

Our total killed were about five hundred; some two thousand wounded, and about five hundred missing.

I have no means of fully ascertaining the rebel loss; but it must be as large as ours. For the most part they fought under cover.

Our captures were eight pieces of cannon, a large stock of small arms and commissary stores, besides the cheering effect the victory had on our troops, and the demoralizing influence on Johnston's. Resaca was, in truth, the first great battle of the campaign. Here the enemy, aided by every advantage of ground and position, made a stand. A fair but desperate conflict ensued, and the enemy were whipped. From that day our army felt they were to be victorious; Johnston's, that they were to be defeated.

CHAPTER VII.

THE PURSUIT.—OUR ARMY CROSS THE RIVER ON PONTOONS AND BRIDGES.—CAPTURE OF A REBEL COURIER.—A GOOD TRICK OF GENERAL THOMAS.—SPLENDID ACHIEVEMENT OF GENERAL SWEENY.—STORMING THE HEIGHTS AT SNAKE CREEK.—DEEDS OF INDIVIDUAL VALOR.—SHERMAN AND THE LONE WIDOW.—A COUP D'ŒIL FROM BUENA VISTA.—DESCRIPTION OF THE COUNTRY.—TROUBLES OF THE CORRESPONDENTS.—PERSONAL ANECDOTES OF SHERMAN.

GENERAL JOHNSTON had pontooned the river just below the bend. He could not cross his trains by the regular road bridge, as the noise would reveal the movement. The troops crossed at several ferries, the major portion over a foot bridge laid beside the railroad bridge.

The rebels had left behind them four guns, in addition to those captured the previous day, immense stores of ammunition, several thousand stands of small arms, a large amount of commissary stores, and all their dead and wounded. They destroyed the railroad bridge, but had not time to demolish the road bridge near it.

The pursuit commenced early next morning. McPherson had crossed over at Lay's Ferry, and the foot bridge left by the rebels. General Thomas had to lay down some additional bridges, and followed up right in the rear of the retreating army.

General Schofield had to make a wide detour to the left, and crossed the Counasauga and Coosawattee, which form the Oostanaula at Fite's and Field's Ferries. Our cavalry were close upon the rear of the rebels, but were not in sufficient force to bring them to a stand.

The troops effected the crossing of the rivers in very good time.

McPherson had his pontoons already established. The rebels, in their haste, had left the road bridge and a foot bridge standing. Schofield, however, had to ford or pontoon the two rivers. All this was done with such despatch that the whole army was in pursuit by noon the following day. It soon became one continual skirmish between the rear guard of Johnston's army and our advance. His intention evidently was to cross the Etowah, fall back to the strong range of the Alletoona Mountains, and there, with his lines extending from the railroad to Dallas, give us battle.

Near Adairsville, — which, by the way, is a pretty village eighteen miles south of Resaca, — Wood's division, of the 4th corps, came upon Hood's and part of Hardee's corps where they were intrenched, with the intention of checking our advance. They opened a heavy artillery fire upon our lines. General Wood formed into line, deployed heavy bodies of skirmishers, and a very brisk little fight ensued, which continued all the evening. The enemy retired after nightfall.

On the 17th Butterfield's division, of the 20th corps, drove the enemy from Cassville. Hooker pressed on, driving them from Calhoun, which village presented nothing but ruined and shattered houses, the inhabitants having fled at our approach — some to the woods, others into the rebel lines. These had been pretty towns, with their neat, white houses, and trim flower gardens, before the scourge of war had swept over them. The country around is extremely fertile, and many a wealthy planter's mansion and farmer's homestead formed bonfires for our destroying army.

The stubborn fight made by Johnston at Adairsville was for the purpose of protecting some wagons and artillery, which he wanted to get off by rail. His main army at this time was but a few miles ahead. Next morning the 4th corps marched through Kingston; in the afternoon they encountered a slight opposition from Cheatham's division and two regiments of cavalry.

Meantime Hooker had moved by River Creek, reconnoitring south, and striking the railroad between Kingston and

Cassville. Butterfield's division was ahead, and encountered the enemy at Cassville, and kept them at bay until Williams's and Geary's divisions came to his support, when the whole corps formed into line, and drove the enemy from the town, after a very hot contest.

The 20th and 23d corps had a slight skirmish with Johnston's flank. The 23d corps occupied the extreme left, harassing the enemy's flank. The 4th and 20th corps occupied the centre. The 14th corps came in on Hooker's right, while McPherson operated on our extreme right. Davis's division of the 14th corps had already moved on Rome, occupying the town with slight opposition.

At Rome we captured a small steamboat on the Coosa River, large quantities of supplies and cotton, and several founderies, all of which were destroyed. Rome is a beautiful little city, embowered amidst trees, and full of pretty flower gardens.

Most of the families had fled. All the able-bodied negroes, men and women, had been carried off. The inhabitants must have left, in hot haste, with the garrison, for provisions and furniture were untouched in the houses; and some of them looked as if the ladies had just gone out to pay an evening visit, and meant to be back to tea.

Our men soon changed the appearance of things, liberally helping themselves to anything they wanted, and then destroyed the rest, and in some cases the houses with them.

On our march a courier from General Johnston to his chief of cavalry, General Jackson, was captured. The despatch was asking information of Sherman's movements on his flank. The poor fellow appeared much terrified, made a generous confession, and looked upon himself as booked for the other world.

General Thomas dressed one of his scouts in the officer's clothing, and sent him off with the despatch. The brave fellow succeeded in his hazardous mission, and returned with valuable information.

Our trains were now following up the army as far as Kingston and Rome, though Wheeler was threatening our communication. On the 24th he made a dash on a train of about sixty wagons belonging to Schofield, which was going to Cassville with surplus baggage. He captured the wagons, but had to burn them, as our cavalry was pressing him; but he took away most of the teams. His men here acted with great cruelty, for we found some of our men with their brains dashed out, and we were told that they were butchered after being captured. Though not crediting all such reports, I cannot ignore them all, for I have met too many savagely butchered myself.

I believe that none of those acts have ever been committed with the cognizance of the superior officers. I give them credit for more humanity on both sides. In all civil wars, and particularly in one carried on with such bitter rancor as this, there must have been many savage acts and brutal murders perpetrated. Our march and battles were characterized by many personal exploits of foolhardy daring that cannot be surpassed.

The crossing of the Oostanaula at those points where the enemy remained to dispute our passage was a noble achievement. General T. W. Sweeny, commanding the second division, 16th corps, had received orders to move to Lay's Ferry, a point south of Resaca, and take possession of the opposite bank. Johnson's brigade, Walker's division, Hardee's corps was fortified on the opposite bank, and opened a galling fire on the advancing troops, who had to charge over an open field to the shelter of some rail fences, and a regular fire across the river ensued.

Meanwhile pontoon boats were launched in Snake Creek, a tributary of the Oostanaula, and six companies of the 66th Illinois and 81st Ohio were ordered to cross in them. The boats, with about three hundred soldiers, pushed down the stream, when a regular storm of rebel bullets whistled around them, toppling some into the water, more into the boats. On they push, blazing away at the enemy in return. The rebel batteries now open, throwing round shot and shell among them, ploughing up the water around, and, in some cases, tearing through their crowded masses.

At length they gained the shore, and with a shout of triumph and derision the brave fellows rushed up the banks, firing as they advanced; then charging right on the enemy, breaking and routing them. Thus did these gallant western men open a passage across the river for Dodge's command.

A private soldier of the 66th Indiana swam the Oostanaula, at Lay's Ferry, during the night, passed the pickets at the other side, scaled the rebel fort, pulled down a battle flag, reswam the river, returning safely to his comrades with the flag as a trophy.

Near Cassville three soldiers belonging to the 23d corps were somewhat behind their command, and not being able to get up to it at night, bivouacked in a small farm-house aside from the road. About the middle of the night they heard a great noise outside, and on looking out discovered the yard full of rebel cavalry. They were betrayed by the people of the house, all of whom they found had left while they were asleep. One of the cavalry, thinking to nab them quietly, gently opened the door, when one of the soldiers ran him through. His comrades fired one volley into the house, the bullets passing through the rotten planks that formed its sides.

The men lay quietly in the most secure positions, and fired out, and then immediately shifted to another corner, the rebels pouring a volley of bullets through the place they had left. This game was played for some time, when those outside, finding that they were paying too dear for it, resolved to burn down the house, though the family protested against it. The house was set on fire, and the dry timbers began to blaze about them. Nothing was now before them but certain death, and they were resolved to sell their lives as dearly as possible, when an unexpected deliverance came. A squad of Stoneman's cavalry, passing near, heard the firing, and hastened to the spot. They attacked the besieging party in the rear, soon putting them to flight, and released their friends.

Johnston had now succeeded in crossing the Etowah, burning the road and railroad bridges near Cartersville. Here General Sherman halted his army for a few days to give it time to rest, and to bring up some supplies.

General Thomas's army lay around Cassville, General Schofield's at Kingston depot and the Etowah Bridge, with General McPherson's about Kingston. In this delightful and fertile section of country, which we found a garden before us, but left a wilderness behind us, the army now halted to rest, and to pillage, too.

It was amusing to observe how the soldiers imposed on the innocent people by giving them forged vouchers. General Sherman, attended only by a single orderly, rode by a small plantation house, where he went in and sat down. The old lady was quite communicative, and Sherman entered into conversation with her.

"Well, have the boys taken much from you?"

"Almost all I have. Sherman was here; he is a right nice un; the poor man said he was hungry; so I got him something to eat; and as he said they were starving, he took a ham and a chicken, but he left me something he called a purtection paper," and she pulled a dirty, scribbled scroll from her breast, and handed it to Sherman. It read, —

"Sergeant Take-them-all gives general protection to this poor, lone widow, with her husband in the army, and to her helpless chickens and roosters; that is, what's left of them."

"And what did the boys say to this?" asked Sherman, who could not help smiling at this novel protection.

"Well, your fellows only laughed at it; it 'pears like they have drefful little respect for their general."

"I am afraid so, madam. If you give me some paper I'll write one they won't laugh at."

"And are you an officer?"

"Yes, ma'am."

"May be you'd have a piece of backer, or a chew; the soldiers didn't leave me a blast."

"Don't use them. Here is a cigar, and a pass that won't be laughed at;" and Sherman mounted and rode off.

While the army is resting, we will devote a brief space to the general appearance of the country, its soil, climate, and geographical position.

Walker County, through which we had just campaigned, is south of Tennessee, and was laid out from Murray County in 1833.

Its general appearance is hilly, or rather mountainous, interspersed with rich valleys of great fertility, covered with a dark, mulatto soil. It has several very prominent mountains, generally running from north to north-west, the principal of which are Taylor's Ridge, — commonly called Rocky Face Ridge, — Lookout Mountain, overhanging Chattanooga, John's Mountain, and White Oak Mountains.

These are separated by some fine valleys, among others Chickamauga, the scene of Rosecrans's memorable fight; Armucha Valley, where Sherman's army sat down before Johnston's intrenched position, along Rocky Face and Buzzard Roost; and Dogwood Valley, where Schofield advanced, threatening Johnston's flank.

It has no towns of importance, Ringgold, Rossville, and Villanow being the leading ones. All these are small places, but remarkably neat and picturesque.

They have become rather historical from the stirring scenes of which they have been the theatre.

This county has been called Cherokee Georgia; and some of the tumuli and remains of the Cherokee settlement are still extant. This county is remarkable for its many caves, the most remarkable of which is Wilson's Cave, which is second only to the Mammoth Cave of Kentucky.

Its great mineral springs are its most remarkable feature, and possessed of strong medicinal qualities. They are situated at the foot of Taylor's Ridge, and are about fifty in number, all located within a space of less than half a mile.

Twelve of these, and the chief ones, are grouped together in less than a quarter acre. These springs held a high reputation among the Indians; and the beautiful valley has been justly called the "Vale of Springs."

The waters are strongly mineral, combining chalybeate, red, white, and black sulphur, iron, magnesia, and salts, in various combinations.

The scenery immediately around the springs is rather of the

sylvan order; but an hour's walk brings you to the mountain, whence you have a view of as picturesque, lovely, and romantic a region as the eye could rest upon. The wood has been cleared from the top of Taylor's Ridge, from which point there is a magnificent stretch of mountain and valley scenery. This is called Buena Vista, and appropriately, for a good view it is.

Here, wearied and fatigued, I slept that summer night of the 7th of May, after helping to drag up that section of artillery to Buena Vista. Here, next morning, I took a bird's-eye view of the camps of the contending hosts, their expiring watch-fires, and their marshalled troops, awaiting the battle. Here, on this point, crowded hundreds of Harker's and Newton's men who were not engaged, anxiously watching the battle raging along the ridge and beneath. How earnestly they watched our advance down Dogwood Valley, as we were steadily driving back the enemy's skirmishers and sharpshooters. And when we dashed into that thick wood beneath, and our huzzas, and the ringing sound of our rifles, told that we were still forcing back the enemy, what a shout went up from Buena Vista! When we emerged from the wood with flying colors, the enemy driven back on their main lines, that shout rang over us, louder even than the din of battle. The men on the summit flung up their caps, and they came down upon us like a shower.

Never before had there been such a party on Buena Vista — never before had there been such a bloody drama played there, and, I trust, never will be again.

Chattooga County, in which Sherman's army was now resting, is next to Walker.

It is rather a beautiful country, even richer in soil than Walker County, and full of hills and valleys, equally fertile and picturesque. It derives its name from its principal river, Chattooga.

It has some splendid plantations, with their wealthy homesteads, and numerous negro surroundings. Summerville is the capital of the county; but we left this on our right flank. Adairsville and Kingston are small but interesting villages. We found them pretty well deserted.

At Cassville, in Cass County, a pleasant spot, the rebels made a decided stand; and consequently it suffered considerably.

Floyd County now lay before us. Johnston had placed the Etowah between Sherman and himself. The Taylor Ridge of mountains continue in a south-west direction through Floyd, dividing the waters of the Chattooga from the tributaries of the Oostanaula.

The Altoona range of hills cross these in a westerly direction. This being a strong natural position, protected by water and mountain and hill range, Sherman justly conjectured that Johnston would avail himself of it.

Floyd County differs little from the others either in soil or scenery.

Its chief rivers are the Oostanaula and Etowah, which, uniting at Rome, form the Coosa. From Rome, the Coosa flows through a rich valley, with beautiful wooded hills and slopes on both sides.

Rome itself is a handsome little town, situated upon an elevation overlooking the river. It did not suffer much from the troops, as we only paid it a passing visit. It is about eighteen miles from Kingston, and is destined to become a flourishing business place. It also has several mineral springs, the most important of which is Cove Spring, on Little Cedar Creek. These gush out from a mountain, forming a pretty considerable creek.

Having so far given a topographical description of the country through which we had operated, I will continue to describe its various features as I chronicle the advance and subsequent achievements of the army, which I left enjoying itself along the banks of the Etowah.

Sherman had his headquarters at Kingston. Here he issued the following order, which rendered the position of newspaper correspondents in the army very uncomfortable.

KINGSTON, GA., May 20, 1864.

. . . . What the commanding general does discourage is the existence of that class of men who will not take a musket and fight, but who follow an army to pick up news for sale, speculating on a species of information which is dangerous to the army and to our cause, and who are more used to bolster idle and worthless officers than to notice the hard-working and meritorious, whose modesty is generally equal to their courage, and who scorn to seek the flattery of the press.

W. T. SHERMAN, *Major General.*

This was by no means complimentary to the press or its representatives, and made the position of correspondents very unpleasant. Every stuck-up jackanapes of an officer, with more assurance than brains, who had lately left the counter or workshop, thought he was privileged to insult gentlemen, and men of learning. However, I must say that no true gentleman in the service ever attempted to do so. I have reason to know that even Sherman's own staff, with the exception of one or two, censured this order. His brother-in-law General Ewing, Surgeon General Moor, Major General Barry, and other gentlemen of his staff, disapproved of it.

As for his adjutant general, Major Dayton, he could not afford to be courteous to a representative of a newspaper.

A respectable member of the associated press once called on him for permission to telegraph just a few lines to relieve the anxiety of the country after an important movement.

His reply was, —

"No, sir. What the h—l do we care about the country? You should go to Washington for news. This is no place to come looking for it?"

Had Sherman issued an order prohibiting correspondents from accompanying the army, I would respect his strength of character; but he knew too well that the war was a matter of history and public interest; that the country was liberally pouring forth its treasures and its blood to suppress treason, and that it would not allow the press to be gagged, and thus shut them off from the most reliable and expeditious source of information relative to the fate of their friends, and the success of their cause in battle.

Thus exposed to petty annoyance from some worthless fops "clothed in a little brief authority," several correspondents left the army.

This order was unworthy of Sherman. Intelligent correspondents had too much respect for themselves and their papers to write anything derogatory to the interest of the army, and if they did, he had his redress in his own hands.

Sherman's abrupt manner of dealing with parties whose business was distasteful to him gave rise to a good many amusing stories about him.

On one occasion a deputation from some commission waited on him for transportation to bring up supplies, and particularly tracts and Bibles to the soldiers.

"Tracts and Bibles, gentlemen," he replied, "are very good in their way, but rations and ammunition are much better. Now, I can't encroach on them."

He was right, for most of these agents were mere hangers-on, living on the country, and giving the supplies to officers and quartermasters to propitiate them, and not to the soldiers, for whom they were intended.

On another occasion Sherman was dining with Howard. A sanctimonious parson present thought the occasion demanded an extra strong grace. With eyes and hands raised piously towards heaven, he was in the midst of it, when Sherman, who sat at the other end of the table unconscious of the chaplain, was bitterly denouncing some officer, and wound up by bringing his hand slap on the table, and exclaiming, —

"Hang the man! Will he ever stop?"

The chaplain, thinking the expression to apply to himself, let fall his hands, and became almost petrified. There was a suppressed titter around the table, and the chaplain did not recover his composure for the evening.

Sherman was at times convivial, and would tell, with the richest humor, racy stories connected with himself, and the many strange characters he had come across.

"I tell you," he said one evening to a party of us at dinner, "I have met more men afflicted with cotton on the brain than any other disease. Some time since a chaplain wrote to me for permission to go south, because, as he had numerous acquaintances there, he could buy plenty of cotton if he only had permission to bring it through the lines. I didn't mind this. Some time afterwards, I got another letter from the same party, renewing the request, but making an offer to give me half the profits. I at once ordered him beyond the lines; and only that I believed he was not quite sane, I would have dealt harder with him.

"At Memphis," he continued, "I was completely pestered about cotton. A little Jew had somehow managed to get into the rebel lines, and buy cotton from private parties, who agreed to send it to some neutral point outside their lines. Our cavalry met them, and brought in the cotton, the parties having no authority for dealing in it. The Jew came to me in a great fright.

"'Ah, monseer jenral, de cavalry took mine cotton.'

"'What right had you to go beyond our lines to buy cotton?'

"'Jenral, I knew de cotton vas dere; and I knew de good government vants it; so I said I'd buy the cotton, and bring it in to you.'

"'You paid for it, then?'

"'Yes; tree tousand dollas down in de gold.'

"'That is, you gave three thousand dollars to the rebels to use against us.'

"'No, jenral; it vas for de cotton.'

"'Well, it's all the same; it went into their hands; and now, as you were so good to them, I order you to pay the same amount to our government, or else I will swing you out of a tree.'

"'And can't I keep de cotton?'

"'Not a pound of it. It's confiscated.'

"We had no more Jews speculating in cotton after that."

CHAPTER VIII.

A CARNIVAL IN THE CAMPS.—RACING AND HUNTING PARTIES.—STRAGGLERS AND MARAUDERS.—EXCESSES OF OUR TROOPS.—MURDER OF REBEL OFFICERS.—CAPRICIOUSNESS OF THE SOUTHERN LADIES.—MRS. MAJOR DASH AND MRS. CAPTAIN SMART.—CONDITION OF THE POOR WHITES.—INCIDENTS AND ANECDOTES.—WHITES AND BLACKS.

The section of country occupied by our encamped army extended some twenty miles, embracing Rome, Kingston, Cassville, and several other minor places. We had established strong posts at Ringgold, Tunnel Hill, and Dalton; also connecting posts to guard our lines of communication.

The country around was very fine, the weather favorable, and the officers and men seemed inclined to employ their days of rest with amusement and recreation.

Races were got up, hunting parties formed; also foraging and visiting parties.

Generals and officers, in their gayest uniforms, rode from camp to camp, making it a pleasing and exciting scene.

The most of the plantation houses were abandoned by their owners, who were either hiding in the woods until we should pass, or had gone on with the rebel army. Old men and women, with decrepit negroes, and squalling picaninnies, were the only persons at home.

The lying press of the south, and all other sources from which they drew information, had so poisoned their minds with stories of our savage and cannibal acts that they trembled at our approach, and looked upon their total destruction as certain. Unfortunately the wanton acts of some of our troops gave color to this. In all large armies there is a class of cowardly ruffians who are sure to slink from battle, and whose only object is plunder.

Owing to the wooded nature of the country, and the vast extent of our lines, these fellows had too many opportunities of gratifying their thieving propensities.

General Sherman had issued an order that the army, as far as practicable, should live on the country.

The soldiers took this as a license for each man to rob and pillage as much as he could; and in truth too many of them seemed well inclined to obey this special order.

For several days a most disgraceful scene of rifling houses, breaking up furniture, ripping up bedticks, and, after making a general mess of things, then firing the houses, ensued.

This was somewhat modified by regular parties being detailed, under command of officers, to forage. Even these often committed the most wanton excesses. I was one evening riding out towards our picket lines, and passing near a house, sheltered in the trees, I heard cries and screams, as if from women in distress. I drew my revolver, and rode into the yard; and what a sight met my view! The yard was covered with the debris of furniture, beds, and bedding; dead poultry and pigs lay around, while soldiers were making desperate charges on others that had not yet fallen. All the beehives were rifled, and the infuriated bees were flying about like so many little demons. I even saw a man wearing the shoulder-straps of a captain, with his hands full of things, rush through a back door at my approach. To add to the savage scene children were rushing about, screaming for their lives; and on going into the house I found four miserable women huddled together in trembling fear. It took some time before I could convince them that they were safe. They were in such a frenzied state, that I remained some time, and put a guard on the house.

Such scenes were of too frequent occurrence; and it often happened that the rebel cavalry came upon these pilfering stragglers while they were rifling some houses, and of course they had no mercy to expect.

On the left of our lines, just outside our picket station, was a very tempting plantation house; still, the men felt a little delicacy in visiting it, as it was pretty close on the rebel lines.

At length a party of volunteers resolved to try the experiment. So they started off in the evening, being favored by the darkness, first having contrived to get the countersign, so that they could return.

It happened that the old planter, a Mr. Hordel, had a son, an officer in Wheeler's cavalry. The young man, being stationed near, availed himself of the opportunity to visit his family.

He, together with two other officers, were in the house when our volunteer party surrounded it.

They were quietly, and, as they thought, securely, sitting around the parlor fire, telling of their hairbreadth escapes and adventures.

Mr. and Mrs. Hordel and their three blooming daughters were the willing auditors.

There must be something strikingly interesting in the adventures of young Hordel's brother officers, who, by the by, were two fine-looking fellows; for two of the young ladies seemed wonderfully pleased at them, and with greedy ears devoured their discourse, and gave them for their pains a world of sighs.

A scout crept softly from the party abroad to the window, and looked through the partially open shutters. He soon reported progress.

What to do now was the question. The front door was locked. The servants were in the back yard, and would give the alarm, should they try to get in that way; and the officers had their revolvers beside them on the table. What was to be done?

It was at once agreed to surprise them from the rear, but to leave three men at the window to fire on the officers if necessary. Two men slipped around, got into the kitchen, but were stoutly encountered by two of the rebel officers' orderlies.

The young officers, hearing the noise, jumped up, and soon a shot from the hall told them that they were surprised.

They grasped their revolvers, and had drawn their swords, when the men at the window fired. One of the officers fell dead, while old Mr. Hordel, who had just at the moment jumped up, received the bullet aimed at his son. The third bullet took effect on one of the young ladies.

CONDUCT OF SECESH LADIES. 81

The men outside joined their comrades, and fired through the windows. Hordel and his living friend rushed into the hall, and joined their orderlies, resolved to sell their lives dearly.

A fierce fight ensued; and as the men outside had set the house on fire, there is no knowing how it would end had not the third orderly, who was outside at the time, made his escape back to a rebel cavalry post, and hurried them up.

They surrounded the party, and killed every man of them except one, who made his escape into our lines, with a most exaggerated report of how they were surrounded, captured, and then butchered. I learned these true particulars from a negro who was in the house at the time.

As a general thing throughout the south, we experienced the most inveterate hate on the part of the ladies. They were bitter against us, and full of the most absurd prejudices. They hated the Yankees; but still, in many cases, they softened down wonderfully; and when we remained any little time, they actually became warm converts to the Union.

When first we entered a town they scarcely showed their pretty faces at all; or, if they did, they wore such a scornful expression that we could well dispense with them.

They tried all those petty modes of annoyance by which ladies can so well show their dislike. You were sure to hear rebel airs floating from Secesh pianos and fair Secesh vocalists.

After a little time they began to mix more freely. They vowed that Captain Smart and Major Dash were ducks of young men. Certainly they could not be Yanks, they were so noble-looking, generous, and polite! Really, though they did not like them, they were too agreeable and too much like gentlemen to be treated rudely. Then they sang so well, and danced so divinely, they should like to meet them. No; they positively could not be mere vulgar "Yanks."

Some of the ladies brightened into sunshine and smiles. "The bonny blue flag" gave way to "The star-spangled banner;" and the farce ended by the prettiest, but most violent of the Secesh ladies, becoming Mrs. Major Dash and Mrs. Captain Smart.

After all, we can hardly wonder that the southern ladies should have exhibited so bitter a spirit. Raised up as they were in luxurious indolence, with slaves to anticipate their every whim, with pampered tastes, and a strong impression ingrafted upon them in childhood that labor of all kinds was dishonorable, the lesson of poverty came home to them with fearful force.

Shut out from all communication with the outer world, they were now deprived of all the luxuries of life, and could barely command its mere necessaries. The price of tea — one hundred and twenty dollars per pound in Confederate money — precluded the very thoughts of it. Coffee was proportionally scarce and dear. Of sugar they could always raise a rough supply from the cane and sorghum.

Their horses were taken for the use of the army, their carriages were rotting in the coach-houses, and their dresses were unfit to appear in public.

They had worn out their fine silks and rich dresses; and such articles now, if they could be got at all, could be only obtained at fabulous prices. So they had to clothe their dainty figures in linsey-woolsey. And because all the able hands, black and white, were gone to the war, either to fight or work in the intrenchments, they had either to labor or to starve.

Their colored servants became sulky and unmanageable, and ardently longed for the approach of the Yankees, whom they looked upon as their friends and deliverers.

Their mistresses, now powerless to coerce them, had to cajole and coax them; while the servants, conscious of their increasing power, gave them as little work, and caused them as much annoyance, as possible.

In their blindness and ignorance they set the Yankees down as the cause of all this; as the murderers of their brothers and husbands, and the destroyers of their peace and happiness. They could not separate cause from effect. Their only argument, as I heard it expressed, was, "Why don't the Yankees let us alone? Why do they endeavor to oppress and conquer us?"

There was another class in the south, who comprised the bone

CONDITION OF THE POOR WHITES.

and sinew of the war, and who, though living in the basest degradation, were not sensible of it. I mean the poorer classes, or, as they are more commonly called, "the poor white trash."

These were scattered over the large plantations, tolerated to squat down and till a few acres in some remote corners, in consideration of the political influence their votes gave their masters. They were too ignorant to know that they were greater slaves than the bondmen whom their masters daily sold.

They learned their politics from their fire-eating masters; from ignorant county newspapers, which, of course, chimed with the planters, who supported them; and from preachers, who doled out whole volumes of sedition, instead of preaching the gospel, and whose only orthodox creed was blind submission to the will of the slave owners.

In such a school, and under such circumstances, can we wonder at the condition of the non-slaveholding whites? They tilled their arid plot, raised a little corn and rye, and, with a few half-starved hogs, which prowled through the woods, they managed to support their miserable lives and half-naked and wholly uneducated children.

As a relief they frequent the dram shanty, where they discuss bad politics and drink worse whiskey.

The planters have given the rudiments of trades to their slaves, and they do their work. They will not, therefore, employ a white man. If they must employ such, it is sure to be some northern man that has settled among them. The very negro servants look down on them with contempt, for they feel that they are much more useful and have more influence.

I had a good instance of the relative values of the black and white races in the south from a colored servant of General John Logan.

Dick was an excellent servant, and was formerly a slave in some part of Northern Georgia. Like thousands more of his class, Dick thought the day of jubilee had come with the Yankees, and turned over to them.

"Dick," said I to him, "was your master kind to you?"

"O, bery much, massa; massa bery kind."

"Did he give you plenty to eat and wear?"

"Bery much, massa; plenty eberyting."

"Never whipped you?"

"Neber whipped dis nigger."

"Then why did you leave him?"

Dick stopped for a moment; then drew up his burly figure to its full height, and exclaimed, "Massa, I had a wife and two children. I have seen oder nigger's wives and children torn from their homes and sold. Why not mine? Massa, I wanted to be free; dis nigger wanted to own hisself."

Dick's logic was sound. Slavery is a bitter draught; and though, in my opinion, the negro was physically better cared for as a slave than he can be during that transition state through which he is now passing, still, I thank Heaven that slavery is abolished. It was a curse to the south, and a degradation to the north.

But to Dick's story.

"I believe, Dick," I said, "a black man was of more value in the south than a white man."

"Yah, yah!" exclaimed Dick. "White man no 'count dere; dis nigger worth fifteen hunder dollars, white man nothing."

"Why, then, Dick, it was better to be a black man than a poor white one."

"Lor bress ou, massa; poor white no value. Massa was sinking a well. It was down bery deep, and Pompey working hard at it, when neighbor Miller comes along, and says, 'Am surprised you leave Pompey down dere; dat will sure cave in. Hire a poor white man.' Massa sent me for one, and put him in dat ere well in place of Pompey; when, sartin enuff, de well caved over him; and Massa Miller says to massa, 'Now see, I am the lucky man to you; I saved you twelve hunder dollars;' and dey went in and had a drink, and left poor white man dere."

This was Dick's story, and I believe it was a true one, for I have seen too many instances of the selfish cruelty of planters to their poor white neighbors.

No wonder that such men, so poor and wretched, should wish for some change. They knew that any alteration in their circumstances could not be for the worse, and all parties, planters, parson, and politicians, told them that if the south attained its independence, their condition would be greatly improved; and they rushed into a war to cut their own throats. I once asked a planter, "Why don't you try to educate the poor of the south, and better their condition?"

"It is hopeless, sir; they are an indolent, good-for-nothing race."

The answer reminded me of a similar one which I once got from an Irish agent, who was clearing off the poor tenants by wholesale. "Why don't you give these people a lease, and encourage them to remain at home?"

"Why, sir, if we gave them leases they would become too independent to vote for the landlord; the only way is to keep them down, sir; keep them down!"

I pondered on his words, and thought therein lies the secret of Ireland's grievances.

Another of the great evils of the south was the land monopoly. A man had no status who did not own several slaves and several hundred acres, no matter though the former were old and feeble, and the latter covered with wood and underbrush. They were the true criterion of the social standing of the owner. I met a lady in Kingston who complained bitterly of her destitute condition. Her husband was a doctor in the rebel army, and the owner of some ten thousand acres of land and some twenty slaves. He had tilled as much of that vast tract as his few slaves could manage, leaving the rest of it a wilderness. He had, perhaps, two hundred acres tilled out of the whole; yet he would not dispose of any of it, except to a few poor white squatters, who were eking out a miserable existence. His dignity and prestige would suffer if he parted with it; so, like the dog in the manger, he lay in his own way, and in the way of others. It was rather amusing to hear his little wife, who was now forced to bustle about and help herself, deplore her fallen state; and of course the Yankees were held responsible for her condition.

"My husband had twenty thousand acres of land, and slaves

at his beck; and look at me now, sir, without a servant!" she exclaimed.

"It's hard, madam, but you have brought it on yourselves. We did not want to come down here, had you not forced the issue upon us."

"No, sir; why don't you let us alone? We'll die before we'll be Yankee servants. You have taken all our slaves, and now want to make slaves of ourselves."

"Such is not the case; we are fighting for the maintenance of the Union; we have not taken one of them; all that can are following us. We cannot nor will not prevent them."

"They are all gone, the ungrateful wretches, except the children and a few old ones, and two the master took along with him, — I am sorry that he did not take the whole batch, — and we so kind to them."

"Why, then, did they leave you, madam?"

"I am sure I don't know."

"They wanted to be free, madam."

"I am sure they were free enough. We never sold but two of them, and we had reared them up idly, and I am sure we had a right to get something out of them. One of them thought to get married to my waiting maid, Chloe, and as we did not want that, we sold them."

"Are the colored people affectionate to each other?"

"Very much so, indeed. It is strange how they take to one another, and fret when any of them are sold away."

"Just so, madam. What would you say if you were sold away from your husband and children — what would you say if you were separated from the man you love?"

"Who dare do it?" said the little woman, defiantly.

"And yet you do it to them; do you believe they are human beings with divine souls, like you?"

"Don't exactly know; guess they may."

"And your Bible tells you, 'Do unto others as you would they should do unto you;' they have deep affections, as well as you, and are you justified in disregarding all these fine feelings?"

"O, that's different; they are black folks, poor ignorant

creatures. It's true they take it to heart very much, but then they get over it."

"Just like you, madam; if you lost your child or husband, you would feel very much: but as people must live after all, you'd get over it."

"But you don't compare the poor ignorant things to us?"

"Certainly not, madam. In some respects, perhaps in human feeling and sympathies, they are your superiors; and if they are ignorant, who made them so? You exclude them from all education and chance of refinement, and then call them ignorant."

"We had better make gods of them, as you do; live with them, eat with them, and sleep with them."

"There you are wrong. We want to give them a fair chance to live, to own themselves and the fruits of their labor; but we do not make them socially our equals; it is you who do so."

"We, sir; no, sir! We are above that; we tolerate them."

"Indeed, madam; look through the window here;" and I pointed out a group of children at play; some of the true Ethiopian jet; some looking as though they had been steeped in a hogshead of tobacco juice; more a rich mahogany color; with others so white that one could mistake them for the doctor's children, only for their short, crispy hair. Who knows whether they were or not? "What do you think of them, madam? Is there not equality between white and black? And these are the children you sell for slaves; your own flesh and blood. No wonder a judgment should come on you!"

The little lady could not see it in this light; and though the wife of a doctor, with twenty thousand acres of land, she smoked her pipe, and freely used her chopsticks and snuff, telling us that "'backer and snuff were tarnation scarce."

The besotted habit of indulging in tobacco and snuff, so peculiar to the lower and middle classes of the south, is equally filthy and demoralizing. It is repugnant to a northern man's sense of propriety and decency to see a pretty young girl swabbing her teeth with dirty snuff, and then asking you for "some 'backer."

I once stopped at a plantation house to rest. I was received by a young girl, as perfect a specimen of female beauty as one could wish to see. She had hair like the raven, eyes like the gazelle, and a bust and frame that might enrapture a Canova. I took off my hat, and bowed in homage to so lovely a creature. She eyed me for some time, assumed a most negligent attitude, and then asked me, "I say, stranger, haven't you got any 'backer you'd let a lady have?"

"I don't use it," I said, in surprise.

"O h—l you don't, old chap! then you might have a cigar to make snuff. I hadn't a swab in a week: curse this d—d war."

My admiration for her beauty soon gave way to a sense of disgust, and a deep hatred for a state of society which could convert a temple so divinely fair into a receptacle for tobacco juice, snuff, and filthy language.

Despite these nasty habits, you will find among the poorest a good deal of homely honesty and hospitality. They will willingly share their last corn-cake with you.

On account of the great extent of most of the plantations, houses are far apart; school-houses few and far between; and therefore the poorer class are extremely ignorant; their clothing, during the war, at least, was of the poorest and meanest description; with the women, consisting of a cotton gown, linsey petticoats, and no head covering. The men wear linsey trousers, stuffed into dirty, heavy boots, a hunting shirt of as many colors as Joseph's garment, all begrimed with filth, and surmounted by a slouched hat or skin cap. Their houses are generally log huts, badly put together, with sufficient interstices to admit the rain, and let out the smoke, which too often escapes from cavernous fire-places at the end. They generally consist of but one room, with a rough floor of hewn logs. The furniture and contents of the hovel are composed of some not over clean culinary utensils, such as a broken pan, a few filthy tins, a dilapidated looking pot, two beds of corn shucks in a corner; a dozen squalid children of all sizes and colors; a couple of half-starved hounds, which show their bloodthirsty propensities by hungry, wistful looks at you. A troop of strange skeletons called hogs, or shotes, besiege the door with their clamorous cries. The old ones, apparently sensible of the folly of expecting anything from creatures so wretched as their owners, have betaken themselves to the woods in pursuit of roots and berries. The owners disdain to work. It is laborious and disreputable. Hunting and fishing are much pleasanter. By fawning and sycophancy, they become the henchmen of young massa, acquire drunken, dissipated habits, and live, swaggering and bullying about, a burden to themselves and a curse to society. These are the general characteristics of that class called the "poor white trash" whom I have met all through Tennessee, Georgia, and the Carolinas, particularly in the latter states. I do not include in this category the laboring poor whites. The men who work for their living, though illiterate and poor, when contrasted with the laboring classes of the north, compare favorably with the laboring classes of other countries. They are a hard-working, plodding people, either working as farm hands on the plantation, or cultivating their own little farms, remote from the bustle of the world and the refinements of civilization, raising the necessaries, and some of the luxuries, of life, enough, at least, to support them. They know little of what is going on outside of their own sphere, and must ask "the master" "Who is president?" or, if there is a new one wanted, "Who will we vote for?" I expect many of them will keep voting for Jeff Davis for years to come. Some northern philanthropists are for extending the franchise to the emancipated negroes. If they do so, be assured they are only throwing so many votes into the hands of the planter, to enable him to reëstablish the power of the land-ocracy, and restore the political status of the south. Many colored folks, no doubt, understand the importance of the franchise; but with four fifths of them it will be as it was with the old nigger, who, when asked, would he not take an oath to support the Constitution, replied, scratching his woolly pate, "By de gor, massa, me hab no dejection to support her; times dreful hard, massa; hab 'nuff to do to support the ole 'oman and de children, I s'pect."

CHAPTER IX.

SCENES IN CAMP.—STORIES BY THE FIRESIDE.—HOW AN ILLINOIS MAN SOLD A HORSE.—THE DOUBLE-ENDER GUN.—MISERY OF THE PEOPLE.—THE HIDING-PLACE IN THE THICKET, AND THE DEAD GIRL.

MANY of my readers have not seen a vast army encamped. What a sight it presents! Here are some showy headquarters, with their numerous surroundings of white tents. Look into these and you will find that officers do not fare so badly even in the field. Neat beds are contrived: some are cots; others lithe saplings or frames covered with a cotton tick, and plenty of covering, probably contributed by some plantation house. On one side is a table laden with books, a box of cigars, and most likely a bottle of "commissary." These, with a looking glass and the officers' equipments, compose the furniture of the tent. Four flies form a mess tent; and as the general and staff are going to dine, we will just see what kind of fare they have. It consists of stewed beef, hashed potatoes, and a couple of chickens, which the Georgian housekeepers were kind enough to rear for them, and most likely a few bottles of old rye, which the planters were kind enough to leave in their cellars for our especial benefit — all these flanked by a respectable force of negro waiters.

Officers and orderlies are always lounging or riding about headquarters, which gives it a very gay and stirring appearance. At some distance from these are the less pretentious headquarters of some brigadier general, or colonel, while a little farther on are the modest tents of the rank and file and company officers arranged in streets.

The men around these are collected in groups, listening to long yarns beside the cook fire, or are formed into little parties playing cards, pitch and toss, or a thousand other games, known only in the army; others, are dining, grumbling at their rations while dining on turkey. The cooks are busy around a huge tin caldron, placed on the fire, in which a joint of bacon and some peas are bubbling and bubbling around as if they were patriotic enough to enjoy being eaten for the good of the soldiers. A smaller vessel simmers near it, but as the lid is on it I cannot see its contents — most likely a brace of chickens under the wing of a fat turkey. This is the way our troops lived on Sherman's campaign. You might ask where they got all these good things? They will tell you, —

"Bedad, cap, hard tack and sour billy were thinning us down like racers, and we sent Belzebub here [a full-blooded grinning negro] to buy these little luxuries for us."

"The villain stole them, though!"

"O, no, massa cap, this nigger sartain he bought dem ere roosters," the hopeful Belzebub would grin out, as he resorted to that infallible remedy of a negro in distress, namely, to scratch his wool. The poor southern women will tell you that they forgot to pay; and I believe them. The rascals became quite epicurean in their tastes in Carolina, good things flowed in such abundance on us.

One evening, in passing by the men while at supper, I overheard one call to the servant, "Come here, you black imp of Satan, and take this turkey; I am tired of it; and bring up that 'ere chicken."

The tents themselves had a very picturesque appearance, scattered over hill and valley, in streets and in clumps, looking like so many canvas villages, or huge gypsy encampments. The groups of soldiers, the lines of soldiers marching to or from picket, the sentries moving statelily on their beats, generals and officers gayly dashing about, make a camp scene gorgeously imposing and impressive.

How greatly is the effect of a camp scene improved by night! For miles around you the camp fires glitter and sparkle like the lamps of a city. If standing on a hill, one circle of dancing lights and sparkling fireflies encompasses you; while from the valleys beneath you the fires also glow, and the noise of song and merriment, of the harmony of music, floats around you.

In some places the fire has ignited the tall pines, and envelops them in one sheet of flame, which leaps from limb to limb, and feeds on the resinous trunks, presenting the appearance of thousands of fiery demons, or huge flaming pillars. Then the men crowded around them, gambling and enjoying themselves by their light, look like so many dark imps, keeping up some hellish orgy; and the sentries, walking up and down with their glittering rifles reflected by the fire, add to the sublimity of the scene.

The officers are in their tents reading, telling stories, or enjoying a drink or a cigar. What strong yarns are spun, what a lot of peach brandy is consumed, particularly if a late discovery has been made, and many casks exhumed; if so, all the officers are collected in the mess tent, a huge fire glows in front; around this their servants are collected, all cheered by the peach brandy, and highly amused at the antics of some six young Ethiopian minstrels — servants and camp followers — who are capering about in the most fantastic manner, singing all kinds of negro songs, timing them by clapping their hands together and on their thighs, thus keeping up the most discordant harmony, all agreeing, "dat de day of Jubelon am come."

It was certainly a strange sight to see these poor youths capering and jumping around to the no small amusement of the officers and men, who laughed heartily, and so highly appreciated the fun of the thing, that they gave the peach to them so liberally that they soon fell off, one by one. One lad made a vigorous stand to maintain his position. He was a musical genius; could produce all kinds of sounds with his voice; imitate a drum, a piano, a fiddle, and the Lord knows what. He was so appreciated, and filled with vanity like any vain white folk, he struggled on for a time, blending all the harmony of the spheres in the most hissing manner, until at length all his vanity yielded to the potent influence of peach brandy, and he fell down beside his brethren.

Improvident and thoughtless soldiers are full of fun and drollery. Looking upon life as a very uncertain tenure, they try and make the most of it. Their motto is, "Eat, drink, and be merry, for to-morrow we die." You would hear more rich, real stories and incidents of battle-fields, beside a camp fire, from a jolly set of happy dogs, who, perhaps, might be shot the following day, than you would your whole life among your city friends. They will lie like troopers, and, I am afraid, steal and swear like troopers, too; but then they make it all right by fighting like troopers.

"I tell you, boys," said one of the men around the camp fire, after taking a pull out of the fire-water bottle, "I once made a good thing out of a strayed horse I cotched. You see, when a poor private meets a streak of luck, if he blabs at all he is sure to be tricked out of his chance. In making 'tracks around the country, while serving in the cavalry, I came on a regular snorter, a coal-black stud, and, taking it for granted that his owner was a sneaking rebel, I brought him with me; and I thought I would keep the matter dark until I could sell him; but the general himself heard of him, and ordered me to turn him over. I had to do so, boys; and didn't I swear he'd be the last horse I'd ever bring in? Well, all the time the thing was heavy wid me, and I felt bad about it. I was orderly to Colonel Shuke, of the —— Illinois cavalry, and he was laid up with an ugly gash he got; so I had my own way. The colonel had a captain's old coat ; so I drew a pair of his long boots over my pants, put on his coat, and turned out a very creditable lookin' captain. Knowing something of the barbering business, I embellished my frontispiece, which is as bare as a pole, with a fine pair of whiskers, made out of horse hair, and a darling mustache, just of the same material. Having fust managed to get the countersign, I rode off through the woods to the general's quarters. Of course, being a captain, no one minded me. I tied my old horse under cover. The night was very dark; so I crept up close to the headquarters; there, sure enough, were all the horses, with a whole lot of orderlies, encamped around them. I had to wait till they went to bed; and there was no one there but the sentry, who occasionally sat on a pile of sacks, keeping watch all the time.

" 'I will be up to that fellow,' says I, and got behind and let fall a bottle of whiskey, and then fell back to my hiding-place. He soon picked up the bottle, looked at it, took out the cork, and smelt it.

" 'Ain't I the lucky dog!' I heard him say. 'Some of the officers dropped this here. Well, they may bid good day to it now;' and he took a long pull out of it, and then sat down on the bags and took another pull, and then got up, went his rounds, and took another pull, and sat down again. I remarked that after every pull he sat longer and longer, until at last he fell asleep.

" 'Now is my time,' says I; so I up and slips off the horse, changes the saddles, and lets old rasper find his way home, which I knew he would. I knew a colonel who wanted a fust-rate horse, and would pay a big price. He was in the 17th corps. So off I started for his quarters next morning.

" 'Is Colonel Strunt in?' says I.

" 'Yes, captain,' replied an orderly.

" 'I want to see him,' says I.

The colonel soon walks out, hitching on his pants.

" 'Good morning, Colonel Strunt,' says I, saluting him.

" 'Good morning, Captain ———.'

I saw he was at a loss about my name.

" 'Sweltonback, of the 4th regulars,' I replied.

" 'Captain Sweltonback. By George, but that is a splendid horse you have; just turn him around.'

The colonel was a great admirer of horse-flesh.

" 'A noble horse, sir; but, colonel, I want to inquire, have you any man named George Sweltonback in your brigade. I have a brother in this corps somewhere.'

" 'Sweltonback, Sweltonback! Well, I think not; but I shall inquire. Captain, wouldn't you be tempted to sell that horse?'

" 'Well, I don't like to part with him, as he is a great favorite;

but as I am going out of service in a few days, sooner than take him home, I'd sell him for a good sum.'

" 'What price do you set on him, captain?'

" 'Well, I can't exactly say. You see I haven't my mind made up. Would you think two hundred and fifty dollars too much?'

" 'It's a big price, captain; but I like the horse. I will go two hundred. I couldn't do more.'

"After much haggling I let him have the horse at two hundred dollars, drank heartily, rode one of his horses the most of the way home, took off my beard, mustache, and captain's coat, and went to my quarters.

"The general kicked up a dreadful row looking for that horse; and when he came across Colonel Strunt riding on the identical black horse, wasn't there a scene? It was as good as a play to see them. At it they went like two fishmongers, and I really thought they would run one another through; for I was present at the interview."

"And how did they settle it?"

"I really don't know, for I soon after left. There was a great fuss hunting up Captain Sweltonback, but he couldn't be found."

"That was a capital trick," said a little wheezy man who seemed particularly attached to the bottle; "but, by gorra, it wasn't as good as how Mick here eschaped from the tarnation murtherers that kilt him."

"Tell us that, Mick," said the others by general acclamation.

"An' sure it was nothing worth talking about," says Mick. "You see I went with a few of the boys to visit the neighbors; and the spalpeens, not having any liking for us, took us prisoners, and kilt one of the boys. We kilt two of them, and they said they'd kill another of us to make the number even; and faith and troth they selected myself, and made me sthand up beside a three. Though I argued and rasonified with them, there was no help; so die I must. Faix, I had no liking for it; but that was no use at all. I had an old gun that was slightly bent, and wouldn't throw fair for the life of you; and I knew there was two charges in it. All I ask of ye boys, honey, is to shoot me with my own gun; it would be a consolation to me. Well, they agreed to please me, seeing I was about to die; so the fellow up and bobs at me; but, murther, he an' I jumped up in the air as if for a wager. That gun was a caution to sinners; it shot both ways, and kilt him deader behind than me before; but I let on being dead all the time; and when they kicked me to see if I were all right, I didn't sthir, but the blood gushed from my side; so they set me down for dead. Well, at night I got up, borrowed one of the dead men's coats, and stole away. The rest of my comrades never came back; so I believe I was best off, after all."

Women and children were dreadfully frightened at the approach of our army. It was almost painful to witness the horror and fear depicted on their features. They were schooled up to this by lying statements of what atrocious murders we were committing.

"Neither life nor virtue is sacred from these northern barbarians; the old and infirm perish by their bloody hands, while lovely women — our wives and daughters — are reserved for a fate even worse than death. Strike, men of the south, and exterminate such polluted wretches — such living demons."

This is an extract from a southern paper. Is it any wonder, then, that the country people trembled at our approach, and hid themselves away in woods and caves? I rode out one evening alone to pay a visit to another camp which lay some six miles beyond us. In trying to make a short way through the woods, I lost the road, and rambled on through the forest, trying to recover it. This is no easy matter, as I soon discovered; for I only got deeper and deeper into the forest. I then turned my horse's head down a valley that I knew would lead me out on a camp somewhere.

In riding along this, I thought I saw a woman among the the trees. I rode in the direction, and saw her darting like a frighted deer towards a thick copse of tangled briers, wild vines, and underbrush.

Fearing some snare, I followed, with pistol in hand; and

heavens, what a sight met my view! In the midst of the thicket, sheltered by a bold bluff, were about a dozen women, as many children, and three old men, almost crazy with fear and excitement.

Some of them screamed when they saw me, and all huddled closer, as if resolved to die together. I tied my horse, and assured them that they had no cause for fear; that I was not going to harm them, but would protect them, if needed. Thus assured, they became somewhat communicative.

They told me that they thought the soldiers would kill them, and that they hid here on our approach. Thinking that we were only passing through, they had brought nothing to eat or to cover them. They were here now near three days, and had nothing but the berries they picked up in the woods. They looked wretched, their features wan and thin, their eyes wild and haggard, and their lips stained from the unripe wild fruit. Some of them were lying down, huddled together to keep themselves warm; their clothes were all saturated from the dew and a heavy shower of rain which fell during the day.

I do not think one could realize so much wretchedness and suffering as that group presented. Some of the women were evidently planters' wives and daughters; their appearance and worn dresses betokened it; others were their servants, or the wives of the farm-laborers.

There were two black women, and some three picaninnies. Under the shelter of a tree, I saw a woman sitting down, rocking her body to and fro, as she wept bitterly.

I went over to her. Beside her was a girl of some fourteen years, lying at full length. As I approached, she looked so pale and statue-like, I exclaimed, —

"What's the matter. Is she in a faint?"

"Yes; in one that she won't waken from," said an old crone near.

"Dead!" I exclaimed.

"Well, stranger, I reckon so; better for her go, poor darling, than have the Yankees cotch her."

It was so. She was dead. I understood she was delicate;

and the hunger and cold had killed her. So much were they afraid of being discovered that they had not even a fire lighted.

I inquired my way to the camp, and soon returned with some provisions. The dead body was removed, and the sorrowing group returned to their homes; but some of them had no homes, for the soldiers, on the principle that all abandoned houses belong to rebels, had laid them in ashes.

CHAPTER X.

ASSAULTS AND SKIRMISHES NEAR DALLAS AND ALLATOONA.—
WOOD'S DIVISION STORMING THE HILL.—CLEBURNE'S REBEL
DIVISION DRIVE THEM BACK.—GALLANT ATTACK OF GENERAL
T. W. SWEENY.—KENESAW MOUNTAIN.—GENERAL FRANK P.
BLAIR ARRIVES.—PERSONAL RISKS OF OUR GENERALS.—
SHERMAN SHELLING A SKULKER.—ATTACK ON A TRAIN, AND
ITS CONSEQUENCES.

WE had secured possession of two good bridges across the Etowah, and had built some others. The army being recuperated and supplied with twenty days' rations, broke camp and moved forward on the morning of the 23d May.

Johnston had now occupied the Allatoona Pass, his lines and works extending along the Allatoona range toward Dallas.

The army of the Tennessee crossed the Etowah at the mouth of Conasaw Creek, and moved by the little town of Van Wirt, on our right flank, and south of Dallas. General Davis's division of the 14th corps had moved directly from Rome to Dallas, following McPherson's route. General Thomas, with the 4th and 20th, and part of the 14th corps, marched by Euharlee and Burnt Hickory, crossing the Pumpkin Vine Creek, on the main Dallas road.

General Schofield, with the 23d corps, was moving still farther on our left.

General Gerrard operated on the flank and rear of McPherson's column; General Stoneman, flank and rear of Schofield, with General McCook guarding our rear.

On the 25th the 20th corps was well in advance on the centre. Williams's division crossed Pumpkin Vine Creek on a bridge partly burned by the rebels. Geary crossed about two miles farther up, and Butterfield about a mile below — all converging toward Dallas.

About three miles south of Pumpkin Vine Creek the enemy opened suddenly, from the dense underwood that lined the roads, at the head of Hooker's column.

A heavy line of skirmishers were deployed, driving the enemy back, on the column which had filed into line of battle on the right and left of the road. The country was hilly and densely wooded, and favorable to a sudden attack by the enemy. Hooker had but one division south of the creek; the others were not up.

The rebels made a fearful attack on Williams's division, but were met with firmness, and a surging, uncertain fight ensued. Williams was barely able to hold his position, for a large portion of both Polk's and Hood's corps were massed against him.

About five o'clock Geary's noble "White Star Division" came to his support, and at once became engaged. Butterfield's division deployed into line of battle, and Williams and Butterfield charged the enemy in the face of a fierce storm of bullets and canister.

Their ammunition was nearly exhausted, and the troops were wavering, when Geary's division, which, after the first assault, had been thrown back in reserve, formed into three lines, and advanced to their support.

Geary reserved his fire until close upon the enemy, and then poured a deadly volley into them, which made them waver; but again they rallied, and the contest lasted until the darkness of night separated them.

Howard's corps was in the rear of the 20th, Wood's 2d division in front, and rapidly hurried up to their support; but on account of the darkness, and a heavy thunder and rain storm, were not able to get up in time to assist them. We hastily threw up breastworks, and the men lay for the night within four hundred yards of the enemy. The rebel troops engaged were Stevenson's, Stewart's, and Hindman's divisions.

Sherman had ordered Hooker to make a bold push for New Hope Church, a point where the Ackworth, Dallas, and Marietta roads meet. In trying to do so, Hooker had thrown out one column as a feeler, and thus suddenly struck the enemy's lines.

ASSAULTS AND SKIRMISHES. 101

During the night the 4th corps, Howard's, moved into position on the left of Hooker's, with Schofield still on the extreme left. On the right of Hooker came Johnson's division of Palmer's corps, while McPherson was still moving on Dallas by the extreme right flank.

Johnston had occupied the Allatoona Ridge, a range of mountains extending in broken spurs. He had established lines along these, tending partly north-east by south-west.

All the hills around were scooped, and grooved, and converted into rifle-pits and batteries.

Our lines were formed in conformity to those of the rebels, but somewhat longer, and threatening to outflank them.

The country here was very poor. Deep, dark valleys, high, barren ridges, all full of underbrush and forest trees, were the general characteristics.

The 26th passed off with heavy skirmishing along our front, both armies trying to secure favorable positions.

Our lines were pretty well established on the morning of the 27th, and the scene opened with a desultory fire between the sharpshooters, growing brisker as the day advanced.

Batteries were established in Hooker's front. These were covering a section in front, which occasionally opened on the enemy.

A rebel brigade of Pat Cleburne's division made a dashing assault on the advance guns, believing they were but partially supported. They came on splendidly, as Cleburne's crack troops always did, but were met by a concentrated musketry fire, and a generous allowance of canister from the guns. They staggered; made another charge; were again mowed down, and then fell back. Similar charges had been made at other points during the day.

Johnston was looking out for a weak point to assault in force, but he soon found that there were no weak points there.

In the afternoon General Thomas J. Wood, commanding the 2d division, 4th corps, made a flank movement, wheeling round the 23d corps. He was ordered to feel the enemy's right flank, and if possible turn it. He had to march through a regular jungle of trees and underbrush, which consumed the most of the day. So it was close on night when he was able to form into line and advance. Wood wished to defer the assault until morning, but his orders were peremptory.

He formed his division into columns of double lines by brigades. General Hazen's brigade in front; Scribner's brigade of Johnson's division, 14th corps, supported Wood on the left.

It was an ugly place to advance. Steep hills, thick brushwood, and a small road that crossed a stream leading up to a place called Picket's Mills, were to be traversed.

The troops moved calmly and steadily up that hill, through the matted wood, crossed the intervening ravine, and gained the crest of the hill. One would think these fine fellows were going to a parade, instead of to death, so calm and composed did they look.

Having gained the crest of the hill, they halted to dress up their lines, and then descended its sides into a deep ravine, which separated them, by about one hundred yards, from the rebel works. Across this they charged with a shout. The rebels had all the time reserved their fire, and had lain down in their intrenchments, to make us believe that they were not in force. As our lines approached, they jumped to their feet. Two masked guns belched forth on us, while a regular sheet of lead and flame seemed to burst from behind the intrenchments.

Under this fierce storm our men rushed up to the enemy's works, many of them sheltering themselves behind them.

It was Cleburne's division that was there. This iron chief, the Stonewall Jackson of the western army, and his famed troops, seemed ubiquitous, for in the early part of the day he was fighting away on our centre.

Our lines were shattered, our ammunition exhausted, and we had to fall back.

The remnant of Wood's division intrenched itself, fearing an attack from the enemy during the night. They also succeeded in bringing in most of their dead and wounded.

Major Hanson, of General Wood's staff, was among the killed. He was a thorough gentleman, refined and courteous;

a true soldier, brave and chivalrous. He died as he lived, a Christian and a soldier.

The loss in Wood's division was very severe, numbering about thirteen hundred, all told. They made a desperate fight, but they fought against every disadvantage.

Fatigued with a trying march, they had to charge over hilly ground on strong intrenchments guarded by desperate troops.

I strayed around that hill-side, where we had laid our dead and wounded that night. My horse could scarcely pick his way through them, so closely were they lying; yet the noble brute picked his steps as safely as if it were clear day. It is strange that a horse will not shy at dead men; and you can scarcely get him to pass one of his own species when dead.

He will walk through piles of dead on the darkest night without touching a single man.

That assault of Wood's division was one of the fiercest I have ever witnessed. One continued file firing was kept up all through. No pattering of bullets, but one unceasing roar of musketry ran along the lines for hours. The officers and men did all that men could do — rallied, charged; but all to no use. Cleburne's division was too strongly intrenched. As the 124th, 41st, and 1st Ohio were bringing in the dead and wounded, the rebels jumped from their works and attacked them. They fought like so many tigers over their prey. When we gained that bloody field we could then see how desperately we fought for its possession.

Dead bodies were found lying just behind the rebel works. The trees in the valley were cut through with bullets, just as if mowed down. The ramrods, fired in the hurry of the moment, were stuck in the trees.

Captain Stenson, of General Howard's staff, was badly wounded, and Howard slightly. General Howard and General Wood remained on the ground until near day, seeing that the troops were all safe and the wounded cared for, and then they threw themselves down, but not to sleep, for shells came hurtling through the trees, bursting near them. A piece of one struck General Johnson, of the 14th corps, in the side, seriously wounding him.

After much marching and manœuvring, and considerable skirmishing, McPherson had taken up his position in front of Dallas. The enemy were not content to leave him inactive. About three o'clock on the afternoon of the 28th they opened an attack on Logan's pickets, and a very sharp contest ensued, and was maintained with great obstinacy on both sides. The enemy being largely reënforced, and Logan not sufficiently supported, his advance had to fall back on the main lines.

It was evident from their manœuvring and feeling our lines, that the enemy meant to make an assault.

About five o'clock the rebels had massed in heavy columns, and charged on General Harrow's division. The rebel column moved boldly up the hill, exposed to a heavy artillery fire. Our troops lay down in their works, letting the enemy come within a few hundred yards of their breastworks, when they jumped to their feet, and poured into that proud, defiant column volley after volley, which made them quail and falter.

Again they rallied and charged, cheering one another on, and dashing right up to our works. We had brought some guns to bear on their flank, thus exposing them to an enfilading fire. Despite this they doggedly persisted in maintaining their position, actually charging right against the works. At length they began to break off in detail, and soon the whole mass followed, making for the shelter of their works and the woods. Scarcely had this assault been repulsed, when they renewed it, in front of Osterhaus's line, repeating the same game with similar effects.

After this there was a considerable lull in the storm of battle, and we thought that the enemy had given up all hopes of renewing his mad assaults; but we were disappointed.

This time they had collected their troops for one more desperate effort in front of Sweeny's division, 16th corps; but they met a stubborn customer in Sweeny.

Was he, brave Tom Sweeny, — who had lost his right arm in Mexico; whose desperate resistance at Stone River was the turning-point of that important battle; who had earned the name of "Bulldog Sweeny," so tenaciously did he hold his own, or scourge the rebels in his fights,—was he now to yield to twice repulsed columns? Certainly not; and Sweeny met their assault with his characteristic dashing bravery, soon driving them back in broken and disjointed masses.

Dallas is about twenty miles from the line of railway at Marysville, and forty-five from Atlanta.

The operations around Allatoona and Dallas were not looked upon in the light of a general engagement, but rather a succession of heavy skirmishes—desperate assaults and repulses. Johnston tried the assault on the right, and was repulsed with great slaughter; we repeated the game on the left and left centre with equal success. The following days we had continual heavy skirmishing and partial assaults along the lines, except in front of McPherson's position, which the enemy desperately assaulted. For twelve days, which were enlivened by continued attacks and heavy skirmishing, we lay around the Allatoona range.

On the 1st of June General McPherson moved to his left, and occupied General Thomas's place. Our left was then strengthened, and swung around, occupying the woods leading to Allatoona and Ackworth. General Stoneman's cavalry advanced into Allatoona, at the east end of the pass, and General Gerrard's cavalry at the west end. Our infantry lines were now closing up, and we had fully accomplished our work in flanking the Alltoona pass.

Johnston, finding his position untenable, fell back to the Kenesaw range of hills. Kenesaw itself comprised twin peaks, rising boldly out of the valley, and commanding the line of railway and the passes to Marietta. Extending on our right was a range of hills, the highest of which are Pine Mountain and Lost Mountain. These form one continuous, irregular link of conical hills, with Kenesaw covering the town of Marietta, and the railroad back to the Chattahoochee. The enemy now occupied these hills with a line fully twelve miles long. The crests and sides of the hills were bristling with batteries, and crowds of men, looking in the distance like so many huge ants, were busy felling trees, digging rifle-pits and intrenchments, and in every way making grand preparations for the impending struggle. Sherman moved by Ackworth, and established a base of supplies at the Allatoona pass. He placed a garrison here, and had the railroad bridge across the Etowah built. He soon had a large store of supplies up.

While at Ackworth we were reënforced by Major General Blair, with two divisions of the 17th corps, and Colonel Long's brigade of cavalry.

General Frank P. Blair is a man of considerable energy and resolution. He is about five feet eleven inches high, with strong, expressive features, covered with a long, sandy beard. Since the time he joined Sherman, until the winding up of the campaign by Johnston's surrender, his military career has been very creditable. In the campaign through South Carolina, a large share of the fighting fell to the lot of his corps, the 17th.

Sherman calculated that these timely reënforcements would supply his loss in battle since the opening of the campaign. I expect, in every way, we must have lost, up to this, about twelve thousand men. Perhaps the enemy's loss was less, as they for the most part fought behind strong intrenchments.

Several curious incidents, showing the danger to which our generals were exposed, occurred at this time. General Hooker's and Thomas's headquarters were very well under range of the enemy's guns, so that shells were falling about pretty fast. A piece of one went through General Hooker's mess tent, and another carried off a camp stool he was going to sit on.

"Very impolite indeed!" said the general, looking after it, and getting another.

As for Thomas, I don't think he was ever guilty of perpetrating a joke; he is too grave and stoical for that.

Sherman, in his abrupt manner, says some good things. He was standing near a battery one day, as we were shelling along the line previous to Wood's advance, and with his glass was closely examining the enemy's position. Seeing them getting up a battery at a certain point, he turned to Captain De Grass, and said, "Look here; do you see that point on the right of the wood?"

"Yes, general."

"Put a shell in them; yes, put them in there; they are trying to start a battery there to sweep this point; start them out of it, you, first."

Sherman himself went to sight the first gun, and while doing so a sharpshooter sent a bullet glancing along the barrel just by his cheek.

"Ha! close shaving, that; well, let us pay them back the compliment — fire!" and right went the shell bang among them.

"Very good, very good," said he with a grin; "that kicked up a dust, and some of their heels, too; give them more of them, with my compliments, captain." And away went Sherman's killing compliments, compelling the rebels to give up the idea of establishing their battery at that point.

A man almost dead with fear had crouched under the roots of an uprooted tree. Sherman chanced to take shelter from a fierce fire near by. When a shell burst close, the fellow would writhe, and cry out, "O Lord! O Lord! if I get out of this, I'll never be caught again. O, dear! O, dear! if I once get home — O, it's dreadful! I know I'll be killed!"

Sherman was so amused at the fellow's cowardice, that in order to increase his terror he would fling stones against the old tree, when the fellow crouched closer, exclaiming, "O, dear! it is awful! it's dreadful! I'll surely be killed!"

"That's hard firing, my man," exclaimed the general.

"Hard! O, it's fearful. I think thirty shells struck this tree while I was here."

"It's all over now, my man; come out." The trembling wretch crawled out and looked about him. There was Sherman standing quite coolly. When the man saw who his tormentor was, he was nearly frightened as much as by the shells, and darted right off for his command, not heeding the shells this time.

A battle-field is one record of stirring incidents and acts of personal bravery, a few of which I will here relate. As a class, the sharpshooters must use a great deal of caution and strategy, both to shelter themselves and induce the enemy to expose themselves. Some sharpshooters had taken down several of our men from behind the shelter of some large trees which protected them. But our boys resorted to a ruse. They sectioned off in twos, and took up favorable positions; then one would dart out from the tree. The rebel sharpshooter, believing that he had a sure thing of it, would expose himself, and pop at the other. This gave the comrade an opportunity of taking a sure shot at the rebel, while the other's motions were so rapid that he most likely escaped. The effects of fear, amounting almost to insanity, sometimes developed in action, are very extraordinary. In General Harker's brigade, the men were under orders to advance, when a sergeant retired to his tent, and shot himself through the head. I have known several cases of the kind. It appears strange that a man from fear of going into battle should kill himself. I have often seen men strip themselves stark naked, and run crazy out of a battle-field. I might suspect their sincerity, but I have seen them rush in this manner, under fire, into the rebel lines. This is caused, no doubt, by the stunning effect of shells bursting around them, and killing their comrades. So great is the terror produced by the explosion of several shells, that I have seen a horse that was under a very heavy fire, tremble, the sweat at the same time bursting out of every pore, and then drop down dead, without being touched by ball or shell. I have also known some noble instances of the affection of the horse for his master. An orderly of General Logan's, while carrying a despatch, was shot. His horse was a great pet, and would follow him and obey his commands. As soon as the master fell, the horse stood up, and turned round, and whined most piteously. Though the noble animal seemed fully sensible of his danger, and would turn about to shelter himself from the shot and shell which were falling around fast and furious, still he remained with the body several hours. He would move away a little by times, and neigh, as if calling for help, and when this failed, would again return to the body. I have known several other instances of affection on the part of the horse. A wounded horse looks at you with the most piteous, upbraiding expression, as much as to say, "It's all your doings; I had nothing to do with it."

AN AMUSING OCCURRENCE.

Johnston's position was now a strong one, besides, he had been reënforced by some ten thousand Georgia and Alabama militia. He now occupied the last strong range of hills north of the Chattahoochee. If driven from this he should fall behind the river, thus relieving us from the harassing attempts made by his cavalry and guerrilla squads, from his flank, upon our rear and lines of communication. We had to garrison the railroad bridge on the river, important posts, and the different towns back to Chattanooga. We had to leave a garrison at Tunnel Hill, Resaca, Rome, Kingston, Allatoona, and other posts. This, of course, considerably weakened Sherman's effective strength. The militia, or one hundred days' men, soon relieved portions of these. The different garrisons, posts, and block-houses had to be connected by a chain of pickets, to prevent squads of cavalry from raiding on the line, and destroying it and the telegraph wires. Still, they often succeeded in misplacing a rail, or placing a peculiar iron crank upon it, thus throwing the train off the track. This was a daily occurrence, and if by any chance it failed, they would open fire from the thickets of the forest on the train. Many passengers and soldiers got killed this way. Many trains were thrown off, until the whole line looked one lying-in hospital of invalid cars. I heard Sherman oftentimes say, "That cursed line is more trouble to me than to whip Johnston."

The following amusing incident occurred to me in one of my dangerous trips on this road. We were crowded inside luggage vans and dirty cars; outside them, in every place that a man could be stowed, a man was perched. The soldiers on the top had their pieces ready, looking out for breakers, while we, inside, were busy with revolvers, and wishing that the rascals dared make their appearance, just for the fun of the thing. Among those loudest in praise of his own heroism was a sutler, who, with a huge navy revolver, swore he was a match for any six of the guerrillas. By some chance we had a lady travelling with us, who appeared very much alarmed, and clung to the valiant Jack Falstaff hero for shelter and protection. This fired his courage. He told her to stick close to him, which she literally did, by putting her arms around his waist. Really, it was delightful to see her clinging to him, and to witness his bold, defiant air, as much as to say, "Let them come on now if they dare." We were passing above Resaca, in a gloomy section of country, without a house within miles of us. We had passed the military post a few miles, when bang goes a volley from the wood at the cars. At the same time the locomotive ran off the track; but as it was going very slow, this was not of much consequence. The volley was returned by the men on the top, some of whom fell off, from the shock of the engine. We jumped up, and I naturally looked to see if our brave hero was mowing down the Philistines. All his courage had evaporated at the sound of lead, and he lay sprawling at the bottom of the car, making frantic efforts with one hand to keep the woman between him and the dangerous side, while with the other he was piling a regular barricade of sacks of corn around him. I took up the pistol, and could not resist the temptation of giving him a very powerful application of my boot, which he must have taken for a wipe of a shell, for he swore and prayed most vehemently, and kicked most spasmodically. If he were under the operations of a most powerful battery, he could not do it better. The woman was almost frightened out of her life by his squalls and antics. Our men soon formed, and drove off the guerrillas. Fortunately, there was no one seriously injured, and the train having been put to rights, we soon got off. Our friend of the buskin courage was quite chop-fallen. He suffered most by the solicitude of the woman, who wanted to know where he was wounded. It was no use denying that he was, for she vowed that she felt the piece of shell hitting him, and he wouldn't halloo so, only he was badly hurt.

CHAPTER XI.

KENESAW MOUNTAIN. — SHERMAN COMMANDS A BATTERY. — DEATH OF BISHOP POLK. — THE MARCH THROUGH THE MOUNTAIN PASSES. — SHERMAN'S STEAM SCOUT. — A FRIENDLY VISIT, AND ITS CONSEQUENCES.

McPHERSON commanded the line of railroad between Allatoona and Kenesaw, marching on parallel roads. General Hooker was on the right, with Schofield a little retired, and General Thomas in the centre, fronting Kenesaw. A heavy fall of rain set in on the 13th and 14th, rendering active operations impossible. A brisk artillery fire was kept up on different parts of the lines.

Towards the right of our line were some strong positions. Lost Mountain and Pine Mountain were separated by intervening hills. On these the rebels had established some batteries. Sherman was manœuvring in order to compel Johnston to fall back from these natural ridges extending from Kenesaw, which would throw open the road by Nickajack Creek, and give him a better chance of flanking his left. On the morning of the 14th some change had been made in our lines. The fourth corps moved forward in the centre, closing up well on Hooker.

Skirmishers were thrown out in order to cover the advance of our lines, and a few sections of artillery were placed in position. The skirmishing was pretty brisk towards evening, and the batteries opened a dropping fire on the rebel position. Sherman rode up to a battery, and turned his glass towards Pine Mountain.

After taking a good view he turned to the officer in command, saying, "Captain Simonson, can you send a shell right on the top of that knob? I notice a battery there, and several general officers near it."

"I'll try, general."

The captain fired, and the general looked on with his glass.

"Ah, captain, a little too high; try again, with a shorter fuse;" and up went the glass to his eye. Away went the shell, tearing through General Bishop Polk in its course.

"That will do," said Sherman, shutting down his glass.

It is said that Johnston and Hardee were on their horses beside Polk when he fell, and when the first shell came they remarked, —

"It is safer to alight."

Polk smiled, and still staid surveying our position, and thus met his death.

We knew that night that he was killed, for our signal officers had discovered the system of the rebel signals, which enabled them to read the despatches along the enemy's lines.

When we took that hill, two artillerists, who had concealed themselves until we had come up, and then came within our lines, showed us where his body lay after being hit. There was one pool of clotted gore there, as if an animal had been bled. The shell had passed through his body from the left side, tearing the limbs and body in pieces. Doctor M—— and myself searched that mass of blood, and discovered pieces of the ribs and arm bones, which we kept as souvenirs. The men dipped their handkerchiefs in it too, whether as a sacred relic, or to remind them of a traitor, I do not know.

Thus fell Lieutenant General Leonidas Polk. He was born in Raleigh, North Carolina, in 1806. He graduated at West Point, but soon after entered the Protestant Episcopal ministry, and was appointed missionary bishop to Kansas and the Indian territory. In 1841 he was appointed regular bishop of the diocese of Louisiana.

At the breaking out of the rebellion he was appointed major general, with command of the district of the Mississippi. The battle of Belmont was fought, and Forts Henry and Donelson fell, while the department was under his command. At the battle of Shiloh General Polk had command of a corps under Beauregard. He also served at Corinth.

Having the command of a corps under Bragg, he participated in the movements through Tennessee and Kentucky. He fought at the battle of Perryville, in October, 1862. Here he showed wonderful presence of mind, for somehow getting into the Federal lines he passed off as a Federal officer, actually ordering a regiment to cease firing. He served at Murfreesborough and Stone River; also during the fearful struggle of Chickamauga. On account of some difference with Bragg regarding that battle he was relieved. In January, 1864, he was again in the field, assuming the temporary command of the department of the Mississippi, in place of Johnston, appointed to the chief command. He commanded a wing of Johnston's army all through the campaign against Sherman, until he lost his life on Pine Knob.

The 15th opened with an irregular artillery fire along the lines, increasing as the day advanced. Our lines had pushed considerably forward at several points. A part of McPherson's command moved obliquely towards the left and the railroad, and soon became engaged with the enemy. Harrow's division, of the 15th corps, took up a position on their left, with Osterhaus in reserve. Towards evening McPherson's command engaged the enemy in front, while Harrow, with his division, wheeled to the right, forming a semicircle. He thus overlapped an outlying detachment of the enemy, comprising the 31st and 40th Alabama. They had soon to surrender. Harrow then fell back with his prisoners, and McPherson closed up his line, shifting more to the left.

Sherman, finding that Johnston had occupied too extended a line for his forces, resolved to break through it between Kenesaw and Pine Mountain, and thus split his army in two. Simultaneously with McPherson's movements the other corps advanced, the 14th corps against the enemy's position on Kenesaw; Howard occupied Pine Mountain, and Hooker against the enemy's intrenched position on Lost Mountain. This assault of Hooker's was one of the most desperate and best sustained of the many charges made on the enemy's position while occupying the stronghold of these mountain ranges. Lost Mountain is a conical-shaped hill, separated by a ridge from Pine Mountain: this ridge runs obliquely, connecting with Kenesaw. The enemy's left rested on Lost Mountain; therefore this strong position was of vital importance. It covered a valley or gorge, which was the only outlet for our army to make a flank movement. Geary's second division formed into line of battle, and moved forward in column by brigade; Colonel Ireland's brigade being in advance, Colonel P. H. Jones's next, and Colonel Candy's next. Geary's division was supported by the first and second divisions.

Heavy lines of skirmishers were first thrown out in order to develop the enemy's strength and position. These were closely followed by the assaulting column, and a fierce fight ensued. For a moment the column was checked, but again they rallied, and charged with such desperate impetuosity that they soon had possession of the enemy's first line of work, driving them towards the crest of the mountain. Geary occupied the intrenchments and strengthened his position. In the course of the evening the enemy made several ineffectual attempts to regain their lost ground. This was a noble charge of Geary's division, and was right nobly sustained and resisted.

Colonel Ireland's brigade suffered heaviest, it having lost in all about three hundred men. For a time it had to sustain the whole charge, but was ably supported by Colonel P. H. Jones's — now General Jones — brigade, which dashed into its support with that daring impetuosity which has characterized itself and its brave young commander. Colonel Jones was wounded at Pea Vine Creek, and had just returned in time to participate in the present fight, in which he lost about two hundred men. Colonel Candy's brigade lost about one hundred and thirty men.

While Hooker was engaged on the right, McPherson on the left, Howard moved on the centre, wheeling by Pine Mountain. The rebels retreated from the hilly knob in front to the range in rear, thus affording Howard only a chance of skirmishing with them. Towards evening his troops occupied Pine Knob, where General Polk was killed. For the last three days we had captured a large number of prisoners, in all about two thousand. Geary, in his assault, captured about one half of these; several of them had deserted into our lines. It is evident that the southern soldiers were then losing heart in their cause. I had been speaking to several of them, and they said, "The newspapers and officers tell us we are going on well; we can't see it, though. Our lines are thinning every day; our officers don't care for our lives, but dash us upon your lines recklessly, and get us butchered; we are falling back every day; if this is going on well, I can't see it."

It is true that our army acted through the intelligence of the mass; theirs through that of their leaders. They appeared to be mere puppets in the hands of the latter. The foreign element in their army was deserting very rapidly. On the 16th a captain, three lieutenants, and fifty-five men came into McPherson's lines near Big Shanty. They assigned as their reason that they were tired of the war. They had served for three years, and did not want to fight any longer. They had been conscripted, and did not want to fight at all against the Union. Now, as they had got the chance, they deserted.

"O mein Gott!" exclaimed a German, "we have got 'nuff of de hunger, and de rout, and am tired of de ting."

I asked an Irishman how it was that he, who had come from an oppressed country, could fight against the government that gave him a home and a living.

"Begor, you see, sir," replied Pat, "we were down here when the ruction was kicked up, and sure there couldn't be a shindy without having an Irishman at one end or tudder; so when we couldn't join the right side we had to fall in wid the wrong."

While around Big Shanty, Ira B. Tuttle, with some four men, made a reconnoissance on the enemy's flank and rear. They struck on a quartermaster's depot, full of forage, some sixteen miles south-west from Atlanta. They made an unexpected dash on the concern, which was poorly guarded. They captured the captain, a lieutenant colonel, and some five men who were lounging about. They secured their prisoners in an out-office, helped themselves to some good horses and equipments, leaving their own sorry nags in exchange, set fire to the store, which contained a large supply of corn and bacon, and returned safely to their own quarters.

The success of our march has been unprecedented. Though our progress had been checked by natural barriers, strong enough to intimidate a less resolute general than Sherman, or less daring an army than his, — though our march lay through the mountain regions of Georgia, through bold, craggy hills, where the men had to drag up their bodies by grasping projecting rocks or branches, through deep defiles and tangled brushwood, where the foot of man had never before disturbed the solitude of the place, nor the repose of snakes and crawling reptiles, — still onward that gallant army pressed, driving before them a stubborn enemy, who doggedly disputed every mountain crag and pass, and whose unerring rifle, like that of the red Indian, hurled death from every thicket. Napoleon's exploit in crossing the Alps stands forth as the *nonpareil* of military achievements. Napoleon's chief foes were the cold and snow. Sherman had to encounter hills, some two thousand feet high, in which a powerful enemy lay intrenched, and which actually bristled with cannons and bayonets. Which is the nobler exploit I leave to history to judge.

Johnston thought himself fully secure in the strong range of hills near Dalton; but Sherman flanked him here, and so managed as to head him from the bold and defensible range of the Chattagata Mountains, crippling him severely by the desperate battle of Resaca. Johnston's next battle-ground was the Allatoona Range. Here, too, he deemed his position impregnable; but he soon found that even the mountain fastness was a poor security. When driven from this, after several days' obstinate fighting, we hoped that he would fall back behind the Chattahoochee, allowing us to debouch on the open country lying between Marietta and the Chattahoochee; but Johnston resolved to defend the strong position at Kenesaw and the neighboring range of hills. Here they firmly intrenched themselves, their left and the batteries from Kenesaw commanding the railroad, their right resting on Lost Mountain, and commanding the pass by which Sherman could debouch on their flank towards the river. The rebel line extended in a south-westerly direction, or rather almost directly from east to west.

Our operations of the 15th and 16th towards the base of the ridge made them fall back, not only from that point, but also from Lost Mountain and Pine Knob.

The enemy kept their batteries on their right flank, commanding the Marietta road, very silent. Sherman was at a loss to know what guns they had there, to see how far an assault was practicable. It was an important position, and McPherson was close upon it.

No amount of artillery fire, or annoyance from our sharpshooters, could bring them out.

Sherman struck on a plan. He ordered a locomotive to be attached to three cars, and to put on full steam.

"Now," said he, "run that down the road like hell!"

On she started, puffing, blowing, and snorting as if she were bent on going right into Atlanta.

The rebels heard the noise of the fiery monster as she came on, throwing sparks from her chimney, as if lashing herself into fury. They sprang from intrenchments, redoubts, and forts, coming to the conclusion that it was laden with troops making a sudden dash into Marietta, on their rear. They opened at it right and left. Every battery was soon playing away at the monster, which, though perforated in several places, hissed and shrieked the more, as if hurling defiance at them.

"That will do," said Sherman, walking away; "I know what they have there, now."

Whether the engine got knocked off the track, or got a shot through her boiler, I can't tell. She did good service, however; for the enemy revealed guns enough to convince Sherman that they were too strong to be assaulted there.

The rebels now commenced threatening our communications. Heretofore, any attempts were mere guerrilla efforts; but on the morning of the 16th, the rebel General Wharton, commanding a brigade of two thousand five hundred men, made a descent on the road between Kingston and Dalton, capturing and burning five freight trains laden with supplies. Reënforcements were hurried up from different points, and arrived in time to prevent them from doing any serious damage. They hovered about for some time, threatening our communications.

While lying in front of Kenesaw, several days would pass over without any fighting, unless a kind of duel between the enemy's artillery on the hills, crests, and sides, and ours beneath them, and some volleys between the pickets, simply to keep their hands in practice, might be called fighting.

We were tired of this, and wanted a battle, or some other excitement, to rouse us up. We were tired of watching the course of the shells as they whirred through the air, and conjecturing as to where they fell, or whom they killed.

"I tell you that fellow fell right in our second brigade," one would say.

"Indeed, it didn't. It was more to the right," was the reply.

"Well, it was a whopper. I am sure it was a sixty-four-pounder."

"Pshaw, there is more of it. How the hell do you know? Now, I'd take my oath it was only a twelve-pound parrott shell."

"But I am confident it was a sixty-four-pounder. Didn't you hear the noise of it?"

"How the deuce could they get up so heavy a gun there; but, whist; here comes another?" and as this fellow was evidently visiting us, we jumped up and hugged some trees most affectionately, until he had paid his flying visit.

One evening, Colonel M—— and myself thought the thing such a bore that we decided on visiting some friends in the 20th corps. A camp is a very hospitable kind of place. From the highest general down to the lowest full private, a drink is the *summum bonum* of hospitality.

Our friend had just raised a barrel of strong apple-jack at the expense of the natives. We found himself and his brother officers in a large hospital tent. They had all come to congratulate the colonel upon his valuable discovery, and also to taste said discovery. Some were joining in a rousing chorus, with their tin cans and fruit cans full of the native, held up for inspection, as they chorused, —

"We won't go home till morning."

Others, who had dropped off, were lying around, enjoying a snooze. We were a welcome accession, and were received with uproarious shouts.

It was getting dark, and a cold, drizzling rain was falling when we started to return.

When we got into the camp of our own division, I remarked the sentry at one post sitting under a tree, consoling himself with puffing a long pipe.

"Colonel," said I, " that sentry hasn't challenged us."

"Where—re — is he, the rascal? I'll have him up," hickuped the colonel, who was stringent in the observance of military duty.

We turned back.

"I say, sir, — do you hear?"

"Well, I reckon I do," said the other, coolly knocking the ashes from his pipe, and placing the gun, which stood upright near the tree, between his knees.

"Why th— h—l didn't you challenge us?"

"Challenge you;" and he took a long pull from the pipe. "Catch me challenging two drunken officers; you might have a taste about you, colonel; the night is raw;" and he resumed his pipe.

This was too much for the colonel; so he turned around, leaving the sentry in peace.

"This reminds me," as Abe Lincoln would say, of a similar incident that occurred to me in the army of the Potomac. I had passed a sentry on a very important advanced post without being challenged. I turned around to reprimand him, asking him why he did not challenge.

"Faith, captain," said he, presenting arms, "I didn't know you.

CHAPTER XII.

A CHAPTER OF FIGHTING. — JOHNSTON ADDRESSES FALSE WORDS TO HIS MEN. — A DISAPPOINTMENT TO THE REBELS. — BATTLE OF CULP'S FARM. — DEATH OF GENERAL HARKER. — HIBERNIAN ANECDOTE.

The duration and the fierce nature of the conflict of our campaign through Northern Georgia is unsurpassed in history. Fifty days from the opening of the conflict we sat down in front of Kenesaw. There were but few of these days that we had not more or less fighting along our lines. The days were followed by weary nights of incessant toil, oftentimes fighting and building breastworks and intrenchments — weary nights of restless anxiety, with the cold, damp ground for our bed, sleeping on wet branches, sometimes on rails, to keep us from the mud; and then how often were our rude couches rendered too hot for us by the pattering bullets which rattled around us!

The rebels disputed every inch of ground with a heroism that has won our admiration, and has caused a feeling of regret that such soldiers had not a better cause.

The 16th passed off quietly. On the evening of the 17th heavy skirmishing opened in front of Stanley's division of the 4th corps. Harker's brigade, of Newton's division, and part of Hazen's brigade, of Wood's division, were also sharply engaged. Towards night the rebels opened a fierce fire along Howard's front, sending shot into our very camps and tents. Bradley's and Bridge's batteries replied with effect.

On the left, near Big Shanty, Logan's and Blair's batteries were also briskly shelling the rebel works on the hill.

Hooker, having repulsed them at Lost Mountain, was pressing on their flank, while Schofield was swinging round on their left, repulsing their skirmishers, and capturing a number of prisoners.

On the night of the 17th the rebels attacked our position. It was a beautiful night. The soft moonlight, beaming from the clear southern sky, floated through the forest trees, lighting them up with a bewitching charm of beauty.

The air was calm and balmy, the sky without a cloud; fireflies, sparkling like diamonds, were flitting around. The cry of the whippoorwill resounded through the forest; and the croaking of the toads rose from the marshes like the tinkling of sleigh bells. Houses that had been burned were yet shooting forth their columns of fire and smoke.

Such was the night! — a grand and solemn night! Soon a dropping shot along the line awoke the wearied soldier as he lay on his rude couch. "It is nothing," he said, and lay down to sleep again, only for a moment, for a rapid musketry fire ensued, and the wearied soldier opened his eyes and jumped to his arms, for he knew it was a night attack. Our batteries soon opened, hurling shell and canister into the rebel works.

The rebels had made a strong attack on McPherson's left, where they vainly strove to regain their lost position, but were repulsed by Logan's 15th corps.

The rebels were foiled in their night attack at all points, and the horrid din of battle soon gave way to a placid stillness. The toads resumed their music in the marsh, and the whippoorwill his in the forest. The tired soldiers again lay down to rest, and dream of a home and fond ones they were never destined to see.

Towards morning a sudden rain-storm burst over us in a perfect deluge. The maxim "When it rains it pours," is very applicable to the south. Next morning the country was one miserable swamp of slushy mire and water.

The rebels had fallen back and abandoned their front line of works. General Howard ordered his whole line to follow them up sharply. General Harker's brigade led the advance, and having come up with the enemy, and being reënforced by Wagner's brigade, they charged forward, driving them from their first line of works.

As we charged on the rebel skirmishers, they fled precipitately back on their intrenchments. A southern Charlotte Corday, a modern Joan of Arc, jumped upon the breastworks, waved a sword, and fiercely upbraided them with cowardice. There she stood, defiantly waving a flag in one hand and a sword in the other. Of course our men could have shot her down, but no rifle was turned on the Amazon. Her reproaches drove many a poor fellow back on our lines to certain death.

The women of the south have much blood to answer for. Bitter and uncompromising, many a brother and lover their sneers and scoffs drove into the army never again to return.

We thought the rebels were retreating, but they were only wheeling round their left to prevent it being outflanked by Schofield, who had wheeled round Pine Mountain, and was pressing along the Dallas and Marietta road. McPherson, too, was pressing closely on their right, and had taken possession of a ridge beyond Big Shanty, and also of Bush Mountain. Thus threatened on the flanks, they had to refuse their centre and compress their lines, for Howard and Palmer were thundering at their centre. They could the more easily depress their lines, as they had good works in their rear, on which the citizens and negroes had been engaged for months.

All their works along Kenesaw were of a formidable and scientific nature, strengthened by salient and traverse lines and angles. From such positions, seemingly impregnable, have we driven them since the opening of the campaign, day after day and week after week.

Our skirmishers pressed on, and having developed their new position, Newton's division on the left and Wood's famed division on the right were thrown into line of battle, with Stanley's division, to the rear of Wood's, held partly in reserve.

The 5th Kentucky, 6th Indiana, and 124th Ohio, Hazen's brigade, and 32d Indiana and 25th Illinois, of Colonel Gibson's brigade, were thrown forward in a heavy line of skirmishers by General Wood.

On their left, Wagner's brigade and the 27th Illinois, of Harker's brigade, were also deployed, and with one gallant, united effort they succeeded in capturing the enemy's first line of works.

Towards evening Captain Goodspeed's battery of five guns, and Bridge's 6th Ohio battery, with sections from Bradley's and Spencer's, opened a raking fire on the enemy, which was enforced by a continuous fire of musketry from our skirmishers. The rebel line, unable to withstand this concentrated fire, fell back, leaving a large number of prisoners in our hands, also Colonel Perdieux, 1st Louisiana battalion, and another colonel, belonging to the 7th Mississippi, dead.

Their loss must have been very heavy. Captain Levy, who was captured with his whole company, stated that his regiment alone lost nearly eighty men.

Our loss was pretty considerable. The 4th corps alone captured two hundred and twenty-seven prisoners; Wood's noble division capturing one hundred and ten of them.

At night the rebels fell still farther back to their works on Kenesaw Hill.

We now occupied the house of a Mr. Wallace, on the Marietta road, from which we had a fine view of the enemy along the slope of Kenesaw. Generals Sherman, Thomas, Hooker, Howard, and several others, had congregated here to watch the effect of our batteries on the enemy's works.

The house and offices were used as a hospital, and military operations were going on in the rear while the doctors were busy amputating inside; one party making cases for the other. Captains Goodspeed and Bradley got their batteries into position; these, with Bridge's in front of Stanley's division, opened all together on the rebel works, making the hillside a pretty hot place. The rebels soon replied with two batteries from the slope and a section of heavy guns from the crest.

A regular artillery duel now ensued. The intervening valley was one dense cloud of smoke, which rose in floating canopies over the mountain.

We could see the sheets of flame, followed by volumes of

smoke, jump out from the mouths of the brazen monsters, and the loud, reverberating sounds echoed along the mountains and valleys.

An assault was now taking place; this heavy artillery fire was merely to cover it.

Stanley was charging the enemy in his front, while Wood and Newton were hotly engaged on his right. The 20th corps had by this time succeeded in crossing Noe's Creek, which had been very much swollen by the late rains. Williams's division had crossed, and was stubbornly engaged on the right. Palmer's and McPherson's batteries were thundering away on our left, while far away on our right the 23d corps was disputing the passage of the swollen stream with the enemy. Early on the morning of the 20th Wood's division, 4th corps, crossed the creek and relieved Williams, who swung round to the right of the 20th corps, thus connecting Geary's division with the 4th corps. A slight tongue-like ridge ran out in front of Wood's division, which presented a first-rate position for a battery. The 49th Ohio advanced along this hill, driving back the enemy. Two guns were immediately dragged forward, and, under the superintendence of General Wood himself, and his truly chivalric adjutant general, Captain Bestow, were put into position and brought to bear on the enemy. Stanley was heavily engaged skirmishing all day; and towards evening our batteries all along the front opened again on the enemy's guns upon the hill, which were becoming troublesome.

Some fifty guns on both sides were belching away with all their might and main within the short range of less than a mile. We could see the shot and shell whizzing through the air like so many imps of hell on their unhallowed mission, the trees toppling over, and the rocks and dirt in front of the rebel batteries flying up in the air.

The infernal din was increased by the incessant rattling of musketry along the lines.

The rebels, finding that we were closing in on their flank, had massed in the centre, with the desperate resolution of piercing through the 4th corps.

We learned from deserters that part of Hood's and Hardee's corps had been massed in the centre with that intention. Under shelter of the heaviest artillery fire, the rebels charged in massed columns on Stanley's front.

Whittaker's brigade nobly met the attack, and repulsed them with loss. They next tried their hand on Kirby's, where they also met a stubborn resistance; but after a fierce conflict of nearly one hour, they gained some temporary advantage, and took possession of a prominent knoll in our front. Cross's and Whittaker's brigades again pitched into them, and a most bloody conflict continued until after dark, with little success on either side. Our position at night was thus: Wood's and Newton's divisions had somewhat advanced, but Stanley's division, having had to bear the brunt of the day's fighting, had barely kept its own. Stanley was hard pressed all the afternoon, and as he was over the creek and poorly supported, great anxiety was felt about him; but he kept his position until reënforced, and then a ringing cheer along his lines apprised us that he was all right.

Early on the morning of the 21st Wood's division moved forward to recover the height occupied by the rebels the previous day. Wood threw forward the 15th Ohio, which pressed on the enemy, taking possession of the hill before the others had come to their support. With it they captured a large number of prisoners.

The fighting for the past three days had been very severe. The air was hideous with one continuous roar of musketry and artillery. Hooker and Schofield were pressing the enemy well on our right; the latter had succeeded in crossing some of his cavalry over Noe's Creek, thus threatening to turn the enemy's left. By this time our lines were within five hundred yards of the enemy at some points, and our flanks were partly encircling them.

The fighting in front of General T. I. Wood's division, 4th corps, had been very severe. The 15th Ohio, under Lieutenant Colonel Askew, and the 49th Ohio, engaged a superior force on the contested hill, routed them, and soon established themselves in their place, though eight rebel guns were all the time vomiting shot and shell on their advance. General Hazen's brigade and the 89th Illinois relieved them, repulsing the enemy still farther. Howard was confronted by Cheatham's troops.

I have stated elsewhere that Johnston had sent his cavalry to harass our rear, and that they had succeeded in tapping the road between Kingston and Resaca. This attempt was much exaggerated, and the rebel leaders made the most of it.

While in front of Kenesaw, Johnston issued a complimentary address to his troops, and, as good news, stated that the railroad was torn up, our supplies cut off, and our army starving, in fact, on half rations for several days.

This order was being read to the troops, and was about receiving a due amount of cheers and huzzas, when all stopped, with their hats in their hands, ready to give the cheer; they listened a moment, and looked towards Big Shanty. What could that shrill loud whistle, and that puffing and blowing, mean? It was the engine, and it seemed to be considerably excited at all the lies the general was telling about it. The men listened a moment, looked at one another, uttered hard names, and slunk back to their quarters, while one loud, ringing cheer from our lines proclaimed that the boys were not starving, despite Johnston's assertion.

Captain L. H. Levey, 1st Georgia, and sixty men, were captured by our pickets. I asked the captain, "Don't you think your cause hopeless?"

"There are," replied the chivalrous captain, "about one hundred thousand high-toned, chivalric southern gentlemen whom ye may extirpate, but can never subdue."

This sounded very fine; but to spoil the chivalry of the thing, it turned out that the captain and his men were surprised on the picket line and captured by a sergeant and seven men, who frightened them into submission by pretending to have a whole regiment at their back.

What forcibly struck us as we marched through the south was, how fully impressed the people were with the notion that the

Yankees were savages, some believed cannibals. This belief was not confined to the poorer classes either; so corrupted were the minds of even the wealthier portions that they had not a much better opinion of us. They fully believed that we were coming wantonly to violate, destroy, or enslave them. On our approach women and children fled in terror into the woods and other places of concealment. If all the menageries and lunatic asylums north, including the late Barnum's itself, were let loose upon them, they could not be more afraid. By degrees they ventured out, and became wonderfully relieved when they found that we did not eat any of them. I heard an old lady, with scarcely a tooth in her head, and shaking with fear and age, say, "Well, well, the Lord be praised; you'ns not so bad after all; the girls all ran away, afraid of you'ns fellows, but I thought I'd stay; and there, not one of you'ns have touched me yet!"

I went into a shanty where an old lady was sitting at one side of the fire, comfortably enjoying a puff from a soldier's pipe, and discussing the war question with the soldier, who occupied the other side.

"And you tell me you'ns fellers have plenty backer, and coffee, and snuff?"

"Plenty, ma'am, more than we can use."

"Dear me! we'ns are badly off; haven't coffee, nor backer, nor snuff. I wish this war was over; when do you reckon it will stop?"

"Can't say; as soon as they stop fighting, or when we have them all killed."

"Well, there is an almighty lot of ye critters in it; I know ye'll eat them up; besides, you'ns fellows don't fight we'ns fair."

"How so?" said the soldier.

"Why, you'ns fight ind ways, and that's not fair," said the old lady, drawing a very indignant puff from the pipe; "besides, you'ns have furruners fightin' for you'ns."

"Not that I know; we are all either Americans or American citizens."

"O, you'ns can't come over me dat way; wasn't them fellers here to-day from a place called New Jersey?"

It is sad to witness the fearful sufferings of the people, particularly the women and children, in those parts of Georgia through which we have campaigned. As for the men, we met but few indeed. All that were able to fight were conscripted; the rest were hid in the woods or caves; some few had the good sense to remain at home, and trust to the humanity of the Yankee soldier. I am sorry to say that our men often wantonly burned down the houses, destroyed their contents, and drove forth their wretched inmates, houseless, homeless, starving outcasts, to perish of cold and hunger. It is true that such acts were not sanctioned, but stragglers and hangers-on, who bring up the rear of a large army, destroy everything, like a swarm of locusts, particularly when they find a place deserted.

I have met, in more cases than those I have already alluded to, frenzied groups of affrighted, starving women and children huddled together in the woods, where many of them perished of cold and want.

Such sad pictures of old and young, gray-haired matrons and timid girls, clinging together in hopeless misery, may be imagined, but cannot be described. I have seen whole columns of brave men melt away before the leaden storm of battle; I have passed through the whirlwind and carnage of many a bloody field; I have heard the groans of fearful agony from the poor sufferers under the surgeon's knife, where piles of legs and arms — the grim trophies of war — attested death's fearful harvest. Yet all these did not move me as did the sight of these poor, innocent, helpless *miserables*.

The morning of the 22d of June opened with brisk skirmishing on our centre, which continued all day, but became hotter towards evening. About 4 o'clock our batteries opened on the rebel works all along the range, to which the enemy vigorously replied. Battery after battery opened, until it became a perfect storm of shot and shell, enlivened by the stirring interlude of small arms.

About 4 o'clock the enemy commenced massing in front of Hooker, with the evident intention of attacking him.

The position of Sherman's army was — Schofield was on the extreme right, moving down the Landtown road; Hooker was on his left, commanding the Marietta road; Howard on the left of Hooker; Palmer next; next came McPherson, extending in front of Big Shanty and Bush Mountain, on the line of railroad. On the evening of the 21st, Hooker ordered Geary to advance his skirmish line, and press back the enemy's, which he accomplished, though the rebels obstinately disputed a commanding hill in his front.

Culp's farm is situated on the Powder Springs and Marietta main road, and about five miles in a westerly direction from Marietta. Contiguous to it are a handsome frame church, a school-house, planters' establishments, including several negro shanties, all of which give it something of the appearance of a small village.

Extending from this, partly in a northern direction, is a valley of reclaimed land, reaching some three miles in length and half a mile in width. This comprises Culp's plantation, also the plantation of a Mr. Greer, whose house is situated in the middle of the valley, and was an important point of attack during the engagement.

The land is rising on both sides, and is compressed in the middle with a small, sluggish stream, fringed with trees; running at right angles with this stream is a deep ravine, with a few thickly-wooded knolls scattered over the valley. This was the field of the battle of Culp's farm.

Hooker, having ascertained that the enemy were in force in his front, ordered General Williams to throw out a heavy line of skirmishers to keep the enemy engaged while he was forming into line, and, if possible, to get possession of Greer's house and the surrounding knolls.

Williams at once deployed the 123d New York, supported by the 46th Pennsylvania, 141st New York, and 5th Connecticut. These advanced rapidly across the plain, and soon became engaged. Hooker had formed line with Williams's division on the right, Rogers's brigade on the right, General Knipe's next, with Colonel Robinson's extending *en échelon* to the rear on the right. Geary's division was to the left of Williams's, but separated by over two hundred yards on account of the ravine and the extended nature of the line. Colonel P. H. Jones's second brigade closed up on the ravine so as to fill up the gap. Butterfield's division was on the extreme left, held in reserve.

Hood's corps was hastily forming in front of the wood on the other side. He had wheeled round the previous night from Kenesaw, thus leaving Loring's corps — Polk's — on their extreme right, and Hardee in the centre.

Hood had formed into line of battle in the following order : Stewart on the right, Stevens in the centre, and Hindman on the left — all massed on the centre, and formed into lines by divisions front.

Our artillery was hurried to the front, and hastily got into position. McGill's and Wheeler's batteries took up position in front of Geary's line, and opened an enfilading fire on the enemy. Captain Wheeler was killed beside his gun. Pinnegar's first New York and Captain Woodberry's were in front of Williams's division.

Hood's corps had now formed in front of Williams's position. Two brigades from Hardee's corps had taken up position in front of Geary's. Two regiments moved along Powder Spring road to turn Hooker's flank, he not being able to extend the line to cover the road. Hood's column was now advancing in magnificent order, as if on parade, with banners flying and officers dashing from line to line. On they came in grand array : —

"Few shall part where many meet;
The earth shall be their winding-sheet."

On came that proud column, with heavy lines of skirmishers in its front. Our skirmishers fell back, but obstinately disputing every inch in order to give our lines time to form, and our batteries to get into position. Colonel P. H. Jones, after a dashing brush with the enemy, now held Greer's house, from which the rebels vainly and repeatedly tried to dislodge him. As the column neared the stream, pressing back our skirmishers with defiant cheers, our batteries along the hill suddenly opened, vomiting shell and canister among them, sweeping lanes through their ranks, and converting many a cheer into a death-groan.

This raking fire from our batteries was fearfully thinning their lines.

Stewart's shattered ranks were now hurled back on Stevens's, who, for a moment, stemmed the torrent.

We could see their officers rush before the men with waving sabres, striving to rally them, but in vain; for our artillery and musketry were showering lead like hailstones right into their lines. After repeated assaults, the panic-stricken rebels, with broken ranks, riderless horses, and trailing banners, fell back to their works.

While the conflict was raging in front of Hooker, the regiments which had gone up the road to outflank him, did not fare any better.

Schofield, hearing the firing, and apprised of what was going on, hurried up. Hascall's division was in front, and the 14th Kentucky, covered by two pieces of artillery, were thrown out as skirmishers. They engaged the advancing regiments, and, after a stubborn fight, repulsed them, thus covering Hooker's right.

The 14th Kentucky lost heavily, but left sixty-nine dead rebels in its front, and brought in thirty prisoners.

Schofield's main body soon came up to their support. Of a small engagement, this was a crushing one. The rebel lines were so exposed that their loss must be about a thousand, while ours was very light.

It was a mad attempt on Hood's part to attack at such a disadvantage. If we had the selection of our ground, it could not be more favorable.

It must be that Hood was under the impression that he was striking our right flank, and that Hooker was moving so carelessly in column that he could outflank and crush him before he could get into line. His sending the troops up the road confirmed this; but Schofield arrived in time to spoil that part of the programme.

I rode over that battle-field when the conflict was ended. Along the little stream ran a rail fence. The rebels had crowded behind this for protection, but were literally mowed down. The torn, bloody knapsacks, haversacks, blankets, and the frequent pools of blood around, were ghastly evidences of how they suffered. The stream was actually choked up with bodies, and discolored with blood. In the ravine, and around the house where the rebels had crowded for shelter, their bodies lay piled on one another.

On the 23d of June, the only fighting was in front of the 4th corps, where heavy skirmishing went on all day, enlivened by an artillery fire from, at least, fifty guns. We had advanced our skirmish lines close upon the rebels. Captain Dalger's battery was threatened by the enemy. He was sent word that he could get no support.

"I want none," he replied; "I'll support myself."

And he did so, soon silencing the rebel battery in his front.

There was considerable activity in front of McPherson during the 25th and 26th.

Our batteries, along the whole line, opened a brisk fire on the rebel position, and our skirmishers crept up, as close as possible, to the shelter occupied by the enemy.

Logan formed Harrow's division on the extreme left, and moved cautiously on the enemy, covering his advance by a heavy artillery fire. Harrow's advance was so rapid and well-timed that he surrounded a rebel brigade lying in advance of the woods, who durst not leave their shelter, and were all captured, to the number of about three hundred. Logan also brought up Morgan L. Smith's division, and took up an advanced position, intrenching himself. Osterhaus also advanced by the left, driving the enemy from their rifle-pits in his front. Blair, whose corps lay between Osterhaus's division and the other two divisions of Logan's corps, advanced his right far enough to complete his line, connecting with Osterhaus's advanced position. Dodge, who occupied McPherson's right, had also pushed forward, and attempted at night to build a fort upon a hill in his front, which resulted in a night fight that did not prevent him from building his fort.

Thus we had our lines so far advanced preparatory to the fatal assault of the 27th.

General Sherman had decided on assaulting Kenesaw, with the resolution of forcing their breastworks, at a point where success would give the largest fruits of victory.

He selected, as the chief point of attack, the left centre, because, if broken through, the head of the assaulting column would reach the railroad below Marietta, cut off the enemy's right and centre from its line of retreat, and could overwhelm it; therefore General Sherman ordered an assault on the enemy's position at two points south of Kenesaw, by Generals McPherson and Thomas's commands. Precisely at eight o'clock, on the morning of the 27th, General Logan, after forming his corps into line of battle, advanced on the enemy's works, with orders to capture, if possible, a small knoll at the base of the mountain. Though advancing under a heavy fire of musketry and artillery, he succeeded in taking the first line of works, and then the second, which he occupied.

On his left Legget's division, of Blair's corps, wheeled round to the extreme left, and, supported by Gerrard's cavalry, made demonstrations on the enemy's right, west of Marietta. This was simply a feint to cover the main attack.

The 16th corps also made an attack on the enemy's lines in its front, without gaining much advantage.

Logan's corps was pretty heavily engaged; but finding that the mountain was too steep and the rebel intrenchments too strong for assault, after a desperate struggle, he had to fall back to the second line of works.

The assault on the right centre was equally unsuccessful, and even more fatal.

Early in the morning, Baird's and Davis's divisions of the 14th corps, having quietly shifted during the night, moved in on the right of Howard. Geary's division, of the 20th corps, had closed up on Davis, so as to engage the enemy at that point. Williams's and Butterfield's divisions were on Geary's right, with Schofield swinging round on the rebels' extreme right.

The programme was this: Newton was to open the ball by an assault on a strong knoll west of Kenesaw, which was a powerful position in the hands of the enemy, and from which their artillery had considerably annoyed us. Stanley's and Wood's divisions were on the right and rear of Newton, somewhat thrown back *en échelon*, but within supporting distance.

Newton's division advanced in column by brigade, the 125th Ohio, Colonel Opdyke, covering the front as skirmishers, supported by the 59th Illinois.

Our lines had to advance through a dense wood, thence up a steep ascent. The enemy were strongly intrenched behind a breastwork, protected by an abatis.

Harker's brigade had the advance, Kemball's on his left, and Wagner supporting.

The 125th Ohio, 74th Illinois, skirmished heavily with the enemy for some time, driving them back on their main lines, but were there received by a destructive fire of musketry. Our lines followed up to their support, when two batteries opened on our front and flank, aided by a shower of musketry in front. Harker's men cheered, and dashed on; but a decimating shower of bullets caused them to waver. Our officers rushed forward to cheer them on; but from concealed batteries and secure breastworks the leaden storm came mowing them down by scores. Our batteries were playing on the enemy's, but regardless of this, the rebels gave all their attention to our advancing columns, which soon gave way, and fell back in confusion. General Harker led this charge in person. With his cap in his raised hand, he cheered on his men; and seeing them falter, he rushed to the front, but soon fell shot through the side. Beside him stood his adjutant general, Captain Ed. G. Whiteside, who, though shot through the thigh, still urged on the men, until his horse was shot under him, and he fell beside his noble general.

There were few more promising generals in the army than Charles G. Harker. He was a native of Mulligan Hill, New Jersey, and a graduate of West Point, and captain in the 15th regulars. He distinguished himself at Chickamauga, where he had his horse killed, and was rewarded by a brigadiership. He was again wounded at Resaca, and had a horse killed under him, also, at Mission Ridge. He was a brave, dashing soldier and efficient officer, and was always foremost where duty and danger called him. He fell in the prime of manhood, being but twenty-seven years of age, but left after him a name that history will record with pride.

Davis's division, 14th corps, was also heavily engaged on the right of Newton, but was also repulsed. Geary's division, 20th corps, and Schofield's corps, were also engaged on our right.

We were repulsed on all sides. Our loss was heavy in field officers and men. Besides the gallant General Harker, Colonel McCook, created general before he died, was mortally wounded; Colonel Rice, 57th Ohio, severely. Our loss in rank and file must be between two and three thousand; while the enemy's must be very slight, as they fought behind their works.

I spent the evening previous with the noble young Harker.

"So, general," said I, "you are to lead the advance to-morrow?"

"Yes," said he, "I lead it, whoever returns."

"I hope, general, your usual good fortune will attend you, and that you will return safe."

"Well, I hope so; a soldier should be always prepared to die, though;" then after a pause he said, "They are powerful works; we can never take them; I will do my best, though."

I saw him when he fell. It was a matter of surprise to me that he escaped so long; for there he was, at the head of the line, cap in hand, rallying the troops, who were falling on all sides around him.

I helped to remove him from the field, and asked him, "General, do you suffer? Where are you struck?"

He placed his hand on his side; the pallor of death was on his brow. A few hours more and he had breathed his last.

As Harker's brigade wavered in front of the rebel works, the colors were lying on the ground,— bearer after bearer had fallen,— when an Irish sergeant of the name of Kelly rushed forward, seized the colors, tore away the abatis with his left hand, jumped on the rebel works, planting the colors there, and calling on his comrades to follow him. He was immediately transfixed with bayonets and pierced with bullets. Finding himself not supported, he jumped backwards, flung the colors over his shoulders into the lines, calling out, "Boys, save the colors!" and then fell dead.

Next day General Johnston sent a flag of truce to Sherman, in order to give time to carry off the wounded and bury the dead, who were festering in front of their lines.

A truce followed, and Rebels and Federals freely participated in the work of charity. It was a strange sight to see friends, to see old acquaintances, and in some instances brothers, who had been separated for years, and now pitted in deadly hostility, meet and have a good talk over old times, and home scenes, and connections. They drank together, smoked together, appeared on the best possible terms, though the next day they were sure to meet in deadly conflict again.

Even some of the generals freely mixed with the men, and seemed to view the painful sight with melancholy interest.

I saw Pat Cleburne, with that tall, meagre frame, and that ugly scar across his lank, gloomy face, stand with a thoughtful air, looking on the work his division had done; for it was his troops that defended the line of works in the centre, and committed such fearful havoc on Newton's and Davis's divisions. He looked a fit type of the lean Cassius. He was certainly to the western army what Stonewall Jackson was to the eastern; and when he fell at Franklin, Hood's army had lost its ruling spirit.

An officer, speaking of this sad burial, said, "I witnessed a strange scene yesterday in front of Davis's division. During the burial of the dead, grouped together in seemingly fraternal unity, were officers and men of both contending armies, who, but five minutes before, were engaged in the work of slaughter and death.

There were Generals Cleburne, Cheatham, Hindman, and Money, in busy converse with a group of Federal officers, mostly Tennessee officers, whom they had formerly known. Cheatham looked rugged and healthy, though seemingly sad and despondent. He wore his fatigue dress — a blue flannel shirt, black neck-tie, gray homespun pantaloons, and slouched, black hat. At first he was very taciturn; but this wearing off, he made inquiries about old friends, particularly about those from Nashville.

General Mooney was less reserved. He was elegantly dressed, as were also several other officers, who looked as if they wanted to cut a shine on the occasion.

Captain Lee, from Columbia, broke the ice by asking Captain Nixon, 14th Michigan, "Do you belong to Mizner's regiment for some time stationed at Franklin and Columbia?"

"Yes, sir; I do."

"Then you are the man who was provost marshal?"

"Yes, sir."

"It is well for you that we didn't get possession of that place and you. I would have hung you!"

"No, you wouldn't," interposed a red-haired, red-eyed major, — Hawkins, — formerly deputy sheriff of Nashville, "for the boys say their folks were better treated by these Michigan men than by any troops ever stationed there."

"That's so," said Major Vaulse, of Cheatham's staff; "boys, you have better whiskey than we have got;" and the major tried the ardent.

Colonel House was in charge of the burying party, and was courteous and affable.

Under the shelter of a pine, I noticed a huge gray Kentuckian rebel, with his arm affectionately placed around the neck of a Federal soldier, a mere boy. The bronzed warrior cried and laughed by turns, and then kissed the young Federal.

Attracted by such a strange proceeding, I went over to them, and said to the veteran, "Why, you seem very much taken by that boy; I suppose he is some old friend of yours."

"Old friend, sir! Why, he is my son!"

"Your son? Good God! how did it happen that you have taken different sides?"

"Well, sir, you see, like many other fools, I was carried away by darn stories, at first. I was told this thing would be over in a few weeks, and then we'd have a free country, and all that 'ere stuff. Well, I'm darned if I believed a word of it; but then I had to join or kick the bucket, like more of my neighbors."

"And your son?"

"Well, he had a kinder likin' for home; but the d——d guerrillas took everything his poor mother had; so he joined you, and is trying to support the old woman with his pay, and I fightin' agin' him!"

The strong man bent his head on his hands and sobbed.

"Don't, father, don't!" said the boy, kissing him; "I guess it will be all over soon."

"I hope so; I hope so, boy. We're fightin' agin' one another!"

I have often witnessed scenes equally as sad and equally as expressive of the horrors of a civil war, where father sheds the blood of his son, and brother that of his brother.

Though I could fill volumes with tales of our pickets, and the battle-field, I think the following was about as amusing a one as I have witnessed.

While squads on both sides were engaged burying the dead, two Irishmen met, who were old friends in the good days of peace and union.

"Musha, God bliss my soul! Jem Gleeson, is this you?" said the rebel Irishman, dropping a body which he was dragging by the leg to the pit for burial, and giving the other a hug that might do credit to a bear.

"Arrah, whisht! is this yourself at all?" was Jem's reply, returning the embrace with equal fraternity.

"By gor', it is my four bones; but how the divil did you get here? I thought you were safe an' sound in the 'ould dart.'"

"In truth, I wish I was, Ned. Sure I don't know the day I will go to some other dart. And you, my ould friend, may be the one will send me there wid an ounce of lead in my sthomach."

"Be gor', that's too bad. If you could only call to me, I'd shoot some other one in your place. But tell me, how did you come here at all?"

"Arrah, shure I came over the say; and then such a lot of frinds as I met in New York, every one persuading me I'd make my fortune and become a gineral if I joined the army; and shure I thought they ought to know best; so I took their advice."

Jem, seeing a canteen hanging by Ned's side, after exhausting their mutual embraces, asked, "Have you got a drop of the cretur' there?"

"Faix, in troth, I have; come over here beyond."

And they went and sat under a shady tree, where they had another big shake-hands and a big talk about old times. They drank one another's health, a health to absent friends, including the "*ould dart.*"

They had quite a jollification of it; so much so that they were oblivious of the fact that the troops had fallen back to their respective lines.

After a time they were seen to issue, arm in arm, from the tree, both proceeding to our lines.

Ned's friends called out to him "to come back, or else they'd fire on him."

"Arrah, hould your tongues," said Ned, waving his hat at them; "shure I must see my friend home, and then I'll go back."

When they approached our lines they stopped to have a parting chat and a *dur a durish;* and the best thing we heard was, "Ned," from our man, "go home, now, and God purtect you; go like a good fellow (hic, hic, hic), and shure I have nothing bad to say to ould Davis; the divil isn't as bad as he is painted!" (hic, hic, hic.)

"That's thrue, Jem, I will; but come wid me; the boys will be glad to see you (hic, hic, hic), and we'll (hic) get another canteen (hic, hic). Come, Jem, let us go home" (hic, hic, hic).

Ned and Jem looked at one another, then nodded, then shook hands, and were parting, when our man turns back, and calls out, "I say, have the boys a dhrop below?"

"Faix, in troth they have; and if you come down, I'll drink ould Abe's health wid you!"

This was too much for the other; he couldn't refuse so honored a toast; so he was actually staggering back to join him, when some of the men interfered, and sent each to his respective command.

CHAPTER XIII.

KENESAW.—CROSSING THE CHATTAHOOCHEE.—SHERMAN OUTWITS AND OUTFLANKS JOHNSTON.—FIRST SIGHT OF ATLANTA.—CRUELTY OF THE SLAVE DEALERS.—THE STORY OF THE NEGRO OSTIN.

KENESAW MOUNTAIN, which will be the Waterloo of the future tourist, and whose sides and valleys are one vast cemetery of patriots, is made up of two high peaks, which almost connect at their summits, and are about nine hundred feet high. Looking at them from our lines beneath them, they have the appearance of two immense mounds, surrounded at the base by smaller ones, separated by fertile little valleys well adapted to cultivation. The outline of the mountain rather curves on the eastern side, describing a kind of half circle, thence sloping toward the west, where it loses itself abruptly in a small valley. The base of the mountain is about five miles from east to west, and about a mile in width. Its sides are covered with thick forests, brushwood, projecting rocks, and huge bowlders. The rebel works around it were of the most elaborate kind, being all protected by their high position, stakes, abatis, and *chevaux de frise* in front, while traverse and salient lines shot out from their main works. These lines of defence extended as far as the summit, upon which were several batteries with guns located at all commanding points, and sharpshooters ensconced behind rocks, trees, and rifle-pits. It was impossible to take such a position by assault.

Sherman did not remain long idle to muse over his repulses. Finding the position too formidable to be taken by direct assault, he resolved to outflank it. Owing to the hilly nature of the country and the great distance from the river, this was not practicable on our left. Ten days' rations were issued, and on the night of the 1st and 2d of July, our troops cautiously changed positions. McPherson wheeled round on the extreme right towards Nickajack; Gerrard's cavalry took McPherson's place around Big Shanty and the eastern slope of Kenesaw. Schofield was also threatening this point, while Stoneman's cavalry were pressing on Turner's Ferry on the Chattahoochee. The effect of this move was instantaneous. Johnston could not suffer us to cross the Chattahoochee, and thus head him off from Atlanta; so on the night of the 2d he evacuated Kenesaw. We captured a large number of prisoners around Kenesaw, in all over two thousand. After Johnston's retreat, we found several officers and men asleep. The 4th corps alone captured three hundred, making in all, since the opening of the campaign, for this one corps alone, thirteen hundred and sixty-five prisoners. General Hazen's brigade captured a number belonging to the 1st Georgian. Several of them came in voluntarily, particularly the Irish and Germans. The 1st Georgian men stated that their regiment started nine hundred and thirty-seven strong, and were now reduced by desertions and the casualties of war to three hundred and thirteen. In fact, the drain on Johnston's army had considerably reduced it, while ours was made good by recruits. When we consider that we had taken about eight thousand since the opening of the campaign, and how Johnston had been decimated by battle, desertion, and sickness, it is evident that it was no longer the proud, boasting army that confronted us at Kenesaw.

The army moved rapidly in pursuit. The 4th and 14th, with two divisions of the 15th corps, followed up the centre towards Marietta, the other columns moving on the right and left. We struck Marietta about 8 o'clock in the morning, the enemy rapidly falling back in our front, making no fight, but keeping up some skirmishing just to cover their rear. A provost guard was immediately detailed to protect the town from plunder. General Thomas came upon a chaplain, a hospital steward, and some darkies pillaging a house, and at once placed the ill assorted lot under arrest. Most of the inhabitants had fled, carrying everything of value with them. Others, finding that the Yankee barbarians were not going to destroy them, returned and mixed with the soldiers. In the centre of the town is a splendid hotel, which Sherman occupied as his temporary headquarters. The military college, the court-house, the churches and private buildings, were all spacious and of a most interesting nature.

Marietta was considered one of the prettiest and healthiest towns in Cherokee Georgia. It is situated on an elevated plain, and is twenty miles from Atlanta by the railroad. It has some very good private and public buildings, is well laid out with good spacious streets shaded by trees. The Military Academy, which is situated on an elevation overlooking the town, is a very fine building, and is well located, both as regards the health of the pupils and the grounds for amusement and exercise. I am informed that General Sherman was at one time professor in this institute. How little did he imagine then, when instructing his pupils in tactics and manœuvres, the building of forts, tangents, intrenchments, and the like, that he would one day define these lessons by practice around this very out of the way little town in Northern Georgia. We found a good many of the houses deserted. The terrible name and reputation of the Yankee had scared the inhabitants. Those who remained appeared so terrified that it was painful to witness their looks. This soon wore off, and they freely mixed with the soldiers, trading little articles of barter, and talking over the stirring events transpiring around them. Before we were an hour in the town, you would see some wearied soldier sitting on a piazza with his rifle resting between his knees, and he entertaining a group of interested women and children with his adventures and campaigns. Beside him is a bowl of milk, from which he occasionally quaffs a deep draught by way of parenthesis. On a more fashionable piazza, in front of a more fashionable house, some officers gayly lounge. The young ladies of the house, rather tastefully dressed, considering that the war has shut them in from the fashionable world, think they have a right to enjoy their own piazza; and of course the officers pay all due attention to them, and they are so surprised to find Yankee officers courteous at all, that they enjoy the thing, soon get into good humor, and evidently become converts to the Union, at least to a man. Marietta had a population of about five thousand. It had also four churches, several hotels, schools, and stores, and was fast becoming one of the most attractive and stirring towns in Georgia. From the many advantages it possesses in climate, soil, and location, it is destined to become a very important place.

When falling back, the rebels tore away the rails of some two miles of the railroad between Big Shanty and Marietta, thus retarding the advance of our trains.

The column halted, and rested for a few hours in Marietta, for the day was intensely hot. We then resumed our march. About three miles from Marietta, near Neal Dow Station, the rebels made a stand in order to cover their rear, which was badly pressed. Stanly's division, of the 4th corps, threw out a heavy line of skirmishers, and also moved forward to the front four pieces of artillery. Newton's division came up on Stanly's left, and Wood on his extreme left. Some brisk musket and artillery firing followed. The programme was, that Schofield and McPherson were to attack on the right, while Thomas was to make a demonstration to direct the attention of the rebels from them while crossing Nickajack Creek, which they were ordered to do at all hazards. Howard had so disposed his troops as to be ready to assault the rebel advance work in the morning, and therefore kept his artillery shelling them all night.

The morning of the 5th opened with brisk firing on both sides, and about 11 o'clock the cannonading became furious. Under cover of this, Stanly's division, 4th corps, in conjunction with King's division, 14th corps, made a dashing assault and succeeded in capturing the enemy's works. The rebels brought up reënforcements from their main line, which were also repulsed. Wood's and Newton's divisions had now come up to Stanly's support, and the rebels fell back. In this conflict, Stanly and King lost about three hundred, among them, Colonel William Stoughton, 11th Michigan, mortally wounded. Schofield had met but little opposition in his front. He repulsed the skirmish line thrown out to check his advance, and captured several prisoners. McPherson's column struck the enemy near Nickajack Creek, and after a sharp engagement, routed them.

It was evident that Johnston only wanted time to get his trains over the Chattahoochee, as also to take possession of the strong line of works between Vining Station and the railroad bridge across the Chattahoochee. Next morning we resumed our march, the 4th and 14th corps moving parallel, the former along the line of railroad, the latter on the road contiguous. Wood's division, 4th corps, had the advance, and again encountered the enemy near Vining Station. Hazen's brigade dashed bravely forward, driving their skirmishers in confusion across the river. The rebels barely had time to cut loose the pontoon and let it swing down the river, so closely was Hazen on their heels.

The Chattahoochee River is one of the largest and most important in the State of Georgia. Its head springs, and those of the Hiwassee, are in the Blue Ridge, towards the northern corner of Habersham. It flows in partly a south-west direction, and after a course of near four hundred miles, it unites with the Flint River, thus forming the Appalachicola. It is navigable to Columbus. It drains a large section of country. In some places, where the country is level, it is low and marshy; in other places, where the lands are rolling, it is very rapid and picturesque. Gold has been found in considerable quantities in its bed, particularly towards its head waters. The water power of the Chattahoochee and its tributaries has been turned to practical use. We struck on several grist mills, saw mills, factories, and tanneries, the most important of which was Roswell factory, at Roswell, on Vickery's Creek. The cavalry seized this while in full operation. It was employed making clothes for the rebel army, and was consequently destroyed. There were at the time about three hundred female operators employed in it, and it was feeling to witness how they wept, as this, their only means of support, was consigned to destruction. They were sent north, or wherever they chose. This factory worked over four thousand spindles, and was certainly the most important in this section of country. A little village

13

called Roswell was rapidly springing up about it, comprising several houses, a few stores, a church, and a female academy.

The nature of the country around here is similar to that we have passed. The surface is broken and rolling, presenting some bold ridges and fertile valleys. The valleys of the Chattahoochee produce good cotton, corn, and wheat. The country around is thinly settled, except in some locations, where the natural fertility of the land has induced settlers to locate. Here little villages, or hamlets, spring up. Between Marietta and Atlanta is a vast section of country, with but a few houses scattered here and there. The forest yet blooms in all its wild luxuriance, as it did some hundred years ago, when it was the sacred hunting ground of the Indian, and resounded with the sound of the chase or the wild war-whoop.

We occupied several important positions along the river. Gerrard's cavalry held the ford. He destroyed the factories which had supplied the rebel army with cloth. A French flag floated over one of these, but of course, under the circumstances, it was not respected. Speaking of the owner, Sherman says, "A neutral, surely, is no better than one of our own citizens, and we do not allow our own citizens to fabricate cloth for hostile uses." General Thomas's flank now rested on the river, near Pace's Ferry. General McPherson held the mouth of the Nickajack Creek. Gerrard's cavalry, with Newton's division, of the 4th corps, held Roswell, while General Schofield moved from his position on the Landtown road on our right, to Smyrna camp ground, near the mouth of Soap Creek, on our left. Schofield seized Soap Creek Ferry, surprised the guards, and captured several prisoners, and took up a strong position on the east bank. So sudden and well-timed was Schofield's move, that the rebels thought his troops were reënforcements coming to join them by way of Decatur.

"I say, Yanks," they hallooed to our fellows across the river, "how do ye get along there?"

"Very well, thank you; how do you get on?"

"Fus rate; won't ye come over to see us? We'll give ye a warm reception."

"Well, the truth is, we have come a long ways to see you, and you show us nothing but your backs, which ain't very clean, either."

"We'll show ye something else in a few days more; we're waiting for reënforcements."

"And where in God's name will you get them, unless you enlist the women?"

"Wouldn't you like to know, Mr. Yank? Well, wait a little."

Deserters, too, told us that reënforcements were coming in. A little time after, they found their mistake, for Schofield had taken up a position commanding their right flank.

The army of the Tennessee wheeled round from the extreme right to the extreme left, to follow in Schofield's track. General Howard effected a crossing at Power's Ferry, and pontooned the river. We had, by the 9th, a large part of our army thrown across the Chattahoochee, above the enemy, and commanding the roads leading to Atlanta. Johnston had intrenched himself between Vining Station and the Chattahoochee Bridge. He also had advance intrenchments and forts guarding the road at Smyrna, with a *tête du pont* at the river. The river forms a deep curve here. Part of Johnston's army held these bends and the bridge, while the rest guarded the fords on the eastern side. There had been some heavy skirmishing during these movements, but nothing amounting to a fight. Wood's division, of the 4th corps, moved down from Power's Ferry, along the bank of the river, and dislodged the force there guarding Pace's Ferry. A pontoon was immediately thrown across the river, and the 14th corps passed over in a few hours. McPherson had now left Johnston in quiet possession, and swung round to the left. Thus we had our main army trains, wagons, and supplies on the Atlanta side of the river, while Johnston was on the other side in fancied security. Finding that his flank was turned, and that Sherman was likely to strike direct for Atlanta, he hastily crossed the bridge at night, destroying it after him. He had all his trains and wagons over before. The crossing of the Chattahoochee was one of Sherman's best movements. A less experienced general would be likely to press Johnston in his works. Sherman knew the strength of these too well, and also knew that by crossing far up on the left, and threatening a flank advance on Atlanta, Johnston would give up his position, and fall back to its relief.

True, such movements would not break up Johnston's army, but it gave us a victory; besides, Sherman and Johnston were watching each other's movements, like two expert wrestlers, to know who would make a slip, for they knew that to attack an intrenched position was likely to prove a defeat.

The admirable way in which Sherman moved his army from right to left, as if it were a single brigade or division, confounded Johnston. To-day Schofield and McPherson were threatening his left flank on the Sandtown road and Nickajack Creek; to-morrow they are operating at Roswell and Soap Creek, several miles up, on his left; and the first thing he heard was, that they had crossed, and were moving down on his flank, with the intention of cutting him off from Atlanta. So bold and rapid was this movement, that even Johnston himself was deceived by it, and looked upon the advancing column as a friendly one.

Deserters and scouts informed us that the enemy were removing rolling stock and government property from Atlanta, and that the utmost panic and confusion reigned there. I am sure the roar of our cannon, as it thundered across the Chattahoochee, hurried their work, and made many a southern heart tremble. I can well fancy their feelings on the night of the 4th of July, as Johnston's couriers hurried to and fro, cheering the fear-stricken inhabitants with the news, that "the Yankees are coming;" and then came the booming of our cannons to confirm it. It was a city of mourning, a city of tears and tribulation.

General Howard had his headquarters at the house of a Mr. Pace, after whom the ferry was named. He was a wealthy planter, and had barely succeeded in getting himself and some thirty negroes across the river when we came up. Behind his house was a high hill, from the top of which Captain Morgan's battery, 14th cavalry, was pelting away at the rebels beyond the river.

From the summit of this hill we could plainly see the steeples and houses of Atlanta; also the smoke from the founderies in the rear, and could almost look into the rebel intrenchments beyond.

We met a striking sight on the top of this hill — the mummy skeleton of a soldier dangling from a tree, tied by a string of hickory bark. In his pocket was his descriptive list and five dollars in Confederate money. His name was T. B. Dunkin, of some Alabama regiment. It is likely that he was some unfortunate deserter, who hung himself. I have known men to shoot themselves sooner than go into battle.

Several of the men said he was a negro; he was certainly black enough to be one. Several other skeletons were discovered in the woods. It was almost impossible to know whether they were those of white or colored people.

There is no doubt, when the negroes heard of the approach of our army, they tried to make their escape to it, and such as were caught were shot or hung. The following story of the sufferings of a poor negro was too well authenticated for me to doubt its truth. I give the real names of the inhuman butchers in the tragedy.

Near Nance's Creek, a few miles beyond the Chattahoochee, lived a planter named Tom House. Tom had some negroes, and traded in their flesh by selling them out to other planters. Among them was a very faithful hand, called Ostin, whom he rented out to a man near Atlanta. Ostin's master was a drunken brute, who ruled his slaves by kicks and floggings. Ostin, of course, came in for a liberal share of this treatment.

One evening his master came home from Atlanta in one of his drunken fits; he seemed to have a dislike for Ostin, for the poor negro's piety and rectitude of life were a kind of censure on him; besides, Ostin, with that privilege given by good masters to their slaves, spoke to massa on the evil of his ways.

The overseer, finding that poor Ostin was in bad odor, reported him as keeping the hands idle by singing psalms and the like.

"Send him to me," said the drunken master, "and I'll knock the d—l out of that fellow."

Poor Ostin humbly presented himself.

"I say, you old scratch of a blasted nigger, why do you be keeping my hands idle? Is it for that I hired you?"

"No, massa; I neber keep de hands idle; dis nigger work like a hoss."

"Didn't Shinton tell me that you are always shouting your blasted hymns among the hands?"

"We only pray to the good Lord, massa, to lighten our work here, and den take us to glory."

"Come, you old woolly skunk, did I buy you to pray or to work? Now, if I hear any more of your d—d stuff, I'll flog the skin off your old bones."

"De Lor' says, massa, dat we can't deny him; and dis ole nigger won't deny the Lor'; but dis poor nigger will work all he can."

Why follow out the conversation between the drunken white brute and the poor negro, whose faith was so firm in the "good Lor'?" Ostin returned to his cabin, and when the day's work was over, was joined by his little congregation in a most pathetic hymn.

His master chanced to be passing by, and rudely broke in on their innocent devotions, and most brutally kicked and abused Ostin. He then tied him to a pole, and flogged him himself. At night poor Ostin made his escape. He had a wife and child at a Mrs. Ballinger's, near Nance's Creek. Hither poor Ostin went. His wife opened her cabin door on hearing his well-known knock; he was all covered with blood and wounds. The wife soon comprehended the matter, and clasped her hands in agony.

"Don't feel bad, Chloe," said poor Ostin; "massa drunk, don't know what he's do, an' de good Lor' tell us to forgive those that don't know what da do."

"But he'll kill you — he bad man."

"No, Chloe," said Ostin, thoughtfully. "If I stay here, de massa send me back, and he whip me to death; they say our savors are comin', and I go meet de Bridegroom."

Ostin had made up his mind, and no persuasion of Chloe's could shake his resolution. So, after providing himself with a hoecake and some food in his wallet, he took an affectionate leave of Chloe and their little picaninny and started off.

Ostin reached the banks of the Chattahoochee before day, but had to conceal himself in the brakes until night would come round again. He knew the country well, and he thought that by travelling by night and lying concealed by day, he could escape to our lines, which were then in front of Resaca.

Poor Chloe did not sleep that night, expecting every minute to hear the pursuit; nor was she long kept in suspense, for early in the morning Ostin's master, Mr. House, a planter named Giles Humphreys, and a Mr. Wemyss, rode up to the house, accompanied by bloodhounds. Wemyss made his living by keeping bloodhounds for hunting down runaway negroes. He had such a keen relish for the business, it was said he could smell out a negro himself. With unparalleled refinement they made Chloe give them an article of Ostin's clothing to help the scent.

The party was joined by several young bloods and idle negroes, for such a hunt promised to be exciting, and created considerable interest. Mrs. Ballinger entered warmly into the spirit of the thing, treated the party liberally to fire-water.. Being fully primed, off they started. The hounds soon took up the scent, and made the woods ring with their bloodthirsty cry.

Poor Ostin heard this. It was his death knell, and as the hounds approached him, he ran along a creek to baffle their scent, and then lay down in the water with barely his head above it, and screened by overhanging branches.

The dogs were put at fault for some time, but were too well trained to the game to be thrown off the track. They ran up and down the river several times, snuffed around, and searched every hole and corner, all the time encouraged by the pack of human brutes behind them, who were impatient to satiate their thirst with blood.

After a long search they discovered poor Ostin, and dragged him out like a drowned rat, amidst the jeers and curses of their ruffianly followers.

The poor fellow appealed for mercy, showed his wounds in proof of how he was treated, said he would be a faithful servant if Màssa House would keep him himself; but poor Ostin was appealing to hearts of stone. Several negroes had fled to the Yankees of late; it was necessary to make a frightful example. Ostin was tied to a tree; his back was placed against it; his hands swung round it, and were pinioned to it. In this condition the hounds were first let at him, to give them a taste of blood. Here an incident occurred that showed even the bloodhound to be capable of more kind feeling than a depraved planter. Among the dogs was an old hound, which was a great favorite with Ostin, who always fed and cared for it. When the other dogs fell to tearing the poor wretch, this dog fell on them, and was only removed with considerable difficulty. They next lighted fires about him, but his wet clothes would not burn.

While this horrid sacrifice was going on, a woman, half naked and frantic, bounded in among them. It was his poor wife, who had followed the hunt, and had now come up. She threw herself upon the maimed and lacerated victim, every embrace only tearing open his wounds. Despite this affecting sight, the groans of the poor, suffering wretch, and the pleadings of his unfortunate wife, poor Ostin was made a victim to intimidate others. The only mercy they showed him was to suspend him from the limb of a tree. No wonder that we discovered skeletons in the woods; no wonder that slavery brought its own curse with it.

Chloe returned home, became pensive, and would not work; but that Christian lady, Mrs. Ballinger, sold her down in Montgomery, Alabama, and retained the child. It is said that this lady kept her hand in practice by flogging some mulatto girls she had.

It is hard to credit that any person could be guilty of such savage cruelty; yet I heard the story from several. In this neighborhood was another man, named Newson, who punished his negroes by nailing their ears to a tree. After flogging one negro, he tied him naked to a tree, and left him there for the flies and mosquitos to feed on his lacerated flesh.

This man was looked upon as a monster of cruelty. His study was how to devise new modes of torture. He took particular delight in flogging his negroes himself. I must say that such savage demons were the exceptions. I have met negroes who seemed to be actually petted by their masters. There were many kind, good masters, whose interest and feelings of humanity induced them to treat their slaves with kindness; but there were some others, demons in human flesh, who only wanted the power and the opportunity to gratify their hellish passions.

CHAPTER XIV.

OUR CAVALRY AT WORK.—HOOD REPLACES JOHNSTON.—THEIR TACTICS COMPARED.—THE BATTLE OF PEACH-TREE CREEK.—ATLANTA SURROUNDED.

THE all-absorbing interest felt in Grant's campaigns in Virginia, and his movements before Richmond, for a time clouded Sherman's stirring and brilliant campaign in Georgia. If the importance of battles be rated by the thousands killed, we had not so bloody a scroll of honor to exhibit; but if continual fighting and incessant and exhausting marching amount to anything, we, too, had suffered. It is true that about thirty thousand would cover our whole loss since the opening of the campaign until we sat down before Atlanta. That would scarcely fill up one battle account in Virginia. I have had some experience in marching and fighting. I have seen something of the endurance of soldiers; but I must say that Sherman's campaign has surpassed my conception of man's capability of endurance. Our march had been one scene of stirring events and self-sacrifice, unparalleled in history.

Our wearied troops had not only to march and fight by day, but were often disturbed from their fevered sleep on the wet ground by the shots of the enemy and a night attack. When repulsed, the men had to build new works and keep on the *qui vive*. Yet these men, with their strong arms, stronger hearts, and bronzed faces, were cheerful under the most trying privations.

True, they may have grumbled a little, now and then, when disturbed from their sleep by the roar of the musket, or if disappointed in their coffee, or some other of the little enjoyments of a soldier's life; but then, after giving vent to their spleen in a strong prayer or two for the Johnny Rebs, they would coolly fall into line, and, with stern looks and knit brows, walk up to the cannon's mouth, not for the bubble fame, but because it was their duty, and for the good of their country.

Though our men were pretty well exhausted when we reached the Chattahoochee, and much in need of some rest, the sight of Jerusalem could not have a more inspiring effect on the devoted pilgrim than the sight of Atlanta had on our troops; it seemed the long-wished-for goal, and all were eager to rush on.

Having safely effected the crossing of the Chattahoochee, General Sherman gave a rest of some six days to his army.

All this time was well employed in collecting stores at Allatoona, Marietta, Vining Station, and other depots, improving the railroads and bridges, and strengthening the guards along our lines of communication.

Sherman now felt secure about Atlanta. Its fall was but a matter of time.

Heretofore the operations of our cavalry were chiefly confined to protecting our flanks, guarding our trains, and patrolling our railroad lines.

Sherman now resolved to organize large raiding parties to operate on the enemy's rear and destroy their lines of communication.

Johnston's cavalry had made such attempts upon us with very partial success; and now the Mississippi Railroad, connecting with Atlanta and Alabama, was exposed, and General Sherman ordered General Rousseau to take command of the large cavalry force concentrated at Decatur, Alabama.

Rousseau's force consisted of the 5th Indiana cavalry, Colonel Tom Harrison; 5th Iowa cavalry, Lieutenant Colonel Patrick; 2d Kentucky cavalry, Major Eifort; 4th Tennessee and 9th Ohio cavalry, with two Rodman guns.

General Rousseau, commanding the district of Nashville, had proposed to General Grant a concerted movement from Decatur upon Selma, which he looked upon as vulnerable to a cavalry attack. This proposition was not entertained at the time. General Sherman, seeing the necessity of destroying the railroad between Montgomery, Alabama, and Columbus, Georgia, ordered General Rousseau to make preparations for a raid on the road between the above points, also at Opelika, the point at which the Columbus road diverges from the Atlanta, West Point, and Montgomery road, thus cutting off Johnston's army from these two important sources of reënforcements and supplies.

The force thus organized numbered about two thousand five hundred, and had about a thousand Spencer repeating rifles.

With this expedition General Rousseau started from Decatur on the 10th, and, according to instructions, pushed rapidly south across the Coosa River, and thence struck directly for Opelika.

In this raid Rousseau had been remarkably successful. He encountered the rebel General Clanton and whipped him; passed through Talladega, struck the railroad on the 16th, twenty-five miles west of Opelika, tore it well up, also the branch line towards Columbus and West Point.

Having fulfilled his instructions, he returned to Marietta with only a loss of about thirty men.

Early on the morning of the 17th we broke camp around the Chattahoochee, and moved forward, every heart throbbing with the hope of entering Atlanta soon.

The French, in their fatal march through Russia, did not look out with more longing desire for Moscow than we did for Atlanta.

The 4th corps advanced on the Atlanta and Roswell road, the 23d corps upon the Decatur and Atlanta road, with the 14th and 23d on the Pace's Ferry and Atlanta road. McPherson's command was on our extreme left, with instructions to direct his course against the Augusta railroad, east of Decatur, near Stone Mountain.

McPherson marched on a right wheel, and reached the Augusta road the following day, at a point seven miles east of Decatur, and with Gerrard's cavalry and Morgan L. Smith's division of infantry, tore up about four miles of the road. Next evening Schofield took possession of the town of Decatur.

Wheeler's dismounted rebel cavalry were on our front, and

annoyed us from the shelter of rocks, trees, and the forest thickness. Wheeler himself had his headquarters in a farmhouse near Buckhead Creek, about six miles from Atlanta. So close was the 4th corps pressing him, that he had only just time to leave before our troops came up.

The day was spent in skirmishing with Wheeler's cavalry and Hood's rear guard, for the latter general was now in command.

After some sharp skirmishing, Schofield succeeded in effecting a crossing over Peach Creek.

The 20th corps had formed a junction with the right of Howard's corps.

Next morning General Thomas J. Wood moved out towards Peach Creek on a reconnoissance to develop the enemy's position. He advanced two brigades beyond Buckhead, and deployed a heavy line of skirmishers, which soon became engaged with the enemy.

The rebels began to intrench, but our artillery and sharpshooters soon made them move.

General Wood, having succeeded in driving the enemy across the creek, sent two brigades over, which succeeded in driving the rebels from their first line of works, and holding their position. They also captured several officers and men of the 2d Tennessee, who reported Hood's main army only a little in their rear.

The creek was too deep and wide for any great force to cross over.

Brigadier General Hazen at once undertook the building of the bridge, which had been destroyed by the rebels in their retreat.

General Hazen, to the cool daring of the soldier, the reflective judgment of the wise general, combined a large share of engineering skill.

While engaged personally on the bridge, his provost marshal, Captain S. B. Eaton, was badly wounded at his side by a sharpshooter, and Major Parkes, of the 79th Indiana, was also wounded in the leg.

Stanley effected a crossing on the left of Wood, and Hooker on the right.

Peach Creek runs somewhat in a westerly direction, and is a deep, turbid stream. At the point where Howard had crossed, it is only about five miles from Atlanta.

On the morning of the 20th a general advance in the direction of Atlanta was begun. By 10 o'clock the 20th corps had reached a range of heights rising between the creek and the city, and skirting the creek on its south bank. The 4th corps had now occupied the centre, with Newton's division beyond the creek, and connecting with Hooker's left, while Hooker's right was supported by the 14th corps.

In the brilliant and desperate conflict that ensued, it was but partially engaged. It came up, though, in time to form a junction with Williams's division, and take a part in the contest.

Before entering fully into the details of this fight, I will give a short *résumé* of the movements of the 20th corps the day previous.

Hood was now in command of the army. General Johnston was removed, because he was not checking Sherman's onward march, and because he would not engage to hold Atlanta at all hazards. Jeff Davis had been at Macon, lately, painting the Confederacy in a most flourishing condition. Among other things he told his dupes that Johnston's falling back was merely a stratagem on his part; that when our communication would be well cut up, he would pounce upon our army; and that Atlanta should, and would, be kept at all hazards.

Wheeler's attempt to cut up the line in our rear gave color to this; and now, in order to keep up the drooping hopes of the Confederacy, it was necessary to make a desperate blow to hold Atlanta. And because Johnston refused to sacrifice an army to do this, he was removed, Hood put in his place, and a new mode of campaigning inaugurated. Johnston proved himself a wise and prudent general, when, finding himself not able to contend against his antagonist in the field, he was keeping his army compact and well in hand for any opportunity that his wily enemy should afford him. Hood was a brave man, but a rash one; all his strategy lay in desperate fighting. This might do well enough if he were superior in numbers, or had the means of replenishing his ranks; but with a decimated army, and no means of replenishing it, it was certain destruction. This he fully proved by his attack on Hooker on the 20th of July, on McPherson on the 22d, on Howard on the 28th, and in his insane attempt to capture Nashville, where Thomas gave the final blow to himself and his army.

Had he followed Johnston's programme, or had Johnston retained command of the army, he would have fallen back toward Macon, giving us the option of garrisoning Atlanta, and contenting ourselves with a trifling victory, or following him up. It took about eighty thousand men to guard our lines of communication to Atlanta. It would take about eighty thousand more to Macon, and thus absorb our whole army. Well, should we follow them up, could they succeed in cutting off our supplies, we were ruined, or, should Sherman make one mistake, such a wily general as Johnston would be sure to take advantage of it.

Hood first weakened his army by mad assaults, and then went on a wild-goose chase to Nashville with what remained, opening the road for Sherman's grand raid, which showed the weakness of the Confederacy, and broke its backbone.

On the morning of the 19th, Geary's division, 20th corps, was ordered to advance. Williams's and Ward's divisions were ordered to hold themselves in readiness to follow Geary's. General Ward had taken command of the third division, General Osterhaus having gone home on sick leave. The 20th corps was encamped, at this time, on the Buckhead road, about two miles from Peach-tree Creek, and six miles due north from Atlanta. Geary advanced to the creek, repulsing the enemy in his front. The rebels destroyed the bridge over the creek, which was about twenty feet wide and five feet deep. The enemy took up a strong position on a range of hills on the other side. After a careful survey of the position, Geary resolved to make a crossing. He got his artillery into position, so as to cover the crossing.

The pioneers having ready the materials for laying the bridge, our artillery opened, and our sharpshooters advanced along the creek, under cover of the fire. A hastily constructed bridge was constructed, and Colonel Ireland rapidly threw his brigade across, and charged the enemy's flank. The whole division soon followed to his support, and succeeded in taking up a position beyond the creek. Meantime the 4th corps was effecting a crossing at Collier's Mills, and the 14th at Howel's Mills.

On the morning of the 20th, Williams's division crossed on the same bridge as Geary's, and Ward's farther on the left.

About 11 o'clock, Colonel Candy's brigade, Geary's division, advanced nearly a mile across a ridge, and established a line there.

This hill was on the flank of a ridge held by the rebel skirmishers.

General Ward soon attacked their position, and met a stubborn resistance.

The 13th New York battery (Bundy's) was placed in front of Candy's brigade, and enfiladed the rebel lines. Colonel P. H. Jones (now General Jones) sent out the 33d New Jersey, under Lieutenant Colonel Furratt, to support Ward's skirmishers and to fortify the hill. General Geary and staff were out reconnoitring, and soon perceived the enemy massing in column for an assault.

The divisions and brigades were formed into line as fast as possible.

Candy's brigade occupied the advance left of Geary's line, Jones's the right, and Ireland's in reserve. Williams's division was on the right of Geary, Ward's on the left; both somewhat refused, forming a kind of semicircle, with Geary's division as the apex.

Newton's division, of Howard's corps, had fortunately moved to the right the night previous, in order to connect with Hooker, and was now thrown back *en échelon*, his left resting on the creek. They had barely time to throw up hurried breastworks of rails in their front, and bring their artillery into position, when the enemy swept over the plain and burst on their front, next on Geary's front and flank, actually wedging between his right and Williams's lines, thus swinging on his rear. Colonel Jones at once wheeled round by brigade front, Colonel Candy doing the same, thus exposing the enemy to a cross fire. The fighting here was close and desperate for some time, the enemy striving to crush Jones's and Candy's brigades, and thus pierce our centre and double up our flanks. Our troops, on the other hand, fully sensible of the imminent peril of the movement, fought with desperate determination, resolved to hold their ground until the lines could close up and support them.

Jones's noble brigade, admirably led and fought by its brave commander, was nearly decimated, and could not hold out much longer; Candy's brigade, too, was fearfully thinned, when Williams's left closed up on the enemy, thus placing them between an enfilading fire. A desperate fight ensued, the troops, on both sides, being exposed, and fighting at close quarters. At some points it was a regular hand-to-hand conflict. Williams succeeded in throwing his whole division on the enemy's flank, which was soon compelled to give way, and was actually mowed down while retreating over the plain to their works. In this short and desperate struggle we lost some valuable officers, among them Captain Thomas H. Elliot, adjutant general to General Geary. Captain Elliot was a native of Philadelphia, son to Colonel K. Elliot. He was a good officer, of splendid executive ability, a thorough gentleman, and refined scholar. Geary suffered much, during the war, in staff officers, all of them being either killed or wounded. Captain Newcomb, of General Williams's staff, was also killed. Several field-officers were either killed or wounded. Among the latter were Colonel Jackson, 134th New York, and Lieutenant Colonel Furratt, 33d New Jersey, both of whom distinguished themselves during the engagement.

Robertson's brigade, of Williams's division, engaged the enemy on the flank, and lost severely. It made a noble fight, stemming the rebel advance until the rest of Williams's division came up. Colonel Loyz, of the 141st New York, was killed, Colonel

McNelty lost an arm, and the brave Colonel McGroarty, of the 61st Ohio, was shot through the shoulder.

About 4 o'clock the rebels came on in massed columns against Newton, without skirmishers, and with fierce yells they bore down upon his line. Newton's division had but partly completed their breastwork of rails, and had barely time to fall into line and seize their guns, before Walker's and Bates's division, of Hardee's corps, burst right on them.

The pickets guarding the interval between the right and left had barely time to jump into the creek and swim for their lives. For a moment everything was in confusion. Newton's line was extended and weak, being thrown back to guard the bridges across the creek.

Captain Goodspeed brought up his guns with great rapidity, and placed them in position. They opened with canister, and poured a deadly storm on the advancing enemy. The gunners worked with frenzied energy, pouring the leaden storm right into their faces, and sweeping whole lanes through their ranks. The rebels poured volley after volley into our line, and, though fearfully decimated, continued to advance. Officer after officer, color-bearer after color-bearer, line after line, went down before the sweeping storm of canister and bullets.

At length their line began to falter and get into confusion. We renewed our energy with a sort of frantic rage, and soon they wavered. One volley, one cheer from our men, and the enemy broke and fled.

General Ward's division, on Newton's right, was struck at the same time. Ward had just halted his men at the foot of a hill, when he discovered that the enemy were gathering in his front, evidently with the intention of making an assault.

Ward formed into line, and the enemy soon came pouring on him. Ward at once advanced up the hill in his front, in order to gain the crest before the rebels. Here the two columns first struck each other; and as both sides fought with muskets, the destruction of life was fearful. Ward had previously sent his artillery to assist Newton.

In Ward's front the men fought, at some points, at close

THE BATTLE DESPERATE. 163

quarters, the contending lines actually intermingling together, and fighting hand to hand with the bayonet and clubbed rifles.

This continued for nearly an hour, the opposing lines surging to and fro, until at length the rebels broke for the woods, leaving a large number of prisoners.

The rebel charge next swept along to the right, striking Geary's and Williams's divisions, which were also exposed, not having time to throw up any works, for the rebel assault came by surprise.

Palmer's 14th corps was partly intrenched on Williams's left, and considerably refused, and consequently did not suffer much during the fight.

Ward captured six battle-flags and a large number of prisoners, besides strewing the field in his front with killed and wounded. The 26th Wisconsin took the colors of the 33d Mississippi; the 105th Illinois captured two colors, and the 129th Illinois one. Some of our men, being out of ammunition, emptied the dead rebels' cartridge-boxes into their own.

Colonel Harrison, 129th Illinois, and four men, captured three officers and thirty men of the 57th Alabama.

A boy about fourteen years old, named Ed. Harvey, 70th Indiana, captured five men, and brought them in prisoners.

This battle was very obstinately contested on both sides. The rebels got mixed up with our lines, when a regular hand-to-hand death-struggle ensued. As soon as we recovered from the first surprise, and got to form our lines, we mowed the enemy down with fearful slaughter.

The battle of the 20th was desperate and stubborn. Hooker was in marching column, and Hood thought he would strike him unprepared. In this he partly succeeded. A large gap intervened between Geary's and Williams's divisions, through which he burst with his massed troops in admirable order. Our troops, for a moment, gave way; but, after recovering from the first panic, formed and wheeled about, presenting two fronts to the rebel column, which had now wedged through them. In this manner a double fire was brought to bear on their lines, and the slaughter was fearful. Along the deep hollow intervening between Geary's and Williams's division the enemy poured along in masses, but only to be mowed down wholesale. Robertson's brigade, of Williams's division, hastened up along the crest of the hill, and facing by the left flank, engaged them. Geary's right struck them on the other side, and Knipe's brigade had formed in line on the right of Robertson and in conjunction with the 14th corps. The enemy also poured down upon Knipe with the same fierceness and desperation they exhibited at the other points.

At this stage the battle raged fiercely; the air became dark and heavy from the sulphurous canopy of smoke which hung over the plain. Wounded men were borne to the rear by scores, the blood flowing from their wounds. Even those sickening sights, and the din of musketry, and the thundering roar of artillery, did not damp the ardor of the contending heroes; for fresh troops bravely advanced to fill the thinning lines which were made by some patriotic hearts, the treasured pride of many a household, sinking, quivering, upon the earth, to fill a soldier's grave and rend a mother's heart.

This was the first of Hood's desperate assaults around Atlanta; and dear was the price he paid for it, and bloody the harvest he reaped.

In their telegrams to General Sherman, General Howard stated that he had buried two hundred, and that there was a large number of wounded in his front; and Hooker reported, "I have buried four hundred dead, and at least four thousand wounded lie in my front."

Sherman himself estimated the rebel loss at about five thousand, and ours at fifteen hundred. He says, "The enemy left on the field over five hundred dead, about one thousand wounded *severely*, seven stands of colors, and many prisoners."

I think myself the rebel loss is over-estimated. Generals, in making their returns, are seldom under the mark; for the greater the loss to the enemy, the greater is their victory. I would set down our loss at about two thousand; the enemy's at least double that. As they were the assaulting parties, and exposed, their loss must be severe.

Next day (21st July) McPherson moved forward and established a line east and south of Atlanta, and within three miles of the town.

Blair's corps, 17th, formed the extreme left, and rested south of the city, his left flank being within two miles of the Macon railroad.

Logan held the Decatur road, his centre resting on it, with Dodge on his right.

Palmer, Howard, and Hooker's corps swung round to the right, forming an irregular semicircle. Hooker's right commanded the Chattahoochee.

The enemy's lines were adapted to ours, their left extending to the river, and covering the roads leading to Atlanta.

Gerrard's cavalry occupied a line along the Decatur, Cross-Keys, and Lebanon road, protecting our supplies at Roswell. Stoneman was north of the river, between the Sandtown road and Vining's Bridge. Gerrard had sent forward a squad of cavalry in advance, which succeeded in cutting the railroad near Stone Mountain. We could see the heavy volumes of smoke rising from the burning of the cross-ties and station-houses.

While Hooker was engaged with the enemy, our centre also skirmished with them. General T. J. Wood swung round on the Decatur road after General Stanley. Stanley soon struck the enemy, and, after some sharp fighting, drove them back to the rear of a Mr. Johnson's house, about four miles from Atlanta. Here the 40th Ohio and 21st Kentucky, which had the advance, struck on a strong line of rebels. Stanley hurried up his artillery, and opened on the rebels with good effect.

Schofield had now connected with Stanley on the left, and had swung round his left towards Atlanta, timing his movement with McPherson's.

On the night of the 21st, Schofield's right and McPherson's left were within less than three miles of Atlanta, so that they could actually rain in shell upon the devoted city.

Our army now surrounded Atlanta in a horseshoe form. McPherson's command stretched beyond the Atlanta and Augusta Railroad, which he had torn up, thus cutting off one source of supplies from the enemy, and preventing them from falling back to Stone Mountain. Our lines were drawing tighter and tighter around the city. It was evident that it would soon fall, unless Hood, by any more of his dashing assaults, could burst through our lines and compel us to retreat. This he tried next day; but the effect was as crushing and disastrous to him as his attempt on Hooker.

CHAPTER XV.

BATTLE OF THE 22D OF JULY.—DEATH OF GENERAL McPHERSON.—HIS LIFE AND SERVICES.—SCENES AMONG THE DEAD AND WOUNDED.

HOOD had now been reënforced by Stephen D. Lee, with about four thousand of the Trans-Mississippi army, and about ten thousand militia, which he had placed to garrison the trenches in and around Atlanta. Johnston had been removed for not fighting his army. Hood was resolved that he would not give any cause of complaint on this score, and if by any good fortune he should succeed, he would eclipse Johnston as a general; besides, things were in such a desponding state, that even in case of failure his reputation could not suffer much.

At a council of war held on the 16th, at which Jeff Davis himself presided, and Governor Brown, Johnston, and Hood were present, Johnston was relieved of his command, and Hood installed in his place. Next day Johnston issued a farewell address to the army; this was followed by an address from Hood, and reckless assaults on our lines. Foiled in his desperate attempt on Hooker, under cover of the night he moved his army from the front of our right wing, and transferred it to our left. He seemed to understand our position thoroughly, for he knew that on McPherson's left was a deep, unguarded gap, through which he could move his columns with the bold intention of outflanking our army. In this he was partly successful, and might have been fully so, only for our superior numbers and the desperate manner in which our troops fought. This movement of Hood's has been very much censured by military critics; to me, it appears a masterly one. Had he succeeded,— and the chances were in his favor,—he would have broken our left wing, and then he could safely capture our immense trains, which were parked around the Chattahoochee, and follow this up by an attack in rear on our right, or centre, while the militia behind the strong works in front were able to keep our advance in check. This assault appeared to me to have more wisdom in its design and execution, than the assault on Hooker's lines. In the latter the advantages were on the side of our army, as Hooker's divisions were close, and he got into position too soon for the rebels to obtain advantage. In the attack on McPherson they succeeded in swinging their columns on our flanks and rear, and under such circumstances few troops will withstand a charge. I have seldom known a case where troops are outflanked and enfiladed but they lose heart and break. Men are judged, not so much by the wisdom of their acts or counsels, as by the result. It was so with Hood; he failed and is execrated; had he succeeded, he would have been idolized.

On the morning of the 22d, Generals Howard and Hooker, finding that the rebels had retired from their immediate front, followed them up close to their first line of works, and captured several prisoners and stragglers. They then threw out strong lines of skirmishers, and established their batteries in good positions. The rebels kept pressing on Hooker's front in order to cloak their assault on the left. Schofield, too, considerably advanced his lines, and skirmished with the enemy. Even the wily Sherman himself was for a time deceived by this movement of the enemy. He thought that Hood was so prostrated by his defeat on the 20th, that he was going to give up Atlanta without striking another blow for it. But Hood was simply carrying out that bloody programme, of which his assault of the 20th was an index.

General McPherson had moved from Decatur with the intention of joining the column that was closing around Atlanta, and marched along the line of railroad with the 15th corps, destroying it as he marched. Blair's corps, the 17th, was on the left of Logan, and Dodge's, the 16th, on his right, and connecting with Schofield near the Howard House.

On the evening of the 21st, Blair's corps had a sharp engagement with the enemy for the possession of a commanding hill, called Ball Hill, south and east of the railroad. This we succeeded in gaining, and it gave us a most commanding range of the very heart of the city itself. General Dodge was ordered from right to left to occupy this position, and make it a strong general left flank. General Dodge was in the act of moving by a kind of by-road for this point when the enemy struck him.

After the repulse on our right, Hood hastily swung round Hardee's corps, followed by the others, on the flank and rear of McPherson. This hurried and unexpected movement partly took us by surprise. Unfortunately, McPherson had no cavalry guarding his front or flank, for Gerrard was out on a raid to Covington, on the Augusta line, and with instructions to send detachments to break the bridge across the Yellow and Uleauhatchee River, tributaries of the Ocmulgee.

At daylight on the 22d, the pickets discovered the rebel works in their front evacuated, as the enemy had fallen back to their main lines. Preparations were made to advance our whole line. Schofield's corps moved up first, and began to reverse the abandoned rebel works. There was much conjecture as to what this movement meant. Could it be that the city was evacuated? Scouts and deserters reported so. Several of the latter, no doubt, came into our lines to confirm this report.

About noon our troops were still moving into position, Giles A. Smith's division occupied the left of Blair's corps; in his rear was General Fuller; while General Sweeny's division brought up the extreme rear. This was fortunate, as, had they been up and in position, there would be no troops to check the headlong dash of Hardee's corps, as it swept around our extreme flank.

The mystery of the falling back by the rebels was soon solved, for about 2 o'clock Hardee's corps had completely got in on our rear. Hardee made his assault on the rear of the 17th corps, repulsing a brigade supporting the artillery, and capturing the battery. When the attack was made, General McPherson was at Howard's House, in consultation with Sherman, when he was apprised of the attack on his lines. The heavy roll of musketry and artillery from the left fully confirmed this report.

He hastily rode off, despatching his staff officers and orderlies to different parts of the lines with commands. He rode right for Dodge's column, in which there had been some changes made since morning. He passed to the left and rear of General Giles Smith's division, which was Blair's extreme left. A gap intervened between the 16th and 17th corps, through which the general passed. Here he fell from the fire of the rebel sharpshooters. His wounded horse returned riderless, and the general's dead body was recovered in the course of the evening. As soon as General Sherman learned the sad news, he at once despatched an aid to General John A. Logan, instructing him to assume chief command.

The death of McPherson was kept secret. He was too much beloved to let his army know that he was no more, at such a critical moment. At night, when his death was known, there was one general feeling of grief and indignation. Strong men, who unmoved saw their comrades fall around them, wept like children.

Logan coolly assumed the command, making no display, so as to conceal the sad bereavement from officers and men. It is said that when the battle was fought and won, General Sherman, looking down on the body of the dead chieftain, exclaimed,—

"Yes, yes; it's all very well, if we could only restore McPherson."

About noon the fight was raging fiercely. Hardee had struck Blair's left flank, overlapping it, and swinging round until he struck Dodge's corps in motion. The fighting was desperate in front of the 16th corps, the line of which ran partly at right angles to the 17th corps. Sweeny's division hastily got into line in the following order: Colonel Rice's brigade faced to the rear, and Colonel Mersey's southward, with Morrill's brigade, of Fuller's division, on Mersey's right. Soon the whole rebel column burst upon them. The 14th Ohio battery opened on their advance, hurling the deadly storm into their faces. The column halted for a moment, and then defiantly came on. The rebel line was now overlapping Dodge's command, and threatened to turn his flank. He ordered the 81st Ohio, Lieutenant Colonel

Adams, and the 12th Illinois, Colonel Von Sellar, to charge on the rebel flank. These regiments moved through a valley, and wheeling round the point of a ridge, suddenly burst on the rebel flank, slaughtering them terribly, and capturing several prisoners and two stands of colors. Sweeny was all this time gallantly fighting his division, stemming the advance of Hardee's corps. Morrill's brigade impetuously charged the enemy, driving them back to the edge of the wood, but was soon overpowered and forced to fall back; again it crossed the bloody field to be again repulsed, but soon rallied, advanced, and held its position.

At the same time Rice's and Murray's brigades were fiercely engaged with the enemy. General Sweeny knew that in a great measure the fate of the day depended on his division; unless he could check the rebel advance long enough for the troops to take up position, they would overwhelm them, flank and rear. With true Celtic chivalry he dashed from point to point, and if he saw any part of the lines wavering, there he was, regardless of shot and shell, encouraging and exhorting the troops.

The attack in front of the 17th corps was steadily made and well sustained. After heavy hand-to-hand fighting, the rebels succeeded in doubling in on the 16th, and capturing several pieces of artillery.

Generals Giles A. Smith's and Legget's divisions were making a stubborn stand against the enemy, who had swarmed upon them. They fought in the old intrenchments, and, being attacked in front and rear, had to fight, now on one side, then jump over it and fight on the other side; the men bayoneting one another in the very trenches.

The attack on the centre was equally obstinate. Logan's 15th corps was fighting for life. Morgan L. Smith's division was almost decimated, and was at length forced to retire. The enemy had captured the most of our artillery, and driven back our lines at several points. That brave young artillerist Captain De Grass sat down and wept like a child for his guns, and, as the enemy turned them on us, he could recognize their sound amidst the din and roar of battle, and wondered how they could be so ungrateful as to turn upon him. The celebrated battery of twenty-pound Parrott's, and Murray's regular battery were all in their hands.

Things looked gloomy now. McPherson was dead, our artillery captured, our troops repulsed at several points, and the stream of bleeding men that was going to the rear told the deadly nature of the conflict.

General Sherman, accompanied by Schofield and Howard, occupied a prominent position near Colonel Howard's house, from which he could superintend the whole proceedings. On a commanding hill near, he placed a battery of the 15th corps, and another of the 23d corps, which commanded a converging, enfilading fire on the enemy. He then sent word to General Logan to mass his troops in the centre and charge.

"You must retake those guns," was his peremptory order. Logan seemed to throw his own fiery spirit into the troops. He often rode at the heads of the columns, to make them believe the danger was not so great. Everything being ready, Wood's first division, 15th corps, was ordered to lead the charge. Wood swung his right around so as to envelop the rebel rear.

The rebel column, looking upon us as completely broken, felt surprised that we should renew the conflict. They moved out in column to meet the assault. Our remaining artillery now opened, the batteries near Howard's house hurling shot and shell among them. A confiding cheer went up from our ranks, and on they swept. The contending lines were now so close that the artillery had to cease — one wild cheer from our lines, one sweeping charge, the men delivering a low and deadly fire into the advancing rebel columns as they came on. The enemy's line staggered, paused, and fled before that glittering forest of bayonets.

This was the turning-point of battle; we charged all along the line. The enemy were soon scattered and broken, and flying on all sides. We recovered all our artillery, except two pieces. Our loss in this battle was about thirty-five hundred, all counted. The enemy's loss was at least seven thousand. Logan buried over two thousand of the enemy's dead.

Hood seemed to be well informed as to our positions, for he selected the only available point by which he could wheel to our rear; besides, he knew that McPherson's immense wagon train was left very poorly guarded at Decatur. He did not know, though, that Colonel Sprague — afterwards General Sprague — had gone with his brigade to guard it.

Hood ordered Wheeler's cavalry to make a simultaneous attack on the train.

Colonel Sprague, with his three regiments, met Wheeler's attack with promptness and firmness. Though Wheeler had two divisions of cavalry, mounted and dismounted, Colonel Sprague, with a loss of two hundred men, repulsed them and saved the trains.

On the whole, this was one of the most desperately contested conflicts of the campaign.

Hood, like the ruined gambler, staked all on one throw. His plans were well and wisely laid; he surprised the cautious Sherman, and had he less brave troops and indefatigable generals to contend against, he would have succeeded. It was a desperate game; the stakes were great, and though he lost, he played his hand well.

The body of McPherson, as I said, was soon recovered. The rebels either did not know his rank, or had not time to remove him, as the lines soon after surged from that point. Two of our skirmishers, who saw the general fall, went over to the spot. The rebel skirmish lines were quite near. The general was scarcely dead when they came up. He was lying on his face and breathing heavily, but unable to speak. They turned him on his back; he opened his eyes, and gave one parting look and a smile, when he saw they were his own men, and then expired.

It was reported that the rebels stripped the body; this is not likely, because, if they knew his rank, they certainly would have carried him off.

One of the two men confessed to me, "You see, sir, we knew we hain't no chance of staying there long, as they were fighting all round us, but we did not want to let the poor general get into their hands; so, though it went sore to our hearts to strip our noble general, we cut off his stars and buttons, so they would not know him. We then hid, and the rebels swept over us; they kicked me up, and took me along. They searched me, and found the general's things with me, which one of them transferred to his own pocket. I watched this fellow; he soon got knocked over; I gave a jump and kicked about as if I were shot too; so they left me there. I returned, and knowing that the dead rebel did not want the things any longer, I took them, and staid with the general's body until it was removed."

McPherson was a great favorite in the army. Several of his brother generals came to bid farewell to the remains; many were seen to weep as they turned away; even the stern Sherman's eyes were not dry. A victory was dearly bought at the sacrifice of such a man.

Sketch of Major General McPherson.

Major General James B. McPherson, United States volunteers, and brigadier general of the regular army, was born in Sandusky, Ohio, in November, 1828, and was consequently in his thirty-sixth year when he was killed. He graduated at the head of his class at West Point, and entered the regular army with the brevet rank of second lieutenant of engineers. He was engaged in different military capacities, both in New York and on the Pacific coast.

In 1861, when General Halleck was ordered to the department of the west, he was selected as aid-de-camp, with the rank of lieutenant colonel. He was chief engineer in the expedition against Forts Henry and Donelson, and for his services promoted to a brevet major of engineers. He served with General Grant during his operations in Tennessee, and until after the battle of Shiloh. He was again promoted for his services at Shiloh to a brevet lieutenant colonelcy of engineers. He was soon promoted to a colonelcy, and again assigned to General Halleck. At Corinth he again distinguished himself, and was soon after promoted to the rank of brigadier general of volunteers. At the battle of Iuka, September, 1862, General

McPherson held a position on the staff of General Grant, and distinguished himself at Corinth by carrying reënforcements to the besieged garrison in October, with the enemy intervening; and next day, at the head of a division, he pursued the flying column of the foe.

For his services he was promoted to the rank of major general of volunteers, to date October 8, 1862. He commanded the column that moved on Lagrange, under Grant, in the fall of 1862. He next commanded an expedition into Mississippi. His history from this time forward is a history of Grant's various battles and campaigns.

He was engaged at Fort Gibson, being then in command of the 17th corps. Under his direction the Bayou Pere was bridged and crossed, the enemy being followed up to Jackson, Mississippi. He again whipped the enemy at Raymond, repulsed them after a severe fight, and again whipped them at Champion's Hill.

In front of Vicksburg he acted a distinguished part, both as a general and in the employment of his splendid engineering qualities. After the fall of Vicksburg, General Grant, in recommending his various officers for promotion, says of him, after enumerating his many battles, "He is one of the ablest engineers and most skilful generals. I would respectfully but urgently recommend his promotion to the position of brigadier general in the regular army." This was granted, and the Board of Honor voted him a gold medal for his gallant conduct during the siege of Vicksburg.

In February, 1864, he commanded a wing of Sherman's army, during the expedition from Vicksburg to Meridian. On Sherman assuming command of the military division of the Mississippi, General McPherson was placed in command of the army and department of the Tennessee, embracing the 15th, 16th, and 17th army corps. He thereupon removed his headquarters to Huntsville; and hence he commenced his movements in the latter end of April, 1864, taking the right of Sherman's army in the Georgian campaign. On the 9th of May he occupied Snake Creek Gap, and the next day was within a mile of

Resaca. Again, he encountered and routed the enemy at Powder Springs, near Dallas, inflicting a severe loss upon them.

At Allatoona he distinguished himself; also in the several engagements around Big Shanty and Kenesaw Mountain. His command did a great deal of heavy marching on the Chattahoochee, now threatening the rebel left on Nickajack Creek, and then suddenly wheeling on their right, crossing the river, moving on Decatur, and destroying the Augusta line. After such brilliant services, he met his death, I might almost say, accidentally, in the desperate charge Hood made on his line on the 22d of July.

In appearance he was near six feet high, of agreeable and engaging manners.

His eyes were dark, his hair and beard, which he wore long and flowing, rather dark brown. He was a man of noble, stately presence, affable and courteous to all.

Though strict in the discharge of his military duties, he was beloved by his officers and revered by his soldiers. In his fall his soldiers lost their friend, the country a true patriot and wise general.

In this battle I had an opportunity of witnessing how little personal animosity men who are engaged in deadly conflict entertain for one another, and again how the terrors of death itself cannot allay bitter personal hatred. Ambulances, with the blood dripping between their boards from the wounds of the poor sufferers inside, were hurrying to the rear. The low groans and the piercing shrieks that issued from the vehicles, as the victims were shaken about by the wheels getting into some deep slough, or bumping against a tree, pierced the very marrow in my bones. A long line of these wagons was continually hurrying from the field to the hospitals.

In passing one of these, I was stopped by an angry altercation going on inside. The ambulance was stopped, and the two wounded men, one of whom was a rebel, the other a Federal, were found to be engaged in a fierce hand-to-hand encounter. We wrenched the bayonets from their hands.

"Shame, shame!" I exclaimed, "for wounded men thus to butcher one another. You should not forget you are enemies no longer."

"Should we, indeed?" exclaimed the Federal soldier. "I hain't forgot it, though. I hain't forgot this here scoundrel burnt the house over my wife and children up in Tennessee; he may thank his stars this leg and arm are shattered, or I'd have pinned him to the wagon here."

It was true. The man's leg and arm were broken, and had afterwards to be amputated.

"O, you are a fine fellow," sneered the other, who could scarcely speak from a bullet-wound through the chest. "Only for this ugly hole in my lungs, we'd see who could crow. I am a poor wounded prisoner now. You can do as you like, but if we met up in Tennessee, when you were on my track with your bloodhound, it would be different. Answell, did you not kill my brother and my father? and why should not I look for vengeance?"

"If I did, it was in fair fight. There was nothing of your d—n skulking, murdering tricks about it."

Seeing the angry feeling between the two men, and that nothing but more blood could satisfy it, we removed one of them to another ambulance. Behind the ambulances were the stretcher-bearers removing the wounded from the field. The stretchers were dripping with blood; and as they deposited their gory burdens, some were senseless, some speechless, others cheerful, and conversing about the battle, treating their wounds very lightly.

On the other hand, some who were not dangerously wounded were limping along on their muskets, hobbling to the rear.

It was no unusual sight to see a Federal soldier kindly leaning on the arm of a Confederate one, who was less wounded than himself.

These men appeared on the best possible terms, and almost wondered why they should be fighting against each other.

As one had a canteen, they took several pulls out of it, and then stopped, and discussed its merits. On the whole, some of these appeared to be the best possible friends. I met one stretcher carrying a very fine young rebel soldier. Beside it was a sergeant, who, as the bearers laid down their burden, wiped the death-damp from his brow, and gave him a drink from his canteen.

The sergeant seemed to suffer as much agony as the mute soldier on the stretcher. I found they were brothers from Tennessee, and had now, for the first and last time, met in four years.

The elder brother, who was now on the stretcher, was in business in Augusta at the breaking out of the war, and, of course, joined the rebel army; the other, who remained at home, joined the Federal army. In the charge on the works, the sergeant had shot down this young fellow, who daringly placed the rebel colors on our works. He then recognized him as his elder brother.

I knew another case in this fight where the father shot his own son.

When the rebels were charging upon our lines, a young officer at their head was conspicuous for the desperate bravery with which he was leading on his men.

"Will one of you shoot him down? or we are undone," exclaimed the officer in command.

A sergeant, who was remarkable for his crack shot, took deliberate aim, and shot the rebel officer; his men gave way, and we occupied the ground. The dying officer was brought within our lines, and the sergeant found that he was his only son whom he had left in business down in Charleston at the breaking out of the war.

This was too much for the wretched father; so in the grand charge that soon followed, he was conspicuous, and, with a frantic desperation, rushed right upon the enemy, and fell, with his body actually perforated with bullets.

I will relate another case, of an Irishman who came to this country in search of a long absent brother. One was north, the other south, and both joined the contending armies.

The day after the battle, a flag of truce was sent out in order to bury the dead.

Our Irish friend was among the parties detailed; and in one of the bodies brought for interment he discovered his long-lost brother.

Another was the case of two Germans. One of our men, detailed for hospital duty, had a young soldier brought in to his care, whose leg had been just amputated. The poor youth was still delirious, and dreamed and talked of absent friends in Rhineland. Then he commenced raving about Karl, a long absent brother, whom his parents commissioned him to find in America.

"O, mine Gott!" exclaimed Karl, covering his face with his hands, "but he is mine broder."

And it was thus they met for the first time since Karl left the other, a prattling babe in the old home on the Rhine. All Karl's care could not save him; but he was conscious before he died, and had the poor satisfaction of knowing Karl, and having a good talk about the old folks, and the grape-clad cottage overlooking the river. Karl heard his last sigh breathed, and bore his last wish to those at home.

He had his body interred beneath a branching cedar, and placed a slab at his head, to tell his name and how he died.

This even was a satisfaction to poor Karl, for he felt that his brother was not huddled into the common pit, where hundreds are flung in to rot together, but had a decent grave to himself.

It is an affecting sight to witness the removal of the dead and wounded from a battle-field, and the manner in which the former are interred. In some cases, deep pits are sunk, and, perhaps, a hundred or more bodies are flung promiscuously into it, as if no one owned them, or cared for them.

In other cases, where the bodies had been recognized, they were buried with some semblance of decency. I was once riding with a column over a battle-field, in which the skeletons of the hastily buried dead were partly exposed.

The arm and hand of a man protruded from one of these sunken graves.

"Arrah, Bill," exclaimed one Irishman to another, "could you tell me what that man has his hand up for?"

"Faith, in troth, I don't know, if it ain't for his back pay and bounty," was the reply.

I have often met skeletons in the woods, with the bones stretched out, and the old rotten knapsacks under the heads, and the remnants of the clothes still clinging around the bones.

These were poor fellows who got wounded in the heat of battle, and retired to the shelter of the forest. Here they lay; and not being discovered, and being unable to get away, they died, inch by inch, for carrion birds to pick their bodies. What must be the suffering of these poor fellows, with their festering wounds, crawling with maggots, without a hand to tend them, without a drop of water to cool their parched lips, with the ravens and turkey-buzzards croaking around them, watching, until they would be too helpless to defend themselves, to pounce on them, and pluck out their eyes, or drag the quivering flesh from their frames.

I have seen others, particularly at the battle of Chancellorsville, who fell, wounded, out in the woods, and who were burned up when the woods took fire, and whom we could not assist, as the rebel skirmishers and sharpshooters took down every man who dared to put out his head.

Their shrieks and groans, as they writhed in the fiery furnace, still ring in my ears.

CHAPTER XVI.

UNSUCCESSFUL CAVALRY RAIDS OF McCOOK AND STONEMAN.—
CHANGE OF COMMANDERS.—HOWARD'S APPOINTMENT AND
HOOKER'S RESIGNATION.—THE BATTLE OF PROCTOR'S CREEK.

Hood's attempt on our left being frustrated, he fell back to his inner line of works, while our lines tightened upon him at all points. The works around Atlanta were of the most formidable nature.

Deep lines of intrenchments, with forts and gabions, protected by palisades, *chevaux-de-frise*, and pits, in their front, faced us on all sides. In these were several sallying-points, from which the skirmishers and sharpshooters could deploy.

Sherman too well comprehended the impossibility of taking such works by assault; so he devised a new plan of action. He issued an order to the army of the Tennessee to be ready to vacate its line, and to shift by the right flank below Proctor's Creek, and move to our extreme right.

At the same time Generals Schofield and Thomas extended their line towards the Augusta road.

Sherman's intentions were to swing the army to the rear of Hood, so as to operate on the East Point road. At the same time he had in operation a great cavalry raid on the enemy's rear. To General Stoneman he gave the command of his own and General Gerrard's cavalry, making an effective force of about five thousand men; and to General McCook he assigned the command of the cavalry returned by Rousseau, under command of Colonel Harrison, and the 8th Indiana cavalry, making an aggregate of four thousand, or a total of about nine thousand cavalry.

With these two formidable bodies, which were to act in

concert,— Stoneman to the left of Atlanta, by McDonough Station, and McCook on Fayetteville,— he expected to whip Wheeler's cavalry, and destroy the remaining routes to Atlanta by railroad. General Stoneman requested permission to be allowed to proceed to Macon and Anderson to release the Federal prisoners confined in those prisons. Sherman left this at his own discretion, in case he felt he was able to do so after the defeat of Wheeler's cavalry, but, at the same time, allowing Gerrard's cavalry to fall back in time to cover his flank.

Both cavalry expeditions started at the same time, and both proved more or less a failure. McCook succeeded in returning with his command, but with a heavy loss of both men and material. Stoneman had the most of his command cut up or captured, while he himself remained a prisoner in the hands of the enemy.

Before I proceed with the siege of Atlanta, I will give a short account of those two expeditions, as they form an important part of the campaign.

McCook's Cavalry Raid.

On the morning of the 27th July, General McCook broke camp at Mason's Seminary, near Sweetwater Town, on the Chattahoochee. His command consisted of two brigades, commanded by Colonel Cloxton and Lieutenant Colonel Torrey, and also Colonel Harrison's command, which had lately returned from Rousseau's raid, and comprised the 8th Indiana, 2d Kentucky, 5th Iowa, 4th Tennessee, and 9th Ohio.

McCook crossed Sweetwater on the main road leading to Villaricka.

After meeting some slight resistance in crossing the Chattahoochee, the command moved on two parallels for Palmetto, skirmishing with Armstrong's brigade all the way.

At Palmetto they tore up about two miles of the railroad, and burned about fifty railroad cars, a large supply of commissary stores, and over five hundred bales of cotton.

They next struck for Lovejoy, over nasty broken roads and a very densely wooded country. On the morning of the 29th they surprised a large baggage train, and burned about one hundred and fifty wagons, and shot about six hundred mules.

Generals Hardee, Loring, and Stewart's headquarter wagons were among the lot.

They next struck Fayetteville, where they captured over four hundred men and officers, and thence marched for Lovejoy, on the Macon line, destroying about two miles of the track and telegraph wire.

According to the programme laid down by Sherman, Stoneman and McCook were to form a junction on the night of July 28th, on the Macon road, near Lovejoy, and effectually destroy it.

McCook now found that a large cavalry force intervened between himself and Stoneman, while another force was pressing on his rear, thus preventing the possibility of a junction; so he had to wheel by the flank for Newman.

Near Lovejoy, the 8th Iowa became engaged with the enemy, and was soon supported by the whole brigade. Kelly's rebel brigade had encountered them, and a sharp fight ensued, with little advantage at either side.

McCook crossed the Flint River, near Whitewater Creek, without opposition, though the enemy was all the time hanging on his flank and rear. Near Glen Grove, the 4th Kentucky, which formed the rear guard, and was commanded by Lieutenant Colonel Kelly, was attacked by two brigades of cavalry, and after making a desperate stand, was repulsed with considerable loss. The main body was all this time too hotly pressed to come to their relief. Early next morning, August 1, the advance struck Newman, but was there confronted with Roddy's command, of about one thousand infantry, to which command he had been lately transferred. These were on their way to Atlanta, to reënforce Hood, and took up a position commanding the main road, along which McCook was marching. The rebel cavalry were now pressing McCook on all sides, with Roddy blocking up his advance—rather his retreat. The 2d Kentucky were deployed to open the road to the left of the town, so as to allow the main body to swing round on Roddy's flank, and force a passage towards the river. Major Starr commanded this brilliant, destructive, but successful charge. After cutting through Roddy's lines, they were confronted by a new line, of dismounted cavalry. Captain Mitchell, of McCook's staff, here came up with reënforcements, and both combined charged on the second line, and, after repeated assaults and repulses, succeeded in breaking it. The second brigade had now formed line in advance, and encountered an assault of the enemy, which was sustained with desperate force, both by their mounted and dismounted cavalry.

General McCook, finding himself sorely pressed, ordered his ambulances and prisoners into a valley, under cover. The 8th Iowa made here another charge, but, not being supported, were mostly all captured. In their former charge they captured Brigadier General Ross.

The enemy had now almost encircled McCook, who, seeing his desperate situation, threw forward a heavy line of dismounted skirmishers, supported by mounted men, and a section of artillery.

Our batteries opened a heavy fire of canister on the rebels, checking their advance.

A desperate assault, headed by Colonel Harrison, and General McCook's staff, was now made, which succeeded in repulsing the enemy; but, unfortunately, the brave Colonel Harrison fell into their hands.

The enemy soon rallied, and swept down upon our front. General McCook ordered the 2d Indiana cavalry to meet the charge, which they did with good effect.

The enemy were closing in their circle, and McCook, finding there was no other way of escape but by cutting his way through, spiked his guns, released his prisoners, abandoned his wagons and ambulances, and rallied his command for one final charge.

It was gallantly made and desperately sustained; but though hundreds fell, the main part succeeded in cutting their way through and through.

McCook, with his shattered command, succeeded in crossing

the Chattahoochee, near Bushy Creek, and reached Marietta on the 3d of August, with about sixteen hundred men.

Large squads came in for days afterwards; but numbers, including one whole regiment, had been picked up by the enemy.

Stoneman's Raid.

Major General Stoneman started from Decatur on the morning of the 27th July, with the following forces: —

First brigade, commanded by Colonel Adams; the second brigade, comprising the 5th and 6th Indiana, Colonel Biddle; the 14th Illinois, 8th Michigan, and McLoughlan's Ohio squadron, formed the third brigade, commanded by Colonel Capron.

The command took the Georgia Railroad, towards Covington, thence south by Monticello, capturing a large number of horses, and about three hundred negroes, whom they mounted on the prizes. At Macon a battalion of the 14th Illinois made a dash on a station called Gordon, near the Oconee River, destroying eleven locomotives and several trains loaded with quartermasters' and commissary stores.

When near Macon, General Stoneman learned that all the prisoners had been sent to Charleston the day previous, and the garrison considerably reënforced. Up to this he had encountered very little resistance, but now he found a strong garrison in his front, with cavalry wheeling on his flank and rear. Stoneman sent out heavy skirmish lines to develop the enemy's strength, but soon encountered General Iverson's cavalry in force.

This was between Clinton and Hillsborough, and about fifteen miles from Macon.

The country around here was very unfavorable for cavalry operations, and he soon found Allan's brigade of infantry had wheeled on his flank, and taken up position on the main road, thus cutting off his retreat.

Armstrong's brigade of cavalry, comprising the 1st and 2d Kentucky, had wheeled in on his left flank, thus completely hemming him in. The 1st and 2d Kentucky, of Adams's brigade, encountered their rebel namesakes, and both fought with all the desperation of contending soldiers, embittered by personal animosities. Stoneman now dismounted some of his troops, who repeatedly charged the enemy in front, but were each time repulsed. A panic seemed to seize the troops on all sides. They were rallied by Stoneman and staff, who charged at their head, but were driven back in disorder. Soon the enemy dashed on his flanks, while the infantry and a battery kept sweeping the lines in front.

Despite the example and exhortations of their officers, the men refused to charge. Major Keogh, of Stoneman's staff, dashed in front, trying to rally the men; and having partially succeeded, went right upon the enemy, but was met by a derisive cheer and sweeping fire.

He was soon deserted, except by some officers. This small, Spartan band swept down upon the enemy, and for a moment appeared successful; but many a saddle having been emptied, the gallant few returned, among whom was their brave leader, Major Keogh.

The enemy were now sweeping the lines on all sides with artillery, infantry, and cavalry. The led horses broke loose, and the frightened negroes rushed frantically about, adding considerably to the confusion.

Stoneman now ordered all the commanders to rally their troops, and cut their way through as well as they could; as for himself, he was resolved on surrendering. Several remonstrated, stating there was yet a chance of making their escape; but he could not be prevailed on to do so. Major Keogh and several more refused to abandon him, though they saw a prospect of escape.

Colonel Adams and his brigade made an escape almost intact. Colonel Capron's brigade also made its escape, but halted at night, and overpowered by sleep and fatigue, and, I fear, by something stronger, too, they slept so soundly that they only awoke in the morning to the clangor and clash of arms.

They had neither sentries, pickets, nor patroles out; or, if they had, they slept so soundly that they did not feel the rebel cavalry sweeping over them.

One scene of wild confusion followed; men jumped from their sleep and rubbed their eyes, but were soon cleft down, while others awoke in the other world. The majority of the brigade was either captured or slain; only a small portion made their escape. It is said that General Stoneman sat down on a tree and wept.

This raid had proved a great failure. McCook succeeded in doing material injury to the enemy, and, though surrounded, cutting his way through, saving the most of his command. Stoneman appeared to have got into a perfect trap, while his men became unmanageable.

Indeed, some accounts state that they imbibed too freely the apple-jack and peach brandy with which the citizens liberally supplied them.

Somehow there appeared to be a want of coöperation among the different raiding parties that started under such favorable auspices; the only one that succeeded effectually being that of Rousseau, who went out on his own responsibility. There was to be a joint coöperation between McCook, Stoneman, and Gerrard.

McCook owed his safety to desperate fighting. General Gerrard moved to Flat Rock, to cover Stoneman's movement to McDonough. Here Stoneman was to join him; but he wheeled off towards Covington, and Gerrard had to return. Thus the three columns were isolated, and afforded an easy prey to the enemy, who seemed perfectly aware of our movements, and was fully prepared to meet them.

Since the fight of the 22d, no important movements took place in Atlanta. The usual daily amount of skirmishing and artillery firing continued. We had pushed our works quite close to the rebels at several points, and had got our lines pretty well around Atlanta. Hood must have been considerably weakened after his late assaults on our lines. The battles of the 20th and 22d fully proved our superiority over the rebels in fair, open fight. Though, in both cases, they took us partly by surprise, unprotected by defensive works of any amount, which gave them a decided advantage in the beginning of the fight, yet they were ultimately repulsed with wholesale slaughter. Had we got such an advantage over them, we would have broken through their lines, crushed in their flanks, and swept them before us.

In the mountain regions, jungles, and defiles, through which we had passed, their natural strongholds, aided by formidable works, enabled them to annoy and often to repulse our advancing columns; but here the tables were turned. Hood was forced to come out of his intrenchments and fight us on open ground, or give us the chance of doing, what we ultimately did, namely, wheel round to our right and destroy the only running line of communication he had open.

About this time some important changes were made in commanders. Major General O. O. Howard was appointed to the command of the army of the Tennessee, in place of the lamented General McPherson.

General Howard had seen much service, both in the army of the Potomac and in the western armies. He served all through the peninsular campaign, and lost his right arm at Fair Oaks. He also commanded at Antietam, Chancellorsville, and Gettysburg. Since his transfer to the western army, he served through all its trying campaigns, and confirmed his high reputation as a brave and efficient general. He succeeded General Granger in the command of the 4th corps, and served with Sherman all through the desperate and protracted campaign from Chattanooga, in which his noble corps took a leading part, hanging fiercely on the enemy's rear in their retreat from Rocky Face Ridge to Resaca. General Howard is not only a cautious general, but also a thorough patriot and practical soldier. Kind and courteous to all, his orders are obeyed with alacrity, while his Christian example has had a most salutary effect on his command.

General Joe Hooker, feeling slighted at Howard's appointment, who was his junior, resigned.

There is but one opinion regarding Hooker while serving in the western armies. No man could do better. His gallant corps, the 20th, distinguished itself in the present campaign, and has suffered fearfully. Since the day it stormed the granite heights of Lookout Mountain, until it hurled back the rebel tide at Peach-tree Creek, it knew no rest. His men were devotedly attached to him, and actually wept when he left.

The command of the 4th corps now devolved on Major General Stanly, a well-tried and efficient officer. Stanly was best known as a cavalry officer; in this branch he had few superiors. He distinguished himself with the 4th corps in its many fights, and commanded that corps at the desperate battle of Franklin, where he got wounded through the neck.

Major General Slocum was appointed to the command of the 20th corps. General Slocum was then in Vicksburg, in the capture of which city he took a prominent part.

General Slocum's reputation was best known in conjunction with the old 12th corps, which he commanded in many a stubborn battle in Virginia and Maryland. His services in the west, though of recent date, had so far won the admiration of General Sherman that he at once had him appointed to the command of the 20th corps. General Williams was now commanding the corps in his absence.

General Palmer also resigned the command of the 14th corps, and General Jefferson C. Davis was promoted to that command.

General Davis was a dashing officer; but his unfortunate affair with the hectoring bully Nelson seemed to retard his career.

The Augusta line was now thoroughly broken up for miles, cross-ties burned, and rails bent in all kinds of fantastic shapes. There was no danger that it could be replaced, and Sherman's object was to extend his right flank, so as to command the Macon line, on the western side of Atlanta.

The army of the Tennessee broke camp on our extreme left flank on the night of the 26th, and noiselessly marched around our lines to the extreme right, to operate on the Macon and Atlanta Railroad. Schofield now refused the left of his line, and Kirby's and Taylor's brigades of the 4th corps took up position on his extreme left, partly *en-échelon*, occupying the old line of rebel works, thus preventing all chances of a flank movement by the enemy on that point.

On the morning of the 27th Major General Howard received his appointment as commander of the department of the Tennessee, and, accompanied by his personal staff and his brother Colonel Howard, who had served beside him from the first Bull Run battle to the present time, proceeded to take charge of his new command, now in line of march, and make preparations for the coming battle, which appeared imminent.

Dodge's corps alone arrived in time to take up position on the evening of the 27th. General Howard, in person, located them on the right, and considerably in advance of the 14th corps, which had formed our extreme right. Early next morning Blair took position on the right of the 16th corps, thus extending our line within a few miles of the Macon line. Logan took position on the right of Blair, but so refused as to cover the right flank and prevent a repetition of the 22d. Davis's old division of the 14th corps was expected up to cover the right flank, but did not arrive in time.

Howard's line now was something in the shape of a horseshoe, with the toe to the enemy, and resting on a wooded ridge with partly open fields in front. Howard, finding the enemy making demonstrations, and fearing that they would strike him before he got into position, had to move cautiously until he occupied the hill, which he at once intrenched.

A rebel battery was all this time playing on his advance. General Logan was ordered to capture this. Logan threw forward his skirmish lines, and his sharpshooters soon silenced the guns; he also soon brought a battery to bear on that point.

General Howard, finding the rebels massing in his front, with the evident intention of trying his flank, sent out his escort as vedettes, for he had no cavalry, to watch the enemy's movements. About 10 o'clock he went to the right to reconnoitre, and try to ascertain the point where the enemy were likely to assault. On his right was an open plain, which his artillery commanded; so he felt satisfied they could not charge over that. Soon after the enemy, in massed columns, burst on Logan's front. Two regiments, which Logan had sent out to capture the guns, were first struck, and fell back to the main lines. This encouraged the enemy to follow up the assault at this point. General Howard ordered up his reserve to support Logan, and prolong his right for fear of being turned.

The attack on Logan was fierce and heavy. One continual fire of musketry and artillery ran along his line. The enemy, though repeatedly repulsed, still continued to charge upon his lines, where they were literally mowed down; some being bayoneted, others clubbed.

After every assault they fell back, leaving in our hands trophies, such as colors captured, officers, and men. This desperate conflict continued, with slight intermission, from 11 to near 4. The muskets of the troops got foul several times from the rapid firing, and regiment after regiment, brigade after brigade, and division after division, had to be replaced.

After sustaining several heavy repulses, and being severely cut up and exhausted, the rebels fell back, leaving their dead and wounded, several stands of colors, and a large number of prisoners in our hands. General Logan handled his troops admirably, behaving with great gallantry, and exposing himself to the enemy's fire. After the battle, as he and General Howard were riding along the lines, they were received with loud cheers.

The attack was chiefly confined to Logan's corps. Blair and Dodge were only partially engaged, just enough to cause a diversion in favor of Logan. The heaviest fighting was along the Lick Skillet road, which was occupied by Stewart's and Lee's corps. Our loss, all counted, was calculated at about one thousand. The rebel loss I should set down as over three thousand.

Among their wounded were Lieutenant Generals Stewart and Loring, also Brigadier Generals Rector, Sphral, Brown, and Walthall.

CHAPTER XVII.

SHELLING ATLANTA.—A SCOUT'S EXPERIENCE OF HANGING.—
THE LADY MAJOR.

While Howard's engagement was raging on our right, a vigorous demonstration was taking place along our lines; the artillery had opened with shot and shell upon the city. Our skirmishers pressed on the enemy's at various points. Indeed, the skirmishing in front of the 4th corps swelled almost into the magnitude of a battle.

Major General Stanly brought his artillery into position, and kept up a warm fire.

General Thomas J. Wood's division captured the rifle-pits in his front, one line of works, and about fifty prisoners.

From several points along the lines we could plainly see the doomed city, with the smoke of burning houses and bursting shells enveloping it in one black canopy, hanging over it like a funeral pall.

The scene at night was sublimely grand and terrific! The din of artillery rang on the night air. In front of General Geary's headquarters was a prominent hill, from which we had a splendid view of the tragedy enacting before us. One night I sat there with the general and staff, and several other officers, while a group of men sat near us enjoying the scene, and speculating on the effects of the shells. It was a lovely, still night, with the stars twinkling in the sky. The lights from the camp-fires along the hills and valleys, and from amidst the trees, glimmered like the gas-lights of a city in the distance. We could see the dark forms reclining around them, and mark the solemn tread of the sentinel on his beat. A rattle of musketry rang from some point along the line. It was a false alarm.

The men for a moment listened, and then renewed their song and revelry, which was for a while interrupted. The song, and music, and laughter floated to our ears from the city of camps, that dotted the country all round.

Sherman had lately ordered from Chattanooga a battery of four and a half inch rifles, and these were trying their metal on the city.

Several batteries, forts, and bastions joined in the fierce chorus. Shells flew from the batteries, up through the air, whizzing and shrieking, until they reached a point over the devoted city, when down they went, hurling the fragments, and leaving in their train a balloon-shaped cloud of smoke. From right, and left, and centre flew these dread missiles, all converging towards the city. From our commanding position we could see the flash from the guns, then the shells, with their burning fuses, hurtling through the air like flying meteors.

"I hain't no objection to be out of that 'ere place," said a soldier in the group near us, who were also intently looking on.

"Rather hot, I guess," said another.

"A little too much so to be healthy, I reckon," was the response.

"What matter whether one is killed there or here? We must all die when our time comes," said a fatalist.

"I have no objection to wait for my time, and not go meet it half ways," said the general's cook.

"You," said a patriot, with disdain, "you don't feel that it is sweet to die for one's country."

"Be gor, then, as for myself, I'd sooner live for my country, any day, than die for it," replied a wit from the Emerald Isle.

"Where is the difference?" replied the fatalist, who also appeared to be something of a deist, "we are all born to die; and must die; death is but a sleep, a rest. What does it matter whether we sleep to-night or twenty years hence? We can't die until our time comes."

"Then you think that we will all die at a certain time?"

"Certainly," replied the fatalist, gravely.

"Bosh! then do you mean to tell me that all the men that

have been killed in this war would die, had they remained at home?"

"Certainly not; but the war was made for them, or, rather, they for the war; so they could not avoid it; it is all fate."

"By George, I believe you're right," said another; "at the battle of Resaca my musket dropped out of my hand, and I stooped to pick it up, and a cannon ball came over my head, killing the two men behind me."

"All chance; nothing more."

This philosophical conversation might have continued much longer, had not a dark volume of smoke shot up from the city in one vast spiral column; and then came a dead, heavy, rumbling report. One of the arsenals was blown up by a shell. This was followed by a fierce fire, which shot up, almost simultaneously, in different points. A cheer came from our batteries, and was taken up along the whole line.

"War is a cruelty," said the general beside me; "we know not how many innocents are now suffering in this miserable city."

"I'm dog gone if I like it," said a soldier, slapping his brawny hand upon his thigh; "I can fight my weight of rattlesnakes, scaramouches, or sneaking rebels; but this thing of smoking out women and children, darn me if it's fair."

"Psha!" exclaimed an orderly near us, on whom the general placed great reliance as a scout, and who went through some hair-breadth escapes; "the women are the worst of them; one of them put the rope once on my neck to hang me."

"Indeed! how was that, Bentley?"

"At the battle of Peach-tree Creek I got captured, and was brought before General Hood to be pumped; and as he could not get anything out of me, he had ordered me back to the other prisoners, when an officer, attended by an escort, rode up and saluted the general.

"'Ha! Mademoiselle Major, how do you do?' replied the general, doffing his hat.

"'Well, general;' and she jumped off her horse, throwing the bridle to her orderly, and politely returned the salute.

"The she-major was strangely dressed; she wore a cap

decked with feathers and gold lace, flowing pants, with a full kind of velvet coat coming just below her hips, and fastened with a rich crimson sash, and partly open at the bosom.

"In her belt she carried a revolver, and by her side a regulation sword. I looked at her; her features were rather sunburned, giving her a manly appearance. Only for her voluptuous bust, little hands, and peculiar airs, I might have taken her to be a very handsome little officer of the masculine gender.

"As I gazed at her, she looked full into my face; and turning to the general, she pointed her whip at me, and asked, 'Who is that fellow, general?'

"'A prisoner that has just come in — a dunce; I couldn't get a word out of him.'

"'Indeed, general, that is a spy;' and she again pointed her whip at me.

"'O, no; he is only just brought in captured.'

"'That may be; but he is a spy. I saw him at General Johnston's, one day, and he was full of lying information, which cost the general many a life.'

"'Is that so?' said the general.

"'On my honor; come here, Hartly;' and she called over her orderly. 'Did you ever see that man before?'

"'Yes, Mademoiselle Major.'

"'Where?'

"'At General Johnston's, where he was giving information as a scout.'

"'What have you to say to all this, my man?' said the general.

"I had nothing to say, for it was true.

"'What shall I do with him; shall I hang him?' said the general.

"'Give him to me,' said she, with a sweet smile; 'I am going to General Johnston's; it might be well to take him there.'

"'I make you a present of him,' said the general.

"After spending some time with the general in the tent, she came out, and placing me between herself and her orderly, rode off. When she came into the wood, she and her orderly alighted, and she pulled out from under her dress a strong, but fine, rope.

"'Sneaking dog of a Yankee!' she exclaimed, looking at me with a vengeful eye, 'you hung the only man I ever loved; I swore I'd have vengeance. I have had it; but I have it doubly now, by giving you a similar death.'

"My hands, all this time, were firmly tied, so I was powerless. While the orderly stood with a pistol before me, she tied the rope firmly around my neck, giving it several good pulls, to make sure it was all right. They then helped me to get up on the saddle of one of the horses, so as to have a fall, while the orderly proceeded up the tree to tie the rope to a limb.

"Now was my time. While the orderly was climbing, I flung my two hands across the rope, and snatched it from him, jumped into the saddle, and drove my heels furiously into the horse's side, which made him plunge and rear. She held him bravely with one hand, while pulling out her pistol with the other. Before she could fire, I got a chance, and struck her with my heavy boot right in the face, spoiling her beauty, and giving the dentist a job. She fell. The horse bounded off with me, and I escaped.

"After that, I believe I would swear against women in general, had not a woman saved my life in return.

"I could not get off the mule chain with which she fastened my hands, though I tugged until the blood was oozing out of them, and my teeth filed almost to the gums. The cord, too, was so firmly tied to my neck that I could not get rid of it. There I was, like a half-strangled whelp, with all my credentials about me. I had no control over my horse; so, fearing that he would take me back to the rebel lines, I slipped from him, and skulked away as well as I could. I got into a little by-road, and thought I would venture up to a shanty where I saw some nigger children playing around the door. They ran in, frightened, when they saw my hands tied, and I trailing my rope.

"I followed them in, when — heavens, how I shook! — there were two rebel soldiers, drinking some whiskey.

"'Hilloo!' said one, 'here is a d—d Yank, that cheated the gallows; well, I hain't against a man settling his accounts; so we'll take care of him until he gets another swing.'

"They questioned me, and taunted me with brutal jeers and laughs.

"At length they took me away; and not having enough of whiskey to get there, they called to another house for more. To make the more sure of me, they locked me into a dark room without any window, so that I could not possibly escape, while they were enjoying their debauch.

"For a time I heard the drunken soldiers, noisy, and singing; and then they evidently had fallen asleep, for I heard their loud snores.

"It was now a bit into the night. I presumed they had made up their minds to remain where they were; so I threw myself down, and tried to sleep. Though death stared me in the face, I had fallen into a sound slumber, when I felt myself gently shook by the shoulder. I looked up, saying, 'I'm ready;' but instead of the two drunken soldiers, a gentle young woman stood over me, with a shaded light in her hands.

"'Make no noise,' she whispered, 'but get up.' I looked at her as I sat up. She took a knife and cut the cord from my neck, and then tried to open the chain.

"'Your poor hands are all torn,' said she, compassionately, as she unloosed the bloody chain.

"'Alas! yes,' said I; 'but why do you try to save me?'

"'Because I am a woman, and true to the instincts of a woman, which is to save and not to kill. Poor boy! some sister or mother would fret for you. If you should ever meet one in such a situation, do as much for him. Now go, but very quietly.'

"'But you! will they hurt you?'

"'No, no. I know them; it would not do for them to quarrel with me; follow me.'

"I glided through the kitchen; the two rebels were sleeping beside the fire. I passed out, then imprinted a grateful kiss upon my deliverer's cheek, fled, and got into camp next day."

CHAPTER XVIII.

THE SIEGE CONTINUED.—SHARPSHOOTERS FRATERNIZING.—A MILITARY GAME OF CHESS BETWEEN SHERMAN AND HOOD.—SHERMAN WINS THE GAME, AND ATLANTA TOO.—CAVALRY RAIDS OF KILPATRICK AND WHEELER.—THE DECISIVE BATTLE OF JONESBORO'.—ATLANTA OCCUPIED BY OUR TROOPS.

In the beginning of August, the fighting around Atlanta had settled down to a regular siege. Every day had its skirmishing, its artillery duels, and an assault and repulse. Like another Troy, the enemy fought outside their walls and intrenchments, and many an amusing combat took place, particularly between the skirmishers. I have often seen a rebel and a Federal soldier making right for the same rifle-pit, their friends on both sides loudly cheering them on. As they would not have time to fight, they reserved their fire until they got into the pit, when woe betide the laggard, for the other was sure to pop him as soon as he got into cover. Sometimes they got in together, and then came the tug of war; for they fought for possession with their bayonets and closed fists. In some cases, however, they made a truce, and took joint possession of it.

It was no unusual thing to see our pickets and skirmishers enjoying themselves very comfortably with the rebels, drinking bad whiskey, smoking and chewing worse tobacco, and trading coffee and other little articles. The rebels had no coffee, and our men plenty, while the rebels had plenty of whiskey; so they very soon came to an understanding. It was strange to see these men, who had been just pitted in deadly conflict, trading, and bantering, and chatting, as if they were the best friends in the world. They discussed a battle with the same gusto they would a cock-fight, or horse-race, and made inquiries about their friends, as to who was killed, and who not, in the respective armies. Friends that have been separated for years have met in this way. Brothers who parted to try their fortune have often met on the picket line, or on the battle-field. I once met a German soldier with the head of a dying rebel on his lap. The stern veteran was weeping, whilst the boy on his knee looked pityingly into his face. They were speaking in German, and from my poor knowledge of the language, all I could make out was, that they were brothers; that the elder had come out here several years before; the younger followed him, and being informed that he was in Macon, he went in search of him, and got conscripted; while the elder brother, who was in the north all the time, joined our army. The young boy was scarcely twenty, with light hair, and a soft, fair complexion. The pallor of death was on his brow, and the blood was flowing from his breast, and gurgled in his throat and mouth, which the other wiped away with his handkerchief. When he could speak, the dying youth's conversation was of the old home in Germany, of his brothers and sisters, and dear father and mother, who were never to see him again.

In those improvised truces, the best possible faith was observed by the men. These truces were brought about chiefly in the following manner. A rebel, who was heartily tired of his crippled position in his pit, would call out, "I say, Yank!"

"Well, Johnny Reb," would echo from another hole or tree.

"I'm going to put out my head; don't shoot."

"Well, I won't."

The reb would pop up his head; the Yank would do the same.

"Hain't you got any coffee, Johnny?"

"Na'r a bit, but plenty of rot-gut."

"All right; we'll have a trade."

They would meet, while several others would follow the example, until there would be a regular bartering mart established. In some cases the men would come to know each other so well, that they would often call out, —

"Look out, reb; we're going to shoot," or, "Look out, Yank, we're going to shoot," as the case may be.

On one occasion the men were holding a friendly *réunion* of this sort, when a rebel major came down in a great fury, and ordered the men back. As they were going back, he ordered them to fire on the Federals. They refused, as they had made a truce. The major swore and stormed, and in his rage he snatched the gun from one of the men, and fired at a Federal soldier, wounding him. A cry of execration at such a breach of faith rose from all the men, and they called out, " Yanks, we couldn't help it." At night these men deserted into our lines, assigning as a reason, that they could not with honor serve any longer in an army that thus violated private truces.

After their late bloody repulses, the rebels seemed to lose heart altogether, and the desertions were very numerous. While on the Chattahoochee, a camp of rebel conscripts on the Hendersonville road, seven miles from Atlanta, was abandoned, and nearly five hundred of them came into our lines.

As I have said before, we had now settled down to a regular siege, pounding away at the beleaguered city on every side. Hood had his intrenchments and forts garrisoned with militia, convalescents, and some worthless conscripts, and had kept the veteran troops on hand to operate when required; they, having the arc of a circle to act on, could hurriedly move from point to point.

Our heavy shelling was regularly replied to by the enemy, who revealed some heavy guns. I weighed one projectile; it weighed sixty-four pounds. It had plunged in among our tents at General Thomas J. Wood's headquarters, but fortunately did not burst, but made a regular fuss and a scare, kicking up a whole lot of puddle; in fact, conducting itself like a miniature volcano.

General Sherman, finding that the right of the army of the Tennessee did not extend to the Western Railroad, ordered General Schofield to shift from the extreme left to the right, and General Gerrard's cavalry to take up Schofield's place. Next he ordered the 14th corps to follow, and move in on the extreme right, below Utoy Creek. The aim of these movements was to get possession of the railroad between Atlanta and East Point.

This accomplished, Atlanta should fall. Right before us, within a few miles of our lines, almost within reach of our guns, runs this great life artery of the rebel city. Once cut this jugular vein, and Atlanta speedily falls. Sherman knew this well, and therefore turned all his attention to it; the rebels knew it well, and therefore were exceedingly vigilant and active to resist all our attempts upon it. They left their strong works to be guarded by the militia and conscripts, and followed up our movements with the utmost promptness and daring. It was evident now that the battle would not come off before Atlanta. Perhaps Sherman could take it by direct assault; but we had learned that assaults were always costly, even when successful. Sherman was cautious and wary, pushing his skirmishers everywhere, beating all bushes, and suspicious nooks and dells. Hood, on the other hand, was watchful to counteract any movement of his wily foe. It was a great game of chess. Hood had castled, and Sherman moved to checkmate him. This had continued so long that we were getting tired of it; so the indication of a new move on Sherman's part was hailed with delight. It appeared now that his tactics were to bring corps after corps from the left to the right wing, in the hopes that the rebels would draw off their forces from the city to oppose us, and thus leave it open to attack on the north. But they, having the inner line, and having been considerably reënforced, continued to keep their works strongly garrisoned, and also to confront us at every advance we made on their flank. Hood also seemed perfectly conscious of all our movements, for when we threw a corps with the greatest celerity on their flank, he hurried heavy masses of troops to confront them. Their scouts must have been cleverer than ours, or they were able to fathom our movements through the tangled woods and ravines of the country.

On the 3d of August, General Schofield, having gained the north side of Utoy Creek, prepared to make a lodgment there. The creek is a deep, narrow channel, running east and west, four miles south of Atlanta. The banks of the creek are very steep, and their sides are tangled with vines and bushes. Hobson's brigade, of Hascall's division, deployed, throwing their flanks across the creek; they soon became masters of the bridge, capturing a captain and his whole command.

Had Schofield been supported next day by the 14th corps, he certainly would have succeeded in getting in on the railroad, as the rebels had not yet taken up position, or intrenched themselves. But two days were lost in a squabble about precedency which gave the enemy full time to understand our move, and counteract it.

General Palmer was ordered to report to General Schofield, while acting in concert with him. This he refused to do, and consequently the delay. It appears that Schofield was his junior; but a battle-field is no place to settle points of etiquette. However, we had few such squabbles, as we were too far from Washington for intriguing generals to flourish.

Palmer resigned, and Jeff C. Davis took the command; and on the morning of the 6th, the 23d corps wheeled to the right of the 14th, in order to attack the enemy's flank, and thus uncover the Macon line.

On the previous day General Reilley's brigade attempted to force the rebel lines, and, after a stubborn fight, were repulsed, with considerable loss.

Cox's division opened the attack early in the forenoon, and was supported by the 2d divisions of the 14th corps, and succeeded in establishing a line almost at right angles with the creek.

A heavy skirmish line was then thrown out in the centre, commanded by Lieutenant Colonel Mott, 12th Kentucky, and charged through a dense wood, though filled with rebel skirmishers, driving them from their pits in fine style; but they were soon forced to retreat, as a heavy line opened upon them, and the rebels, charging over their works, pursued them.

The 8th Tennessee, having got too far in advance, was surrounded, and mostly captured, with their colors.

The 2d division sustained the 3d, and also lost heavily, without effecting any material injury on the enemy.

We had gained no advantage at any point. We simply held the creek, with our right reaching within three miles of East Point, and about two miles from the railroad.

After the fight, the 23d corps held a position nearly at right angles with the 14th corps, and facing southward, the 2d division slightly refused to protect the flank, and rested upon a strong and easily defensible ridge.

Our works now in front of Atlanta were formidable, and held by very light lines. Indeed, they might be said to be impregnable. The same might be said of the rebel works confronting us. We were thus far fairly matched.

On the 16th of August, General Sherman drew up his programme for the grand flank movement on the right, in order to command the western line, and thus control the supplies of the city. This was to commence on the 28th. This movement contemplated the withdrawal of the 20th corps to the intrenched positions around the Chattahoochee Bridge, and the march of the main army to the West Point Railroad, near Fairborn, and afterwards to the Macon road, near Jonesboro', to start with fifteen days' provisions.

A larhe force of almost seven thousand cavalry, had wheeled on our rear in order to cut off our supplies, and was operating near Adairsville, and had succeeded in capturing about eight hundred head of cattle.

This movement induced Sherman to suspend the execution of his plan.

He ordered General Kilpatrick, who had lately returned, recovered from his wounds, to collect all the cavalry he could, and move on West Point and Fairborn, and there break the railroad, and thence proceed to Macon. He could the easier do this, as Wheeler was raiding upon the Chattanooga line.

Kilpatrick's Raid.

His forces comprised the 3d division of cavalry, over two thousand strong, and Minty's and Long's brigades, of the 2d cavalry division, about the same strength.

Colonel Minty, in the absence of General Gerrard, commanded the 2d division.

The expedition started on the 18th of August for their rendezvous at Sandtown.

Colonel Minty broke camp, and made Sandtown, under shelter of the darkness, in order to cloak the movement from the enemy.

To show how well informed the rebels were of all our movements, a letter was captured on the 20th, dated the 18th, giving Hood full particulars about the movement, its destination, and the force engaged.

Minty arrived at Sandtown on the morning of the 19th, reported to General Kilpatrick, and received his orders. At night, the whole command, numbering five thousand men, started forward, striking for the West Point Railroad, near Fairborn.

The rebel General Ross encountered the 3d division, and checked its advance. Minty and Long moved to the front, and slowly drove the enemy back on Flint River. Here the destruction of the bridge and depth of the stream checked our advance; besides Ross's and Ferguson's brigades were drawn up in line on the other side.

Our artillery at once hurried up, and with the dismounted skirmishers, soon cleared the bank, and our troops crossed over.

Minty hurried on to Jonesboro', a town on the Macon Railroad, twenty miles south of Atlanta, the 4th Michigan covering his front as skirmishers.

The rebels fell back to the shelter of the houses, from which they opened a sharp fire on Minty's advance. Minty brought up his artillery; but the rebels vacated the houses, mounted, and rode away.

Minty charged after them into the town. The third division quickly came up, and commenced destroying all rebel property, the depot, and some railroad stock. While so engaged, Ross and Ferguson, who had been reënforced by some infantry from Atlanta, at this time were forming south of them. Kilpatrick moved east, towards Lovejoy Station, with the purpose of destroying the railroad.

As we were leaving Jonesboro', more infantry came in from Griffin. Next morning, the enemy followed us up.

The 4th Michigan, having struck the railroad, commenced tearing it up; the 4th regulars were sent out to support them. Before they could get into line, a brigade of infantry pounced down upon them, sweeping over them, killing, wounding, and capturing the most of those engaged in burning the tracks. Long's brigade immediately came up, with artillery, and repulsed the rebels.

While engaged with the infantry, the rebel cavalry, comprising Ross's and Ferguson's brigades, swept down on our flanks.

Minty's brigade hastily formed on the right of the road. The 3d brigade formed in the same manner on the left of the road. Kilpatrick was now completely surrounded. There was no means of escape, but a sharp sabre, brave heart, and strong arm.

Minty was ordered to charge.

At the words, "Attention! forward! charge!" away went his brigade, followed by a host of darkies, on pack-mules, who, with kettles and pans rattling, and darkies flying for dear life, almost made the scene ludicrous as well as grand.

On came Minty and his troops. The rebels were drawn up behind a hastily constructed barricade. They met them with a scattered fire, but, being unable to withstand the charge, broke, followed by Minty's men, who cut them down by wholesale on the retreat.

This gallant charge of Minty's brigade gave Kilpatrick time to collect and form his scattered troops. It also deterred the enemy from trying to bar his passage.

Minty's men captured three stands of colors, the 4th United States two, and the 4th Michigan one. Minty had his horse shot under him. The 3d division now struck for the McDonough road. Long's brigade soon came into collision with a brigade of Cleburne's division, and was repulsed. General Long was here wounded. Kilpatrick now made the best of his way back, and reached Cotton River on the night of the 21st, where he bivouacked until next morning.

Thence he moved forward by South River, over which the bridge was destroyed; so he had to swim it, losing one man, several animals, and some wagons. They reached Lithonia on the following day, and on the next reached camp in rear of our infantry lines.

This raid was more brilliant than successful, effecting little real good. As for the portion of the railroad they succeeded in destroying, it could be repaired in one day.

Wheeler's Raids.

Hood, being repulsed in all his assaults, sent Wheeler's cavalry to operate on Sherman's lines of communication.

Wheeler moved on our flank, with the intention of tapping the Chattanooga line as far as possible from Sherman's main army. Wheeler's first attempt was on Dalton, which had a garrison of only four hundred men, commanded by Colonel Seibold, who, in reply to Wheeler's letter demanding a surrender, returned the following soldierly reply:—

I have been placed here to defend the post, but not to surrender it.
B. SEIBOLD, *Commanding United States forces.*

Wheeler made a bold attack, his men swarming into the town, and would have succeeded in crushing the little garrison, had not Major General Steedman come to his rescue.

The garrison rallied out to support Steedman, and, joined by Colonel Morgan's 14th United States colored troops, charged on the enemy, soon clearing them out.

Wheeler had torn up some miles of the track near Calhoun, and captured about fifteen hundred head of cattle, the most of which were retaken, or stampeded.

He next moved round towards Cleveland, with the expectation of destroying the Knoxville line, but was again met by General Steedman, near Graysville, and well whipped. The rebel cavalry was now divided into raiding parties, operating on our communications at various points.

Major General Steedman commanded the district of Chattanooga, and rendered the most efficient services by keeping the line open, and sending forward troops to the different points threatened, thus frustrating Wheeler's raiding assaults.

Wherever Wheeler threatened in force, there he was sure to encounter Steedman in person, and to get well whipped to boot.

These important movements of Steedman's culminated in the successful part he took in Thomas's great battle of Nashville, where his troops were the first to strike Hood's flank, turn it, and thus materially contribute to that crowning victory.

Though Steedman was reckoned one of our fighting generals, his promptitude and exertions proved him also to be one of our thinking generals.

The government fully appreciated his services, and placed Major General Steedman in command of one of the most important of the southern departments.

Rousseau's cavalry also contributed to frustrate the designs of Wheeler and Morgan, and to restore our communications, which, for a time, were interrupted.

We now come to Sherman's crowning victory — to that great strategic movement which confounded Hood, and placed Atlanta in our hands.

The works which Johnston had built around Atlanta, during his slow but masterly retreat, were of the most formidable character and strength. It was truly a city of intrenchments and fortifications.

For some time it became apparent to Sherman that he could not take them by direct assault, and also that the Western Railroad was too well guarded to be effectually destroyed by cavalry raids, or casual attempts.

On the other hand, it would take, at least, two hundred thousand men to completely invest the place so as to prevent sallies and cut off all communications, as the trenches were garrisoned by old men, militia, conscripts, and mere boys, who would do very well behind works, but would prove an encumbrance in the field.

Sherman's purpose now was to deprive Hood of this strength, and the protection of his works, by compelling him to take the field, or suffer his supplies to be totally cut off. Hood, then, had no alternative. He should come out and fight; and in a regular battle, the chances were largely in favor of our veteran troops.

In order to prevent Hood from falling back on our communications, the 20th corps was to guard the Chattahoochee Bridge; and being strongly intrenched there, it was capable of resisting any attempt of Hood's in that quarter. This apparent retreat of Sherman's was one of the most masterly movements of the war, and was, for a few days, heralded forth to the world by the rebel press, as a disastrous rout, attributable to the weakness of Sherman's army, and the injury inflicted by the raiders.

Our Flank Movement, and Battle of Jonesboro'.

The commanders of the armies of the Ohio, Cumberland, and Tennessee, by orders from General Sherman, had sent across the Chattahoochee River all surplus supplies, — wagons, horses, and material not absolutely necessary for the expedition, — and had loaded their best wagons with sufficient quantities of bread, meat, sugar, coffee, and other necessaries, to last fifteen days, and a good supply of ammunition.

These trains were quietly made up near Utoy Creek, in the rear of the right of the main army.

General Kilpatrick moved to Carp Creek, while Schofield covered the Campbelltown road.

General Slocum, who had now arrived from Vicksburg, and assumed command of the 20th corps, occupied the works around the Chattahoochee, with instructions to hold them at all hazards; also, to guard the packed trains, and the pontoons across the river, as well as the depot at Vining's Bridge, and Marietta.

All dispositions having been made, on the night of the 25th of August, General Stanly, commanding the 4th corps, moved from the works on our extreme left, leaving a light skirmish line and cavalry pickets to cover the movement. He wheeled to the rear of our lines, south of Proctor Creek, touching on Utoy Creek, and behind the right centre of the army of the Tennessee.

Gerrard's cavalry followed up, and took position behind Peach-tree Creek, in order to cover our movements and check the enemy, should they attack our rear.

General Howard followed, crossing Utoy Creek, and moving by the most direct road towards Fairborn, halting at Carp Creek.

Thomas massed the 4th and 14th corps below Utoy Creek. Schofield's command moved parallel with Howard's.

From Carp Creek, General Howard moved the army of the Tennessee, in conjunction with Schofield's army of the Ohio, directly for the West Point Railroad, in the direction of Fairborn, Kilpatrick's cavalry heading his advance.

General Thomas's army followed in two columns, well closed up.

Gerrard's cavalry brought up the rear, and had some light skirmishing with the enemy. Our vast trains were well guarded, and kept under cover as much as possible.

Thus, on the 30th, Sherman's army occupied the following positions: —

Howard, on the right of the line, crossed the West Point Railroad, near Fairborn, and then pushed forward in an oblique direction for Jonesboro'; Schofield moved in a more direct line, crossing near Red Oak, for Rough-and-Ready Station, on the Macon line; Thomas, with the army of the Cumberland, moved into the centre, filling up the gap between Schofield on the left and Howard on the right. This gave our lines an extension of about twelve miles.

Since Kilpatrick's raid, Hood had intrenched a corps of troops around Jonesboro'. The remainder of his army was at Atlanta. Sherman was, therefore, right between his two armies.

Hood was now at Atlanta himself, and looking on Sherman's evacuation as a retreat, he sent a detachment of cavalry to reconnoitre, which soon struck against Slocum, and got well beaten.

The citizens all rushed out to see our abandoned works, and congratulated one another on their supposed victory. Rifle-pits, intrenchments, and old camps were eagerly examined and souvenirs brought home.

How short-lived was their joy! It was but a new version of the deluded Trojans and the wooden horse.

Hood soon awoke from his fancied victory, but it was too late.

Howard found the enemy in force at Jonesboro', and at once intrenched himself, extending a salient angle within a mile of the railroad.

Schofield and Stanly struck the railroad some five miles beyond the East Point Junction.

At about 4 o'clock in the afternoon the rebels attacked Howard's position. Their chief assault was on the 2d division, 15th corps, now commanded by Brigadier General Hazen.

This officer formerly commanded a brigade in the 4th corps, but in the translation of Major General Howard to the command of the army of the Tennessee, he, knowing his worth and great military acquirements, got him transferred to his command, and assigned him to a division. He fully justified his expectations, and, for his brilliant assault on Fort Pulaski, was made major general.

Hazen's division met the assault with firmness, repulsed the enemy, and took possession of a hill which commanded Jonesboro', and might be justly called the key of the position.

On this hill Hazen rested for the night, the other divisions being on his right and left. The 16th corps, somewhat retired, formed on the extreme right, and the 17th corps on Hazen's left. The enemy lost sorely in men and officers in their attack on the 15th corps.

In Hazen's front alone the dead and wounded were actually piled on one another. Hazen captured two flags and several prisoners.

Next morning, the 1st September, the 14th corps, under General Davis, marched along the Macon line, destroying the track for several miles, and about 4 o'clock took up position on the left of the 15th corps, which was drawn up in line of battle.

The 14th corps was ordered to assault the enemy's intrenched position. Cavalry and infantry steadily advanced, under a surging fire of musketry and artillery. They had to cross a cornfield, then a deep ravine, and strike up a slope to the enemy's works. The 14th corps stood the ordeal well; swept over the valley, charged right on the works, where a regular hand-to-hand conflict ensued, which lasted for nearly two hours, but finally terminated by our men gaining the works and capturing two batteries. They turned these guns upon the flying rebels, mowing them down by wholesale.

One of these batteries was Loomas's celebrated battery of five guns, which had been taken from us at Chickamauga.

They also captured another battery of four guns, several battle-flags, and a large number of prisoners, including many general officers, thus swelling our list of prisoners captured in the expedition to about two thousand. General Govan and his adjutant general were among the prisoners, General Cummings among the dead.

It was now night. Our troops had closed around the town to renew the attack in the morning.

During the night the enemy, finding it impossible to hold Jonesboro', retreated along the Macon road in a southerly direction, and took up a position at Lovejoy's Station, seven miles from Jonesboro', and twenty-nine miles from Atlanta. Here they hastily intrenched themselves. Early next morning Sherman ordered a rapid pursuit, and towards noon General T. J. Wood, of the 4th corps, reached their new position, and gallantly assaulted it. General Wood was shot in the foot, but refused to leave the field.

Sherman, finding that he could not prevent a junction between S. D. Lee and Stewart's corps, issued orders to fall back to Atlanta, which was now occupied by Major General Slocum.

As soon as Hood discovered Sherman's real object, he at once saw that his position was untenable; and on the night of the 1st September he blew up all the magazines and ammunition, destroyed all the supplies he could not remove, comprising eight locomotives, and near one hundred cars laden with ammunition, small arms, and stores, and then retreated. Next morning General Slocum sent forward detachments from Ward's, Geary's, and Williams's divisions on a reconnoissance.

On advancing near the city they met no resistance. Finally, observing that it was evacuated, they entered it about 11 o'clock, on the morning of September 2, 1864. They were met outside by a deputation, comprising the mayor, Mr. Calhoun, the high sheriff, and some of the most respectable citizens, who made a formal surrender of the city to General Ward, simply making the following request: —

BRIGADIER GENERAL WARD, 3D DIVISION, 20TH A. C.

SIR: The fortune of war has placed the city of Atlanta in your hands. As Mayor of this city I ask protection for non-combatants and private property.

JAMES M. CALHOUN,
Mayor of Atlanta.

General Slocum arrived soon after, and took formal possession of the town. A large share of government property, four engines, and fourteen pieces of heavy artillery, fell into our hands.

CHAPTER XIX.

ATLANTA OURS.—SHERMAN'S ENTRANCE.—FEELING OF THE CITIZENS.—SKETCH OF THE CITY.—BURIED ALIVE IN A BOMB PROOF.—THE CITIZENS SENT NORTH AND SOUTH.—AN INHUMAN FIEND.

ATLANTA was now in our hands, the crowning point of Sherman's great campaign. Hood had been outgeneralled, outmanœuvred, and outflanked, and was now trying to concentrate his scattered army. On the night of the 1st, when the rebel army was vacating, the stampede was frightful to those engaged, but grandly ludicrous to casual spectators.

Even war has its laughable scenes amidst all its horrors, and the retreat from Atlanta was an illustration of that. Conveyances were bought at fabulous sums, and when all were crowded, those who could not procure any — men, women, and children, old and young—followed the procession, bearing bundles of all contents and sizes. The delicate drawing-room miss, that could never venture half a mile on foot, with her venerable parents, now marched out, joining the solemn procession. Confusion and disorder prevailed in every place, considerably increased by the eighty loads of ammunition now blowing up.

Shrieking, hissing shells rushed into the air, as if a thousand guns were firing off together. We plainly heard the noise at Jonesboro'. How terrifying must it be to the trembling, affrighted fugitives, who rushed to and fro, and believed, with every report, that the Yankees were upon them — to slay, ravage, and destroy them.

But yesterday, they had exultingly gazed upon our abandoned works; to-night, how changed!

I had left Jonesboro' on the morning of the 2d, and being provided with an escort of cavalry, through the kindness of

General Gerrard, I started for Atlanta. There was no communication opened, as yet, between Sherman's army and Atlanta; and as deserters and militia squads were along the roads, the attempt was rather hazardous, and was attended with some amusing incidents. We had twenty-one miles to ride over an enemy's country. At one point a horseman came out of the woods into the main road, and, seeing us, dashed off at a fearful rate. Two men went in pursuit, and not being able to overtake him, fired on him, which brought him to.

He turned out to be a full-blooded negro. I have never seen such a scared animal in all my life. He could scarcely speak when we came up; but there he was, with his mouth and eyes opened to their fullest extent, and the latter looking as if they would roll out of his head.

"Have courage, man; we are not going to kill you."

"O, massa, me done nothing, massa; spare dis nigger, massa!"

He found it a great relief when we were not going to eat him, and became quite communicative.

As we parted from him, one of the boys fell in love with his horse, which was a fine animal, and borrowed him. I expect he forgot to return him.

The people knew nothing of what had taken place; they thought that General Hood was yet in Atlanta, and it was ludicrous to witness their terror when the Yankee cavalry hailed them, and told them how things stood.

Two of the men, who were dressed in butternut jackets, rode up to a house in search of refreshments. A lady was inside, and they asked for something to eat and drink.

"Why, you scamps, you're worse than the Yanks; you won't leave we'ns a bit or a sup in the house. You'ns have taken everything I have."

"O, well, get us something now, and we won't call any more."

"Won't you'ns? Often you've said that. I wish the Yanks come and cleared you'ns out."

"Well, madam, you have got your prayer; we are the Yankee cavalry."

"Git out; you'ns not."

"Come here;" and he took her to the door, and pointed out the men drawn up on the road.

"O, laws me, but you'ns are;" and she clapped her hands together, and nearly went into a fit with fright.

We called into another house, and asked for some bread and milk, which the lady brought down. She was a very garrulous old lady, and had a little too much lip loyalty to be sincere.

"We'ns are so glad to see you'ns, gentlemen; and if my Johnny was here, he'd be so glad! Eat enough, gentlemen. Didn't you'ns ever hear of my Johnny?"

"No, madam."

"Dear me, dear me; I thought every one knew Johnny McGowan. I wish you could see Johnny; he'd be so glad to see you."

"Is Johnny a rebel, madam?"

"O, dear me, gracious, no; my Johnny is one of the best boys in the country; he wouldn't hurt a fly. O, gracious, no; Johnny wouldn't fire a shot for the life of him, for fear of hurting any one."

"Where is he now, madam?"

"Gracious me, I don't know; I think he is looking for you'ns critters to help ye."

All this time some of the men were making a tour of inspection about the rooms, and one of them telegraphed to me from the door. I went with him into a room. The beds looked as if they had been just slept in; and on turning down the coverlets we exposed a little arsenal of rifles and small arms.

"Madam," said I, "what brought all these firearms here?"

"O, gracious me, you'ns won't mind them; Johnny is such a sportsman; he's never tired shooting. Dear me, if you knew my Johnny — I wished he was here."

"I wish so, too, madam; and for fear he'd injure himself shooting, we'll break these guns; and when we are passing this way again, we'll bring this Nimrod a small field-piece."

"O, dear, how kind! and if you'ns let me know when you are coming, we'ns will have dinner ready."

We so fully appreciated her generosity that we took two fine mules, and, not thinking the place very healthy, took our leave.

We reached Atlanta about nightfall. As we approached the city, troops were drawn up before us, not knowing but we were rebel cavalry. We floated a white handkerchief, and soon joined old comrades, and were received with loud cheers, which were redoubled when we told them all about the victory at Jonesboro'.

I at once went to report events to General Slocum, for we were the first to reach Atlanta from Sherman's army.

Next morning Sherman resolved to retire to the defences of Atlanta, there to give his wearied army time to recuperate, after its unparalleled campaign of four months' marching and fighting.

His own entry was without parade or ostentation — no beating of drums, no flaunting of colors, no firing of salutes, to humble the pride of the conquered.

Sherman and staff, accompanied by several general officers, simply rode through to his headquarters. There was not even a shout or huzza to welcome him.

The citizens looked out from their doors and windows, eager to catch a glance of the man whose name had now become so famous. The soldiers lined the sidewalks, quietly looked on, and passed their own remarks on "Old Billy."

Officers, mounted on prancing steeds, looked far more consequential than the great conqueror himself, and cast their eyes from window to balcony to see if any fair eyes were admiring their gracious selves.

The fair eyes had fled, and those remaining would fain wither them with their basilisk glances.

Sketch of Atlanta.

Atlanta has acquired much importance as the great objective point of Sherman's campaign through Northern Georgia, and on account of the trying siege it withstood, and the desperate conflicts that raged outside its walls.

It is a new city, that has sprung up in the desert. Some

thirty years ago its site was a wilderness. The princely oak and pine had given way to stately houses and shady streets; the war song and dance of the swarthy Indian was replaced by the hum and bustle of commerce and trade, and where once stood his wigwams now a mighty city was springing into existence. In 1845 the site was laid out, and in 1861 its population was estimated at about fifteen thousand, which was swelled up during the war by government employees and officials to about twenty thousand.

This rapid, almost unparalleled, growth was owing to its position. It was the great central point where the leading railroads of Georgia met, and consequently became a flourishing market for grain and cotton and other market produce. Atlanta is the great depot of the following railroads: The Georgian road, connecting Atlanta with Augusta; the Macon and Western road to Macon, and the Western and Atlantic road to Chattanooga; the Lagrange branch connects Atlanta with West Point, on the Chattahoochee River, on the Alabama line. By these different converging lines Atlanta lay in communication with all parts of the United States. By railroad it is one hundred and seventy-one miles from Augusta, one hundred and one from Macon, two hundred and ninety-two from Savannah, and one hundred and thirty-eight from Chattanooga, Tennessee.

It was a beautiful and rapidly progressing city previous to the war. The streets were wide and airy, and all converged towards the railroad depot, which was in the centre of the town. It had several good hotels, a tasty court-house, churches, public schools, and several fine blocks of buildings.

Atlanta owed its wealth to its location and trade, for the country around was rather barren and uncultivated; but south, towards the valleys of the Chattahoochee and Etowah, are some fine valleys of great fertility. Atlanta is situated partly on an elevation, and on this account was considered remarkably healthy.

In a military point of view, Atlanta was of vital importance. Jeff Davis felt this when he said at Macon, "Atlanta must be held at all hazards." It was the key to the network of railroads extending to all portions of the Gulf states, and on the inception of the war was at once selected as a government depot and manufacturing centre; so rolling mills, founderies, machine shops, laboratories, and shops for the manufacture of all kinds of government articles were established here.

It was therefore the cradle from which the southern armies drew their supplies, and consequently of vital importance. The government works here were of the most important nature. The Atlanta rolling mill was one of the most extensive in the south. It employed two hundred hands. It furnished the iron for the Merrimac, Arkansas, and several other boats. There was a rolling mill for the manufacture of shot and shell, and another for the manufacture of pistols, employing about three hundred hands. On the other side of the railroad was a government arsenal, which was built during the war, and was kept in vigorous operation, making and repairing arms, gun-carriages, and the like. Above these were the machine shops and round houses of the Georgia Railroad and Banking Company.

Three miles east of the city was the government laboratory. North of the depot were the naval laboratory, railroad foundery, and machine shops. Besides these and others, there were several government depots, pork-packing and oil establishments, clothing and other factories. With such important manufactories and stores for army supplies, it is no wonder that the Confederates should risk a large army for the protection of Atlanta, and that Davis should be so anxious to hold it.

The material effect of the capture of Atlanta was the first great death-blow to the rebel cause; thenceforward they began to lose hope, and consequently became disintegrated.

. The city had suffered much from our projectiles. Several houses had been burned, and several fallen down. In some places the streets were blocked up with the rubbish. The suburbs were in ruins, and few houses escaped without being perforated. Many of the citizens were killed, and many more had hair-breadth escapes. Some shells had passed through the Trout House Hotel, kicking up a regular muss among beds and tables.

One woman pointed out to me where a shell dashed through her house as she was sitting down to dinner. It upset the table and things, passed through the house, and killed her neighbor in the next house.

Several had been killed; some in their houses, others in the streets.

When the rebels were evacuating, in the confusion several of our sick and wounded escaped from the hospitals, and were sheltered by the citizens.

Almost every garden and yard around the city had its cave. These were sunk down with a winding entrance to them, so that pieces of shells could not go in. When dug deep enough, boards were placed on the top, and the earth piled upon them in a conical shape, and deep enough to withstand even a shell. Some of these caves, or bomb-proofs, were fifteen feet deep, and well covered. All along the railroad, around the intrenchments and the bluff near the city, were gopher holes, where soldiers and citizens concealed themselves.

In some cases it happened that our shells burst so as to close up the mouths of the caves, thus burying the inmates in a living tomb. I learned the following case from the sufferer himself: Private James Newcomb got wounded in the battle of the 22d of July, and was captured and brought into Atlanta hospital, where his right arm was amputated. To use his own words,—

"I hain't nothing bad to say against them at all. They treated me well enough, but still I liked to join our own boys. Ladies came round the hospitals every day, and always had a kind word or some little delicacy for us. I got on very well; my arm began to heal, and then I began to look round for a chance to escape. I could easily get out of the hospital, but how to get into our lines, that was another thing. Every day I heard the shells whizzing about the city, and hurtling over the hospitals. I thought of the boys, and wished to get back to the camp, and have a long talk about all I saw and went through. We had a nigger servant of the name of Moses, who seemed to take to me rather kindly. One evening we were sitting outside the hospital, watching the shells my old friends were sending to visit me.

"'Moses,' said I, 'come here, and fasten this bandage on this stump.' Moses went on one knee before me, and began to fasten the bandage, but started and looked scared as a shell whirred over our heads.

"'Moses,' said I, 'you shouldn't be scared about them; every shell of them is unbinding the chains that fetter you.'

"'Don't say so, massa;' and he looked up into my face.

"'Moses, would you like to be free — to have no massa to whip you or kick you?'

"'Dat I would, massa.'

"'These Yankees, of whom you are so much afraid, are trying to set you free.'

"'Specks so; but Massa Joe says they'll kill us all, or sell us up nor', to work like de horses; besides, they won't get in here, massa; specks dey are running back.'

"'I think not, Moses; your folks say we are retreating every day, though, as you see, we are but getting nearer.'

"'Dat a fact, massa.'

"'Moses, will you help me to escape, and come with me?'

"'O Lor', massa, I wish I could;' and he raised up his hands and looked into my face.

"'You can, when it's dark; you know the back ways; let us slip away, and, by wheeling around by Decatur, we will get into our lines.'

"Moses was true to his appointment; the guards were very negligent about the hospital; so I took up a large bread basket and shook the flour over me. The guard, taking me for the baker, let me pass. I had on a rebel jacket and homespun pants; so we passed through the streets without any observations. As we were approaching the suburbs, a squad of soldiers drew near.

"'Moses,' said I, 'we had better hide, and let these pass.'

"'O Lor', yes, massa. Come here;' and he opened a little wicket leading into a deserted house, at the end of which was a cave.

"'Here, massa, down here;' and in we got into the cave, Moses drawing an old barrel after him to stop its mouth.

"We were scarcely settled in it, when we heard the soldiers follow after us; so we thought we were done for. It appeared they were going to bivouac in the deserted house for the night. They soon stacked their arms right around us, and lighted fires. We could plainly hear them talking, and their tramp over us.

"The fear was now that any of them would come down into the cave; so Moses and I trembled as we lay down on the cold ground. There was no chance of escape, as the mouth of the cave faced the veranda, on which the men were now sleeping; besides, the sentries' beat was right by it. There were some dry boards in the cave; so we lay on these, and slept. In the morning the soldiers moved off; we heard them say they were going to Jonesboro'.

"Moses returned to the hospital for something to eat, and was not suspected. I durst not venture out now in the day, but resolved to wait until night.

"Moses returned with some bread, and the disheartening news that our men were retreating, and that I was missed, and they were hunting me up. An occasional shot was still fired on the town; so I could scarcely credit it.

"It was near the time that Moses was to return to accompany me, when I heard the whir of a shell; and a crash, and mortar and bricks came tumbling down the mouth of the cave, completely blocking it up. The volume of dust that rushed in nearly smothered me.

"The place became as dark as the blackest night; the dust was suffocating me, and either a slow, miserable death from starvation, or a death equally wretched from suffocation, stared me in the face. All my dependence was now on Moses. I lay here I don't know how long, expecting him to relieve me; but no Moses came. O, the horror of such a death! I pulled the bricks to clear away the entrance, but more rolled in. I then piled some of the bricks under my feet, and tried to pull down the roof. It seemed to mock my efforts. I threw myself down, prayed and cried by turns. I shouted, but the place was deserted, and no one heard me. I was buried alive in my tomb. I don't know how long I was in it. I had eaten the scraps of bread Moses had brought me, and chewed some belts. My tongue was swollen; my throat was parched. O, if I could but die! I heard a rumbling noise — the cave shook around me — I thought it was an earthquake. I jumped up with fear, but soon threw myself down exhausted, to die.

"I thought I heard voices over me, and some one calling my name. I screamed, partly with terror, partly with hope. I heard people rapidly clearing away the bricks. The light soon burst upon me, and there stood Moses. I fell into a swoon. When I came to myself I was lying on the piazza with some four or five negro boys around me, who quickly supplied me with coffee and food. When Moses left me that evening, he was forced off by an officer who was going in pursuit of the retreating Yanks. They discovered the Yanks at the Chattahoochee, and got a peppering reception from General Slocum. In the confusion Moses managed to escape to our lines, and was with the first of the Union troops that entered the city. He at once came to the cave, rather through curiosity than with any expectation of finding me there. He heard my scream in reply to his call, and collecting a squad of negroes, soon cleared the opening. A round shot struck the end wall of the house, toppling it down upon me. The great noise I heard was caused by the rebels blowing up their ammunition. I was, in all, five days in that cave. It was dreadful what I suffered. My hair was jet black when I went in; it is now well tinged with gray. Moses has saved my life, and he and I have sworn a bond of lasting friendship."

Sherman's army was now grouped around Atlanta in the following order: The army of the Cumberland in and around the city; the army of the Tennessee at East Point; and the army of the Ohio at Decatur. Hood had made a desperate struggle for Atlanta.

One of Davis's leading organs declared, "Atlanta is the gate city from the north and west to the south-east. Its fall would open the way for the Federal army to the Gulf on one hand, and Charleston on the other, and close up those rich granaries from which Lee's armies are supplied. It would give them control of our network of railways, and thus paralyze our efforts.

"The capture of Richmond would prove of greater advantage to our enemies in a political point of view, than any other sense, With our capital in their possession, we would find additional influence brought to bear against us abroad; but as a material loss, its fall would in no manner compare with the disadvantages which would result from a defeat of General Johnston, and the occupation of Georgia that would follow. The first point is near our boundary lines, the second is our great centre. To lose the one would be as the loss of a limb; should we be driven from the other, it will be a terrible blow at our most vital point."

Hood, too, in his boastful mood, stated, "We cannot lose Atlanta. If we do, the Confederacy is broken. For my part, I'll fight while a man stands by me, even until the streets of the city run with our blood." Very fine indeed. He meant his soldiers' blood, for Hood went by the sobriquet of "Butcher Hood."

In falling back to Atlanta, we destroyed fifteen miles of the Macon and Western Railroad.

The enemy were now in position between Lovejoy Station and Jonesboro'.

On the 8th of September, General Sherman issued a congratulatory order to his troops, thanking them for the bravery and unshaken fidelity with which they sustained so arduous a campaign. On the same day he issued an order desiring all citizens of Atlanta either to go north or within the rebel lines within a certain day. At first this order appeared cruel, almost savage; but his subsequent destruction of Atlanta justified such a harsh measure. A truce of ten days, from September 12 to September 22, was declared, in order to carry out this order. In the mean time, transportation was supplied as far as Rough-and-Ready Station, to all who desired to go inside the Confederate lines.

Sherman's comprehensive mind was already clearing the way

for the Georgian campaign. He knew that Atlanta might again be rendered formidable in the hands of the enemy, and had resolved to destroy, or, to use his own words, " to wipe it out." War is at best a horrid cruelty, and cannot be refined. Expediency and necessity justify acts savage enough to make the angels weep. Friends and foes suffer indiscriminately from its ravages, and too often the innocent suffer, while the guilty escape.

In Atlanta we had strong proofs of the military despotism of the Confederacy. We captured in the trenches feeble old men, with gray heads and tottering steps, and mere striplings, who were too young to be taken from their mothers' leading-strings. Everything had been made subservient to the army. It swallowed up the blood and wealth of the land, leaving its poor, deluded dupes stripped of everything — of the enjoyments of life itself. The people, after awakening from the first shock inspired by the terrible barbarities they heard of the Federal soldiers, seemed to welcome the new order of things. They were now protected, and could walk abroad in security. General Slocum's administration of Atlanta was so impartial and rigidly enforced, that life and property there were as secure as in the city of New York. Near the depot were several slave marts, with their glaring signs, announcing, " Slaves bought and sold here," " Slave auction rooms," " The great slave mart," and such like. As the soldiers passed these they read them with a mocking laugh. As the poor negro passed these human shambles of his former degradation, his heart became light, for he no longer dreaded the galling chains, or the lash, or the auctioneer's hammer that was to consign him to a new master, and separate him from his wife and children.

As soon as General Sherman had issued his order, several families prepared to go south at once. They were merely joining their friends, while the men who had concealed themselves from conscription, who had been persecuted by rebel authority, whose friends had been shot down or hung up for their Union sentiments, who concealed our wounded men and fed them, and who screened our prisoners and aided their flight, who longed for us as their friends, did not well know what to do. They found our friendship as destructive as the rebels' enmity. Some few went north; the most of them remained, hoping, like Mr. Micawber, that something better would turn up.

"Could you tell me who are our friends?" said an old, respectable citizen to me.

"If you tell me your politics, I will," said I.

"At the breaking out of the war I owed large sums to northern merchants, and I paid them. I had neither hand nor voice in bringing on this war; I wanted to live under the old flag. During the war I gave every assistance in my power to relieve Union prisoners, and my only son was caught aiding one of them to escape, and shot. The rebels then stripped me of my property, and called me a d—d Yank. Only for my age, they'd hang me."

"Well, I think you are a Union man," I replied.

"I have given proofs enough, at least; and now what's my reward? You hunt me from my house and place in my old age. Do you think but I am suffering for my country? I have the alternative of going north and starve, or going into the rebel lines and being hung."

Alas! he spoke the truth. There were hundreds like him; but war makes no distinction. Those going within the rebel lines seemed to enjoy the thing. The cars taking them down were loaded with a miscellaneous cargo. In some were crowded together tottering old age and maidens in their youthful bloom. The former fretted very much at being thus rudely torn away, root and branch, from the soil on which they grew, and in which they hoped soon to rest their wearied hearts. As for their young companions, they seemed to treat the thing as a kind of sentimental journey. I fully understood this when we reached the rebel quarters, when I saw with what a warm greeting the rebel officers and soldiers received them. Some even carried their enthusiasm so far as to welcome them with warm kisses and embraces. In addition, the wagons were crowded with a heterogeneous medley of poodle dogs, tabby cats, asthmatic pianos, household furniture, cross old maids, squalling, wondering children, all of which, huddled together, made anything but a pleasant travelling party, which I accompanied. We were kindly received by Major St. Clair, who was in command of the rebel party. Everything went on in the most friendly way — visits paid between Federals and Confederates, exchanges made, friendly intercourse kept up. One could scarcely realize that these laughing, chatting groups were deadly enemies, who to-morrow would strive for one another's blood.

Among the most notorious of persecutors of Union men in Atlanta was a Mr. Jones; he kept a livery stable in the rear of the mayor's. He was a devil incarnate; kept bloodhounds for hunting up men skulking from the conscription, or Federal prisoners trying to make their escape. Woe betide the wretch that got into his hands. Like all tyrants and ruffians, he was a coward, and bought exemption by his valuable services as a spy and dogger. This black-hearted ruffian used all his influence to get the poor men executed who attempted to destroy the bridges and run off with the train on the Chattanooga line. He succeeded, and as the poor victims were dragged along to the place of execution by the halters on their necks, this foul scoundrel followed them, goading them on, and mocking them. He was also accompanied by his bloodhounds, as he said, "to give them a smell of Yankee blood." The executioner had to enjoy the exclusive privilege of tying up his victims, and then drawing the plank from their feet. As their bodies dangled in the air, he swung them round, knocking the convulsed breathing frames against one another. All this time his bloodhounds barked and jumped at the dangling feet of their victims, and as they caught them they swung from them until the flesh gave way. Honest men shuddered at such fiendish cruelty, but durst not resent it. They dreaded the tyrant's power. I hope this fellow has met his deserts before this; if not, that all honest men will treat him with scorn, and society exclude him from its circles. Such a fellow is only fit to associate with his brother demons.

CHAPTER XX.

A NEW CAMPAIGN.—BATTLE OF ALLATOONA.—SHERMAN SIGNALLING FROM KENESAW MOUNTAIN.—WHO PLANNED THE CAMPAIGN AND MARCH THROUGH GEORGIA, SHERMAN OR GRANT?—THE CONFLAGRATION OF ATLANTA.

THE truce having expired, Hood inaugurated a new campaign. Hood had been informed that two divisions of troops had been sent to Tennessee to strengthen our positions against Wheeler's and Forrest's cavalry, which were now threatening us at different points, and had succeeded in capturing some small post and a few block-houses. Athens, too, though garrisoned by about six hundred men, strongly intrenched, and commanded by Colonel Campbell, shamefully fell into their hands, even without a fight.

Hood had been also informed that two divisions more were gone to Kentucky to recruit, and that Blair's corps had gone home, their term of enlistment having expired.

He was led into this error, because, about this time, the 16th corps was broken up, and consolidated with the 17th.

Under the delusion that Sherman's army was now considerably weakened, he resolved to fall back on our communications with one corps, and keep the remainder on hand to watch Sherman's rear.

Forrest's cavalry was certainly causing us a great deal of trouble about this time; and it looked feasible enough that by forming a junction with him, or causing a heavy diversion in his favor, he would succeed in destroying the railroads and cutting off our supplies, which would be ruinous to Sherman, as he had but a small amount of supplies on hand at the time, and the country all round was stripped of provisions.

Acting on this programme, on the evening of October 29, Stewart's corps, of Hood's army, broke camp, and marched to the Chattahoochee in the following order: Loring in advance, Walthal in the centre, and French in the rear. They crossed the river at Pumpkintown. Next day they moved by New Hope Church for Big Shanty and Allatoona.

But Sherman was not to be caught napping, for he had thrown a couple of divisions to strengthen the most important points along the railroad, and Steedman had also sent all the troops he could spare from Chattanooga to guard around Bridgeport, Decatur, Dalton, and other threatened points.

Forrest had lost too much time enjoying his victories at Pulaski, Athens, &c., instead of striking direct for Bridgeport, or some other important points on the Chattanooga line. Had he done so in the beginning, his chances of success were very good; now, we had too strongly reënforced them for any cavalry raid to be effective against them.

Previous to this movement Davis had paid his annual visit to the western department and to Hood's army, which was then encamped near Newman, in order to cover Columbus, Ga.

Here Jeff Davis visited the army, and finding general dissatisfaction prevailing against General Hood, in order to allay this and completely shelve Johnston, towards whom he did not entertain a very good feeling, he appointed Beauregard commander of the department of the south-west, Hood simply retaining his position as commander of the army of the Tennessee. Davis now laid down the new programme of action for Hood, and urged on him its immediate adoption.

S. D. Lee's corps followed Stewart on the following day. The army, however, made but a short march; for on the night of the 30th of October they encamped near the old battle-field of New Hope Church.

Here Hood concentrated his forces, being Lee's corps and Wheeler's cavalry. Full of enthusiasm at having successfully crossed the Chattahoochee River, he divulged his plans, and assured his men that "success was certain; Sherman had but forty days' rations of meat, and no bread. I will certainly

BATTLE OF ALLATOONA.

compel Sherman to retreat. Forrest is doing good work on the left, and Wheeler is now going to operate on the right."

Next day he resumed his march. Wheeler struck Marietta, and skirmished about it without any success. Stewart moved on Big Shanty and Ackworth, capturing those places and their small garrisons, and destroyed about ten miles of the track.

General G. French moved farther to the left and north, making for the important and narrow pass of the Allatoona Mountains, through which the railroad runs, and where we had a large depot.

General M. Corse, of the 15th corps, had been ordered from Rome to guard this pass, and just reached in time to take up position before French's assault. The rebel assault here was desperately made and vigorously sustained.

Corse met them with equal fortitude, and a very stubborn battle ensued, which lasted nearly seven hours.

At one time the rebels had seized on a pile of stores at the depot, of which we had over a million rations, and each man was carrying off a box of hard tack, or pork, when a brigade came up, charged on them, and shot them down wholesale, with their loads. Sherman was anxiously looking on from the top of Kenesaw, and signalled to Corse, —

"Keep on. I'm sending reënforcements."

Corse's reply was, "I'll fight to the last."

This was a very severe fight, but ended in favor of the Federal troops. Our loss in Corse's division, which alone was engaged, was about five hundred, while the rebel loss was computed at nearly one thousand.

General Corse was slightly wounded. A bullet grazed his cheek.

Hood continued his march, moving slowly north in the direction of Dalton.

In the mean time Sherman had not been idle. He left Slocum's corps to garrison Atlanta, and followed Hood with his main force. On October 12, Hood made his appearance at Resaca, and demanded a surrender of the place, kindly informing the garrison that if he should take the place by storm, he would give no quarter.

Colonel Weaver, 8th Iowa, commanded the garrison, and bravely repulsed Hood's superior force.

Hood next moved on Dalton, commanded by a Colonel Johnson, which surrendered. It had only a garrison of one colored regiment, and a company of white troops.

Sherman was now pressing so closely on his rear, that he had not time to take away or destroy a store of supplies he captured at Ringgold.

Hood now, finding Sherman on his rear, Chattanooga strongly garrisoned, and Steedman threatening his advance, wheeled for Villanow in two columns, one column moving by Snake Creek Gap, and the other by Buzzard Roost.

Stanly's 4th corps struck the column passing through Snake Creek Gap, and repulsed them. Sherman crossed in their rear, and encountered them at Villanow, where he captured some two hundred prisoners. Cheatham's corps retreated direct to Summerville, the other two corps through Ship's Gap.

On the 26th Sherman's headquarters were at Gaylesville, North Alabama, a little village on the Chatoogata River, six miles from its junction with the Coosa.

Here Sherman rested for six days. It was a very fertile locality, and well supplied with provisions. The enemy had taken up position near Tallidaga.

Lee's, Stewart's, and Cheatham's troops picketed the south bank of the Coosa, while Wheeler and his cavalry were intrenched at Turkeytown, on the north bank.

The 15th corps moved out on a reconnoissance on the 25th, but effected nothing, except developing the position of the enemy.

General Stanly now commanded the army of the Cumberland, in the absence of General Thomas, who had removed his headquarters to Nashville, as the most central point of operation, General Thomas J. Wood taking Stanly's 4th corps.

Hood attempted to capture Decatur, Ala., but was repulsed. He next attempted to cross the Tennessee River near the conflux of the Bluewater, but was confronted by Stanly.

He next marched towards Muscle Shoals, and succeeded in effecting a crossing at Florence.

Sherman now gave up the pursuit. He was but playing with Hood all along.; and now, when he had him across the Tennessee, he commenced preparations for that great march which he had long since matured, and now designed to carry out. He left the 4th and 23d corps under General Schofield to check Hood's advance on Nashville. This they nobly did, keeping Hood's whole army at bay, and defeating it in the glorious fight at Franklin, where Cleburne and the flower of Hood's army fell.

After this they gallantly participated in the great battle and victory before Nashville.

Thomas had taken up his headquarters at Nashville in order to concentrate.

Schofield's instructions were to keep Hood in check as well as possible while Thomas was concentrating.

Major General Steedman had fortified Chattanooga, which, with its immense stores, was a place of considerable importance. When he marched to form a junction with Thomas at Nashville, in order to prepare for the coming battle, which was imminent, he was succeeded by General Thomas F. Meagher, who had taken command of a division of convalescents and others, returning to join the army of the Tennessee. General Meagher's military government at Chattanooga gave general satisfaction. He organized the citizens, and compelled them to man the trenches, or help to build them up; thus rendering the place impregnable.

When General Steedman returned, after the battle of Nashville, he issued a general order, thanking General Meagher for his able military administration in his absence.

Sherman now returned, and encamped his army from Dalton to the Chattahoochee. In his absence, the rebel cavalry, under Iverson, had made several dashes upon General Slocum's lines. Slocum had contracted his lines around the city, and was able to repel their assaults.

Provisions began to run short, and he had to send out frequent raiding parties. One of these, under General P. H.

Jones, of Geary's division, had a brisk fight with the enemy, but succeeded in bringing in a large supply of provisions for "man and beast." Iverson's and Young's cavalry hung round Atlanta all the time, watching some chance of dashing in there; but Slocum was too tried and cunning a soldier to be caught napping.

There had been much conjecture as to whether Sherman planned the programme of his great marches through Georgia and the Carolinas himself, or whether they were planned by Grant, and merely carried out by Sherman.

From my own observation, I know that the programme of the campaign originated with Sherman himself, at Gaylesville, but, of course, was submitted to Grant's approval. I know his instructions were, if possible, to drive the enemy across the Chattahoochee. Having done so, Atlanta lay in too tempting proximity, and was too easily within his grasp to be resisted.

Again, in his marches through Georgia and South Carolina, when cut off from all communication, how often had he to change his line of march and programme, in order to baffle and isolate the enemy's forces!

Sherman knew the weakness of the Confederacy thoroughly. He knew they had no army capable of impeding his march through Southern Georgia. Hood's army was the only one capable of opposing him. Davis and Hood, in their blindness, had thrown this out of his way; and now the course was clear, and he meant to take advantage of their blunders. Travelling with Sherman, seeing all his movements, my firm impression is, that he was the originator, as well as the operator. Grant always said that the Confederacy was a shell. Sherman knew that, and intended to prove it, too.

Before we start with General Sherman, on his great raid through Southern Georgia, we will give a short *résumé* of events.

Sherman occupied Atlanta on the 2d of September. As soon as he took possession of the "Gate City," he began to plan his fall campaign. There was much conjecture as to what this would be, but he very wisely kept his counsel to himself.

About the 24th of September, General Hood suddenly transferred his army, by a flank movement, from Lovejoy's Station, on the Macon Railroad, to near Newman, on the West Point road.
This movement looked as if Hood had divined the intentions of Sherman, and was making preparations to foil his plans.
The incautious language of Jeff Davis at Macon led the country to suppose that this movement was preliminary to one more extensive; and General Sherman's suspicions were, accordingly, aroused, for we find him sending his spare forces, wagons and guns, to the rear, under General Thomas, and, at the same time, sending Schofield, Newton, and Corse to take up different points in the rear of Atlanta.
On the 27th, General Gerrard reported a move on the part of Hood towards the Chattahoochee. On the 1st of October, Generals Ransom and Fuller made a reconnoissance towards Newman, and discovered that Hood had crossed the Chattahoochee River on the 29th and 30th of September. Sherman immediately followed, declaring his intention to destroy Hood before he could commence his campaign through Southern Georgia. As Hood had a good start, Sherman felt it rather difficult to bring him to an engagement. However, he pressed so closely on his rear that he had not time to occupy the small posts along his route.
This pursuit continued, with occasional skirmishes, until Hood slipped from Sherman at Gadsden, and crossed the Tennessee River.
Sherman exclaimed, "Let him go north; our business is down south."
Rousseau and Wood's 4th corps, and Schofield's 23d corps, and Morgan's division, of the 14th corps, were along the Tennessee River. Steedman held Chattanooga, Bridgeport, and that line of railroad.
Thomas was in Nashville, and General Smith was hurrying up his Mississippian army, all concentrating to meet Hood. They were more than a match for Hood in force, while there was no danger but the cool Thomas was able to meet him in strategy.

Sherman now determined to resume his original intention. He gave up Hood, exclaiming, "If he will go to the river, I'll give him his rations."

On November 4, the 14th, 15th, 16th, and 20th corps had all concentrated near Atlanta, and were making rapid preparations for a march, they knew not whither, nor did they care; all they knew was, "it was all right; Old Billy knew what he was about."

Sherman telegraphed, "Hood has crossed the Tennessee; Thomas will take care of him and Nashville, while Schofield will not let him into Chattanooga or Knoxville. Georgia and South Carolina are at my mercy, and I shall strike. Do not be anxious about me; I am all right."

Sherman had laid down his programme, and there was nothing to obstruct him now. He knew he could reach the sea without a battle.

On Sherman's return to Atlanta he issued an order for its immediate evacuation by all citizens who had not left in compliance with his first order.

A great many, of thorough Union sentiments, had remained, expecting the trouble would blow over. It was generally understood that the city was to be evacuated and destroyed. It was pretty well known that Sherman was going to cut loose from all communications, and to destroy all the factories, founderies, railroads, mills, and all government property, between Atlanta and Chattanooga, thus preventing the rebels from using them in his rear.

The citizens who had not joined the first exodus were afraid of being abandoned to the tender mercies of the rebels.

The depot presented a scene of confusion and suffering seldom witnessed.

Women and children were huddled together, while men, who had lately been millionaires, were now frantically rushing about, trying to procure transportion, and forced to give their last dollar to some exacting conductor or railway official. An order had been issued by General Easton providing all these people with free transportation; but several of his employees and railroad officials could not see it in that light. They saw that the thing could be made to pay, and they did make it pay.

General Easton knew nothing of this shameful extortion. Of General L. C. Easton I must say, few men contributed more to Sherman's success. As chief quartermaster he was energetic in getting forward supplies, and in overcoming the many difficulties that opposed their transmission. It is highly creditable to him how admirably such an immense army was fed, and at such a distance from its base.

The question of supplies was an important one, and one on which depended the success or failure of the campaign; and to General Easton's credit be it said, that during our arduous campaign to Atlanta the army never ran short of a single day's rations.

He knew nothing, though, of the extortion practised on the poor fugitives. He had assigned that department to a Captain S——, who, I am credibly informed, had collected some valuable furniture, under pretence of keeping it safe from those who left at first.

He had also gone to reside in a lady's house who had gone north, with the promise of protecting the place and furniture. He is said to have acted in collusion with railway conductors and officials, and transported all this north. In his employ was a tall, lean, lank ruffian, named P——, who was fit for nothing but plots and dark deeds, who did all the dirty work, and handsomely feathered his own nest. These fellows were afterwards court-martialed, I do not know with what result.

Colonel B——, too, is said to have acted with offensive hauteur towards the poor people. If any complained to him, he arrogantly told them he had nothing to do with such things; they were a lying, rebel pack.

They were afraid to complain. They were too anxious to get off, and the dishonest employees told them for days that the next train would be the last that would go. In some cases they gave all they had to be let go, and in many cases paid as high as one hundred dollars to conductors and others to get off, though all the time provided with free passages.

In some cases they managed to divide families, so that they could extort the more from those remaining.

I wanted myself to get a poor soldier, who was going home to die, inside on one of the cars. Though they were full of strapping, healthy negroes, who were either servants to the extortioners, or had the almighty dollars to pay their way, I could not gain admittance for the poor fellow. A few dollars in a conductor's pocket were of more importance than his comfort or safety. I gave him my blanket and oil-cloth, but I have since learned he never reached home, for when taken off the top of the cars at Chattanooga he was found dead.

I simply mention these facts as a caution to generals not to place too much confidence in employees, unless they are well tried and tested.

The Burning of Atlanta.

Sherman's orders were, that Atlanta should be destroyed by the rear-guard of the army, and two regiments were detailed for that purpose. Although the army, cantoned along the Chattanooga line of railroad, towards Kingston and Marietta, did not pass through until the 16th, the first fire burst out on the night of Friday, the 11th of November, in a block of wooden tenements on Decatur Street, where eight buildings were destroyed.

Soon after, fires burst out in other parts of the city. These certainly were the works of some of the soldiers, who expected to get some booty under cover of the fires.

The fire engines were about being shipped for Chattanooga, but were soon brought in, and brought to bear on the burning districts.

The patrol guards were doubled, and orders issued to shoot down any person seen firing buildings. Very little effort had been made to rescue the city from the devouring elements, for they knew that the fiat had gone forth consigning it to destruction. Over twenty houses were burned that night, and a dense cloud of smoke, like a funeral pall, hung over the ruins next morning.

THE BURNING OF ATLANTA. 237

General Slocum offered a reward of five hundred dollars for the apprehension of any soldier caught in the act of incendiarism. Though Slocum knew that the city was doomed, according to his just notions of things it should be done officially. No officer or soldier had a right to fire it without orders.

It was hard to restrain the soldiers from burning it down. With that licentiousness that characterizes an army they wanted a bonfire.

The last train for Chattanooga left on Saturday night, November 12. Next morning, the 14th, 15th. and 17th corps commenced their march from Kingston and Marietta, where they had been resting ten days, while Sherman was making preparations for his new campaign. They destroyed Rome, Kingston, and Marietta, on their march, and tore up the track, setting on fire sleepers, railroad depots, and stores, back to the Etowah.

An immense amount of government property, which we could not transport to the rear, or carry along with us, had been destroyed at the different depots. Coffee sacks, cracker boxes, sugar and pork barrels, bales of blankets and boxes of clothing, were burst open and strewn about and burned. Soldiers were loaded with blankets and supplies, which they got tired of before night, and flung away. It is said that about three million of dollars worth of property had been destroyed in this way.

On Sunday night a kind of long streak of light, like an aurora, marked the line of march, and the burning stores, depots, and bridges, in the train of the army.

The Michigan engineers had been detailed to destroy the depots and public buildings in Atlanta. Everything in the way of destruction was now considered legalized. The workmen tore up the rails and piled them on the smoking fires. Winship's iron foundery and machine shops were early set on fire. This valuable property was calculated to be worth about half a million of dollars.

An oil refinery near by next got on fire, and was soon in a fierce blaze. Next followed a freight warehouse, in which were stored several bales of cotton. The depot, turning-tables, freight, sheds, and stores around, were soon a fiery mass. The heart was burning out of beautiful Atlanta.

The few people that had remained in the city fled, scared by the conflagration and the dread of violence.

Some ruffians ran with brands to fire the churches, which were considerably retired. The Roman Catholic minister, Father O'Reiley, who was the only minister that remained in town, met them, and upbraided them for their impious sacrilege. Even these hardened men of war shrank before virtue and truth, and the good priest not only saved his own church, but also those of his fellow-Christians.

The Atlanta Hotel, Washington Hall, and all the square around the railroad depot, were soon in one sheet of flame.

Drug stores, dry goods stores, hotels, negro marts, theatres, and grog shops, were all now feeding the fiery element. Worn-out wagons and camp equipage were piled up in the depot, and added to the fury of the flames.

A stone warehouse was blown up by a mine. Quartermasters ran away, leaving large stores behind. The men plunged into the houses, broke windows and doors with their muskets, dragging out armfuls of clothes, tobacco, and whiskey, which was more welcome than all the rest. The men dressed themselves in new clothes, and then flung the rest into the fire.

The streets were now in one fierce sheet of flame; houses were falling on all sides, and fiery flakes of cinders were whirled about. Occasionally shells exploded, and excited men rushed through the choking atmosphere, and hurried away from the city of ruins.

At a distance the city seemed overshadowed by a cloud of black smoke, through which, now and then, darted a gushing flame of fire, or projectiles hurled from the burning ruin.

The sun looked, through the hazy cloud, like a blood-red ball of fire; and the air, for miles around, felt oppressive and intolerable. The Tyre of the south was laid in ashes, and the "Gate City" was a thing of the past.

CHAPTER XXI.

THE MARCH TO THE SEA COMMENCES. — HOW THE ARMY SUP-
PLIED ITSELF. — SHERMAN AMONG HIS MEN. — SACK OF MADI-
SON. — NEGRO AUXILIARIES. — FARM-YARD AND PLANTATION
SCENE

ATLANTA had fallen; it was in ruins. A new campaign was inaugurated, and was about to start. Conjectures were rife as to what was its object or destination. The politicians and *quidnuncs* of the north discussed the subject; it was a prolific one. The newspapers speculated about it. What Sherman had next in hand was the question of the day. The most absorbing interest as to his future movements was felt on all sides: not only through the north, where thousands speculated financially and commercially upon it, and through the south, whose destiny seemed to hang on the issue, but also in Europe it was a matter of doubt and conjecture whether Sherman would attempt a march through Southern Georgia. Croaking prophets augured all sorts of evil.

Sherman, removed from his supplies, in the heart of an enemy's country, with the hand of every man, woman, and child raised against him, — "What can he expect but defeat and disaster?" asked one.

"Then," said another, "how will he support his army?"

"On the country, to be sure."

"All very fine; but the enemy's cavalry, and the inhabitants themselves, will burn and destroy all provisions in his track; they will leave the country a barren waste, a howling wilderness. He will perish himself, and his army with him. It will be a second edition of the French retreat from Moscow."

So said the croakers; so said the rebel sympathizers; so said the English press, — for with them the wish was father to the thought. The London *Post*, speaking of it in anticipation of its results, said, —

"The Federal papers several weeks ago announced the determination to transfer the winter campaign to the cotton states, and this, it would seem, is the preliminary movement. Whichever of the two movements Sherman has in view, it is evident that he calculates largely upon the weakness of the country through which he designs to march, or its disloyalty to the Confederacy. In both calculations, we are induced, with good reason, to believe that he will be greatly mistaken. It will be the fault of the people inhabiting those countries, if his army be not utterly destroyed long before it shall have reached either Mobile, Savannah, or Charleston."

The London *Times* said, "The movement seems, as far as we can judge, to resemble the celebrated march of Napoleon in 1814 to St. Dizer, by which he threw himself upon the communications of the allied armies, then marching on Paris. If this enterprise be brought to a successful termination, General Sherman will undoubtedly be entitled to the honor of having added a fresh chapter to the theory and practice of modern warfare. The worst of such enterprises as Sherman's is, that they allow nothing for the chapter of accidents, proverbially so potent in war, and that the slightest and most unforeseen causes may lead to their defeat and ruin. We had our own experience in the tremendous disaster of Saratoga, undertaken, it might be thought, under auspices far more promising than the expedition of Sherman; in the ruin which overtook Braddock; and in the failure of the expedition against Quebec, by the brave American general, Montgomery. It will be strange, indeed, if the army of General Sherman should arrive before Savannah, after such a march, conducted under such difficulties, in condition to attack and storm a town so well fortified and so strenuously defended."

The Liverpool *Courier*, and other leading foreign journals, spoke of it as one of the boldest military movements on record, but agreed that it was more likely to be disastrous to Sherman and his army than to the Confederates.

The southern press, too, in their usual boasting manner, declared that Sherman had now thrown himself into the trap prepared for him; that he was surrounded by enemies on all sides, and would be starved and crushed. All these kind warnings had no effect on Sherman. He had weighed the consequences and calculated the means, and was now prepared to test the issue. Sherman thoroughly understood the strength of the south; he knew its weak points. At the very inception of the war, he showed his complete knowledge of the magnitude it would assume; for when asked how many men it would take to crush the war in the south-western states, he replied, two hundred thousand. Two hundred thousand! The government at Washington, including Stanton and Halleck, thought he was mad; and the papers, to some extent, indorsed the assertion. He was like a man possessed of some great idea, which he saw through clearly himself, yet he could not get others to believe him. The subject was too stupendous and complex for them. So it was with Sherman; but subsequent events proved his foresight and his true knowledge of the nature of the struggle.

There was another class, whose confidence in Sherman was unbounded; that is, his soldiers. They never stopped to question where they were going. I overheard the following conversation near a camp-fire, which gives a good idea of the faith of the soldiers in their leader. A long, dark streak of smoke obscured the heavens along our line of march, illumined here and there by a blazing farm-house. The men were seated around the fire, smoking, and talking, or sipping their coffee. One man exclaimed, —

"Look around, boys; I reckon 'Old Billy' has set the world on fire."

"Why, darn it, 'Old Billy' has nothing to do with it; it's ourselves that are making the bonfires."

"Specks so; guess it's all right, anyhow."

"Why wouldn't it be right? Old Billy wouldn't have done it otherwise."

"True," was the reply.

"But," said the other, "any of ye reckon, boys, where we are going to?"

"Yes," said another, winking around to his comrades; "I had a private talk with Old Billy himself, and he told me that we were going, going — would ye guess it?"

Some of them guessed different places; and the man that asked the question replied, tartly, —

"To hell!"

"O, no," said the other. "I have no doubt but that will be the end of your journey; but we are going — somewhere."

There was a general laugh at the sell; then an old, gray-headed veteran said, —

"I tell ye, boys, we should never ask where are we going, or what are we going to do. Obedience is the duty of a soldier; and whatever Old Billy says or does is right. He does the plotting and flanking; let us do the fighting, and things will go on well."

"Bully for Old Billy! we'll follow him," was the response of his audience.

Sherman issued a special field order, dated Kingston, November 8, in which he informs his troops that he had organized them into an army for a special purpose, well known to the war department and to General Grant. "It is sufficient for you to know," he said, "that it involves a departure from our present base, and a long and difficult march to a new one. All the chances of war have been considered and provided for, as far as human sagacity can." And further, he exhorted the men to maintain discipline, and not scatter about as stragglers or foragers, and also instructed the officers to send all surplus baggage, servants, and non-combatants to the rear.

On the following day he issued another order, in which he said, —

"For the purpose of military operations, this army is divided into two wings, viz.: The right wing, Major General O. O. Howard, commanding the 15th and 17th corps; the left wing, Major General H. W. Slocum, commanding the 14th and 20th corps.

"The army will forage liberally on the country during the march. To this end each brigade commander will organize a good and efficient foraging party, under command of one or more discreet officers. To regular foraging parties must be intrusted the gathering of provisions and forage at any distance from the roads travelled.

"As for horses, mules, wagons, &c., the cavalry and artillery may appropriate freely and without limit. Foraging parties may also take mules or horses to replace the jaded animals of their trains, or to serve as pack-mules for the regiments or brigades."

These orders were all right, if literally carried out; but they were soon converted into licenses for indiscriminate plunder. The followers of an army, in the shape of servants, hangers-on, and bummers, are generally as numerous as the effective force. Every brigade and regiment had its organized, foraging party, which were joined by every officer's servant and idler about the camps.

These, scattered over the country, without any order or discipline, pounced like harpies on the unfortunate inhabitants, stripping them of all provisions, jewelry, and valuables they could discover.

In most instances they burned down houses to cover their depredations, and in some cases took the lives of their victims, as they would not reveal concealed treasures. These gangs spread like locusts over the country. In all cases where the foraging parties were under the command of a respectable officer, they acted with propriety, simply taking what provisions and necessaries they needed. They might as well have stripped the place, though, for soon came the bummers, and commenced a scene of ruin and pillage. Boxes were burst open; clothes dragged about; the finest silks, belonging to the planters' ladies, carried off to adorn some negro wenches around camp; pictures, books, furniture, all tossed about and torn in pieces. Though these wretches were acting against military orders, there was no one to complain. The planter and his family were thankful if they escaped with their lives; and as to their comrades, they were too deep in the pie themselves to complain of a system which was enriching them.

The notion seemed to prevail south that Sherman would strike for Macon; therefore all available troops, comprising Iverson's cavalry, and some scattered militia force, were guarding the Jonesboro' road.

On the morning of the 15th of November, the 20th corps moved out on the Decatur road unopposed.

At daylight next morning the different columns had taken up their line of march; the 17th corps on the McDonough road, the 14th on the Augusta road, with the 20th corps on the left flank, and the 15th on the right.

The first day's march was rather slow, in order to give time to sluggard wagons and teams to get into position. The troops were noisy and cheerful; full of hope and excitement. Though all superfluous baggage and trains had been sent to the rear, still our train numbered about two thousand wagons, and would, if stretched out in one line, extend about twenty miles.

The left wing was moving in a north-easterly direction, and the opinion gained ground that we were striking for Augusta. We passed by Stone Mountain, the column winding along its base.

Stone Mountain is a remarkable curiosity. It is said to be over two thousand feet above the level of the plain, and is about seven miles in circumference. The view of this mountain is exceedingly grand and imposing. One side presents almost a perpendicular surface, or wall, nearly nine hundred feet high. The eastern side is not perpendicular, but exhibits a broken and jagged surface, deeply marked with furrows. After a heavy fall of rain these channels are the beds of thundering waterfalls, with the angry surge flashing and sparkling, and bounding from rock to rock.

On the summit of the hill are the ruins of an old fortification, whose history and purpose are both unknown. Two deep fissures, like caves, cross one another on the mountain. At its foot is a clear spring of cool, sparkling water, gushing from a bed of white sand.

This strange mountain stands alone, looking like a huge loaf of sugar — a puzzle to antiquarians and geologists, and a source of wonder and pride to travellers.

We crossed the Yellow River in the afternoon. As the bridges had not been destroyed, it was evident that there was no enemy in our front. When approaching Social Circle, Lieutenant Colonel Hughes, in command of the 9th Illinois mounted infantry, which was covering the advance, dashed into the village, and nearly succeeded in capturing a wagon train. He burned the depot, and captured a rebel surgeon and about three thousand dollars in gold.

Social Circle was a dirty little village of shanties, superannuated negroes, woolly picaninnies rolling in the dust, and squatting like huge monkeys on the fences, and half-naked, snuff-begrimed white women, who seemed to look upon the whole thing as a grand review for their especial benefit. An old negress raised her hands piously and bowed. "I'm bressed if I thought there were so many of God's critters in de world at all."

In the evening we halted near Ulcofavuhachee, a miserable, muddy stream, with a high-sounding name.

"Living off the country" was fast becoming the order. The men knew that Sherman had started with some sixteen days' supplies, and they wished to preserve them if possible; besides, they thought that a change of diet would be good for their health. There was nothing to be got the first two days' march, as the country all around Atlanta had been foraged by Slocum's corps while hemmed in there. Now we were opening on a country where pits of sweet potatoes, yards of poultry and hogs, and cellars of bacon and flour, were making their appearance. A new spirit began to animate the men; they were as busy as so many bees about a honey-pot, and commenced important voyages of discovery, and returned well laden with spoils. Foragers, bummers, and camp followers scattered over the country for miles, and black clouds of smoke showed where they had been. Small lots of cotton were found near most of the plantation houses. These, with the gins and presses, were burned, oftentimes firing the houses and offices. Near Madison we passed some wealthy plantations; one, the property of a Mr. Lane, who was courteous enough to wait to receive us, was full of decrepit, dilapidated negroes, presided over by a few brimstone-looking white ladies. They were viciously rabid, and only wished they could eat us with the same facility that the troops consumed all the edibles on the place, and eloped with plump grunters and indignant roosters, and their families.

The 20th corps encamped near Madison that night. The cavalry had the advance, burned the depot, and cleared out the town pretty well. Madison is situated on the Augusta line, and was a town of near two thousand inhabitants before the war. It is the county seat of Morgan County, and is about one hundred and two miles from Augusta. The face of the country about here is undulating. The lands are of the richest and best kind of mulatto soil, from Madison, extending across the country from east to west, bordering on the waters of Little Oconee and Apalachee Rivers, and Indian and Sugar Creeks. Madison is said to be remarkable for the beauty of its buildings and streets, and its pretty women. About the women I cannot say much, for we saw none but either the decrepit or wizen-faced, who were too old to fear any assault. The pretty ones kept inside doors, if at home at all. I expect they were, though, for several shutters were half open, and blinds half raised, particularly while the bands were playing "Dixie;" but as soon as it struck up "Yankee Doodle," they were suddenly dropped and slammed to. Some of the houses were very fine — built of brick, surrounded with lovely lawns, flower-gardens, and conservatories. In the centre is the Court House, where law, and not justice, was administered to the white man, and stripes to his black brother.

Our troops entered the town next morning, and a brigade was detailed to destroy all the works around the depot and railroad track, also to burn a pile of nearly two hundred bales of cotton in a hut near. While this work was being executed, the stragglers, who manage to get to the front when there is plunder in view, and vagabonds of the army, crowded into the town, and the work of pillage went on with a vengeance. Stores were ripped open; goods, valuables, and plate, all suddenly and mysteriously disappeared. I say mysteriously, for if you were to question the men about it, not one of them admitted having a hand in it. Grinning negroes piloted the army, and appeared to be in their element. They called out, "Here, massa; I guess we gwine to get some brandy here." The doors would at once be forced open, the cellars and shelves emptied, and everything tossed about in the utmost confusion. If a good store chanced to be struck, the rush for it was immense. Some of those inside, being satisfied themselves, would fling bales of soft goods, hardware, harness, and other miscellaneous articles, through the windows. I have seen fellows carry off a richly gilt mirror, and when they got tired of it, dash it against the ground. A piano was a much prized article of capture. I have often witnessed the ludicrous sight of a lot of bearded, rough soldiers capering about the room in a rude waltz, while some fellow was thumping away unmercifully at the piano, with another cutting grotesque capers on the top-board. When they got tired of this saturnalia, the piano was consigned to the flames, and most likely the house with it. The wreck of Madison was pretty effective, too. All the stores were gutted, and the contents scattered and broken around. Cellars of rich wine were discovered, and prostrate men gave evidence of its strength, without any revenue test. A milliner's establishment was sacked, and gaudy ribbons and artificial flowers decorated the caps of the pretty fellows that had done it. Their horses and the negro wenches, too, came in for a share of the decorative spoils. One fellow created a great deal of amusement by riding down the street, kissing and embracing a female form, which he hugged before him on the saddle, and then squeaked and cried, as if she was kicking up a rumpus at such liberties.

"I say, Ned, where did you catch the prize?" called out one of his comrades.

"Why, Fred, is that you! Up there; there is a little colony of them in it; go get one for yourself."

"I guess not, Ned, if she makes such a fuss as that one about it."

"Isn't there any one in the crowd will protect a poor, lone female from such violence?" squeaked Ned for the figure. "O, O! is there any man here at all?" sobbed the female.

An officer who heard the appeal, riding up to Ned with a cocked pistol, demanded, —

"Halt, you scoundrel, and let go that lady."

"Now, captain, I reckon I'm no more a scoundrel than you; and as to the lady, you may take her with pleasure."

Ned bobbed her around in a most helpless way.

"Dear me," exclaimed the captain, " she is in a faint."

"By h—l, she hasn't a word," said Ned.

"Ruffian, hand her to me, tenderly!" and the captain alighted to take down the poor lady. Ned handed her to him, and then rode off. Fancy the captain's indignation when he found that it was only a wire and wax figure, richly dressed for a show window. He soon let it drop, mounted his horse, said some very hard prayers, and rode off amidst the suppressed titters of the delighted crowd.

This scene lasted until the head of the column under General Slocum arrived, when the town was at once cleared out of these marauders, and guards placed while the troops were passing.

The left wing had destroyed the Augusta line along their march. The right wing had moved by McDonagh to Jackson without encountering an enemy. The rebels were making some little show to the cavalry on our flanks, but did not as yet attempt to give battle. The negroes were joining us in crowds. Near every cross-road and plantation, we would meet groups of old men and women, and young children, who received us with shouts of joy, exclaiming, " Glory be to de Lord; bress de Lord, the day of jubilou is come; dis nigger is off to glory," and fell in with their sable friends in the rear, without even asking where we were going, or what we would do with them. Such was their simple faith that they trudged along, " bressing de Lord, de day of jubilou is come." Many of them had reason to regret their desire for liberty. With them, liberty too often meant plenty to eat and wear, and nothing to do. They found that it meant hardship, hunger, and cold; for many of them perished along the way from fatigue and the hardship of the march.

When the columns halted, or when we bivouacked for the night, Sherman was always poking around by himself.

On one occasion he was crossing to a certain general's quarters; but losing his way, he called at an officer's tent. The flies were down, and the officer was enjoying a snooze for himself. Sherman knocked at the canvas.

"Who is that?" said the officer, impatient at being disturbed.

"Could you tell me where General ———'s quarters are?"

"How the h—l do I know?"

"Ain't you a quartermaster in his division?"

"That's not the reason I'd go fish up his quarters for every one that comes hunting them."

Just then a clerk was going into his master's tent, most likely to tell him whom he was addressing.

Sherman tapped him on the shoulder, and said, "My man, I'm General Sherman; I want to go to General ———; will you please show me the way?"

"General Sherman!" exclaimed the lazy consequential quartermaster, jumping up and stammering out a host of confused apologies, "I'll go with you."

"No, no," said the general, sneeringly; "you are too well engaged; I won't trespass on your time; this man will come with me."

The snubbed quartermaster, who was puffed up with vain conceit and a little brief authority, slunk back, while Sherman and his guide went on their way.

When we discovered large quantities of molasses, there was sure to be such a rush for it, that oftentimes more was wasted than used. On one occasion the men had a regular squabble about a new discovery, and, in their impatience, had upset a barrel. There was a furious crush, and every appearance of a little shindy. Sherman chanced to be strolling about, and, with much trouble, edged his way in among the crowd, and dipped his finger in the sirup and tasted it, remarking,

"Boys, that's good! see all you have spilt here by your crowding; if you only keep order, there is enough for all here; fall back, now, and let only a couple at a time fill their canteens."

He then placed a guard over the sorghum, to prevent any more of it being wasted.

From Madison General John Geary's command made a detour, in light marching order, to Buckhead Station, ten miles on the Georgia Railroad, and destroyed all the railroad buildings and tore up the track. Thence he marched to the Oconee River, and burned the railroad bridge over that stream. He then moved along the left bank of the river, burning several bridges, mills, and tanneries on his route.

Sherman's left was now threatening Augusta; his right, Macon. The enemy, believing that he was aiming at those points, had concentrated there, leaving our right unimpeded. Kilpatrick, who was covering our extreme right, had instructions to demonstrate against Macon. This he did, thus confirming the rebels in their ignorance.

The country lying between Madison, Covington, and Milledgeville, is a perfect garden; and though not literally teeming with milk and honey, it was teeming with something better — farmyards well stocked with hogs and poultry, stacks of corn fodder, corn-houses, and bins filled with corn and grain. Sweet potatoes and negroes seemed to grow spontaneously. Hogs grunted a welcome on every side — fine, sleek hogs, that strutted about with snobbish dignity; young, petulant hogs, that cocked up their noses in disdain at the Yankees. The Yankees, not to be outdone in politeness, soon cocked up their feet. Poor, timid sheep, and submissive cattle, swinging huge bells, as if tolling a requiem over the desolation around, looked wonderingly upon the foragers as they came down in fell swoop upon the farmyard, and patiently submitted to their fate.

The left column was now closing on Milledgeville. They had struck the Eatonton Branch Railroad, twenty-two miles from Milledgeville.

We revelled in the splendid homes and palatial residences of some of the wealthy planters here. The men, with that free and easy, devil-may-care sort of way, so characteristic of soldiers, made themselves quite as much at home in the fine house of the planter as in the shanty of the poor white trash or the negro. They helped themselves, freely and liberally, to everything they wanted, or did not want. It mattered little which.

When near Milledgeville, an amusing incident occurred at the plantation of a Mr. Jordan, who was said to be worth a mint of money.

Mr. Jordan was quite taken by surprise at General Sherman's visit, and was not able to clear out anything but himself from the Yankee Vandals. The house was richly furnished and adorned with pictures, paintings, rich furniture, and plate. He left his overseer, who was formerly from New York, to receive his friends, which he did in the most generous manner.

He received the officers with open arms and smiling countenance. His eyes were actually wet with joy at the unexpected pleasure. The cellar was emptied of its best and richest wines. Venerable brandy bottles were exhumed, frowy with age and mellowness, and he drank, batch after batch of officers, out of the house. He was voted a brick, and a guard placed on the house. As for the rank and file, though they threw many a wistful glance in through the windows, they had to confine themselves to a skirmish with the poultry and hogs around the yard, which they soon cleared out. Mr. Allen had succeeded in drinking a whole division, when he encountered Colonel H. Barnum. The colonel is something of a wag, and was well versed in all the arts and sciences of compounding mixed drinks.

"Colonel, isn't that splendid?" remarked Mr. Allen, holding a full glass of old Burgundy between him and the light.

"Yes, I must confess it's very good; but just try some of this!" and the colonel took out a flask, and poured out a large glassful of it, remarking, "This is some of our northern strong wine; I guess they made none of this there in your time!"

"I should say not," replied Mr. Allen, draining the contents.

Mr. Allen now became very noisy, insisting that every one should drink, men and all, while there was a drop on the premises. He soon reeled about, and keeled over. The officers took him up, and placed him on the bed, laid a sheet over, with a label, for the information of following officers: "Dead drunk, by his own acts."

I am sure Mr. Allen felt rather surprised, when he came to himself, both at finding himself abed, and the house untouched.

CHAPTER XXII.

THE ARMY IN MILLEDGEVILLE.—FLIGHT OF THE GOVERNMENT AND LEGISLATURE.—A MOCK SESSION IN THE CAPITOL.—OUR CAVALRY MOVEMENTS.—THE JEW AND THE GENERAL.—THE WAY SHERMAN'S ARMY LIVED ON THE COUNTRY.

ABOUT noon, on the 22d of November, the advance of the left wing reached Milledgeville.

General Slocum was received by the mayor, who surrendered the city, requesting that life and private property might be respected.

The troops entered playing national airs, and their banners flying. Soon after the stars and stripes floated from the State House.

Governor Brown had delivered a very inflammatory speech to the legislators, on Saturday the 17th, telling them that the Yankee Vandals were approaching the capital, to destroy, pollute, and devastate all before them. He exhorted and entreated every member here present to seize his musket and meet the ruthless invaders. As for himself, he was resolved to defend his home to the last.

His glowing philippic seemed to infuse a spirit of patriotism into the legislative body. The members loudly cheered, and went home to furbish their arms. A report ran through the city that the Yankee cavalry were approaching; and then all their courage, like Bob Acres's, ran through their fingers' ends.

They hastily packed their traps, and fled, Governor Brown heading the runaways, on to Macon. This was followed by a regular stampede, which was greatly accelerated next day by the appearance of Captain Duncan and some ten scouts, who made a dash into the town, scaring away all the men, except the poor craven mayor, who went into hysterics.

The women, of course, remained, but were saucy and indignant enough to fight it out themselves. One lady, whose lord had joined the retreat, and who felt very bitter at such a mean piece of cowardice, informed us how it all took place.

"The cowardly, mean set!" she exclaimed. "I tell you, I'd sooner see my husband dead at my feet than such a skunk. Some Yankee scouts came dashing, pellmell, into the town, when the men — the mean, craven-hearted wretches! — skedaddled, leaving our baby mayor to surrender the town unconditionally to five greasy Yankees, ten miles in advance of the army. Faugh on them! the chicken-hearted wretches! and the mayor a puffed-up old fool. Had I been in town I'd have collected all the women, and driven the skunks out with mop-handles and broomsticks!"

Milledgeville, the capital of Georgia, is rather a pleasant looking town, with a population of about three thousand. It is situated on a bluff, in the midst of a fine cotton-growing country, on the west side of the Oconee River.

Some of the residences are very fine, and built of brick. Delightful gardens, tasteful lawns, and spacious streets give the whole place an air of comfort and elegance.

The Capitol, which is a very imposing brown stone building, is built on a ten-acre square, in the centre of the town, and is flanked on each corner by a small, but tasteful, church.

Trophy-hunters, boisterous negroes, who did not know what to do with themselves and their freedom, drunken soldiers, all revelled now about the State House. The library was ransacked by the literati, and archives and books carried off in loads. Minerals, fossils, state bonds, and state money were at a discount.

Stacks of Georgia state money were found in the treasurer's office. There were millions of dollars there, the most of it not signed. The men loaded themselves with it; the negroes fought over it, and "bressed de Lord, dey were richer dan poor massa now."

This money circulated freely, on the march, in exchange for chickens, bacon, and other little luxuries, and the poor people were gratefully surprised at the liberality of Uncle Sam's Yanks.

The fright of the honorable body of legislators must have been amusing. They scarcely knew where to run or what to do. They heard that our left wing was moving on Augusta, and they felt secure. Then Howard threatened them from McDonough and they shivered again. Then our cavalry and right wing were striking for Macon, and they became valiant again, and made fiery speeches of the last-ditch style. News came that a column was moving right on the capital, and the cavalry were in sight of the city.

This was too much for the Falstaff heroes, and they fled in such confusion that the railroad cars became crowded to an excess with furniture, private property, and goods, and fabulous sums were given for any kind of conveyances. They were frantically running about, like King Richard, exclaiming, "A horse, a horse, my *estate* for a horse!" Buggies, barouches, and other vehicles fetched thousands of dollars. They had only the one outlet for escape, and they trembled lest the Vandals would pounce down on them every minute.

General Sherman took up his quarters uninvited at the executive mansion, Governor Brown, with very bad grace, not waiting to receive him.

General Slocum had placed a provost guard through the city, with strict orders to arrest any one found pillaging, and to protect all private property.

Colonel Hawley, of the 3d Wisconsin, was appointed commandant of the post, and established his headquarters in the State House, after which all scientific and literary investigations were put a stop to.

The only property destroyed were the magazines, arsenals, depots, factories, the penitentiary, which some lawless soldiers had fired, and released the inmates for the benefit of Georgia society, and storehouses, with near two thousand bales of cotton.

No private property was destroyed, and the people began to think that the devil was not so black as he was painted, after all.

Convening the Legislature.

As Governor Brown and the congregated wisdom of Georgia had taken a French leave of absence, and as striking events were developing, it was thought advisable that an extraordinary meeting of the house should be convened. In pursuance of said call, a full house had assembled. The halls and chambers were crowded with honorable members in blue. The meeting was held in the Senate Chamber; the subject under discussion was, the reorganization of the State of Georgia.

Colonel J. C. Robinson was elected president; Lieutenant Colonel H. C. Rogers, clerk; Captain W. W. Mosely was appointed sergeant-at-arms to assist the pages, Mayors Gwindow, Crane, and others, in keeping order and decently laying out under the table any member seized with Bourbon fits, which disease was rather prevalent among the honorable members. The honorable body took their seats in the usual riotous, scrambling manner of such bodies in general, and with the strictest observance of legislative usages.

The business of the house was opened by a general drink, and a Committee on Federal Relations appointed, comprising Colonels Watkins, Carman, Zulick, Thompson, Ewing, Coggswell, who retired, and were soon engaged discussing the merits of a strong bottle of brandy. Snatches of songs and laughter, which floated up from the committee room, proved that the honorable gentlemen were liberally and cheerfully engaged.

Pending their return, General Kilpatrick regaled the convention with a full and highly-embellished account of a very dashing raid he had made on a cellar.

"Though," said the honorable gentleman, "I am a very modest man, that never blows his own horn, like other gentlemen whom I could name, I must honestly tell you that I am Old Harry on raids. My men, too, have strongly imbibed the spirit, and are always full of it. I must confess that my fellows are very inquisitive. Having come so far to visit the good people of Georgia, who are famed for their hospitality, they live in the free and easy style among them; and if, perchance, they discover a deserted cellar, believing that it was kindly left for their use by the considerate owner, they take charge of it. It sometimes happens, too, that they look after the plate and other little matters. Coming to my own particular raid, it was one of the handsomest and most brilliant affairs of the war I ——"

"Mr. Speaker, I must raise a point of order. I believe it is always the custom to treat the speaker." This interruption came from a lobby member, who appeared suffering from an ague fit.

"Yes, I believe it's customary to treat the speaker;" and he produced a huge brandy flask. "I beg to inform this honorable body that I am going to treat the speaker;" and he gravely put the bottle to his mouth, and seemed to enjoy most lovingly its contents. This interruption was received by cheers from some, and cries of Order, order! from others. Before the honorable gentleman could resume his address, the committee returned, some humming, "We won't go home till morning," "Marching, marching along." A noisy debate ensued, every one edging in his own word, the chief tenor of which was a strong wish of cultivating a closer acquaintance with Joe Brown and Company, and regretting their unparliamentary absence from the meeting.

After several calls to order, the chairman of the Committee on Federal Relations read the following set of resolutions: —

1. That the ordinance of secession was highly indiscreet and injudicious, and ought to be discouraged.

2. That aforesaid ordinance is a d——d farce, and always was, and is hereby repealed and abrogated.

3. That Sherman's columns will play the devil with the ordinance and the state itself

4. As the Federal relations with the state are not very friendly, that a committee be appointed to kick Joe Brown and Jeff Davis, and also to whip back the state into the Union.

A lobby member suggested that Sherman's committee of safety, comprising Uncle Sam's blue jackets, would do that, and proposed that the reconstruction of the state be left in their hands.

The resolutions and amendments were submitted to the house, and were loudly ratified, *nem. con.*

The legislature rather hastily adjourned, after the style of Governor Brown, first regaling itself with Bourbon and brandy smashers.

Thus terminated the sittings of this important body of Yankee representatives, who had brought back the state into the Union *vi et armis.*

Here, as elsewhere, we found the ladies to be uncompromising rebels. One lady, who kept a perfect harem of young lady boarders, paid a guard which had been assigned her, liberally in greenbacks, which she had got from officers who had dined there.

"Why do you do that, madam?" asked an officer present.

Assuming something of the Charlotte Corday expression of contempt and disdain, she haughtily replied, —

"Sir, I don't keep the vile trash. I'm no traitor."

On the 22d Kilpatrick struck the Macon and Western road, destroying the bridge at Walnut Creek. Next day Howard's column reached Gordon, and began the destruction of the Georgian Central Railroad.

The only fighting we had since we left Atlanta was between Kilpatrick and Wheeler's cavalry. Kilpatrick made a demonstration on Macon, and when near Gordon the enemy showed fight, and threw forward some infantry. Howard sent General Walcott's brigade of infantry to support Kilpatrick, and a very hot little engagement ensued at Griswoldville. Before I describe this, I will give a *résumé* of the cavalry operations since we left Atlanta.

The first brigade of Kilpatrick's cavalry was commanded by Colonel E. H. Murray, of the 3d Kentucky, and the 2d brigade was under Colonel Atkinson, 92d Illinois mounted infantry.

Kilpatrick covered our right flank, moving on the Jonesboro' road. At Lovejoy they were opposed by dismounted infantry and some militia, in Hood's old works. They had two guns in position. They were soon routed from this position. Kilpatrick pursued them to Bear Creek Station, where

BATTLE NEAR GORDON.

they made another stand, being reënforced. A sharp engagement took place here, but the rebels were finally driven from their breastworks. On the 18th Kilpatrick reached the river at Planters' Ferry. On the 20th he occupied Clinton, and moved by Cross Keys, with the intention of demonstrating on Macon.

The enemy were pretty strongly intrenched on the heights around Macon. Kilpatrick skirmished with them. His instructions were to threaten Macon, but not attack in case of resistance.

Next day he tore up the railroad towards Gordonsville, and burned a number of factories and machine shops.

On the 22d he arrived near Gordon, where the enemy made a decided stand. While the cavalry were engaged here, the rebels sent forward an infantry force, under General Philips. Howard, being apprised of this movement, sent General Walcott's brigade, of the 15th corps, to support the cavalry.

Walcott's infantry swept down on the rebel militia with sovereign contempt. The latter did not immediately give way, but seemed to show fight, as much as to say, "We'll show you that militia can fight."

Walcott opened a heavy fire of musketry and artillery upon them, and replied with a good deal of steadiness. Walcott formed into column and charged right down on them, sweeping them before him. General Philips did all he could to rally his troops, and partly succeeded; but they did not long stand our fire and charge, but fled panic-stricken, leaving Philips and a large number of prisoners in our hands. The fight was rather a tough one, and ended in the rout of the rebels, with a loss of about three hundred, while our loss could be no more than forty to fifty. General Walcott was wounded in the engagement.

Thence Kilpatrick passed through Gordon, crossing the Oconee River, and joined Sherman at Milledgeville.

Howard's column had encountered no opposition as yet, except General Walcott's engagement at Griswoldville. He had destroyed several miles of railroad, stores, mills, factories, and cotton.

The quantity of cotton destroyed was immense. The women

and children, and a few old men, and Jews, who managed the *shent. per̈ shent.* part of the Confederacy, looked on with a morbid kind of apathy.

We found that a large portion of the cotton was, or pretended to be, in the hands of the Jews. We seldom got up a cotton burning that Solomon the Jew, or Isaac the Jew, or some other Jew, did not claim it as his lawful property. They strongly pleaded their neutrality, and appeared horrified when they found that dodge no go.

In one case in Carolina, a Jew, true to his money-making instincts, seeing a fine pile of cotton preparing for the torch, rushes up excitedly, and exclaims,—

"General, you don't mean to say that you are going to burn dat 'ere pile of cotton?"

"Certainly."

"Ah, mein Gott! what a pity! three hundred bales!"

"Four hundred, friend," said the general, amusing himself at the poor Jew's expense.

"An' de cotton as high as fifty cents a pound."

"Sixty-five cents in New York," replied the general, piling up the agony still higher.

"O mein Gott! mein Gott!" exclaimed the Jew, wringing his hands and looking most affectionately at the tempting pile, which his avaricious mind had already converted into a regular mint of gold dollars.

"Come, men, fire it!" exclaimed the general; and the men snatched up the brands from the fire, and were about thrusting them into the pile. This was too much for the Jew: was all his anticipated wealth thus to end in smoke? and raising his hands he exclaimed,—

"Don't fire dat! don't fire dat!"

The men stood with the brands raised. The Jew ran over to the general, and taking him confidentially by the coat, whispered in his ear,—

"What vill I give you for de whole lot?"

The general thought he would keep on the joke.

"Well, taking the risks and everything into account, I should think fifty thousand dollars enough for it."

"Fifty tousand! the risks are great, general!"

"True, then say forty."

"O, dat too much, too."

"What do you say to thirty thousand?"

"De rebel cavalry might come and burn it."

"Well, what do you say yourself."

"General," he whispered into his ears, "I'll give you ten tousand gold dollars, and let de cotton be, and no one be de wiser."

"It won't do; fire the cotton, men."

"No, no, general, I'll make it de twenty."

The general shook his head; the cotton was beginning to blaze up.

"Stop dem, general; I'll make it de thirty."

The pile was in one blaze.

"It is too late now," said the general, and the bewildered Jew looked on in horror.

"Look here," said the general, tapping the Jew on the shoulder, and giving him a look that made him quail, —

"I want thirty thousand dollars from you."

"Mein Gott! for what?" exclaimed the affrighted Jew; "de cotton is all burned now."

"Exactly so; you are a rebel agent; otherwise you could not pay such a sum for this cotton."

"O, no, mein Gott, I hate de rebels; but I wanted to make one little money; me no agent."

"Well, well, you'd buy that cotton for the rebels, if we left it here; of course it would get into their hands. Are you a Union man?"

"O mein Gott, yes; I alvays for de Union."

"You'd do as much for the Union as for the Confederacy?"

"Mein Gott, much more."

"Then you were ready to pay thirty thousand dollars for that cotton, which would fall into the rebel hands; now, I demand the same amount for the Union cause."

The poor Jew was in a trap; he had baited a snare for himself. It was amusing to see how he wriggled and shivered between the fear of being strung out of a tree and the dread of losing his thirty thousand dollars.

The general kept him in a state of suspense for some time, during which he swore by Jacob, Abraham, Solomon, and all the prophets of the old law, that he was a strict Union man, and had not thirty thousand dollars in the world.

"Why did you offer it then, or how did you mean to pay it?"

"O, mein Gott, general, I knew ye wouldn't ax de money until I'd sell de cotton in New York."

This subterfuge so pleased the general that he dismissed the Jew, who, I am sure, never tried to buy cotton from Yankee generals again.

It is a notorious fact that Jews hung around the army like crows around carrion, and as soon as we got possession of a town, they at once got all the good stores and trade privileges.

I have known instances where men, who had served in the army, wanted trade privileges, and could not get them, while Jews, who had never smelled gunpowder, could get what they pleased. I have seen, in a certain town in Tennessee, ex-officers, who wanted permits, left to cool themselves in presence of the Great Mogul,—the treasury agent,—while some wealthy shoddy Jew was getting a lengthened audience, and enjoying a pleasant *téte-à-téte*.

When the ex-officers and others were received by the little great man, it was in the tone of one "clothed in a little brief authority."

"What do you want?"

"Trade permits."

"I can't attend to them. More applications than I can grant."

Again, I have seen Jews walk unchallenged into the office of a certain general, military governor of a certain town in Georgia, while others had to go through a regular course of ceremonies and passes before they reached the august presence of his high mightiness.

I admire the pluck and enterprise of the Jews, and wish them every success; but I don't see why they should be more favorably treated than Christians.

Somehow I think they have discovered the golden sesame.

A friend of mine once complained to a Jew that he could not get any favors from a certain party. "Though," said my friend, "I am asking nothing but what I am entitled to."

"What would you give for the privilege you want?"

"I'd give one or two hundred dollars to any one that would get it."

"Indeed! Well, I take one hundred and fifty dollars from you and get the permit; but mind you," said the Jew, who seemed to feel ashamed of what a Christian delighted in, "one cent of this does not go into my pocket; still it is necessary to get you the permit."

"I understand, and am grateful to you," replied the other.

He soon got his permit.

The Jew has shown his wisdom throughout this war. As a class they were the only people that kept clear of it. While Christians were slaying their brother Christians, and rose up in bloody enmity against one another, the Jews traded and bartered, bought and sold goods, houses, and property, gave and took in marriage, as if the world were at peace, accumulated wealth, and now enjoy in ease the fine homesteads, spacious stores, and rich plantations of the poor victims of pride and ambition.

Verily, they are wise in their generation.

It takes an old raider to appreciate how completely and quickly a railroad can be destroyed. At the first start of railroad raids, the rails were simply turned over,—the men ranging themselves at one side, and raising in one huge swath hundreds of yards at a time, and then tossing it over. This only caused some delay, but left the material for use again. We improved on the thing like all other sciences of war. The rails were torn from the sleepers by a kind of drag, with a lever attached for a handle. Then the sleepers were piled up, and set on fire.

The rails were placed on top, and soon became so soft that

they could be twisted like a corkscrew, or wound around a tree like an *anaconda. Future antiquarians will rack their brains conjecturing how these iron monsters twisted themselves around the trees. I should not wonder if some Barnum of the twenty-fifth century should exhibit an immense rail as the " fungated boa-constrictor found buried in the heart of a huge oak tree, where it must have lain for hundreds of years," with, perhaps, another that has been modelled into a duck of a corkscrew, as " a corkscrew used by the aborigines of America in the days when there were giants upon the earth."

These will be looked back upon as the good old times, though, truly, we have found more harm than good in them.

Near some stations we found several locomotive houses inhabited by a very peculiar people. Some western squatters live on rafts; the Chinese have their floating populations, and the poor Irish their mud cabins; but here we found new tenants who inhabit the box-cars that have been thrown off the track, or switched on sidelings. In some of these were families of blacks, whose masters had been burned out, and they were now shifting for themselves. All the able-bodied men had been carried off by massa, leaving the women and children to enjoy the combined luxury of freedom and starvation.

Greasy negro wenches stuck out their heads through the windows to survey us, while young picaninnies rolled and tumbled about like porpoises on the land.

Some had the octoroon lightness of color and clearness of features; others approached the brown olive of the Indian; while others displayed the thick lips, woolly heads, and dusky skins of the pure Ethiopian.

Such a medley would send your miscegenation disciples into ecstasies; but it would take a whole herald college to trace their relationship to one another. I learned that the octoroon boy, whom, if you met with, you would set down as the child of white parents, was the offspring of brother and sister. His mother was the child of a planter, and his slave; while the boy was the child of the planter's son.

"Did you know," said I to the boy's mother, who was certainly good-looking, "that he was your brother?"

"Specks I did."

"And why did you live with him?"

"Me gwine to oppose massa? Catch a slave do it."

"And have you been kept a slave all the time."

"Yes; but old massa sold my sister, and young massa says he'll sell me if I don't be good."

Two box-cars near the black colony were inhabited by white families. They did not appear to be a bit better off than the blacks. Their clothing was scant, and their sense of shame or moral rectitude, if they ever had any, was perfectly blunted.

In one car I found two young and rather good-looking women. They had three children between them.

"Where are your husbands?" I asked.

"We never had none," was the reply.

"How do you manage to live?"

"Well, I reckon as well as we can. Can't get no coffee nor snuff, now. Have you a chew of 'backer, stranger?"

These wretched families appeared content in their filth, and rags, and wretchedness.

They found very little change in the times. True, they became a little hard since the war took place; still, they were able to live, while, at the best of times, they had a struggle to do so. Their huts and persons were equally dirty and squalid; though a stream of water ran near them, they appeared to have a hydrophobiac dread of it.

It was the policy of the rebel government to abandon the cultivation of cotton for the raising of corn crops, and this was fully carried out by the planters.

I had been informed that for the past two years there was not above one fifth the quantity of cotton planted that had been in former years. This I am sure was the fact; for besides the desire to raise food for the armies, the able-bodied negroes were employed on military works, and the whites conscripted into the army.

As cotton requires watchful care, the planters had not hands to cultivate it.

In our march we daily traversed immense cornfields of hundreds of acres in extent. These were formerly devoted to cotton.

The rich extent of country west of the Savannah River was the great granary of the rebel army of the west. Lee's army drew the bulk of its supplies from the states east of the Savannah, chiefly about Columbia.

How we lived on the Country.

Our campaign all through Central Georgia was one delightful picnic. We had little or no fighting, and good living. The farm-yards, cellars, and cribs of the planters kept ourselves and animals well stored with provisions and forage, besides an occasional stiff horn of something strong and good, which, according to the injunctions of holy writ, we took "for our stomachs' sake."

Indeed, the men were becoming epicures. In passing through the camp one night, I saw a lot of jolly soldiers squatted outside the huts in true gypsy style, and between them a table richly stocked with meats and fowls of different kinds, flanked by several bottles of brandy.

They were a jolly set of scamps — talked, laughed, jested, and cracked jokes and bottles in smashing style.

Chase's financial speculations were nothing to theirs; and as for their war schemes, Stanton's and Halleck's were thrown in the shade by them. On the subject of eating they were truly eloquent, and discussed the good things before them with the gusto of a Beau Brummel.

They thought campaigning in Georgia about the pleasantest sort of life out, and they wondered what would become of the poor dog-gone folks they had left with their fingers in their mouths, and little else to put in them.

Many of our foragers, scouts, and hangers-on of all classes, thought, like Cromwell, that they were doing the work of the Lord, in wantonly destroying as much property as possible. Though this was done extensively in Georgia, it was only in South Carolina that it was brought to perfection.

When we reached Milledgeville, we had about thirty days' extra marching rations.

It is impossible to enter into the details of the many ways an army can live on the country. Besides the regular detailed forage parties, there are the officers' servants and cooks, black and white, all wanting something nice for massa general or the captain's mess. Some of these black and white rascals draw largely on the mess fund, with the honest intention of paying for what they get, but somehow forget doing so. I once had a negro servant, a very pious negro, by the way. He was a kind of preacher, collected his "bredern" at night, and with them shouted out psalms lustily enough to take heaven by storm. He was a pious negro, and pointed out the road Zion-ward to his "errin' bredern."

"I'm gwine out, massa, wid de boys, and I want money." This was one morning when we were preparing to march.

"For what, Moses?"

"Well, you, massa, hain't a chicken nor butter for dinner."

"Moses, why can't you forage, like the rest? I declare, our mess is costing us a pile, while others are living on the country."

"Dat's true, massa," said Moses, with a look of offended virtue; "but dis chil' never steal his neighbor's goods."

I stood rebuked by this unsophisticated son of the wilderness, and, feeling ashamed of myself, handed him a five-dollar bill. In the course of the day, passing a poor shanty, I heard a great uproar in the yard, and the voice of a woman in angry remonstrance. I dismounted in time to see Moses and the cook charge out of the yard, both flanked with chickens and roosters tied to their saddles.

"O, the murthering thieves," exclaimed the woman, "they hain't left me a morsel; they have even taken my blanket, and a little crock of butter, a few pieces of bacon an officer left me, and myself and the children will starve; and here is what they gave me;" and she showed a twenty-dollar Confederate note.

At night Moses had a very nice dinner for me, no doubt; the chickens were elegantly done, the bacon was rich and juicy. I could have enjoyed the thing immensely at any other time; but somehow the widow and orphans seemed to look on upbraidingly.

Moses, however, took it very complacently, and even rebuked me because I sat down without saying grace.

"Any change for me, Moses?"

"Change, massa? I declare, dese 'ere things dreadfully dear! Cost a heap!"

"Indeed! what did you pay?"

"You see, massa, she was a lone woman; so I gave her ten dollars."

"So I owe you five;" and I took out a Confederate bill for the amount.

"This 'ere thing no good," said Moses, handing it back to me, in disdain.

"You hypocrite!" I exclaimed, "it is as good as the one you gave the widow; and by Jove! if you practise any more on me, I'll have you tied up and well flogged."

Moses was quite crest-fallen, and never asked me for money again on the march.

This is a mild case, and gives but a poor notion of the exploits of the grand army of foragers and bummers.

War is very pleasant when attended by little fighting, and good living at the expense of the enemy.

To draw a line between stealing and taking or appropriating everything for the subsistence of an army would puzzle the nicest casuist. Such little freaks as taking the last chicken, the last pound of meal, the last bit of bacon, and the only remaining scraggy cow, from a poor woman and her flock of children, black or white not considered, came under the order of legitimate business. Even crockery, bed-covering, or cloths, were fair spoils. As for plate, or jewelry, or watches, these were things rebels had no use for. They might possibly convert them into gold, and thus enrich the Confederate treasury.

Men with pockets plethoric with silver and gold coin; soldiers sinking under the weight of plate and fine bedding materials; lean mules and horses, with the richest trappings of Brussels carpets, and hangings of fine chenille; negro wenches, particularly good-looking ones, decked in satin and silks, and sporting diamond ornaments; officers with sparkling rings, that would set Tiffany in raptures,—gave color to the stories of hanging up or fleshing an "old cuss," to make him shell out.

A planter's house was overrun in a jiffy; boxes, drawers, and escritoirs were ransacked with a laudable zeal, and emptied of their contents. If the spoils were ample, the depredators were satisfied, and went off in peace; if not, everything was torn and destroyed, and most likely the owner was tickled with sharp bayonets into a confession where he had his treasures hid. If he escaped, and was hiding in a thicket, this was *prima facie* evidence that he was a skulking rebel; and most likely some ruffian, in his zeal to get rid of such vipers, gave him a dose of lead, which cured him of his Secesh tendencies. Sorghum barrels were knocked open, bee-hives rifled, while their angry swarms rushed frantically about. Indeed, I have seen a soldier knock a planter down because a bee stung him. Hogs are bayonetted, and then hung in quarters on the bayonets to bleed; chickens, geese, and turkeys are knocked over and hung in garlands from the saddles and around the necks of swarthy negroes; mules and horses are fished out of the swamps; cows and calves, so wretchedly thin that they drop down and perish on the first day's march, are driven along, or, if too weak to travel, are shot, lest they should give aid to the enemy.

Should the house be deserted, the furniture is smashed in pieces, music is pounded out of four hundred dollar pianos with the ends of muskets. Mirrors were wonderfully multiplied, and rich cushions and carpets carried off to adorn teams and war-steeds. After all was cleared out, most likely some set of stragglers wanted to enjoy a good fire, and set the house, debris of furniture, and all the surroundings, in a blaze. This is the way Sherman's army lived on the country. They were not ordered to do so, but I am afraid they were not brought to task for it much either.

CHAPTER XXIII.

HOWELL COBB'S FAST MARE.—JOE, THE FORAGER.—CONTRA-
BANDS.—CAPTURE OF FORT MCALLISTER.

SLOCUM'S column left Milledgeville on the morning of the 24th, and crossed the Oconee, diving into a dense pine forest.

On the afternoon of the following day, Wheeler's cavalry disputed their passage across Buffalo Creek. Here was a wide swamp, crossed by nine bridges, which the rebels had burned, and consequently easy of defence. A regiment forded the creek, cleared the opposite side, and the engineers soon threw up bridges, and corduroyed the approaches.

Carmon's brigade, of Jackson's division, skirmished up to Sandersville, and Colonel Hughes and his cavalry dashed into the town, but were forced back with the loss of one man.

Southern papers magnified this into a great victory by Wheeler's cavalry.

The infantry soon came up, and made short work of the cavalry. This neat little town was soon pillaged, and an inventory taken of the stock of every store in it.

Here we learned that Wheeler's force was about fifteen hundred men and four guns, and that Hardee was marching to the assistance of Savannah.

Howard had arrived at Swainsboro', on the Great Chopee River, moving towards the great railway centre at Millen. Kilpatrick was on his right, and the left wing was converging in the same direction. Howard had met little opposition, except at the Oconee Bridge, which was burned, and stoutly defended by Major Hartridge, of Wheeler's cavalry.

In a swamp near Milledgeville we picked up a valuable pacing mare of General Howell Cobb's. She was a splendid animal, but the poor fellow that captured her paid a dear price for her, for while testing her speed he ventured too far from the command, and was found with his throat cut.

Cobb's plantation was well stocked with decrepit negroes, and his granaries well filled with corn. The gallant owner had removed all the able-bodied men, women, and animals from the place, leaving a miserable-looking set of negroes to receive us, whom he had soothingly informed that the Yanks would cut their throats for them, or yoke them into their wagons. These wretched creatures were cooped up in their leaky, half-sheltered cabins.

The poor of the south, black and white, were kept in this state of terrorism by the planters. The most ignorant black had a kind of instinctive feeling that we were their friends. Not so with the poor whites. We found male children hid in all sorts of out-of-the-way places; for they heard that we would kill them, to prevent their growing up to fight against us.

On the contrary, the negro knew that massa hated the Yankee; and massa being, in too many cases, their tyrant, they felt that the Yankee must of necessity be their friend.

"Massa can't come dat over dis 'ere nigger," said a grayheaded negro; "massa nebber cared for us. Why does he want to tote us off now dat you'ns a coming? No, massa; we know dat you set us free; de Lord tell us so."

His strong, abiding faith was remarkable. The negro believed in a millennium; and now he thought his belief was about being realized.

General Sherman ordered a generous supply of Howell Cobb's good things to be divided among the negroes. The bummers helped themselves to them next day. Why should they feed Howell Cobb's niggers, if the chivalric, liberty-loving major general deserted them?

These same bummers were wonderful at discovering hidden treasures, concealed goods, and the like; in fact, they appeared more perfectly conversant with the occult sciences than all the clairvoyants of New York. I once saw a body of them riding over a wide, open field. On a sudden the leader halted his scraggy Rosinante with such a jerk as to throw him on his haunches, and to set the score, young and old, roosters and chickens, that wreathed his saddle, into a perfect roar of agonized torture.

"Stop," he exclaimed.

They all stopped, and looked about them, somewhat scared; a vision of Wheeler's cavalry and gaping throats, cut from car to car, crossing their minds.

"What's the matter, Joe?" exclaimed one of the party.

"I'm dog gone if I don't smell a hog."

"Fudge, man! let us ride on; this doesn't look a very comfortable place to be, and we so far out."

"Narry ride, then," replied Joe, "until I make sure. A good fat hog would be such a pleasant change from chicken and turkey."

They all urged Joe to come on, but without effect. Soon they heard a grunt quite near them. They all chimed in with Joe; but where was the hog, though? There was nothing but an open field around them.

Joe remarked that there couldn't be a porcine grunt without a hog, and dismounted to make a closer inspection. By probing with their ramrods, they discovered a hollow place, and were not long in digging it up, when, lo! they discovered one of the fattest and tidiest hogs I have ever seen, buried in a nice cave, which was covered in with boards and earth.

After this exploit Joe was voted the prince of bummers.

On another occasion we had halted at a farm-house, when the lady of the house, with some dozen children clinging round her, came out wringing her hands, beseeching us to leave something for herself and her starving children. They looked miserable and squalid enough to be in want. We felt for her, and had placed a guard on the house, and given her a supply of provisions. When I said "we," I should leave out Joe, who was present, and received her appeals with the unfeeling exclamations of "bosh!" and "bumpkin!" When the grateful woman went in, Joe remarked,—

"I reckon a coon's hide that 'ere woman hain't so poor, neither."

"Miserably so," we replied.

"Waal, we'll see;" and Joe walked off, but soon returned with his whole gang laden with bacon and flour, which they had disinterred about the premises.

Joe was a lean, lank-looking customer, a cross between some roving Tennesseean and a half savage Cherokee. Some of Wheeler's men spoiled the best forager in the army by cutting Joe's windpipe, having first treated him to a pill of lead.

After Joe's demise I think the palm of merit should be given to Chowler, a huge dog, half Newfoundland and half bloodhound. Chowler — I am afraid I am nicknaming the noble brute; it wouldn't be pleasant if he felt offended and met me alone any time, for he had an ugly way of throttling things, which soon brought on a stoppage of breath — Chowler belonged to Captain De Grass, and did the foraging for the whole battery.

He had a delightful way of wringing the heads of poultry, and upsetting hogs, and sheep, and cows. It took but a few minutes for Chowler to pile the peaceful denizens of the farmyard in gore around him; and woe betide the intruder that dare attempt to take any of them. Chowler was more fortunate than Joe; he has outlived the war, and ought to be brevetted for his services. Many a man that did less than Chowler has been.

I think my readers have, by this time, a pretty good idea of how we "lived off the country," not consuming our rations, but accumulating our stock, which, at one time, amounted to about ten thousand head of cattle, which also lived on the country. So I will now resume my narrative of how and where we marched.

We still moved in four columns, each corps in separate columns, but all within sufficient distance to support each other if required, with the cavalry, as usual, operating on our flanks.

On the evening of the 28th the head of the left wing reached the Ogeechee River. The bridge was burned, and the river widened into one of those marshy bayous which became numerous as we approached the coast. We laid our pontoons, and built nearly a mile of railroad.

Baird's and Morgan's divisions, of .the 14th corps, moved on Louisville, by Fern's Bridge, on the Upper Ogeechee, which place they sacked.

It is the county seat of Jefferson County, and was the first capital of the state.

The 20th corps tore up the railroad between Davidsboro' and the Ogeechee River.

Howard had arrived at Swansboro', on the Great Chopee, striking for Millen.

Blair's corps had followed the railroad, destroying it in his march. The 15th corps, commanded by General Osterhaus, in the absence of General Logan, moved in two columns west and south of the Ogeechee. The whole army was now moving southward, swinging on Millen.

The rebel leaders appeared to be confounded by Sherman's movements. Davis and Kilpatrick were all the time threatening Augusta. Here they had concentrated their militia, and a couple of regiments of North Carolinians, and a portion of Hampton's legion; in all about eight thousand.

Hardee, now seeing that Savannah was our objective point, had fallen back to its defences.

Our left wing had pressed on the cavalry in our front all the time. Davis's corps was thrown forward as a strong arm all through for this purpose. Kilpatrick, too, had cleared our flanks, now with Howard on the right, and next with Davis on the left.

At Waynesboro', Kilpatrick had succeeded in destroying the bridge; Slocum moved eastward through Birdsville. The 15th corps, now moving in two columns on the right bank of the river, had taken up the flank movement, and were a day's march in advance.

On the afternoon of the 2d of December, Howard struck Millen, having effectually destroyed the central road from Macon to that place. Millen is a place of little importance, and only remarkable for being the prison of the Federals removed from Andersonville. The stockade, or prison pen, was located in a dense pine forest, some six miles from Millen.

It was a square of fifteen acres, enclosed by a high log fence. Inside this was the dead line,— a single rail fence,— and beyond the burrows and huts where thousands of brave fellows had to endure a sickening confinement more fearful than death itself.

It was a perfect village of kennels, holes, and huts huddled together, whose desolate, forlorn look was enough to crush the feeling of hope out of a brave man's heart.

In the centre was a rather tasty brick kitchen, a palace when contrasted with its miserable surroundings.

At the south end stood a square earthwork, built to command, with its two guns, the whole bastile.

The hospital was a quarter of a mile from the pen. Here were accommodations for three hundred patients; but this was not sufficient. The long row of graves outside the hospital, numbering six hundred and fifty, told the fearful mortality, though our men were confined there only about a month.

In one of the huts was an unburied body. Poor fellow! he little thought that his comrades would lay him in a decent grave.

Contrabands.

As these proved very dark and troublesome on our line of march, and as they are still continuing a dark and tough subject, I will treat about them more fully than I have done.

Georgia and South Carolina were plentifully stocked with slaves. Most of the able-bodied men were from home, either with their masters, or doing the hard work for the army. As soon as the Federal army struck through Central Georgia, a regular stampede took place of bondmen and bondwomen, and bondchildren too. They were invariably dressed in their best, and had packed into bundles their most valuable dresses and a small stock of provisions, and then, feeling happy and jubilant, fell in with the sable column that flanked the roads and brought up the rear on all sides. Parents seemed to part from their families, children from their parents, with the most apparent unconcern. I had just dropped into a clean negro shanty to rest and await the column.

Its occupants were an old patriarch," who had no hair on the top of his head, the place where the wool ought to grow," two young picaninnies, and a good-looking negress in a fair way of soon increasing the slave population.

The old man was quite communicative, and enlightened me very much on the blessings of slavery. Soon a strapping negro rode up to the door, and, hitching his horse, ran in in the best possible spirits.

"Whar you gwine, Jake?" said the young woman.

"I'm gwine wid de rest, to be sure. De Lord has sent 'em to burst our bondage."

"Am I gwine wid you?" asked the wife.

"No, no, Sal; a lady in you'ns state ain't fit to travel. Jist do pack up, and I'll gwine along."

"What will become of your father and family?" I asked.

He scratched his head, and replied, —

"Well, I guess de Lord will take care of dem."

So he packed up a few things, and with scarcely a parting good by, jumped on the miserable animal which he had helped himself to from massa, and joined the moving throng.

Was all this indifference or resignation?

This question of slavery is but poorly understood in the north, and the men who preach most about it for political purposes, know the least of it, its rights and duties.

The slave is now free to all intents and purposes. To leave himself and his old master to settle the issue between them is the wisest policy. Self-interest will compel them into an understanding.

For the most part generals and officers encouraged the slaves to join the army, simply because they knew it would sound so well at home, that General This or Colonel That liberated so many slaves, and fed them on the march. They fed them while they could live on the enemy's country; but what became of them afterwards? What has become of the fifteen thousand that followed our army through Central Georgia? What has become of the twenty thousand that joined us in Carolina? The waters of the Ogeechee and Ebenezer Creek can account for hundreds who were blocking up our columns, and then abandoned, the pontoons taken up, after being encouraged " to gwine along." The poor affrighted darkies crowded around the Jordan of their simple faith; but it proved to them a Red Sea, for Wheeler's cavalry charged on them, driving them, pellmell, into the waters, and mothers and children, old and young, perished alike!

Many of them died in the bayous and lagoons of Georgia, and the bones of many of them mark our track through South Carolina. When food was getting scarce, we turned them adrift, to support themselves or perish; and philanthropists may congratulate themselves that over thirty thousand brothers have shaken off the shackles forever.

As we passed through Georgia, colonies, squads, whole families, from the feeble old folks, supported on their canes, and tottering under heavy bundles, down to the muling infant in the mother's arms, while her back was burdened with a heavy bundle, fell in. The young and the old left home, at a moment's notice, to go, they knew not where, nor asked where, in search of freedom.

Black children of all ages and sizes, I might add, of all shades, toddled along in rags and filth, urged on by the application of the maternal rod. Babies squealed in their mothers' laps. Old buggies and wagons, that they took from massa, blocked up the way, and literally lined it with their debris. Galled and jaded mules and horses carried hampers and bags, stuffed with children and wearables, balanced on each side. It was no unusual sight to see a black head, with large, staring eyes, peeping out of a sack at one side, and a ham of bacon or a turkey balancing it at the other.

Even here beauty conquered, for the good-looking led luxurious lives, stowed away in baggage-wagons during the day, and feasted at the servants' mess at night.

It would be vexatious to the Grand Turk or Brigham Young, if they could only see how many of these dark houries were in the employment of officers' servants and teamsters. I have seen officers themselves very attentive to the wants of pretty octoroon girls, and provide them with horses to ride.

At night, when the poor "snow-balls," and "beauties," as they were ironically called, halted, the men lighted large camp-fires of rails and fallen trees, and around these they collected in circles, and partook of their frugal meal, if they had any; then they all joined in a kind of hymn, "bressin' de Lord." Their finely modulated voices, chiming in one solemn chorus, rang through the still camp.

What nobler subject for a painting than these bright fires, sparkling and glowing amidst the pine trees, the sombre grandeur of the forest, the white tents of the officers, the solemn tread of the sentry, and then those dark groups bursting forth in one impassioned song of thanksgiving to "de good Lord."

The country from Millen to Savannah is one vast forest of pines, cut up by creeks and bayous, and streams flowing to the Ogeechee and Savannah Rivers. Swamps are plentiful all the way, making the roads almost impassable, and compelling us to corduroy miles of them. At Horse Creek, in Scriven County, the 20th corps and train had to wade through some thirty yards of water four feet in depth.

This was on General Slocum's line of march to Springfield, where the enemy were said to be in force, with the intention of disputing our advance on Savannah.

Howard had met no serious resistance in his line of march, and still kept the west side of the Ogeechee River.

On December 9, the left wing had pushed ahead to a point near Eden, on the Central Georgia line, and formed on the left of the 17th corps. The 14th corps, with its left resting on the Savannah River, was moving steadily down, despite the feeble attempts of a gunboat to prevent it.

We were now about twenty miles from the city, with a complete line stretching across the Peninsula, from river to river.

Fearing that we should detach a force to destroy the Gulf Railroad, the rebels pushed a force across the Ogeechee, covering it by a strong line along the river.

General Corse threw his division between the Little and Great Ogeechee, twelve miles in advance of the main column, to the canal which runs from the Ogeechee to the Savannah

River. He bridged the canal, crossed his division, and intrenched himself, thus edging in on the rebel works, and compelling them to fall back to the fortifications around Savannah.

The rebels had thrown up works at the head of an impenetrable swamp, near Monteith Station, on the Charleston Railroad. Here they opposed the advance of the 20th corps. Jackson's division had the advance; Colonel Robinson's brigade was sent to the left, and Carman's to the right, while Selfridge's advanced directly down the road.

The flanking brigades waded through the swamp for over a mile, until they reached solid ground. They at once formed and dashed on the enemy, who soon made long tracks for Savannah with his guns. It was defended by the 40th North Carolina, under a Major Stevenson. Morgan's division, of the 14th corps, had also driven back the enemy from an intrenched position, and whipped Ferguson's cavalry, which had got in on his rear and flanks. The 17th corps, on the right centre, had also a brush with the enemy, in which, of course, it was successful. At 12 o'clock at night we crossed Ebenezer Creek, and encamped on Fort Greene.

Fort Greene.

This fort has been named in honor of the distinguished revolutionary general of that name, and is said to be the spot where that hero defended Savannah River against the British. A Lutheran church, erected in 1769, stands near the river. It is an old, red brick structure, surmounted by a modest cupola, which looks as if undecided whether it will stand or fall. The interior of the church is even more unassuming than the outside. The pulpit is a plain, rude affair, and gives one the impression of an old desk. The floor and pews were clean, and the seats painted and moulded.

It is a venerable structure; and though looking as if it had taken a bad cold, or was afflicted with the rheumatism, it is likely to last near another century.

The citizens say it was used by General Greene as a hospital.

As the most of the fighting fell to General Kilpatrick and his cavalry, we will follow up the *résumé* of his operations since his fight at Griswoldville.

From Milledgeville, Kilpatrick started on the 24th November for Millen, with the intention of liberating our prisoners.

He crossed the Oconee, and rations for a long march had been issued, and transportation cut down to jockey weight.

Next morning the command broke camp and marched to Long Bridge, on Town Creek. As the bridge had been destroyed, and the creek was deep, they had some difficulty in fording. They passed the Ogeechee Shoals into Warren County.

On the 26th, Captain Estes, A. A. G., and Captain Hays, proceeded with two hundred men towards Waynesboro', in order to destroy the bridge on the Waynesboro' and Augusta Railroad, over Brier Creek. This bridge was sixty miles away, and their orders were to reach it that night. They did so; had a sharp skirmish, destroyed the bridge, and a rebel train, and returned.

The main column of cavalry had marched rapidly through Sylvan Grove to Louisville, in order to draw attention from the two hundred.

On the 27th, Colonel Murray's brigade was vigorously attacked by Wheeler, who repeatedly charged his position with no effect.

The artillery was brought to bear on Wheeler, compelling him to retire. In the course of the day Kilpatrick pushed on rapidly, and was again opposed at Turkey Creek. The enemy closing in on Colonel Atkins's command, Kilpatrick fell back to Big Creek, near Louisville, skirmishing with the enemy all the way.

On the 1st December, he moved for Waynesboro', and was supported by Baird's division, of the 14th corps.

The country around Waynesboro' was partly open, and favorable for cavalry operations.

The rebel pickets were charged five miles outside Waynesboro', and driven in on the main works, which Kilpatrick charged. The 10th Ohio dashed on the rebel works, and were hurled back; they re-formed, and again re-charged, dashing over the rebel works, mowing down the enemy with the sabre. In this charge they captured about one hundred prisoners, including several officers.

The enemy's next line was carried in like manner; but their third, which was at the west end of the town, and protected by a swamp and woods, offered more resistance.

After a sharp fight, Kilpatrick whipped Wheeler out of the town.

Here Kilpatrick and Wheeler entered into a little conversation. As I have said, the enemy's position was a strong one, and *le petit général*, with a flag in his hand, called over to Wheeler's men, "Come out, now, you set of cowardly skunks; you claim that you whip Kilpatrick every time! Come out, now, and try it; and I'll not leave enough of you to thrash a corporal's guard. I am Kil himself!"

Wheeler did not come out, but Kilpatrick went in and thrashed him out.

The engagement here was pretty severe, and the losses rather heavy.

Wheeler was now driven to the rear of Hood's infantry line. Kilpatrick was between him and our trains, covering the rear, as we closed in on Savannah.

Kilpatrick next struck for Sister's Ferry, on the Savannah River; but finding a strong infantry force here, he wheeled for Savannah, moving on the flank of the right wing. He had to cross cypress swamps, where bridges were burned, and everything done to impede his march.

One brigade crossed the Ogeechee at King's Bridge, the other fell back to the rear to guard the new position taken by the army.

Brevet Major General Judkin Kilpatrick rendered very important services to Sherman in his campaigns through the south. He is remarkable for his unwearied activity, and continually harassed the enemy, now at one point, next at one remote from that. He has few equals as a raider, for he appears to be ubiquitous, and strikes the enemy when least expected.

As a general, he is more brilliant than solid; perhaps somewhat deficient in the judgment of a cool planner, but eminently qualified for movements that require despatch and rapid execution. In appearance he is of middle height, rather slightly built, but wiry and muscular. He has a gay, pleasant appearance. He talks and acts with nervous rapidity, and swears at the rebels just as vigorously as he fights them.

The left wing invested Savannah on the 11th, taking up position on the right and front of the city; the left of the 20th corps extending as far as the river, and the right of the 20th corps resting on the Ogeechee. Howard had swung into line, with the 17th corps on the right centre and the 15th in reserve, in order to open communications with the fleet. The enemy had opened the dikes of the canals and flooded the country, making it very unpleasant for the troops. We compelled some prisoners we held to rebuild the gaps, and the water soon fell.

Some of our foragers lay in ambush for a steamer on the river, and picked off her pilot and several hands. She surrendered, and was burned. She proved to be the Water Witch, captured from our fleet.

Slocum had struck the Savannah and Charleston Railroad, where it crosses to the west side of the Savannah River, thus severing the communications between Charleston and Savannah. The 11th and 12th were spent in putting troops and artillery into position, erecting breastworks, and making the necessary preparations for the thorough investment of the city. Baird's division protected Slocum's rear from Wheeler's attacks, and also established batteries on the river to check the gunboats. The line now was about ten miles long, extending from the Savannah, where Slocum's left rested, just three miles from the city, to the Gulf Railway, ten miles from the city, where Howard's right rested.

Kilpatrick moved rapidly through Sudbury to Kilkenny, and found the United States ship Fernandina, Captain West, in sight down the bay. Captain Estes, assistant adjutant general, and one of Kilpatrick's most brilliant officers, attended by Captain Messenger and one or two other officers, went out in a small boat and boarded the ship; so General Kilpatrick was able to inform General Sherman that the fleet had been found, and was ready to lend any coöperation to his movements. Understanding that Fort McAllister was to be taken by assault, Kilpatrick asked from General Sherman the privilege of assaulting it with his cavalry.

Owing to the swampy nature of the ground, and the light artillery of the cavalry, Sherman did not think it practicable for artillery. General Hazen's division, of the 15th corps, was selected for this important attack.

Hazen captures Fort McAllister.

To Brigadier (now Major General) Hazen, commanding the 2d division, 15th corps, was assigned the honorable position of conducting the assault on the fort. Sherman well knew that he could not intrust it to a better or more experienced officer.

General Hazen rose rapidly in his profession. He was a West Point graduate in 1854, and served with distinction in the Indian wars on the frontiers and in Mexico, where he got badly wounded. He returned home, and led a domestic life until the breaking out of the war, when he again took up arms, and raised a regiment. He distinguished himself at Shiloh, and subsequently through the western campaign. He conducted some of the most daring assaults on the Atlanta campaign. On Major General O. O. Howard assuming command of the army of the Tennessee, he got General Hazen transferred from a brigade in the 4th corps to a division in the 15th corps. Hazen is an educated general, cautious and reticent in organizing his plans, and energetic in executing them. He is a strict disciplinarian, a good engineer, a thorough soldier, and refined gentleman. He possesses a dignified appearance, and frank, cheerful manners.

With such a prestige, and being only in the prime of manhood,—about thirty-four years of age,—it is no wonder that he is as much admired by the ladies as he is esteemed by his brother officers.

Fort McAllister commanded the river. It was a strong, casemated fort, and mounted twenty-one heavy guns. In front of it was an open space of six hundred yards, through which an assaulting party should advance without any cover. This, too, was thickly studded with torpedoes and sharp stakes.

The 15th was General Sherman's old corps, and the 2d division his old division. Sherman sent them word that they should take the fort by assault; and his old soldiers appeared as well pleased at this mark of confidence, as if he had sent them a wagon load of brandy.

On the evening of the 12th Howard relieved Hazen by a part of the 17th corps. Hazen moved across the Little Ogeechee. The enemy had destroyed King's Bridge across the Great Ogeechee, and this had to be repaired. Captain Reese, topographical engineer of Howard's staff, with the Missouri engineers, bridged this one thousand feet during the night. Hazen crossed over next morning, and moved towards the point where the fort commanded the river. Hazen had to march thirteen miles before he got into position. It was now evening, and Hazen had formed into line, investing the fort closing his flanks, which he swung around it, and evenly converged to the fort as a general centre.

Hazen brought no artillery, as the ground was too swampy to move it, and he had decided on taking the fort by a bold dash and at the point of the bayonet.

As soon as the line commenced moving over the open space, the fort opened all its guns upon them. Hazen, moving in a single line, did not suffer much.

Their loss was mostly from torpedoes, which now and then blew up, hurling piles of dirt on the column, and knocking some poor fellows over. The column was all this time rapidly closing up; not a man wavered; each resolved that the fort should be taken. As soon as they got near enough, they poured a steady fire in through the embrasures, knocking off a good many of the gunners. We afterwards found their bodies lying beside their pieces. The first obstruction they met was a thick abatis, which they tore up and crawled through. The column had now closed in around the fort; the guns were silenced, as nothing could live near them, so deadly was our fire. Only a deep ditch, studded with spikes, now separated us from the enemy. Into this the men jumped, tearing away the palisade, climbed up the crest, and mingled in a fierce hand-to-hand conflict with the garrison. Shouts, groans, and curses, the whir of the bullet, and the clash of steel rang from the enclosure.

The contest was of short duration, for soon our troops burst in on all sides, overpowering the enemy, who fought desperately — some of them being bayonetted at their pieces. The officers did all in their power to rally them; several of them refusing to surrender, preferring death to dishonor.

The contest was over; the palmetto had trailed in the dust, and the stripes and stars had floated in its place. The fort was ours,— thus opening the navigation of the river,— with its splendid guns, and large supply of arms, and a full cellar of rich old wines. This was one of the noblest exploits of the campaign, and proves how much quick, determined action can accomplish. Had Hazen sat down before this, to take it by regular siege, it would keep us days at work and cost us more lives. As it was, our loss in killed and wounded scarcely amounted to one hundred.

During the assault, Generals Sherman and Howard and staffs occupied a Dr. Cheroe's rice mill, opposite the fort on the Ogeechee. Sherman was on the roof of the mill. He had signal officers Berkely and Cole there, to communicate with Hazen. While anxiously looking out for Hazen's signals, Sherman's eagle eye descried smoke in the distance seaward. As yet he had received no intelligence from the fleet, though Captain Duncan, chief of Howard's scouts had started on the hazardous enterprise of opening communications with them as early as the 9th.

Sherman looked; his bronzed features lighted up as he exclaimed,—

"Look, Howard; there is the gunboat!"

Soon after the guns of the fort opened one fierce fire, while puffs of smoke curled along Hazen's line, showing that they were replying. Hazen signalled,—

"I have invested the fort, and will assault immediately."

Berkely announces a signal from the gunboat. All anxiously look out for it. The signals inform us that Foster and Dahlgren are within speaking distance, and ask, —

"Can we run up? Is Fort McAllister ours?"

"No; Hazen is just ready to storm it. Can you assist?"

"Yes; what will we do?"

Another moment the thunders from the fort grow fiercer, the metallic rattle of small arms increase, and are borne clearly across the three miles of intervening marsh. Sherman looks towards the fort intently with his glass, and exclaims, —

"How grandly they advance! not a waver!"

He strains his eyes, and again exclaims, —

"Look, Howard, look! magnificent! See that flag, how steadily it advances! not a man falters — grand! grand!"

Again he looks, and turns to Howard, —

"They are closing in; there is no faltering there; no flinching. Stop; it has halted — they are wavering. No, heavens! it's on the parapet! There they go right over it! See! see! there is a flag, and another, and another on the works! Hurrah, it's ours. The fort's taken!"

Glasses were lowered, the firing had ceased, the stripes and stars were floating from the fort, the key to Savannah, — the key that opened the river to the fleet, — and a new base was in Sherman's possession.

Sherman looked about him, his features lighted up with joy, and turning to Howard, he exclaimed, —

"Howard, Savannah is mine! As the old darky remarked, 'Dis chile don't sleep dis night.'"

Turning to one of his aids, he remarked, —

"Have a boat ready for me; I must go over there," pointing to the fort, which was now crowned with half a dozen battle flags, looking glorious with the golden light of the setting sun sparkling with a strange halo around them. It was the consummation of his great and noble project.

It was the fulfilment of his covenant with his troops, when he told them that he would lead them to a new base; and with the nation to which he had sent his last message, not to be uneasy about him; he would take care of himself.

Fort McAllister was under the command of Major Anderson, Captain Clinch, chief of artillery, and Captain White, engineer, and about two hundred men, regulars and militia.

As I have said, the officers fought desperately, refusing to surrender. Though all the guns were in our possession, Captain Clinch refused to surrender, until he was disabled by three sabre and two gun-shot wounds, and faint from loss of blood.

These men fought with recklessness, for with their guns and the outlets of the fort in our hands, any further resistance was madness. The regiments engaged in this brilliant assault were 6th Missouri, Lieutenant Colonel Von Dusen; 30th Ohio; 116th Illinois, Lieutenant Colonel Maddix. These formed the right of the line, and were commanded by the gallant Colonel Theodore Jones. The 47th Ohio, Colonel Perry; 111th Illinois, Colonel Martin, and 54th Ohio, of the 2d brigade, and commanded by Colonel W. S. Jones, formed the left. The 48th Illinois, Major Adams; 90th Illinois, Colonel Stewart, and 20th Ohio, Lieutenant Colonel Philips, from the 3d brigade, commanded by Colonel Oliver, occupied the centre.

Our loss in officers was three killed and eight wounded, among the latter Colonel W. S. Jones, commanding the 2d brigade.

When the history of the daring exploits of this war is written, brightest on the pages will appear that daring charge on Fort McAllister. The fame of Hazen and his gallant troops will stand prominent among those heroes whose names posterity shall record with admiration. The old 2d division served with distinction on many a bloody field, under the fiery John Logan; but it remained for it to gain its crowning laurels under Hazen at Fort McAllister.

Next day several vessels from the fleet came up to the fort, and landed officers from the navy and Foster's command, who were warmly received by Sherman's officers. Sherman had remained in consultation with Dahlgren and Foster until the 17th, when he and Admiral Dahlgren came up in the flagship Massachusetts.

We had opened a base on the Great Ogeechee, opposite Fort McAllister, and distant from either wing from five to fifteen miles. Several transports and vessels, and seven tons of mail matter, arrived at our new base.

The results of our campaign were more glorious than the most sanguine could anticipate. We had passed through in our march over forty of the wealthiest counties of Central Georgia; occupied over two hundred depots, county seats, and villages; captured about fifteen thousand negroes, — doubtful prizes, — about ten thousand head of cattle, horses, and mules; destroyed nearly two hundred miles of railroad, burned all the gins, cotton mills, and government property throughout the country; also about fifty millions worth of cotton and Confederate bonds and currency, besides supporting our army and cattle on the country.

SAVANNAH INVESTED. 289

CHAPTER XXIV.

EVACUATION OF SAVANNAH.—SURRENDER TO GENERAL GEARY.—
HIS JUST AND CONCILIATORY GOVERNMENT.—DESCRIPTION OF
THE CITY.

THE capture of Fort McAllister opened up communications with the fleet of supply ships waiting in Ossabaw Sound. Owing to the difficult channel of the Ogeechee, no stores were landed at King's Bridge before the 19th. From King's Bridge roads had to be corduroyed over the swamps and plantations to the different encampments.

Our lines were now pretty well closed up around Savannah. The 20th corps held the extreme left, with one brigade of Geary's on Hutchinson Island. Next came the 14th corps, then a gap of some miles of impassable land, covered only with pickets. Before the 15th and 17th corps intervened the flooded and almost impassable rice fields. A mile of these artificial lakes lay between us and the rebel lines. Hazen's division had crept up pretty well to the rebel works, even at this point.

The only approaches to the rebel lines confronting us are by the river road, the Charleston Railroad, and the Central Railroad, and wagon road which ran beside it.

All these were well guarded by intrenchments and redoubts, mounting several guns, which they kept continually firing along the different approaches. They even ran some guns up to our lines, on platform cars, puffed a few volleys, and then fell back.

There were some four or five mills on Hutchinson's Island, which were busily employed for the benefit of *le grande armée*, and particularly for the support of the negroes, who were quartered here, living on rice.

This is a low, swampy, miserable rice island, four miles long

25

and one broad, in the Savannah River. The shore around is low and marshy, liberally colonized by alligators.

Captain Viele, of General Geary's staff, went out on a reconnoissance to this island, in order to view the rear of the enemy's works. He struck upon a colony of escaped negroes, who hailed him as the savages did Captain Cook. In fact, Paul Rooney among the Cossacks never created such a sensation. They showered blessings, sweet potatoes, and rice indiscriminately upon him. They sang hymns, danced, and capered, and could scarcely believe their senses when told that they were free. I am afraid that the idea of freedom was a very vague one with most of them; their perception of it was something about changing places with their masters.

General Sherman had intimated to military commanders that the first one that would enter Savannah should be military governor. This helped to wake up the troops wonderfully. Men would build little platforms and bridges on logs, advancing them every night, or crawl along trees, until they approached within pistol range of the enemy, and pick them off from their guns.

On the 16th December, General Sherman addressed a note to Lieutenant General W. J. Hardee, demanding a surrender of Savannah and all it contained. Sherman was facetious, and concluded his demand with Hood's message for the surrender of Dalton, namely, "No prisoners being taken in case of a refusal." He informed Hardee that he had the city closely invested, and that there was no chance of its holding out.

Hardee replied next day to the effect that he had plenty of supplies and men, and could hold out as long as he chose.

The gunboats brought up plenty of ammunition to Sherman, a supply he rather needed; so he commenced preparations to bombard the town.

Six thirty-pound Parrotts landed from the Delaware and Sylph were placed in front of Corse's division, 15th corps, and in front of the 14th corps. They had plenty of pills with them, which they prepared to administer to the inhabitants; but Hardee changed his mind, and did not wait for the dose.

EVACUATION OF SAVANNAH.

Preparations had been made for assaulting the enemy's works on all sides. Dikes had been bridged in front, and everything got ready for a general assault.

Hardee, being fully apprized of the contemplated movement, took measures to evacuate the city.

On Monday afternoon he opened a fierce bombardment on our lines; all his guns were at work, and shot and shell fell fast and furious within our lines, but did little harm.

Few understood the object of these spiteful demons'rations, but the events of the following day made it clear. In the first place, they wanted to deceive us by a thundering show; in the second place, they wanted to expend a large portion of the ammunition they could not carry off.

Hardee evacuated on the night of the 20th December. After dark he threw his men, on rafts and steamboats, across the river to the South Carolina shore, and escaped up the Union Causeway, having first sent off all the able-bodied negroes, who had been collected in the city, under guard into South Carolina.

The night was dark, with a fierce gust of wind from the west, deadening the sounds of the wagons and tramp of the troops.

General Geary, commanding the 2d division, 20th corps, ever on the alert, holding the extreme left of the line, resting on the Savannah River, heard the movement crossing the bridge, and ordered his division under arms. At midnight General Geary, feeling convinced that they were evacuating the town, apprised General Sherman.

Geary advanced his pickets, who, meeting no opposition, pushed still farther, crawled through the abatis, floundered through dikes and ditches, scaled the first line of works, and found it deserted. General Geary pushed on his division, and was near the city, when Mayor Arnold, with five or six others, rode up, and formally and unconditionally surrendered the city, expressing a trust for the safety of the lives and property of the inhabitants.

General Geary received them kindly, giving them every assurance of protection in his power, and then entered the city first, despatching Captain Viele, of his staff, with four hundred men, to take possession of Fort Jackson, and another officer to General Slocum to inform him of the surrender. The officers and men could scarcely credit that General Geary was in Savannah. It was too startling news, too glorious news to be true.

At 8 o'clock in the morning all the enemy's works were in our hands. Captain Viele held Fort Jackson and Fort Barlow, finding about sixty heavy guns in them.

When our colors floated from the parapet of Fort Jackson, the ram Savannah, Commander T. W. Brent, which lay on the river, opened on the fort. The guns in the fort were all spiked; so General Geary had to wait for some pieces to come up to bring her to her senses.

General Geary's advance was quite on the heels of Hardee's rear guard. Hardee lost some guns and men in his hasty crossing.

Our losses during the siege were very small. About six hundred would cover all during the eleven days the town was invested, and about double that number since we started from Atlanta, — now one month and six days.

In Savannah we captured one hundred and forty-five pieces of ordnance, of different kinds and caliber, an immense quantity of ammunition, over thirty thousand bales of cotton, besides a large supply of rice, grain, stores, and supplies of different kinds.

Hardee had burned the government ship-yard, where a rebel ram was being built; this and other gunboats were destroyed. The iron-clad Georgia was sunk by its commander, and the Savannah, after kicking up a rumpus all day, and sailing up and down in mock defiance of our light guns, was blown up by her commander, who sent his crew on shore and fired the magazine.

First came a flash of light; then, as if from the crater of a volcano, an immense volume of flame shot up, illumining the heavens for miles; then came the fearful report, and the rebel ram Savannah was no more. The concussion was fearful, rocking the city and the vessels at anchor.

The Waterwitch, which was at Thunderbolt, was also destroyed on the night of the evacuation. She was under Acting Master Vaughan.

The Isonidago, Lieutenant R. D. Dalton, also the Macon and Resolute, gunboats, went up the river.

We captured the Samson, Lieutenant Marmaduke, and the Firefly, M. M. Skinner.

The navy, which the rebels had constructed at so much expense, added nothing to the defence of the town. It never amounted to anything, because the mouth of the Savannah was closed against their iron-clads. It was finally destroyed at their own hands.

When we entered the city we found few of the citizens in the streets. The poor classes were grouped around, apparently well pleased with the change, for they had nothing to lose, and had suffered much during the war.

In the first rush, several stores were broken open, and the straggling poor eagerly joined the soldiers in rifling them of their contents. This was soon put a stop to by General Geary, who immediately appointed a provost guard to protect and patrol the city. Indeed, there was not much in the stores to rifle, for on the night of the evacuation Wheeler's cavalry broke into them, carrying off everything of value, and throwing the remainder into the streets.

Wherever Wheeler's wild and reckless freebooters halted, a reign of terror commenced. They inspired a perfect dread among the inhabitants wherever they went. They rifled and plundered everything of value, and, if opposed, burned down the houses. Indeed, they were more dreadful to their friends than to their enemies.

General John W. Geary, commanding the 2d division, 20th army corps, commonly called the "White Star Division," was placed in command of the city.

He divided the city into two districts, the eastern and western, under command of Colonel Wood and Colonel Barnum.

They had a strong provost guard at their disposal, and were to see that order was preserved, and to perform all other duties belonging to their office, which they did with general satisfaction.

General John W. Geary has had great experience both as a soldier and as an executive officer. In his former character his name has been prominent before the country. In the latter capacity I mean to treat of him now.

He was long the alcalde of San Francisco, and subsequently mayor. His firm administration as governor of Kansas in troublous times helped much to tranquillize the disaffected there. He has firm administrative abilities, is a man of great force of character and resolution, and of a kind, accessible disposition. He patiently listens to the complaints and entreaties of all, but administers justice with a firm, impartial hand.

His government of Savannah gave great satisfaction; and when General Sherman was about commencing his campaign through Carolina, a deputation of the most respectable citizens waited on him, requesting that he would leave General Geary in command of the city. General Sherman could not well spare so active an officer from the field, and therefore declined.

The people learned to regret General Geary the more since his successor, General Grover, did little to conciliate the people, but much to dishearten them.

His rule gave a great deal of dissatisfaction; even tender ladies felt it so humiliating that they left the city.

A wiser and better man, Major General Steedman, now commands the department, and will, no doubt, do much to render fair and impartial justice to all parties.

The following were the officers of Geary's staff: —

Captain W. T. Forbes, A. A. A. G. and Chief of Staff.
Captain S. B. Wheelock, A. A. Ac.
Lieutenant Colonel A. H. Jackson, Inspector.
Captain Moses Viele, A. D. C.
Captain John J. Cantine, A. D. C.
Lieutenant W. C. Armor, A. D. C.
Captain G. L. Parker, Post Q. M.
Captain James Gillette, Post Commissary.

MEETING OF THE CITIZENS. 295

General Geary and the above officers will be long and kindly remembered in Savannah for their upright administration and courteous bearing to all parties.

Savannah soon became dull and quiet. All apprehensions on the part of the inhabitants wore away by degrees, and each day witnessed an increase of the citizens on the streets, surprised and gratified to find that no insults were offered, or wrongs committed by Federal troops. They found that the terrible stories of outrage and crimes committed by our army in captured cities were mere fables got up to fire the southern heart against the Federal army.

The falsity of these absurd and extraordinary stories has been proved by the conduct of our soldiers since their occupation of Atlanta.

While marching through the country, where military restraint cannot control all, excesses may be committed; but where military influence is concentrated, it is impossible for them to go unpunished.

The southern people now see the effects of their mad course. So much suffering has ensued, so many families have been bereaved, commerce has been so completely destroyed, and industry so paralyzed, that all sigh for a return to the old *régime*, or some one at least that will restore quiet and business activity.

The mayor convened a meeting at the Masonic Hall, which was well attended, and a committee was appointed to draw up resolutions giving expression to the sense of the meeting. The preamble embraced the sufferings of the people, and resolutions were passed submitting to the new order of things, among which was the following: —

Resolved, That we accept the position, and, in the language of the President of the United States, seek to have "peace by laying down our arms and submitting to the national authority under the constitution," leaving all questions which remain to be adjusted by the peaceful means of legislation, conference, and votes.

Such were the views of the leading men of Savannah; but General Sherman, in one of his special orders, defined for them clearly the line of policy he meant to adopt to meet the present emergencies. In his order he stated that "the city of Savannah and surrounding country will be held as a military post, and adapted to future military uses.

"During war the military is superior to civil authority, and where interests clash, the civil must give way; yet where there is no conflict, every encouragement should be given to well-disposed and peaceful inhabitants to resume their usual pursuits."

General Sherman's orders placed military interests paramount to all others.

He seemed anxious to consult for the civil as well as the military government of the city.

General John W. Geary issued a more generous and elaborate order for the government of the city, in which he said, —

"All public and private property will be protected; and wherever necessary for such purposes special guards will be assigned. No private property will be taken or used against the consent of the owners."

General Geary did all in his power to encourage the citizens at the same time to establish friendly relations towards the Federal government, and to make them feel that their interests were reciprocal. There was a great deal of poverty in Savannah at the time of its occupation. Even some of the most respectable families were suffering, and were forced to sell cakes and corn-dodgers to soldiers through their basement windows for a livelihood.

Rations of bread and meat were soon issued; and the north liberally responded to the wail for bread that came from the conquered city. Two ships, freighted with bread-stuffs and meats, soon steamed into the harbor with their precious cargoes.

A committee was appointed for their distribution, and the good work went on. General Geary and staff spared no exertions to alleviate the sufferings of the people.

Upright and just in the discharge of his duties, attentive to the wants and wrongs of the people, General Geary's short administration gained him a reputation for heroism and justice that will be long remembered in Savannah.

Description of Savannah.

Savannah is the largest and most important city in Georgia, and is situated on the south bank of the Savannah River. Previous to the war, it had a population of about sixteen thousand whites and twelve thousand blacks. It is built upon a sandy terrace, some forty feet above low-water mark.

It is a scattered kind of city, with wide streets, densely shaded with trees, and abundance of small shady parks or squares, of which it counts no less than twenty-four.

Some of the streets have four rows of trees, the centre being a grass promenade, with carriage drives on both sides.

It has some very fine buildings, such as the Custom House, the City Exchange, the State Arsenal, besides some very imposing churches, and other buildings.

There is a fine Doric obelisk erected to the memories of Generals Greene and Pulaski in Monument Square, opposite the Pulaski House. The corner-stone of this monument was laid by Lafayette in 1825.

Another very elegant monument to Pulaski stands in Chippewa Square.

This general, who was a distinguished Pole, fell in an attack on the city while occupied by the British in 1779.

Close by is the cemetery of Boneventure, a strange and solemn home of the dead, amidst the shades of the green forest trees, which look like so many gigantic mourning plumes fretted with their dark pendent moss. Many of these old tombs have now fallen into decay, and the tangled oaks, pines, and vines give the place something of a gloomy forest air.

Savannah was founded by General Oglethorpe in 1732, and was conspicuous during the war of independence.

It fell into the hands of the English in 1778, but was recovered in 1783.

Though the old mounds, and ditches, and forts of revolutionary times are now obliterated, new ones have sprung up in their place to excite the curiosity of other men and other times. Savannah is considered pretty healthy. The climate in winter is delightful.

The non-cultivation of the rice swamps around it have materially contributed to its sanitary condition. The country around Savannah is flat and sandy, — in some places barren, in others very fertile, — possessing a rich alluvial soil. The drives and walks about the city are very pleasant, shaded as they are by the bay, the magnolia, and orange trees.

There are a great many places of revolutionary interest around Savannah.

At Gibson's plantation, a battle occurred in 1782, between General Wayne and a body of Creek Indians, commanded by Garistersigo.

The British landed at Brewton Hill preparatory to their attack on the city in 1778. Its chief river is the Savannah, which divides Georgia from South Carolina and Alabama. The principal towns on this river are Augusta and Savannah, the latter eighteen miles from its mouth.

The head waters of the Savannah are, the Chattooga and Terrora, which unite and form the Tugalo. This makes a junction with the Kiowee, thus forming the Savannah.

Savannah has some important islands, the largest of which is Tybee, at its mouth, five miles long and three miles wide.

Near Savannah there are large swamp tracts, with luxuriant groves of oaks, and pines, and tangled vines, shrouded in that strange dark-gray moss which hangs in heavy bunches from branches, and stems, and trunks. The country along the river is flat and marshy, intersected by numerous sedgy inlets, bayous, and swamps, a fit home for the numerous alligators that inhabit these shores, and bask and sun themselves in perfect security among the tall reeds or sedgy grass.

They are not pleasant customers to come across, particularly if you chance to pick up a close acquaintance with a venerable gentleman some twelve feet long, who might, without any boasting on his part, claim to be that venerable individual "the oldest inhabitant of the place."

Savannah was strongly fortified, and with a well-provisioned garrison might withstand a large army for a long siege. The taking of Fort McAllister, on the Ogeechee, gave us a base and access to the city without encountering the works on the Savannah River.

Fort Pulaski, named after Count Pulaski, is a powerful, massive brick structure, and could mount one hundred and forty guns, though it had nothing like that number when captured.

It commanded the mouth of the river.

Fort Jackson, called after Governor Jackson, is on the south side of the city, distant about three miles. It had perfect command of the Savannah River. Besides these old works, the rebels occupied several others of their own construction. The city was strongly protected by intrenchments, forts, and redoubts, making, on the whole, a formidable place to attack.

CHAPTER XXV.

THE MARCH INTO SOUTH CAROLINA.—BUMMERS.—SHOOTING BLOODHOUNDS.—THE PETS OF THE ARMY.

WE now come to Sherman's last and crowning campaign through the Carolinas. While he remained in Savannah he was busily employed refitting the army and making proper dispositions of captured rebel property. By the middle of January he was ready to resume his march, but the broken state of the weather and other causes retarded it.

General Grant had sent Grover's division, of the 19th corps, to garrison Savannah, and had drawn the 23d corps, Major General Schofield commanding, from Tennessee, and sent it to reënforce the commands of Major Generals Terry and Palmer, operating on the coast of North Carolina.

Sherman's campaign through the Carolinas is not to be judged by hitherto recognized military rules or precedents, for he proved himself not only a great fighter and flanker, but also a great strategist. He inaugurated a new code of tactics, which completely bewildered and defeated the enemy. *He discarded the old, effete style of sitting down before natural barriers and fortified places, to take them by assault, or tire them out by siege. Had he done so, owing to the nature of the country over which he had to operate, his march would have been slow indeed. Discarding such movements, he swept over the country in separate columns, now throwing one ahead, now another, thus flanking the most formidable positions.

The opening campaign to Atlanta was through a country beset with natural obstructions of the most formidable kind, which Johnston knew too well how to improve.

Those we encountered through South Carolina, though of a

different nature, were no less difficult. True, we had no Buzzard Roost nor Kenesaw to scale, but we had to cross wide rivers, whose sedgy, oozy banks were covered for miles with dismal swamps. Through these we had to build roads or cross on single causeways, barely sufficient for four men abreast, and in many cases to dislodge an intrenched enemy at their heads.

After all the vaunting gasconade of the southern press and people, South Carolina prostrated herself at our feet even more than Georgia. They boasted, on the opening of Sherman's campaign, that the great Palmetto State would whip the pusillanimous Federals, though they were deserted by all the other states. Alas for human degeneracy, or rather human humbug! The Spartan State cringed before Sherman's legions. This state, that had hatched treason from the beginning, and had worked itself into such a fury at sight of the Yankee legions, has bitterly paid the penalty of her disloyalty. Her cities are in ruins; her plantations are devastated; her domineering aristocrats are houseless, homeless outcasts, scattered over the world, while a wail of anguish goes forth from her widows and orphans.

A new *régime* has been established. The *canaille* has risen to power on the necks of their lords and masters. The poor, whipped, scourged, despised slave is now his own master.

No general order had been issued by General Sherman relative to the campaign, as the special order on the opening of the Savannah campaign was still in force. All baggage and transportation were reduced to the lowest possible standard. Wall tents were prohibited, except as offices, and one for headquarters.

We started with about thirty days' rations and eight days' forage.

According to the plan, the army of the Tennessee was to take the right wing, — the 17th corps moving on the extreme right, and the 15th corps on the right centre, — taking up their line of march from their temporary encampments around Beaufort and Pocotaligo, along the roads between the Coosawhatchie and the Combahee Rivers.

The army of the Cumberland, under Major General Slocum, occupied the left, the 20th corps the left centre, and the 14th corps the extreme left, — both marching from Savannah, on the right of the Georgia Central Railroad, crossing at Lester's Ferry and Union Causeway, then keeping to the right until they formed a junction with the army of the Tennessee. Kilpatrick's cavalry operated partly in front and partly in flank of the left wing, extending well in on the river.

General Sherman travelled for the most part with the right wing.

As to Sherman's intentions and destination, they appeared a mystery to all. I believe he had no definite course laid down, for his movements were controlled by those of the enemy. Had he struck right for Charleston, the enemy could concentrate and mass in his front, thus retarding his march, and forcing him to a general engagement, which he did not wish to bring on; for he was too far from his base, and not in a position to care for his wounded. The same would hold good had he moved for Augusta, or any special place. He moved his army in four columns, each strong enough to resist any force the enemy could bring against it, yet moving near enough to concentrate, should a large force threaten either. Their separate movement foiled the enemy. They had to detach their forces to try and keep us in check. By Sherman's masterly movements they soon found themselves isolated and helpless. Sherman's object was first to destroy the network of railroads running through South Carolina, connecting Charleston with Richmond, Augusta, Columbia, and other important points. In this he fully succeeded, compelling them to evacuate Charleston, and rendering Augusta and other points of no military value to the enemy.

About the 16th of January the 17th corps and three divisions of the 15th corps were conveyed in transports from Savannah to Beaufort. The 17th corps proceeded to Pocotaligo Landing, where they had a slight encounter with the enemy, but soon took the fort, with the loss of a few men. Brevet Major General Corse, 4th division, 15th corps, took up his line of march with the left wing, which crossed the Savannah River at Sister's Ferry. It was also the intention to send the 3d division by land, across the Savannah River and an estuary of the sea at Union Causeway; but the flooding of the country by the heavy rains and freshets forced them to cross in transports. The same cause retarded also the general advance of the army, which was to take place about the 20th of the month. The fall of rain, which was the heaviest remembered in Savannah, flooded the whole country, converting it into one sea.

Some of the troops who had commenced their march were forced to bivouac on rice swamps and islands for several days, being unable to advance or retire. In some cases supplies had to be conveyed to them in boats. So intense was the flood that the country was covered over for miles. The men were up to their waists on the plantations, and the pontoons on the river were swept away; even some men and teams were lost. The 14th corps, and two divisions of the 20th corps, had fared in like manner. Geary's division remained in the city until he was relieved by Major General Grover, who now assumed command.

General Sherman transferred his headquarters to Beaufort on the 23d, and expedited the transportation of troops and supplies, the last of which had passed over by the 29th. His able chief quartermaster, General Easton, displayed his usual energy and zeal in furnishing transportation and forwarding troops and supplies.

On the 26th of January the 20th and 14th corps took up their line of march towards Sister's Ferry, along the Georgia side of the river.

On the evening of the 29th, the 17th corps, commanded by Major General Frank Blair, broke camp around Pocotaligo, and moved towards the Combahee River, resuming their march next day, on the right of the Savannah and Charleston Railroad, where they had some slight skirmishing with the rebel cavalry, whom they shelled out of the woods on the opposite side of the river.

The 15th corps, commanded by Major General John A.

Logan, took up their line of march along the Beaufort road, and encamped on the night of the 30th between the railroad and McPhersonville.

The army of the Tennessee rested on the 31st, to allow the left wing to come up, and also to have all delayed troops and supplies join their command.

Movements of the 17th Corps.

General Frank Blair broke camp near Pocotaligo Landing on the 30th of January, and moved on the Saltketcher road, on the south bank of the river.

On the 1st they continued their march, General Mower's division in advance, to Whippy Swamp Creek. Here the 9th Illinois infantry, Lieutenant Colonel Hughes commanding, skirmished sharply with the 3d South Carolina cavalry, driving them back on the main road towards the swamp. The causeway over the swamp was spanned by seven bridges, which the enemy had burned on their retreat, thus flooding the roads, and rendering them almost impassable with slashed trees. General Mower crossed his entire division (1st) over the swamp by wading, and over fallen trees, keeping up a fire all the time with the enemy. General Howard, Colonel William E. Strong, Lieutenant Taylor, and their orderlies, advanced to reconnoitre, when the rebels opened on them, badly wounding Lieutenant Taylor.

Next morning the whole column took up its line of march for Braxton Bridge, meeting the enemy's cavalry, who made a stubborn resistance. General Mower deployed his advance brigade; found Braxton Bridge burned by the enemy, and they occupying a strong position on the other side with three brigades of infantry and two batteries of artillery. General Mower left one regiment to skirmish with them there as a feint, and pushed the rest of his command for River Bridge, where he was joined by Colonel Hughes's cavalry, which engaged the enemy, making several spirited charges on their lines. In one of these Lieutenant Colonel Kirby, of General Blair's staff, had his horse killed, and was himself wounded in the leg. The rebels had been pressed so closely that they were not able to burn all the bridges crossing the numerous inlets to the Saltketcher. They commanded River Bridge with two pieces of artillery. Mower's skirmishers advanced close on the river, so as to command the enemy's works. Here Colonel Swayne, 43d Ohio, lost his leg by a shell.

The next morning General Giles A. Smith's division (4th) reconnoitred along the Saltketcher, above Braxton Bridge, for a position to cross, and finally succeeded by wading through a deep swamp. General Mower succeeded in crossing two brigades above River Bridge, thus turning the enemy's position. Heavy skirmishing continued all day, but the enemy fell back in the night.

General Logan moved on towards Beaufort Bridge, which he found destroyed by the enemy. This bridge crosses the Salkahatchie River near the church, on the Owensboro' road. Here we learned that the 20th corps, which was on our right, was within connecting distance, and that it had communication with the 14th corps, whose march had been considerably delayed by the bad state of the roads. They were well under way now, meeting but slight resistance from the enemy's cavalry. Kilpatrick's cavalry was advancing on the front and flank of the 14th corps.

Next morning, February 5, we crossed Whippy Swamp, encamping on the other side. Whippy Swamp is a dense marsh, of about one mile in breadth and several in length, well colonized by snakes and alligators. The rebels commanded this causeway by a strong intrenchment, with redoubt and lunettes. Here a regiment could keep a whole army at bay; but the movement of the 17th corps turned this strong natural position.

Our line of march now lay along the Savannah and Orangeburg road — the very road over which Marion marched during the revolutionary war.

Wheeler's cavalry, commanded by himself in person, made a vigorous stand near Orange Church, on the Little Salkahatchie. Their front was protected by a deep swamp, formed by the extension of the river, and easy of defense. Colonel Weaver's brigade, of General John A. Smith's division, deployed and charged right through the swamp, up to their hips in mud and water, and soon dislodged the enemy.

Wheeler had his headquarters in a house beyond the river the previous night. Sherman and Logan occupied it the following night.

About five miles above the Coosawhatchie Bridge the enemy occupied a redoubt in a curve of the river, which they had mounted with four guns. These considerably annoyed our right, but were silenced by our sharpshooters.

On February 1 we broke camp before day, marching along the McPhersonville road towards Hickory Hill.

The road was flooded in several places. The rebels had felled trees across these bayous, which were soon cleared off by our pioneers.

In front of our column the 29th Missouri mounted infantry and 7th Illinois, under command of Major Buckhart, kept pressing on the rebel videttes and skirmishers.

Major Buckhart rendered very efficient services all through with his command, in skirmishing with the enemy, ascertaining their position, and feeling their lines.

At Sand Hill the column halted for some time on Mr. Peoples's plantation.

Harris's brigade of Tennessee cavalry disputed our passage across the Coosawhatchie Bridge. Colonel W. H. Ross, chief of artillery, 15th corps, ordered up a section of the 12th Wisconsin battery, which shelled the woods, while our sharpshooters covered the bridge. Major Generals Sherman and Logan occupied the house of a Mr. McBride as their headquarters.

This place is at the head of the causeway that crosses the Coosawhatchie Swamp, and about thirty-five miles from Pocotaligo Landing.

We had some slight skirmishing in our front all day, the rebel cavalry making a feeble show of resistance. We met a few dead rebels along our line.

A few miles farther on, near Beech Branch, where we bivouacked for the night, was a splendid marble-fronted residence, belonging to a Mr. Bostick, who had been an extensive planter and slave-owner. He was said to have about one thousand slaves on his different plantations. He had taken all the able-bodied through the rebel lines, leaving but the young and infirm.

We now got into a rich tract of country. There were large clearings along the line of road, with some fine plantations and negro surroundings. Though the houses were mostly deserted, they were well stored with provisions, showing that their owners took French leave.

I had been lunching with Major General Hazen as General Sherman came round.

After some conversation, General Hazen, seeing a thick smoke, remarked, " There goes the bridge."

" I am sorry," replied General Sherman. Then, after gazing a few minutes, he exclaimed, " No, Hazen, no ; that's a house ; it is not the bridge. A bridge would not emit such a dense smoke."

He was right. It showed what an observer he was even of small things.

Generals Sherman and Logan had their headquarters at night near Duck Creek, on the Coosawhatchie. General Howard travelled with the 17th corps.

General Logan had some smart skirmishing with a cavalry brigade on our front, but finally dislodged them.

About 10 o'clock, on the morning of the 7th, the 29th Missouri mounted infantry struck the Charleston and Savannah Railroad at Banbury. This station is some fifteen miles west of Branchville, and nearly equidistant from Charleston, Augusta, and Columbia. We were so close on the rebels that they had to unload several cars of cotton. Major General Wood's division, which was in advance, immediately commenced tearing up the track, which they destroyed for several miles. About the same time the 17th corps struck it at Midway.

At Hamburg we burned about three hundred bales of cotton and some stores. We also captured a mail-bag. It contained several letters from soldiers to their friends, all in the most desponding tone.

On the evening of the 8th, General Hazen ordered General Jones's brigade (2d) out on a reconnoissance towards Cannon's Bridge, on the Edisto River, the enemy being intrenched on the other side. Three companies of the 54th Ohio were deployed as skirmishers. After wading through a dense swamp for about three hundred yards, they got to the edge of the river, and commenced skirmishing. This was intended merely as a feint.

Next day we reached this village, where we destroyed the track along our route, burned the railroad and several bales of cotton. Here Hazen's division diverged north, taking the Savannah and Augusta line; thence proceeding to Holman's Bridge, on the South Edisto.

The enemy were strongly intrenched on the opposite side of the river, and had burned the bridges in their front. The first brigade, Hazen's division, was sent down some distance as skirmishers. The 55th Illinois crossed the river considerably above the bridge, so as to strike the enemy's flank. They had to cross over on trees and floats, and then wade near a mile through a miserable swamp before they effected a lodgment.

Next morning I rode down to the bridge, where I found the hero of Fort McAllister — General Hazen — guiding the movements of his pioneers, who were felling trees for the troops to cross over. This had to be done for about a mile, as the swamp was at some places four feet deep.

The rebel defense was poor indeed. They had about three hundred infantry and some cavalry here; yet they made no stand before a handful of men, who had to wade across a swamp as best they could for about a mile.

On the evening of the 9th, the 17th corps succeeded in effecting a landing at Binneker's Bridge, where the enemy had been intrenched. General Mower had crossed below the bridge during the night, and pontooned the river and corduroyed the road. The rebel position being now turned, they retreated.

On the 11th Blair marched about eighteen miles, and skirmished with the enemy on the north fork of the Edisto, the enemy using artillery. They were strongly intrenched on the other side, and extended their flanks to correspond with ours.

On the 2d of February, when the right wing was fairly on its march, the left wing was trying to extricate itself from the mud and swamps around Sister's Ferry, and moved on to Lawtonville, which was burned by the 20th corps, when they went into camp on the evening of the 8th. Next morning they moved for Barnwell, which they left in ashes on the 11th.

Next day they tore up ten miles of the Charleston and Augusta Railroad, and on the 13th they crossed the South Edisto, and the following day the North Edisto. Up to this they had encountered no opposition from the enemy, except some slight skirmishing, which was carried on by our foragers. The 14th corps encountered a slight obstruction from the enemy near Lexington, and destroyed the most of that place.

Kilpatrick did not meet the enemy until his advance reached the river, near Barnwell, where a small force of the enemy kept him some time in check. Thence he moved for Blackwell, on the line of the Augusta and Charleston Railroad. Kilpatrick, learning that Wheeler, with a corps of cavalry, and Cheatham, with a corps of infantry, were cut off from the main rebel army at Branchville, being deceived by our feint on Augusta, marched along the line of railroad to Johnston Station.

Colonel Spencer, commanding the 3d brigade, encountered a large force of rebel cavalry under General Hagan. A very sharp engagement ensued, in which Colonel Spencer succeeded in repulsing the enemy and capturing three battle-flags, and a considerable amount of guns, sabres, and blankets.

On the 11th the cavalry struck Aiken, and encountered the enemy in force. The 2d brigade, under General Atkins, had been thrown out in advance, and met the enemy, Wheeler having massed his cavalry around Aiken.

The 92d Illinois and 9th Michigan cavalry made a stubborn resistance, but were subsequently driven back to Kilpatrick's main line, near Johnston Station. Here Kilpatrick remained in camp until the 13th, and then moved towards the South Edisto.

Nothing of great interest occurred until the 27th, save crossing the north fork of the Edisto River and the Saluda River. On that day, owing to the many reports concerning the capture and murder of men belonging to his command, General Kilpatrick arranged for an interview with General Wheeler, at Lancaster, in regard to an order from General Sherman, that prisoners in our possession should be shot in retaliation for the murder of our men by Wheeler. This answered a double purpose: first, giving an opportunity for a more perfect understanding relative to the alleged atrocities; second, causing the enemy to believe our point of attack to be Charleston.

The interview was very pleasant, considering the circumstances, and had the desired effect. Nothing was known of the murders by General Wheeler, and he positively asserted that no such thing had been committed by any organization of his command, and, furthermore, he would endeavor to learn if there were any truth in it.

There can be no denial of the assertion that the feeling among the troops was one of extreme bitterness towards the people of the State of South Carolina. It was freely expressed as the column hurried over the bridge at Sister's Ferry, eager to commence the punishment of "original secessionists." Threatening words were heard from soldiers who prided themselves on "conservatism in house-burning" while in Georgia, and officers openly confessed their fears that the coming campaign would be a wicked one. Just or unjust as this feeling was towards the country people of South Carolina, it was universal. I first saw its fruits at Rarysburg, where two or three piles of blackened brick and an acre or so of dying embers marked the site of an old revolutionary town; and this before the column had fairly got its "hand in."

At McBride's plantation, where General Sherman had his headquarters, the out-offices, shanties, and surroundings were all set on fire before he left. I think the fire approaching the dwelling hastened his departure.

If a house was empty, this was *prima facie* evidence that the owners were rebels, and all was sure to be consigned to the flames. If they remained at home, it was taken for granted that every one in South Carolina was a rebel, and the chances were, the place was consumed. In Georgia few houses were burned; here, few escaped; and the country was converted into one vast bonfire. The pine forests were fired, the resin factories were fired, the public buildings and private dwellings were fired. The middle of the finest day looked black and gloomy, for a dense smoke arose on all sides, clouding the very heavens. At night the tall pine trees seemed so many huge pillars of fire. The flames hissed and screeched, as they fed on the fat resin and dry branches, imparting to the forests a most fearful appearance.

Vandalism of this kind, though not encouraged, was seldom punished. True, where every one is guilty alike, there will be no informers; therefore the generals knew little of what was going on. The only cases I knew of theft being punished was on one or two occasions.

General Davis caught two soldiers stealing female apparel out of a house, leaving the family almost naked. He ordered the ruffians to be dressed out in the women's clothes, and made to march behind a wagon, tied to it, for six days, amidst the scoffs and jeers of the men.

General Geary caught a captain plundering a house; he took his sword from him and ordered him to be tied up behind a wagon. Major General Stanly caught a soldier coming out of a house with women's clothing; he gave him such a hearty application of his boot that the ruffian rolled head foremost into a deep sink-hole.

Captain Wiseman, of General Morgan's staff, detected a man taking the coverlets from a bed, and ordered him out, when the man seized his gun and turned on the captain, who drew his sword, parried the blow, and cut the fellow's ear off with one stroke. Had every officer done likewise, the respect and *morale* of the army would have been improved.

The ruined homesteads of the Palmetto State will long be remembered. The army might safely march the darkest night, the crackling pine woods shooting up their columns of flame, and the burning houses along the way would light it on, while the dark clouds and pillars of smoke would safely cover its rear.

Foragers and bummers heralded the advance of the army, eating up the country like so many locusts. These fellows, mounted on scraggy old mules, or cast-off horses, spread themselves in one vast advance guard, and oftentimes went twenty miles ahead of the main columns. They returned at night with strings of chickens, bacon, turkeys, and geese, embellishing themselves and their horses, or with a buggy or carriage, which they had borrowed from the owner, well laden with supplies.

Sometimes some adventurous youths, who had gone too far, to have the first haul, got captured, and most likely had their throats cut.

The bummers of different corps sometimes fought among one another about the spoils, and at other times fraternized together, in order to dislodge some troublesome enemy.

I was standing on the piazza of a plantation house, watching the burning dwellings around. The owner turns to me with an exultant look, and says,—

"There, I knew it would be so; I told the d—d fools it would come to that, but they only laughed at me. There is Jennings's mills on fire; well, serves him right; he was always preaching secession, the d—d scoundrel. I hope they will hang him! Then, there is Milken's house in a blaze, too; and there is Harrison's following them. I told them it would be so; but the fools laughed at me, and called me a Yankee. Well, now they know who was the fool, and I don't care a d—n how soon my own follows them."

A Teutonic member of the 9th Michigan cavalry walked into camp one day with a rebel prisoner. The captor was unarmed, while the prisoner had a rifle slung on his shoulder. On reaching headquarters, the Dutchman saluted, and said,—

"Captains, dere ish un brisner."

"Where did you get him?" inquired the adjutant general.

"Well, yer see, I was in der perginning of der fight, and gut cut off; and, without der gun or horse, hid in der swamp.

Pimepy, I sees der Shoney coming up; so I shust shumped pehind der tree to grab hims. Der tam fool didn't comes close ter nuff, an' I sheps out mit 'Surrender!' I shook hands mit him, and we made une compact to strike for ter camp; and, if it so pe we make rebel lines, I was to pe his brisner; and, if der were ter Unions lines, he is to pe mine brisner."

The story seemed so improbable that the rebel was appealed to, and confirmed the Dutchman's tale, merely adding, —

"I were tired of toting the gun, and wanted to sell out cheap for cash or hard tack."

I came up to a retired plantation house, just set on fire. The soldiers were rushing off on every side with their pillage. An old lady and her two grandchildren were in the yard alarmed and helpless. The flames and smoke were shooting through the windows. The old lady rushed from one to another, beseeching them at least to save her furniture. They only enjoyed the whole thing, including her distress. I turned to them, and said, —

"Boys, look at that poor, crazy woman, and those helpless children; you all have mothers, some of you children; think of them, and any of you that are men will follow me."

They did follow me, and soon a thousand dollars' worth of splendid furniture was rescued from the burning house. I was near losing my life in saving a photograph of her husband, which hung over the mantel-tree in one of the rooms on fire.

The word "bummer" has so often occurred in this work, that I think it well to give an account of the signification of the name. Any man who has seen the object that it applies to will acknowledge that it was admirably selected. Fancy a ragged man, blackened by the smoke of many a pine-knot fire, mounted on a scraggy mule, without a saddle, with a gun, a knapsack, a butcher knife, and a plug hat, stealing his way through the pine forests far out on the flanks of a column, keen on the scent of rebels, or bacon, or silver spoons, or corn, or anything valuable, and you have him in your mind. Think how you would admire him if you were a lone woman, with a family of small children, far from help, when he blandly inquired where you kept your valuables. Think how you would smile when he pried open your chests with his bayonet, or knocked to pieces your tables, pianos, and chairs, tore your bed clothing in three-inch strips, and scattered them about the yard. The bummers say it takes too much time to use keys. Color is no protection from these roughriders. They go through a negro cabin, in search of diamonds and gold watches, with just as much freedom and vivacity as they "loot" the dwelling of a wealthy planter. They appear to be possessed of a spirit of "pure cussedness." One incident of many will illustrate: A bummer stepped into a house and inquired for sorghum. The lady of the house presented a jug, which he said was too heavy; so he merely filled his canteen. Then taking a huge wad of tobacco from his mouth, he thrust it into the jug. The lady inquired, in wonder, why he spoiled that which he did not want. "O, some feller'll come along and taste that sorghum, and think you've poisoned him; then he'll burn your d—d old house." There are hundreds of these mounted men with the column, and they go everywhere. Some of them are loaded down with silver ware, gold coin, and other valuables. I hazard nothing in saying that three fifths (in value) of the personal property of the counties we have passed through were taken by Sherman's army.

It is strange what a fancy soldiers had for pets in general. It was no unusual sight to see a squirrel contentedly perched on a soldier's knapsack, as he trudged along, or to see an unhappy coon, led by a string at his side, timing march with him. As for chickens and roosters, they held secure possession on the wagons, evidently well contented with their lot, and assuming a great many swaggering airs. The hot blood, which the roosters vented all day in defiant crowing, was often allowed to cool at night; for if we got into camp in good time, dog and cock fighting enlivened the evening. Groups of officers were collected with two roosters in the centre, with erect feathers and defiant heads, sparring and fencing, until at length one of them lay quivering on the daisy, to the no small satisfaction of all parties present, except the defunct warrior and his backers.

Not far from this gentlemanly sport, you might see a larger group excitedly swaying around and crying out, "Stick to him bully!" "That's a good dog, Jeff!" and on looking you saw two great mastiffs, or bloodhounds, fiercely tearing one another. Speaking of dogs in the army, I must say that few bloodhounds were allowed to live, except some peculiar one that took the fancy of an officer. As for the general run of these animals, they were relentlessly shot down, the men simply remarking, "Here goes to spoil that 'ere dog's scent for Union prisoners or niggers;" and a bullet did for the poor brute.

As we came near deserted houses, it was pitiful to see the poor, half-starved cur go up to the men with a most melancholy countenance, as much as to say, "I have seen better days, but am now starving; just let me go along, and I will be a good, dutiful dog." Sometimes he gets a kick or a bullet for his confidence; at other times he is not noticed, and he strives hard to look as if he belonged to some one. He seems to know full well what it is to be nobody's dog there; the fate of others warns him, and he knows his fate is sealed if he is once detected to be an outcast. He will follow an officer who calls him, wag his tail as if it would twist off, appear most grateful, and would fain follow him to the end of the earth if allowed; if not, he slinks back, with a heavy heart, but with a cheerful look, as if he had met his master and was hunting up. He lives well on the offal of the camp, and if any one gives him protection he is all right; or if he can pick up a friendly acquaintance with some lucky dog, who claims a colonel or a captain for master, under his patronage he is sure to get along.

We also had a variety of poodle dogs, with collars and flossy hair, and screaming paroquets.

Seth had picked up a most interesting parrot. It was an educated and highly-trained bird. Polly did not like the change of owners, and freely expressed her dislike by calling every one that went by, "nasty fellow."

It was touching to hear her use some of her favorite expressions: "Papa, dear papa, come to tea;" "Welcome, Massa James;" and "Miss Lizzy, Polly is hungry, Polly is hungry."

The poor bird seemed to droop for the want of Lizzy's fostering care. Alas, where was Miss Lizzy now? Most likely a terrified outcast from home and friends. Where was "papa," or "Massa James," whether brother or lover? Perchance they are rotting beneath the shade of some pine tree, while the dear ones they cherished are without a protecting hand to guard them or food to support them.

I must here speak of another class of animals, which have been wretchedly abused in the army; I mean horses and mules. These noble brutes were flogged, kicked, cursed most unmercifully by rude teamsters, oftentimes for no offence at all, but to gratify the bad passions of their brutal masters.

If an officer or wagon master censured a teamster for any neglect, he was sure to revenge it on his mules. Should he loiter on his way, he made up the time by flogging and cursing the animals. Should his wagon get stuck, they were urged on by a stout hickory applied to their heads and ribs. I could tell you the disposition of a teamster by looking at his mules. If they were fleshy and cheerful looking, he was a kind master; if lean and dispirited looking, with straggling harness, he was a blaspheming, blustering bully. As for blaspheming, I often thought the teamsters had taken a special contract to do the swearing for the army. Indeed, I think they prayed in oaths. Though soldiers in general swear terribly, I assure you they could not hold a candle for our teamsters. Cavalry horses, too, have not been treated much better. They are ridden almost to death in search of booty through the country, and are soon used up and unfit for service.

I would suggest the propriety of establishing a regular veterinary corps, who should see that animals are properly treated.

As we picked up some of the first-blooded horses of the south, which, of course, are appropriated to Uncle Sam's use, or to the use of his officers, though some of them were with foal and had to be led, we could not help trying their mettle. Therefore, if we only halted a day, we were sure to get up a race, which was generally well attended. One of these came off in

Georgia, near a stream, with the enemy at one side and we racing at the other. It was a very exciting race, and bets were freely laid and taken; but as the enemy became spiteful, and did not seem to relish the thing, we had to deploy a heavy line of skirmishers along the stream to keep them amused, and prevent them from spoiling our fun.

27 *

CHAPTER XXVI.

DESCRIPTION AND APPEARANCE OF SOUTH CAROLINA.—VISIT TO WOODLANDS.

THE sea islands of South Carolina extend along the coast from Winyaw Bay to the Savannah River, and are composed of a rich, vegetable loam of great fertility, producing sea island cotton, corn, and rice. The orange tree and palmetto flourish among these islands. The tide flows a considerable way inward among the rivers, irrigating the immense extent of marsh land that borders the rivers. These lands, though unhealthy, are very valuable as rice plantations.

The region between the tide swamps and the sand hills of the middle country extends for nearly one hundred miles.

The river swamps here, too, are immense, extending in some places six miles in width, and are unfit for cultivation, but afford a safe retreat for water fowls and alligators. Across these dismal swamps our armies had to force their passage. Beyond these the sand-hill region extends for some thirty miles towards Columbia, and includes the extremes of sterility and fertility. The high, poor lands are covered with pitch pine, black jacks or dwarf oaks, while the low lands bordering the rivers produce corn, cotton, and rice in abundance.

The country extending from the sand-hill region to the mountains, some ninety miles, possesses a pretty uniform character. The surface is clay, covered for the most part with a rich soil, mixed with sand or granite. The rolling nature of this tract of country gives it rather a picturesque appearance. This tract extends along the Broad River, in York and Spartansburg districts. The mountainous country is confined to Pendleton and Greenville districts, and, though the soil is rather sterile, the country is pleasant and healthy.

At Woodlands, about one mile south of Midway, is the residence of the poet and novelist, Mr. Simms. It is an old-fashioned, unfinished brick building, with massive, ungainly porticos. It is a strange, castellated-appearing affair, with something of a weird look about it. Our skirmishers and foragers paid a hasty visit to Mr. Simms, and, as he was not at home, they thought they would do the honors of the house themselves, and fell to helping themselves liberally. On hearing this, Major General Frank Blair placed a guard over the place to protect the house, furniture, and fine library. Mr. Simms is a thorough, rabid secessionist, full of southern prejudices, and a fierce calumniator of northern character and institutions.

Mr. Simms's plantation is a good type of the lowland plantations of South Carolina. Since we left Savannah the country was one vast lowland plain. Large plantations, with their numerous surroundings, fringe the road, while behind the cultivated lands, — which, by the way, here as well as in Georgia, are converted into corn, instead of cotton fields, — the dark pine forests raise their evergreen heads. The cypress and wild vine, too, festoon the forest. In front of Mr. Simms's house are some venerable trees, beneath which the vine and cypress have formed fantastic bowers, with their delicate foliage and garlands of hanging moss. Not far from the residence is a dark, solemn swamp, formed by the expansion of the Edisto over the lowlands. This is full of fallen trees, Gothic arches of cypress and vines interlacing their branches in strange shapes, while the ever-pending moss waves its funereal-looking pall over the miasmatic, poisonous air of swamp lands. Here revel in secure enjoyment wild fowl, serpents, and alligators.

Such dismal swamps are frequent in Carolina, but chiefly abound along the sea coast from Savannah to Charleston.

The people of South Carolina, despite all their boasted chivalry, submitted to Yankee rule and usurpation with neither grace nor dignity. In Georgia, we had to respect the high-toned feeling of the planters, for they yielded with a dignity that won our admiration. In Carolina, the inhabitants, with a fawning, cringing subserviency, hung around our camps, craving a bit to eat, while our foragers disinterred barrels of pork and sweet potatoes around their premises.

In every instance the negroes have proved our friends, giving us valuable information relative to the enemy's movements; also acting as scouts and spies, informing us where the enemy had concealed their cattle, and the like. The poor, despised negroes looked upon our arrival as fulfilling the millennium — the days of "jubilon." In most cases they have been faithful friends, sheltering and feeding our prisoners, and giving us valuable information. They possess a large share of shrewdness, and take a more just view of the present struggle than we generally gave them credit for. They look upon the Yankees as their friends; on their old taskmasters, as their inveterate enemies.

A man named William Clark, formerly of Colonel Walford's cavalry, came into our lines. He was an escaped prisoner, and had been concealed for eight weeks by the poor negroes. He remained in the swamps by day, and joined his kind protectors at night. Though they would be liberally rewarded for betraying him, still they were faithful. We have always found the despised negro to act so. Their masters have lately tried to conciliate them. An old negro said to me, "Massa 'come so kind; though massa cross, he'd drink out of the same gourd with the poor nigger."

While halting at the plantation of a Mr. People, I had a quiet chat with an old, patriarchal negro.

Mr. People chanced to be at home, and all his young and old negroes crowded around, to gape and wonder at the much dreaded Yankee army. Among them was a venerable African.

"How do you get on, father?" I asked.

"Well, massa, dis 'ere nigger gets on poorly, as you see. Massa calls me a young man, and makes dis nigger work like a hoss."

"Has massa any money here?" asked some of the boys.

"Lots of dis 'ere dead money."

"Why do you call it dead?"

"Well, you see, if a hoss is cut, you call him 'ere wounded; if he is scotched terbly, he dies like dis 'ere moncy."

"How do you like the Yanks?" I asked the old African.

"Yeah, yeah! Yanks fine; not like the tallow-faced rebs look, who lib on corn coffee and swash all dere lives."

While the old African was making this philosophical distinction, I overheard a little picaninny whisper, —

"Mamma, the Yanks have good feet; not like de debbil, as massa says."

The planters told all sorts of absurd stories to their slaves about our men, to frighten them at our approach. They informed them that we were killing all the male children, and yoking the men and women as oxen, or selling them in Cuba.

A white slave came into our lines and reported to General Logan. His name is James Le Roach, of French descent by his father. His great grandmother was a pretty Indian girl, and reared by a Mr. Torrens, by whose son she had a daughter, who was sold to a Mr. Western, of Charleston, who had a daughter by her. The latter was the mother of our slave, and kept in servitude by her half sister, a Mrs. Smith, who afterwards sold both mother and children to heartless traders, who trafficked them over the country. This man was about forty years of age, slight build, long, sandy hair and whiskers, and evidently without a particle of African blood in his veins; yet he was the bondman of his kinsman.

Plate and valuables were buried everywhere — out in the swamps, in the beds of streams, under newly-made flower gardens, and even in graves. In no place were they safe from the prying Yankee or traitorous slave.

The graves were even ransacked, and though sometimes the coffins yielded golden treasure, at other times a decomposing corpse, perhaps a woolly negro, rewarded the sacrilegious gold seekers.

The following very amusing incident, showing how a Yank was outdone, came under my own observation.

Some soldiers were foraging round a house owned by some pretty secesh ladies.

One of the men, seeing the earth in the garden freshly turned up, asked, "What is buried there?"

"Nothing," was the reply.

"You can't come it over a Yank that way. I guess I'll find something worth looking after here."

He fell to digging, the lady appearing quite distressed, and requesting that he would desist. This only fired his cupidity, and he dug the more vigorously, until he had got down some six or eight feet. He would not even suffer any of his comrades to help him, claiming the whole as his perquisite.

It chanced to be an old well that had recently been closed up. At length the young girl told those looking on, when a good laugh was had at his expense. He got up, put on his coat, and made tracks, using very strong language to soothe his injured feelings.

I inquired of an old lady who was intently gazing at us whether she ever saw any Yankees before. "O, yes; we often seen your fellows with a pack on their backs, or with a monkey and organ!"

On the 11th of February, all the army was on the railroad from Midway to Johnston's Station, thereby dividing the enemy's forces, which still remained at Branchville and Charleston, on the one hand, and at Aiken and Augusta, on the other.

The 17th corps crossed the south fork of Edisto River at Binneker's Bridge, the 15th at Holman's Bridge.

The approaches to this river were protected by the usual swamps, trees, and brush. We had ascertained from one of General Logan's orderlies, who had been captured, and was afterwards recaptured by the 29th Missouri mounted infantry, that the enemy were intrenched along the north-east bank. We had also ascertained that these works were guarded by Chalmers's brigade. Early in the morning, General Logan ordered General Hazen to feel the enemy at Shilling's Bridge.

The 2d brigade, Colonel Well Jones, at once proceeded to try the passage here.

The 111th Illinois and 53d Ohio deployed as skirmishers, and after wading through the swamp up to their waists, they opened a sharp fire on the rebels, which was briskly responded to.

The 47th Ohio had gone up the river some distance, and not finding the enemy there, crossed over on rafts, while Colonel Theodore Jones's brigade (the 1st) had been equally successful some miles lower. At the same time General Blair's corps (the 17th) was striving to effect a crossing in front of Orangeburg. The enemy had a section of artillery here, which opened upon them. Soon, finding that we had crossed on their flank, and were threatening their rear, they retreated at all points. Our loss was only two killed, and about six wounded. Hazen's division captured about fifty prisoners; the 17th corps some more.

About four o'clock the head of Blair's column entered Orangeburg.

Orangeburg is on the Columbia branch of the South Carolina railroad, ninety-seven miles from Charleston, and forty-seven from Columbia. It had been a pretty place before the war, and had a population close on two thousand. It was built upon a rising bluff, one of the first we met since we left Savannah. It possessed some historic relics of the revolutionary war. It was formerly looked upon as a healthy, pleasant retreat, and was, therefore, rather a fashionable little place.

When I reached the city, it was in flames. Our men say that they found several houses, in which cotton was stored, on fire when they entered it. Be this as it may, the whole town was soon in flames, and by the following morning one heap of ashes.

The tasteful churches, with their tall steeples, and about fifty private houses, alone escaped. A large amount of cotton was also consumed. It was a sad sight next morning to witness the smoking ruins of the town, the tall, black chimneys looking down upon it like funeral mutes, and to see old women and children, hopeless, helpless, almost frenzied, wandering amidst the desolation.

The Orphan Asylum is somewhat in the rear of the town, and then contained over two hundred children. It is a branch of the Charleston House. During my visit there, the children went through their exercises, — sang songs and hymns in a most creditable manner. It was presided over by a New York lady, — A. R. Irving, — a very sensible lady, who talked freely about the present troubles. Her sympathies were with the south. She felt very keenly for her helpless charge, now that the railroads are torn up, and the country devastated. She saw nothing but starvation before them. Alas! I could not hold forth one ray of hope to her.

Our columns were now fast closing in about Columbia. We averaged, at this time of our march, nearly fifteen miles a day. Sherman had deceived the rebels. Those in Augusta were completely cut off by the destruction of the Charleston line. Those at Branchville were also bewildered as to our movements.

After the capture of Orangeburg, our troops made a rapid march, meeting but little opposition from the enemy, until they approached Little Congaree Creek. Here they seemed resolved to make a stand. Logan's corps had marched through by-roads until they struck the state road, near Sandy Run. Blair's corps had followed the state road from Orangeburg, and formed a junction with the rear of the 15th corps at Sandy Run post office.

Major General Wood's division (1st) had the advance, and skirmished with the enemy for some time, driving them back behind the creek. Here they were strongly intrenched, and commanded the bridge by a section of artillery; besides, their left was protected by the Congaree River, while a deep stream, with soft, marshy banks, lay in their front.

A regiment waded the river on their right and left, compelling the enemy to give up their position. Our skirmishers pressed so closely on them, that their cavalry wheeled round and charged them, but were speedily repulsed.

Their artillery kept up a continuous fire all night on Major General Hazen's headquarters and command, wounding several, and taking the leg off of one of Colonel Jones's staff officers, in his quarters.

Early on the morning of the 15th, Major General Hazen threw forward his skirmishers, and ascertained that the enemy had fallen back behind the Congaree, burning the fine bridge that spanned the river just on the edge of Columbia. Hazen had now occupied the front with detachments from his command. Major Generals Howard, Logan, Blair, and others rode to the front, to join Hazen and reconnoitre the position, though the rebel battery was sweeping the road with round shot and canister.

Colonel Ross, chief of artillery, 15th corps, ordered up Captain De Grass's battery. This splendid battery, under its dashing young captain, took up position, and silenced the rebel battery that commanded the road. A section was placed close to the bridge, so as to sweep the streets of the city, which were crowded with soldiers, citizens, and wagons, clearing out of the town.

The shells soon burst among them, making them file right and left in double quick time. Captain Zickerick's 12th Missouri battery, and also some guns from the 17th corps, soon took up position on a commanding hill, and opened on the trains that were leaving the depot. We were within five hundred yards of the city, which was situated on a rising bluff on the other side of the river, so that we could smash it to pieces in a short time by bringing sufficient artillery to bear on it. It appeared to be Sherman's intention to shed as little innocent blood as possible.

We expected every moment that the city would be surrendered, for it now lay hopelessly in our power. About nine o'clock General Sherman and staff arrived; also Generals Blair and Slocum. As the rebels seemed inclined to defend the place to the last, and as the river at this point, from its wide and rapid nature, did not appear favorable for pontooning, General Hazen ordered General Oliver to send his brigade to Saluda, and try and effect a crossing near that village, and, if possible, to save the bridge.

General Oliver sent forward the 99th Indiana and 15th Michigan, but found that the bridge had been burned. After some skirmishing, General Hazen, in person, ordered men to cross over in boats and on rafts, which they succeeded in doing without any loss.

While this was taking place, our mounted infantry, comprising the 29th Missouri and 7th Illinois, dashed into Saluda, a small village on the banks of the Saluda River.

This place contained the Columbia Mills, the largest manufactory in the south, and gave employment to about four hundred hands, chiefly females. Near the village is one of the prison camps of our men, and called Sorghum Camp, as this article composed their chief diet. It was situated on a sandy bluff. The huts were formed of logs, their sides thickly covered with earth. Here they had no fire, as was evident from the absence of chimneys, and the appearance of the woods around. As several succeeded in escaping from this, they were removed to the Asylum enclosure for security. As I intend giving a detailed account of the sufferings of these martyrs of the Union, I will now pass over the subject. It was sad to see in Saluda groups of female operatives weeping and wringing their hands in agony, as they saw the factory, their only means of support, in flames. It is truly said, " War is a cruelty." Neither can it be refined ; for the innocent suffer for the crimes of the guilty.

Towards evening we had pontooned and crossed the Saluda, and charged the rebels across the tongue of land which separates it from Broad River. Though our men were close upon them, they succeeded in burning the bridge, having covered it over with combustible matter. Towards morning two regiments of Colonel Stone's 2d brigade, Mower's division, 17th corps, crossed the river in rafts and boats.

General Logan selected a narrow point of the river, where some men crossed over in boats, the men on our left moving down on the rebel sharpshooters.

It was a lovely sight ; the morning sun rose glowing and beautiful, its sparkling rays lighting up the house-tops of the doomed city, and dancing over the bright waters like diamond gems, bathing the river with its silvery rays. The shadows of the forest trees advanced along the sparkling waters as the boats shot over its surface, and the click of the rifle and whir of the bullet echoed around.

The engineers at once proceeded to lay the pontoons, while the high bluff on the margin was crowded with officers and men. There was General Sherman, now pacing up and down in the midst of the group all the time, with an unlit cigar in his mouth, and now and then abruptly halting to speak to some of the generals around him. Again he would sit down, whittle a stick, and soon nervously start up to resume his walk. Above all the men I have ever met, that strange face of his is the hardest to be read. It is a sealed book even to his nearest friends.

Sitting on a log beside him was Howard, reading a newspaper, and occasionally stopping to answer a question of Sherman's, or make a comment on some passage.

Howard always looks the same — the kind, courteous general, the Christian soldier.

Another of the group was Frank P. Blair, with his strongly-marked features, indicative alike of talent, energy, and ability.

John A. Logan, too, was there, with his dark, almost bronzed countenance, and fiery, commanding eye, the true type of the dashing general.

Not least was General Hazen, the hero of McAllister, with his frank, expressive features, and finely-moulded head, betokening the warm-hearted gentleman, the soldier of mind and brains.

These, with several other generals, with a host of gay officers and orderlies in the background, formed a group worthy the pencil of a Rubens or Vandyke.

Colonel Stone's brigade were now advancing on Columbia, and when within about two miles of it, he met the mayor, Mr. Goodwin, and three members of the City Council, coming out in a carriage to surrender the town.

Colonel Stone, Major Anderson, of the 4th Iowa, and Captain William B. Prett, aid-de-camp of General Logan's staff, and several other officers, proceeded with the deputation into the city, when the mayor delivered up the keys, and made a formal surrender. The 13th Iowa, Colonel Kennedy, claims to be the first to hoist the stars and stripes upon the old capitol, where the first ordinance of secession originated. The 31st Iowa claims the honor likewise. However, the 13th Iowa was the first official flag that floated from it.

As soon as the pontoon was laid, General Sherman, accompanied by several other generals, their staffs and orderlies, forming a brilliant cavalcade, rode into the city amidst a scene of the most enthusiastic excitement. Ladies crowded the windows and balconies, waving banners and handkerchiefs. They were the wives and sisters of the few proscribed Union people of Columbia. As for the rich, haughty secessionists, they had all fled. Negroes were grouped along the streets, cheering, singing, and dancing in the wild exuberance of their new-born freedom. Perhaps the most flattering compliment paid to us was by a negro, whom, with upturned features and clasped hands, I heard exclaim, "At last! at last! our saviours!" Ringing cheers and shouts echoed far and wide, mingled with the martial music of the bands as they played "Hail, Columbia," "Yankee Doodle," and other national airs. It was, indeed, an exciting scene, and one well worth living to witness.

Our march through the city was so orderly that even the southerners began to bless their stars that the reign of terror was over, and that a reign of peace and security, like that at Savannah, was about being inaugurated. Alas that the scenes of the night should mar so auspicious a beginning!

CHAPTER XXVII.

DESCRIPTION OF COLUMBIA.—THE CITY ON FIRE.—DREADFUL SCENES IN THE STREETS.—WHO IS RESPONSIBLE.—SUFFERINGS OF THE PLANTERS' FAMILIES.

COLUMBIA, the capital of South Carolina, is one hundred and twenty-eight miles from Charleston by railway. It has been a beautiful city, situated just at the conflux of the Saluda and Broad Rivers, which form the Congaree. It was famed for its fine public buildings, its magnificent private residences, with their lovely flower gardens, which savored of Oriental ease and luxury. It is hard to conceive a city more beautifully situated, or more gorgeously embellished, with splendidly shaded walks and drives, with flowers, shrubberies, and plantations. Birds of splendid plumage sang and sported in its gardens under the delicious influence of the sunny skies.

The city was laid out in 1787, and had rapidly increased in beauty and population, the latter amounting to about ten thousand previous to the war. Most of its stores and public buildings were of brick, while most of the private residences were framed, neatly painted, with piazzas hanging with plants and creepers. Its churches, insane asylums, colleges, and other public buildings were very fine. The new capitol, built of fine granite, would be a magnificent building if completed. Columbia College, the Alma Mater of the Tazewells, the Barnwells, the Rhetts, the Hamptons, and other distinguished men, is a splendid educational establishment. The Park is a lovely promenade, while the private residences are unsurpassed in the elegance of their finish, the beauty of their grounds, and the luxury of their fittings. A spell of ease and voluptuous luxury seemed to pervade the place. Flowers, pictures, statuary, select libraries, all that the arts and sciences could contribute, adorned its halls and private residences. In the house of General John C. Preston, formerly United States minister and senator, where General Logan had his headquarters, I have seen works in literature, painting, and statuary, that would enchant a savant. In the basement, in a box unpacked, was a Venus, of Italian marble and finest workmanship, worth, at least, from ten to fifteen thousand dollars. As General Logan gave orders not to have the house burned, I hope it has escaped. Woodlands, the residence of General Wade Hampton, was a magnificent place, but has been burned down by our soldiers. He is married to Preston's sister. It is no wonder that Eve was discontented in Paradise, when a people with so much to gratify the most epicurean tastes rebelled.

The rebels left forty-five pieces of artillery, fifteen locomotives, immense government stores, of all kinds, besides a large amount of cotton. Piles of cotton were burning along the streets, but a great deal was yet untouched. I understand there were no fewer than nine generals and the governor in Columbia just a few hours before our occupation. These included Johnston, Beauregard, Hampton, Wheeler, and Butler. They were expecting, up to the last moment, to be reënforced by Lee's troops from Branchville, and Dick Taylor's from Augusta. Besides, hearing of Sherman's army threatening Augusta and Branchville, they thought there was nothing but a small raiding party marching on Columbia. They little knew how they were out-manœuvred, baffled, and isolated.

I spent the evening in the capitol looking over the archives and libraries. Part of Colonel Stone's brigade — I think the 13th Iowa, Colonel Kennedy's regiment — was on duty there.

Towards night, crowds of our escaped prisoners, soldiers, and negroes, intoxicated with their new-born liberty, which they looked upon as a license to do as they pleased, were parading the streets in groups.

As soon as night set in there ensued a sad scene indeed. The suburbs were first set on fire, some assert by the burning cotton which the rebels had piled along the streets. Pillaging gangs soon fired the heart of the town, then entered the houses, in many instances carrying off articles of value. The flame soon burst out in all parts of the city, and the streets were quickly crowded with helpless women and children, some in their night-clothes. Agonized mothers, seeking their children, all affrighted and terrified, were rushing on all sides from the raging flames and falling houses. Invalids had to be dragged from their beds, and lay exposed to the flames and smoke that swept the streets, or to the cold of the open air in back yards.

The scene at the convent was a sad one indeed. The flames were fast encompassing the convent, and the sisters, and about sixty terrified young ladies, huddled together on the streets. Some of these had come from the north, previous to the war, for their education, and were not able to return. The superioress of the convent had educated General Sherman's daughter Minnie. He had assigned them a special guard of six men; so they felt secure, and were totally unprepared for the dreadful scene that ensued. Some Christian people formed a guard around this agonized group of ladies, and conducted them to the Park.

I trust I shall never witness such a scene again — drunken soldiers, rushing from house to house, emptying them of their valuables, and then firing them; negroes carrying off piles of booty, and grinning at the good chance, and exulting, like so many demons; officers and men revelling on the wines and liquors, until the burning houses buried them in their drunken orgies.

I was fired at for trying to save an unfortunate man from being murdered.

The frequent shots on every side told that some victim had fallen. Shrieks, groans, and cries of distress resounded from every side. Men, women, and children, some half naked, as they rushed from their beds, were running frantically about, seeking their friends, or trying to escape from the fated town. A troop of cavalry, I think the 29th Missouri, were left to patrol the streets; but I did not once see them interfering with the groups that rushed about to fire and pillage the houses.

True, Generals Sherman, Howard, and others were out giving instructions for putting out a fire in one place, while a hundred fires were lighting all round them.

How much better would it have been had they brought in a division or brigade of sober troops, and cleared out the town, even with steel and bullet!

General Wood's 1st division, 15th corps, occupied Columbia. Colonel Stone's brigade was the first to enter the city and hoist the flag over the capitol — enviable notoriety, had not the drunken, riotous scenes of the night sullied its honor.

This scene continued until near morning, and then the town was cleared out, when there was nothing more to pillage or burn.

In the hospitals were some hundreds of rebel wounded. The agony and terror of the poor, helpless fellows while the fire raged around them were fearful; but, fortunately, the buildings did not catch fire.

While the streets were crowded with murdering groups of demons from all the corps in the army, hundreds of noble-minded officers and civilians were exposing their own lives to save the lives and property of the citizens.

Who is to blame for the burning of Columbia is a subject that will be long disputed. I know the negroes and escaped prisoners were infuriated, and easily incited the inebriated soldiers to join them in their work of Vandalism. Governor McGrath and General Wade Hampton are partly accountable for the destruction of their city. General Beauregard, the mayor, Mr. Goodwin, and others wanted to send a deputation as far as Orangeburg to surrender the city, and, when evacuating, to destroy all the liquors. In both of these wise views they were overruled by the governor and Wade Hampton, the latter stating that he would defend the town from house to house.

On the other hand I must honestly say that I saw nothing to prevent General Wood, who was in command there, from bringing sufficient troops to clear out the place, or his superior generals either from putting a stop to such disgraceful scenes.

The houses of the Prestons, Honystons, and other wealthy

secesh were occupied as official quarters, and were preserved. Several soldiers and citizens must have been buried in the ruins of falling houses, or caught by the devouring flames. Next morning I saw a lady, a crazy inmate of the asylum, whose child had been burned during the night.

The 18th of February dawned upon a city of ruins. All the business portions, the main streets, the old capitol, two churches, and several public and private buildings were one pile of rubbish and bricks. Nothing remained but the tall, spectre-looking chimneys. The noble-looking trees that shaded the streets, the flower gardens that graced them, were blasted and withered by fire. The streets were full of rubbish, broken furniture, and groups of crouching, desponding, weeping, helpless women and children.

The Park and Lunatic Asylum, as affording the greatest chance of safety, were crowded with these miserable outcasts. In one place I saw a lady richly dressed, with three pretty little children clinging to her. She was sitting on a mattress, while round her were strewn some rich paintings, works of art, and virtu. It was a picture of hopeless misery surrounded by the trappings of refined taste and wealth. General Sherman ordered six hundred head of cattle and some stores to be left for the nuns and the destitute.

The scene of desolation the city presented next morning was fearful. That long street of rich stores, the fine hotels, the court-houses, the extensive convent buildings, and last the old capitol, where the order of secession was passed, with its fine library and state archives, were all in one heap of unsightly ruins and rubbish. Spendid private residences, lovely cottages, with their beautiful gardens, and the stately rows of shade trees, were all withered into ashes.

The ruins alone, without the evidences of human misery that everywhere met the view, were enough to inspire one with feelings of deep melancholy.

The ruins of Pompeii and Herculaneum deeply impress the mind, and make it reflect the days of their glory and splendor before the molten tide of lava shrouded them.

Here was desolation heightened by the agonized misery of human sufferings.

There lay the city wrapped in her own shroud, the tall chimneys and blackened trunks of trees looking like so many sepulchral monuments, and the woe-stricken people, that listlessly wandered about the streets, its pallid mourners.

Old and young moved about seemingly without a purpose. Some mournfully contemplated the piles of rubbish, the only remains of their late happy homesteads.

Old men, women, and children were grouped together. Some had piles of bedding and furniture which they saved from the wreck; others, who were wealthy the night previous, had not now a loaf of bread to break their fast.

Children were crying with fright and hunger; mothers were weeping; strong men, who could not help either them or themselves, sat bowed down, with their heads buried between their hands.

The yards and offices of the Lunatic Asylum were crowded with people who had fled there for protection the night previous.

Its wards, too, had received new subjects, for several had gone crazy from terror, or from having lost their children or friends in the flames.

The churches were full of people, who had crowded into them for shelter. · The Park was sought as a refuge, and in one corner of it the helpless nuns and their timid charges were huddled together. Most of the young ladies were from the north.

They had been sent to school there before the breaking out of the war, and were not able to return. The nuns supported them all through, though not able to get remittances from their friends. In this they were aided by generous people in the south.

These young ladies felt bitterly the treatment of those calling themselves their friends, as they saw their convent in flames, and soldiers rushing through the fire after pillage.

Sunday was a day of quiet in the city. The Sabbath bells tolled from the few churches remaining; but there was something solemn and melancholy in their chime, and sorrowing hearts knelt to the Lord for hope and comfort.

Some men of the 63d Illinois were detailed to cart the ammunition from the rebel arsenal to the river. When pitching the boxes into the water, they let one fall, which exploded, igniting the whole wagon load of shells, killing four men and wounding twenty. Among the killed was Captain Davis, Company F.

Some of our men, escorted by negroes and escaped prisoners, paid a visit to a noted ruffian, a second Legree, who kept a pack of bloodhounds for the purpose of hunting down negroes and escaped Union prisoners. The boys disposed of his dogs, as they have done with all the bloodhounds they come across, burned down his house and place, then tied himself to a tree, and got some strapping negroes to flog him, which they did with a will, repaying in the *lex talionis* style.

The scenes I witnessed in Columbia — scenes that would have driven Alaric the Goth into frenzied ecstasies, had he witnessed them — made me ponder a little on the horrors of war.

Those who are unacquainted with war cannot realize the fearful sufferings it entails on mankind. They read of it in papers and books, gilded over with all its false glare and strange fascinations, as a splendid game of glorious battles and triumphs, but close their eyes to its bloody horrors. The battle-field is to them a field of honor, a field of glory, where men resign their lives amidst the joys of conquest, which hallow the soldier's gory couch and light up his death-features with a smile. This sounds well in heroic fiction, but how different the reality! Could these fireside heroes but witness a battle-field, with its dead, its dying, and wounded, writhing in agonizing tortures, or witness the poor victims under the scalpel-knife, with the field-hospital clodded with human gore, and full of the maimed bodies and dissected limbs of their fellow-creatures, war would lose its false charms for them. Could many a tender mother see her darling boy, uncared-for, unpitied, without one kind hand to stay the welling blood or wipe the death-damp from his brow, her gentle, loving heart would break in one wail of anguish. War, after all, has horrors even greater than the battle-field presents. The death-wound is mercy compared to the slow torture of languishing in prison-houses — living charnel-houses of slow putrefaction — pale, spiritless, uncared-for, unpitied, gasping and groaning away their lives in hopeless misery. And then think of the sacked and burned city; think of helpless women and children fleeing in terror before the devouring element, without a home to shelter them, without bread to feed them; think of the widows and orphans that water their scant bread with the tears of sorrow; think of all the sufferings, misery, ruin, death, war entails on mankind, and you will curse its authors, and wish that God had otherwise chastised his people. Though war may enrich the Shylock shoddies, paymasters, contractors, and speculative politicians, who sport gorgeous equipages and rich palaces out of the blood of their countrymen, it crushes the people under its wheels, like the car of Juggernaut, and oppresses the millions with taxation.

From the prisoners who escaped at Columbia we heard some fearful accounts of their ill treatment.

Private individuals showed that charity is universal by attending them under all risks. They spoke in the highest terms of the attendance of the Sisters of Charity in the different bastiles. The ill treatment of our prisoners is the greatest blot on the reputation of the south.

I give the following short account from an officer; and *ex uno disce omnes:*—

"Lieutenant Meyer was captured at Point of Rocks, Maryland, on June 17, 1863, two days after the battle of Winchester. From this he and several other officers and privates were marched back to Winchester, by way of Staunton, thence to Richmond, and was consigned to Libby Prison, where he was detained for eleven months. It is needless to detail the elegancies of Libby life, of which he fully partook. On the 4th of May, 1864, he, in company with about a thousand others, were transferred to Danville, Virginia, where they remained but four days. Thence they were sent to Macon, where they arrived, after nine days' travelling on filthy cattle-cars, on the 18th. Here they were confined to the stockade, on the usual allowance of short rations, dirt, and neglect. At this time there were about fourteen hundred officers, and the following five generals, prisoners there: Brigadier Generals Hickman, Thellon, Wessel, Scammon, and Seymour, all of whom have since been exchanged. On the 28th day of July they were sent to Charleston, where they arrived next day. Here they were consigned to the city jail, with convicts and women of loose character. Here they were detained fifteen days, and transferred to Roper Hospital, where their treatment was pretty good. The Sisters of Charity attended them here, bringing the sick delicacies, such as fruits, fowls, and the like. Here they could see the flashes of the guns from James Island, and two shells struck the building.

"On the 4th of October, about twelve hundred were transferred to Columbia, and placed in a camp near Saluda Factory, two miles from Columbia. Here they were placed right down in the woods, without a hut or tent of any kind. After two weeks they were supplied with some tools, with which they made huts of logs, with their sides covered with earth. While here, several died from want and exposure, and three were killed while trying to make their escape, one of whom was Lieutenant Eikaws, 2d New Jersey. While here, a rebel officer kept six bloodhounds at the headquarters. They were regularly drilled every morning, in presence of the men, and often exercised in hunting down and capturing escaped prisoners. One morning the dogs came down to the well where the men got their water. Here they seized them and cut their throats, and threw them into a deep hole. When they were discovered, the officer remarked, 'Yankees will suffer for this.' After this our officers were shot.

"While at Charleston and Columbia, two Shylock brothers, named Quinby and Potter, took bills of exchange by power of attorney — for gold, five for one; for greenbacks, two for one. We were glad to enter into this swindle, in order to save life. Their bill of fare here was: Five pints of corn meal, two spoonfuls of rice, two spoonfuls of salt, and one pint of wretched sorghum molasses. These were the rations issued for five days. They did not get soap enough to wash their hands, not to speak of their clothes. So many had effected their escape from this place, we were transferred to the Lunatic Asylum enclosure, which was a large yard with a high brick and stockade fence sixteen feet high. Here we built twelve houses, each house containing thirty-six men. They then stopped supplying us with lumber; so the remainder of the officers had to manage as best they could, some lying under houses, and some beside the walls. Here they remained until the night of the 14th February, when, on the approach of Sherman's army, half were placed on the train for Charlotte. Many of these escaped by making holes, in the night, through the cars with saw-knives, which they concealed on their persons. The night was dark and rainy, and favored their escape. I have not the names of many of these. On the 15th the balance of the officers was sent off. Some sixty of them managed to escape in the following manner: In the yard were two hospitals. These were temporarily built with some space under the floors, and also between the ceiling-boards and roof. Into these the men managed to creep and conceal themselves, where they lay for forty-eight hours without anything to eat or drink. Here they lay concealed until they heard the firing in front of the city. They then got out, and were hid by the citizens until our army restored them to liberty, I might say to life."

Marching orders were issued in the evening, February 10, for 7 o'clock the next morning. At General Logan's headquarters I witnessed a most affecting sight. Hundreds of Union citizens, who were burned out, begged to be taken off. A regular train was organized for them under Major Reynolds, an escaped prisoner. The escaped officers were trying to get off those who were kind to them while in prison, and who had concealed them. It is thought that about two hundred officers and several hundred men had escaped — some by getting into cellars, holes, citizens' houses, and other places; more of them bribed the guards and conductors on the train, who gave them an opportunity to escape by cutting through the floors of the cars.

The scene in the morning was truly exciting. Ambulances,

buggies, carriages, and every kind of conveyance were put in requisition, and all kinds of Rosinantes in use. Old men, women, and children were crowded together, willing to undergo all the hardships and dangers of the campaign in order to escape certain starvation and the infuriated rage of the southern soldiers. Men and women, who were not able to get off, wept like children.

A refugee train was organized, and such as could or wanted to get off joined it.

These, added to the thousands of negroes who had already fallen in, swelled our train to huge dimensions; and it was a large drain on the resources and larders of South Carolina to support them.

While the right wing is resting at Columbia, we will give a *résumé* of the march of the left wing.

Saturday, February 11, the 20th corps marched to the Edisto River. Nine distinct streams, flowing sluggishly through a swamp half a mile in width where the road crossed, were the obstacles to be surmounted here. Two hundred rebel cavalrymen disputed the crossing for a while; but a strong skirmish line, plunging through the swamp, dispersed them or drove them away in a body, and the corps crossed. General Williams's corps was now between the two forks which form the Edisto River. The balance of General Slocum's command was well up on the left, with Kilpatrick farther on that flank. The road across the point formed by the two branches was fourteen miles long. The corps marched to the north fork before night on the 12th, and went into camp. The two hundred rebels who had been driven away from the Lower Edisto had concentrated here; their force was augmented somewhat, and with the assistance of four pieces of cannon they made considerable noise. Skirmishing was kept up all that Sunday night, the pioneers working upon the bridge meanwhile. Monday morning the enemy were gone. General Ward's division being in advance, that general mounted his kicking stallion, took two companies for skirmishers, and advanced towards Lexington and Columbia at a rattling pace.

All day Tuesday the regiment of rebels skirmished with our advance, but they were easily brushed away. Once they made a dash behind the advance, and captured Captain Reynolds, inspector of General Robinson's brigade, and chased Captain Ward four miles or more. The enemy appeared in blue clothes, and were frequently hailed as Union soldiers.

At 5 o'clock in the afternoon of Wednesday, February 15, General Barnum's brigade, of Geary's division, was at Two Notch road, two miles from Lexington and twelve from Columbia. General Slocum had calculated upon Davis's corps being in the town at that hour; but the rains and vile roads had prevented even that swift travelling corps from coming up. General Barnum's brigade was pushed into town, but arrived there just too late to strike a blow at the rear of the rebel cavalry column, which had been pouring through all day towards Columbia. Only a dozen shots were fired. Barnum's brigade was withdrawn, and the 14th corps marched up on a line with the 20th.

General Slocum's wing of the grand army of invasion was concentrated for action Wednesday night, ten miles from Columbia, facing towards that town; and he issued the order for an advance on the capital early next morning, with the expectation of a fight. Ward's division, of the 20th corps, closely followed by Jackson's, moved down the road parallel with Jeff C. Davis's troops, who had "gone through" Lexington, and struck the 17th corps on the banks of the Congaree, opposite Columbia, shortly after noon. By having the shortest line of march, the right wing had reached Columbia first.

From the front of Columbia, General Slocum's command moved to the left, across the Saluda and Broad Rivers, to the Greenville and Columbia Railroad, and destroyed that for thirty miles. Cheatham and S. D. Lee, with twenty thousand men from Hood's army, were reported by Kilpatrick as crossing the river at Newberry, and General Slocum's idea was to prevent a junction between them and Hardee's Charleston troops. We pushed rapidly on to Winnsboro', the capital of Fairfield district, where it was expected the rebel cavalry would give us a fight. They were known to outnumber Kilpatrick's command two to one. Wade Hampton, Wheeler, and Butler were in command. Fairfield district is wealthy. Forage began to roll in; more meat and breadstuffs than I saw at any one time during the Georgia campaign, were brought to the roadside day by day.

General Slocum double-quicked the advance of his column into the village of Winnsboro' to save the town from the torch of his foragers. General Pardee's brigade, of Geary's division, was in advance, and every effort was made to beat the stragglers from the grand army into town. They were not successful. The town was pillaged and set on fire before any organized body of troops got in. All officers turned their attention to the fire, and arrested the progress of the flames. Generals Slocum, Williams, Geary, Pardee, Barnum, and all, worked with their hands, burned their whiskers and scorched their clothes, to prevent the repetition of Columbia scenes. Nine or ten buildings were burned on the main street, before the fire was stopped, also the house of a Mrs. Pope, said to be the property of a man in New York city. Guards were posted at every house in town, and other fires were quenched as they burst out. Unfortunately the church building of the Episcopalian society was destroyed.

Citizens of Winnsboro' told us that Mrs. Lunderdale, a rabid secession woman, set fire to her own property, rather than have it fall into Yankee hands, and so destroyed the property of her neighbors.

From Winnsboro' the left wing marched to the Catawba River, striking it at Rocky Mount Ford, the scene of one of the South Carolina skirmishes during the revolution. Rocky Mount was one of Cornwallis's line of outposts. The Catawba here is about a thousand feet wide, and runs through a very hilly country. A pontoon was thrown across, and the 20th corps hurried over. The rain we feared cut off Geary's division, and the troubles increased. The red clay made heavy mud, and plenty of it. No idea can be formed by outsiders of the difficulties of the Catawba crossing. Wagons were hauled down the steep hill to the pontoon, dragging loads of mud by the axles, the wheels not moving; artillery horses floundered, and cannon were stuck fast. Virginia campaigners said it eclipsed Stafford Court-House. When the crossing was made, the ascension of the hill was just as difficult. Two days were spent by the 20th corps in this labor through the mud. The history of the troubles of the 14th corps would fill a volume.

Dwight's Creek and other streams were crossed in rapid succession, and the 20th corps reached the town of Chesterfield on Friday, the 3d of March. A brigade of rebels was driven out by General Jackson's skirmish line, and possession taken of the paltry town. A brick court-house and six houses comprise the village.

From Chesterfield the left wing marched to the Great Pedee River, near the state line. Howard's wing was already in Cheraw. The Great Pedee, or Yadkin, of North Carolina, is quite a formidable stream to an army depending on pontoon boats; and we were delayed on its banks two days. Crossing the cavalry and the 14th corps, General Slocum plunged into the State of North Carolina.

The 14th corps moved in a parallel line with the 20th, being about fifteen miles from Columbia, and met no enemy.

February 20, the army of the Tennessee broke camp around Columbia and resumed their march. The 17th corps destroyed about thirty miles of railroad, clear up to Winnsboro', thence crossed the Wateree at Pey's Ferry, moving through Russell Place to Young's Bridge, all the time threatened by a squad of Hampton's cavalry, who durst not attack.

Logan marched through Red Hill and Flat Rock to Tiller's Bridge, on Lynch Creek.

On the 24th the rebel cavalry, which was hanging on our flanks, attacked our foragers, killing six, two after surrendering, capturing several, and seven wagons. General Logan in person went out with a regiment, and repulsed the rebel cavalry after a brisk skirmish.

He ordered two prisoners to be shot in retaliation for our two men, and sent a prisoner to inform the rebels that he would shoot five men for every prisoner of ours shot.

We captured about ten refugee trains to-day, with valuable stores and supplies; also several animals. Among those captured were two officers, who were riding in a carriage when the Yanks pounced on them. They were well armed, but made no resistance. They said they were a principal and a second, going to fight a duel, and that the other parties had gone before them to the place of rendezvous. The officer captured was Captain W. F. De Pass, a celebrated duellist of South Carolina. His would-be antagonist was a Captain W. Courtney, a fighting quartermaster. Being chivalrous and obliging, we made every effort to catch the latter, in order to let them finish their little affair of honor in our presence, but failed. It shows how ignorant they had been of all our movements, when officers could be so foolishly engaged at such a critical moment.

The 29th Missouri captured about one hundred and twenty militia to-day, who had a wagon carrying their arms. Some of them were old, gray-haired men, barely able to move along; others, too young to be taken from their mothers' leading-strings. They had been quietly marching along, with their guns in a wagon, and powder in casks, to keep it dry. General Hazen supplied some of these veteran militia with staffs. They were all let go at Cheraw.

Major General Hazen's foragers approached Camden, and skirmished with some cavalry, driving them into the town, and, following them, soon took possession of it. They were supported by the 112th Illinois, Colonel Adams, of Corse's division (4th). We found about fifty thousand rations of corn meal, and four thousand bales of cotton, which we destroyed. Major Generals Howard and Logan sent in detachments next morning, who destroyed all government property, public stores, the depot, and some public buildings. Captain John H. Devereux, of Charleston, post commissary at Camden, while retreating, rode into the head of General Hazen's column, and was captured.

The mayor and city council had prepared a very pretty speech and address to General Sherman on surrendering the city. It was rather mortifying to them to have it unceremoniously occupied by some foragers.

Camden is a beautiful town, situated on the Wateree River, which is navigable for boats of light draught to that point, and is about thirty-five miles east of Columbia, and one hundred and forty miles from Charleston. It has some very pretty private residences, and appears to be a very healthy and fashionable resort. It is also a place of considerable historic interest. In August, 1780, a battle was fought here between the Americans, under General Gates, and the British, under Lord Cornwallis; and another was fought in 1781, on the eastern slope of Hobkirk's Hill now called Kirkwood, over which we skirmished, between General Greene and Lord Rawdon. A monument still marks the grave of Baron De Kalb, who fell in the former battle. The foundation stone was laid in 1825, by Lafayette.

On the market-house stands a well-executed metallic effigy, ten feet high, of King Haiglar, a famous chieftain of the Catawbas.

I have entered so fully into a description of the negro followers in our march through Georgia, that it is needless for me to repeat it here, or to dwell on the wholesale burning of houses, and devastation of property. Suffice it to say, that the swarms of negroes who had flocked in front, and rear, and flanks of our columns, were something to remember. All ages, sizes, and both sexes, were either mounted on broken-down mules or horses, or crammed into some rheumatic old coach, or were laboriously toiling along, faint and sweating, rendering the air not very pleasant to the olfactory nerves.

As for the wholesale burnings, pillage, devastation, committed in South Carolina, magnify all I have said of Georgia some fifty fold, and then throw in an occasional murder, "jist to bring an old, hard-fisted cuss to his senses," and you have a pretty good idea of the whole thing.

An apparently wealthy planter, feeling that he was quite safe under the ægis of the British lion's paw, pompously walks up to General Logan, with his hands stuffed in his capacious pockets, and his hat independently on, saying, "General, you see I want protection from these here houtrages;" and he points at two soldiers, one in pursuit of a young grunter, which seemed as indignant as his master at the outrages inflicted on a Hinglish subject; another was carrying on an excited chase after a rooster, timing the amusement by an occasional fling at some members of the rooster's family that crossed his path.

"Why should I give you protection?"

"Sir, I claim protection. I am a Hinglish subject!" he exclaimed, with the air of a Lord John Russell.

"A what?"

"A Hinglish subject, sir;" and he actually swelled out, like the frog in the fable, at his own importance.

"What the h—l, then, are you doing here if you are? The boys will take every hog and chicken you have, though you are a British subject. British subject be hanged!"

The last thing we heard from the old gentleman, as we rode away, was, "I'll have redress," "Hingland shall hear of this," and the like, while the boys were making flank movements on all sides, well loaded with the rich spoils of the farm-yard. I think the number of muskets we picked up, with the Tower stamp on them, did not dispose the general very favorably towards Hinglish subjects.

Our foragers had a great penchant for honey. It was rather amusing to witness their encounters with the bees, who spitefully resented their intrusion on their rights.

At first the men upset the hives, and dragged out the honey, while a swarm of the bees flew around, stinging them and making them cut up all kinds of capers and gymnastics.

However, practice makes perfection, and they soon learned how to smoke them. Or, if in a hurry, they would snatch up the hive on their shoulder, with the mouth backwards, and run off with all speed. The bees, wondering what the deuce was the matter, would issue out and instinctively fly for their old quarters, assailing men and horses in their way.

I have often seen a regular stampede among a squad of foragers and bummers, caused by swarms of infuriated bees assailing them.

The bees would stick around the heads and ears of men and

animals. The latter would kick and prance, throwing off their riders, and collections of meat and fowl, while the former would swear lustily at the bees and mules together, at the same time making insane efforts to keep off the bees and urge on the refractory mules.

It was certainly an amusing sight to see perhaps twenty mules and bummers kicking up as mad a rumpus as if every one of them was demented.

We had halted at a very nice plantation house near Columbia, and the officers sat down on the piazza, while the men commenced raiding on the good things around. Soon, a Babel of cackling roosters, grunting hogs, and barking dogs ensued.

The house seemed to be inhabited by three ladies of doubtful age; the eldest was on the wrong side of forty, while the next was close to her, and the youngest was certainly a young lady of thirty, *in her teens*. They were dressed alike, all in black, and looked as much alike as possible. They were pale, thin, attenuated young ladies, and wonderfully reticent, so much so that I was for a time under the impression that they were all dummies. My mind was soon relieved; for when the helpless denizens of the yard set up their useless uproar, the weird sisters came out on the piazza in single file, regulated by age, and, with hands and eyes raised, began a hymn. They passed in at another door, but soon returned. After repeating this round twice, they flung themselves on their knees near, and burst out in one loud psalm of supplication to the Lord, informing him that his servants were now ready to depart this life. I know we departed quick enough, bummers and all, for this strange incantation, which reminded one of the scene in *Der Freischutz*, had a stronger superstitious influence on the bummers than a squad of Hampton's cavalry.

So much terror had our name and acts inspired, that even the negroes were wary; afraid, in some instances, to trust themselves among the men who made this fearful work on the country. White table-cloths were suspended from windows, with "Have mercy on me!" for a legend, and the fiery spirit of South Carolina was tamed effectually. Occasionally, in

Georgia, a man could be found who had the courage to say that he voted for secession; but these abject men were afraid to own that they lived in a seceded state.

In most cases, the slaves betrayed their masters, revealing their property and joining in its destruction. I have known cases, too, where the slaves refused to leave their masters, or to betray them, though threatened with death.

Cruel masters reaped the fruits of their tyranny now, while the property of kind ones was in many instances saved by the tact and discretion of their slaves.

The men had surrounded a plantation house, were smashing up the furniture, and preparing to fire the house, when an old slave, of venerable appearance, came out of his shanty, and looking on, said, —

"I taught de Yanks, Lor' bress dem, were too good to hurt dere friends."

"So we are, old woolly head; but you don't reckon this here fellow was our friend."

"I speck he was, dough, and de nigger's friend, too."

"Then why did he join the rebel army, and leave his place here?"

"You see, massa, when dem poor Yanks was running away from Columbia, massa says to me, 'Cæsar, if you meet any of dem, conceal dem here.' So I did, and massa helped me to get dem away. Massa had enemies, and when dey heard dis, dey come and took massa off and stuck him in de army, and den his wife went to her father's, leaving dis nigger to take care ob de place."

"Is all that true, father graybeard?"

"May dis nigger never see de good Lor' if it is not so."

"Well, boys," said the leader of the gang, shouldering his musket, "I think we have done enough here." And they marched off.

The morning after the burning of Columbia, I was passing near a private residence which had been destroyed. Some clothes and furniture were piled up in the yard, and near them sat a lady, with a pretty child beside her, and two younger ones unconsciously sleeping on a sofa near.

The lady appeared much distressed; her head rested on her hands, and her eyes were red from weeping. A likely mulatto girl sat near her, watching her mistress, while near them, trimming a fire, and trying to prepare some food, was a stout negro.

"Chloe," said the negro, "the fire is good; come and get some coffee for missis."

"No, Pompey, no; I can't use any," said the lady.

"But missis knows young massa and Missa Jane and Emma had no supper."

"That's true, Chloe," said the lady; "get the poor children something." After their poor breakfast, the lady looks at her servants, and asks, "Well, Pompey and Chloe, what are you going to do?"

"Missis, I remain wid you," said Chloe.

"And I too; missis has been good and kind to dis nigger, and he is not going to leab her now."

"But I am so poor, you see, I have nothing; nothing to eat, for you or my children."

"Missis," said Pompey, standing before her, "look at dis arm; it's strong. Pompey will work dat arm to de bone before missis want, and de good Lord will take care of us."

The lady bowed her head and wept, and taking a hand of each of her sable friends, she said, —

"Pompey and Chloe, I'll not forget this if I am ever restored to wealth; you are henceforth free."

On our march we halted at a farm-house, in which was a woman and a very fine little boy of about five years. The lady, who represented herself a stanch Unionist, expressed great respect for our flag, and requested to be allowed to examine it, as she had never seen a flag before. Her request was granted, and the little boy also appeared highly interested with it. At length he turned to his mother, and said, —

"O, mamma, isn't it very like our flag, that papa had here?"

This was letting the cat out of the bag. We of course only smiled, and the lady blushed.

I was riding one day with a Mr. B., of the Christian Commission. We stopped at a house, and the lady complained bitterly of how the rebel cavalry robbed her of seventy dollars in gold. My friend turned to me and said, —

"Hell will not be full until Jeff Davis and his followers are there. Just think you; to rob this poor woman! Bad as our men are, they would not do that."

At night we had to sleep on the stoop of a house, with our horses tied in front of us. Mr. B. had a very fine overcoat tied behind his saddle, which was stolen while we slept. In the morning, when he missed it, he turned to me, exclaiming, —

"Well, after all, hell will not be full until some of our chaps get there, too."

It makes a great difference whose ox is gored.

CHAPTER XXVIII.

CHERAW.—CROSSING THE PEDEE.—KILPATRICK'S FIGHT WITH
WADE HAMPTON.—FAYETTEVILLE.—COMMUNICATION WITH
THE SEABOARD.

The right wing had broken up the railroad from Columbia to Winnsboro', and then turned for Pea's Ferry, the 17th corps moving straight on Cheraw by Young's Bridge, and the 15th by Teller's and Kelly's Bridge.

Our march had been somewhat retarded by the heavy falls of rain, which flooded the creeks and cut up the roads, so that we had to corduroy the most of the way. A person unacquainted with the work an army has to do, the length of roads it has to corduroy, and bridges to build, would deem it almost fabulous. On this campaign alone I think we must have made over one hundred miles of road, and built several miles of trestle work and bridges. This is necessary in a country where the roads sink and cave in from the wear of our immense wagon trains.

Lynch's Creek detained us two days, it being considerably swollen by the freshets. Major General Hazen had to build a bridge two hundred yards, and corduroy over three hundred yards before the troops could cross. The stream was so wide and full of snags that it was impossible to pontoon it. One division crossed at Teller's Creek. Black Creek had also to be pontooned, as the water extended over one hundred yards beyond the bridge.

Captain Duncan, 15th Illinois, with his company, the 4th Ohio independent, and some fifteen men of the signal corps, encountered the 7th Carolina cavalry, and had a sharp skirmish with them, in which we had three men, and Lieutenant Quinn, chief of General Howard's scouts, badly wounded.

The rebel loss was five killed, including an acting brigadier general.

The 17th corps crossed the creek at Young's Bridge, two regiments wading through the water. They also had to bridge the creek, and corduroy near a quarter of a mile. Next day (28th) they moved within thirteen miles of Cheraw, crossing Black Creek at McDonald's, and passing near Sugar Loaf Mountain.

On the 3d they marched on Cheraw. Mower's division, being in advance, skirmished with the enemy. The rebels burned Coit's Bridge, on Thomas's Creek, and disputed the passage for some time. Mower opened a few pieces of artillery, and pushed his right to Cheraw. The enemy fled over the Great Pedee, firing the bridge, which they had covered with rosin, after them. General Mower took possession of the town, establishing a brigade as provost guard.

Our mounted infantry, 9th Illinois, and 29th Missouri, with some squads of foragers, made a dash on Society Hill, driving the rebels from the town, and succeeded in burning a train of cars and the railroad depot, and also in tearing up a mile of the track.

Cheraw is near the northern line of the state, and about one hundred and fifty miles from Charleston, and ninety from Columbia. It is a pleasant-looking town, with near two thousand inhabitants. It is on the Great Pedee River, and at the head of the steam navigation. Here we captured twenty-five pieces of artillery, among which was a Blakely thirty-two pounder gun, with the inscription, " To the Sovereign State of Carolina. By a citizen abroad. March 4, 1861."

We also captured twelve cars, one locomotive, eighteen tons of powder, several thousand bales of cotton, and a large supply of stores. In the hospitals we found about two hundred prisoners. A few houses were on fire when we entered the town. We burned the railroad depot and buildings.

Little of importance had varied the march of the left wing. Davis halted and parked his wagons at Youngsville while tearing up the line of railroad from Columbia to Blackstock, a distance of fifty-four miles. The 14th corps was also delayed at Kingsbury Ferry for three days, their pontoon boats, which they had laid across the Catawba, or Wateree, having been carried away by the flood. For two or three days the swollen state of the Catawba prevented the 14th from crossing, and the right wing was cut in two. The delay thus caused to one corps of course extended to the whole army. Sherman at last got impatient, and on March 1st ordered Slocum to send that portion of the 14th corps which was cut off to destroy the wagons, spike the cannon, shoot the mules and horses, ferry the men across on rafts, and come on. The army was now twenty miles in advance. General Slocum rode back to the Catawba at night, unattended, save by a couple of orderlies, and through a country where rebels abounded, and consulted with Jeff C. Davis. That general begged for a delay in the execution of the order. Generals Slocum, Davis, "Jimmy" Morgan, Baird, and Buell went vigorously at the work of saving the 14th corps, and succeeded in getting them across without loss of material. Then, by forced marches, when the endurance of the men was most taxed, they came up and took their place again in the front line, facing towards Virginia.

The whole army was now partly concentrated, with the intention of giving the impression to the enemy that Charlotte was our objective point.

The left wing passed near Hanging Rock on the 2d of March.

This is among the most celebrated points on our line of march, as it bears a revolutionary interest, being the theatre of a battle between Sumter and the British and North Carolina tories, in which the Prince of Wales regiment was nearly annihilated. Mills, in his "Statistics," says, —

"The Hanging Rock is a real curiosity, as are many other rocks near it. They form an irregular group, on the east side of the creek, and are fantastically piled, one upon another, along the declivity of a steep hill. That called Hanging Rock, in particular, is a single mass about twenty feet in diameter, which is, on the side nearest to the creek, scooped into an arch, forming overhead a figure of an exceedingly regular kind, resembling the segment of a concave sphere, or rather paraboloid. This arch is capable of sheltering several persons; and, indeed, it seems fires have been kindled there, supposed by hunters, for the edge of the arch appears tinged with smoke. It is a singularly interesting object, but yet of the minor kind. Another of these huge stones rests upon a larger rock, supported at only two points, so that one is apt, at first view, to suppose that a small force would hurl it from its base down the steep hill, into the creek below. There are many other similar rocks here, but these two are among the most remarkable. As I descended the hill, and viewed this latter rock, it forcibly gave me the idea of a ship resting upon the summit of a cliff, the form of the side and stern being aptly represented to the fancy.

The formation of these rocks is also singularly curious. They are not formed of lamina or strata in planes, as other rocks are, but seem to be composed, more generally, of strata in concentric circles. I saw several masses split off by the force of frost. Some, of immense size, had fractures so even that one might suppose they had been sawn through, yet evidently without any seam.

The substance composing these masses is also curious. The principal matter consists of small, flinty stones, of all sizes, from one eighth to one half of an inch, irregularly hexagonal, mixed with very small, black, glass-like, brilliant particles, about a tenth of an inch in diameter, the whole cemented together by another substance.

The rock is broken without difficulty, so that the agglomerated particles are easily separated. One cannot resist the belief that these rocks were formed in a very different state of the world from the present. These rocks abound in this district. The earth, even in the valleys, rests wholly on rock, though sometimes it is twenty or thirty feet deep. The springs are abundant. The water gushing through the fissures in these rocks renders wells unnecessary.

The Flat Rock is close to the battle-ground of Hanging Rock. It is a huge mass, almost level, composed of a kind of very hard gravel, cemented together. On the surface are several circular pits or cisterns, a few inches deep, which the people here suppose were dug out by the Indians. (Just such tales they tell in the West Indies of the pirate's rocky Punch Bowl.) I stepped across the rock, and found it five hundred feet in diameter. The naked part is about four acres, and the whole extent about twenty. I saw two other rocks of this kind, but on a smaller scale. Indeed, the greater part of the country seems to have such a basis. Immediately before coming to the creek you pass through the battle-ground. The country was then all in woods. The conflict began on the hill, and was continued in the vale.

Four miles from Caston's Tavern is the Anvil Rock, so named from its shape. It stands, a curiosity of the tiny kind, close by the road, about ten feet high, eight feet wide at top, and perhaps five at the bottom, the sides irregularly worn away by frosts and rains. It is composed of the same kind of aggregated particles as the Hanging Rock, and all the numerous flat rocks that lie scattered through this country.

One mile from Hanging Rock Creek there is a mineral spring, four hundred yards from the road. It is very transparent, bubbling up through clear sand, and is intensely cold. It deposits about the well and the stream a great deal of the yellow matter common to chalybeate springs. The taste and smell are sensible. It acts as a gentle aperient, and is strongly diuretic. A gentle descent leads to the spring. It is delightfully shaded by trees, and has a fall for a plunging or shower bath."

The Pedee River was deep and about one hundred and forty yards in width at this point, with high shelving banks, and therefore took some time to pontoon. The 17th corps crossed on the evening of the 4th and morning of the 5th, and was followed in the evening and next morning by the 15th corps. The 20th corps also crossed at the same point, while the 14th corps and cavalry crossed some twelve miles farther up the river, at Sneidsboro'.

In our line of march for Fayetteville, after crossing the Great Pedee, the 17th corps branched off towards Gallipolis, the 15th moving by Laurensburg, and crossing Lumber River at Gilchrist

Bridge to Rock Fish Creek. The 17th corps had moved along the plank road, both corps crossing at Davis's Bridge.

South and North Carolina are separated by an imaginary line. Where we marched, the only object to inform us that we had got into North Carolina was a sign-board with the learned inscription, "fift 3 mils to Fatville," which, I suppose, meant fifty-three miles to Fayetteville. The schoolmaster had likely been lately abroad, when this was written. The country is wretchedly poor — a regular pine region. The troops did not burn or destroy property as they did in South Carolina.

The roads in North Carolina were firm and sandy, for the most part, through these endless gloomy forests.

The trains were able to move in the centres, with a column of troops on each side, thus expediting our march.

The slaves around Laurensburg, at the opening of our campaign through Carolina, had organized a party with the intention of forcing their way to our lines. The plot was discovered, and at one of their meetings they were surrounded by parties of the home guards, captured, and after a kind of mock trial, twenty-five were hung. Captain Robert Johnson, Colonel Robert Dacker, and Captain Tate, of Richmond County, were the leaders in this barbarous business.

We moved rapidly, but with caution, on Fayetteville, for we knew the enemy were concentrating there. Cheatham's corps from the west, and the garrison of Augusta, had reënforced Beauregard; and Hardee, having evacuated Charleston, had crossed Cape Fear River, all endeavoring to form a junction with Johnston and Hoke in North Carolina. Sherman knew all this; he also knew that a battle was inevitable, and moved with prudence.

Kilpatrick's encounter with Wade Hampton was the only military event of any importance that occurred between Cheraw and Fayetteville. This was one of the most stubbornly contested cavalry battles of the campaign. After being surprised, two brigades of our cavalry held and finally drove from their camp in confusion Wade Hampton's entire cavalry corps. It was discovered, on the morning of the 9th, that Hardee was making forced marches to reach Fayetteville, in advance of the infantry of Sherman. General Kilpatrick at once put his column in motion to strike Hardee in flank, or to intercept Wade Hampton, who was following in the rear with his cavalry. General Kilpatrick reached Coleman's Grove just after Hardee's rear had passed. Hampton was a few hours behind.

Our cavalry had not all come up, owing to the bad state of the roads; Colonel Spencer's brigade and Colonel Way's command were at once placed in position, and waited the attack of the rebel cavalry. Just before daybreak on the morning of the 10th, and before the brigades of General Atkins and Colonel Jordon had arrived, Hampton came in front of Kilpatrick's position, and massed his troops, consisting of three divisions, under Hume, Allen, and Butler. The attack was made in three columns,— Wheeler led the right, Hampton the centre, and Butler the left,— and was perfectly irresistible. Kilpatrick's first line, under Lieutenant Colonel Way, was actually ridden over, headquarters and artillery captured, and, at one time, the entire camp, including the whole staff, and Colonel Spencer, commanding the 3d brigade, were in the enemy's possession. But General Kilpatrick made his escape, joined the brigade of Colonel Spencer, which was falling back on foot, stubbornly disputing every inch of ground. A large portion of the enemy halted in and about the camp for a moment to plunder. *This was fatal to them.* Kilpatrick's cavalrymen rallied under the leadership of their officers, retook the hills upon the left, and then, with one wild shout, swept down upon the rebels, who were swarming about the captured artillery and Kilpatrick's former headquarters. In a short time the artillery was in their possession, and turned upon the enemy. At this moment the general's red battle-flag, recaptured from the enemy, floated out in the presence of friend and foe. This animated the troops on our side, and though hard pressed and deprived of the animating presence of their general, they charged and repulsed the enemy, driving him from the field, thus converting a surprise into a victory. Our loss did not much exceed one hundred killed and wounded. The enemy left upon the field a number of officers and seventy-six soldiers dead, besides many wounded, and at the lowest estimate could not have lost less than three hundred killed and wounded. The whole affair was indeed most brilliant, and reflects great credit upon the cavalry, and adds yet another laurel to the many won by them since leaving the hills of Georgia.

Fayetteville is a town of some four thousand inhabitants. The first to come into the town was Captain Duncan, commanding the scouts and mounted men of the army of the Tennessee. He was repulsed by Hampton's cavalry, and himself taken prisoner. His party was reënforced by the foragers, and again attacked the place, taking it. General Giles A. Smith's 4th division, 17th army corps, soon came up, also the head of General Slocum's column, and hoisted the flag over the markethouse. The mayor surrendered the town to Colonel William E. Strong, of General Howard's staff, then to General Slocum, who had just come up. As the rebels were retreating over the river, they opened two guns on the town, and then fired the bridge, which was covered with rosin.

Fayetteville is a poor, straggling kind of a town, with few buildings of any importance. It is at the head of the Cape Fear River navigation, which gives it some importance. It was a place of considerable interest during the revolutionary war, as also being for several years the residence of the celebrated Flora Macdonald, whose name has been so poetically associated with the outlawry and sufferings of the last hope of the Stuarts — the exiled Charles Edward. With a woman's tact and tenderness the faithful maiden shielded the unfortunate Pretender. Though the prince's last words to her were, "Gentle, faithful maiden, I hope we will meet again in the Palace Royal," never had the exiled monarch a chance of displaying his gratitude. In 1775 she and her husband sailed to America, settling in Fayetteville. The tottering ruins of the house are yet to be seen where they resided. The troubles of the revolution soon followed.

The chief of the clan Macdonald having accepted the commission of general from George III., his kinsman in North Carolina joined his standard as captain, but was captured in

1776, near Cross Creek, and detained a prisoner for some time. After his release, broken down in hopes and fortune, he and Flora returned to Scotland, where she died in 1790. Her shroud was made of the sheets in which Charles Edward had slept at Kingsburg.

Foote remarks that Massachusetts has had her Lady Arabella, Virginia her Pocahontas, and North Carolina her Flora Macdonald.

Fayetteville is about one hundred and twenty miles from Wilmington by the river. Though the river banks were known to be occupied by the enemy, a noble little tug and her gallant crew ran the gantlet. They were fired on twice by the enemy, but fortunately no lives were lost. They were received with cheers by our men on her arrival. The sail back to Wilmington, which I accompanied, was extremely interesting. We had a mail boat in convoy, with two guns; and though we saw the abandoned picket fires of the enemy along the river, we were not molested. The night was lovely, with a full moon shedding its rays over the sparkling waters as we shot along the silvery stream. All were cheerful, for it was like waking to a new life, after being so long shut from the outer world.

Never before has an army accomplished so much with such little sacrifice of either life or property.

We had been about forty-five days out since we left Savannah. Our march had been one continued success. Sherman's capital manœuvres completely split up the rebel army, breaking them into isolated bodies, thus destroying their power.

We had been somewhat retarded by the heavy falls of rain, which flooded the creeks and swamps, and cut up the roads so that we had to corduroy over a hundred miles of road, and build several miles of trestle work and bridges.

Besides compelling the enemy to evacuate Charleston, we destroyed Columbia, Orangeburg, and several other places; also over fifty miles of their chief lines of railroad, and thousands of bales of cotton.

At Columbia we captured forty-three cannon, two hundred thousand cartridges, ten tons of powder, nine thousand rounds

RESULTS OF THE CAMPAIGN. 359

of fixed ammunition, about ten thousand muskets, over one hundred government presses, besides an immense amount of public property, locomotives, rolling stock, and other kinds of government stores, too numerous to mention.

At Cheraw we took twenty-five cannon, eight caissons, and two travelling forges.

At Fayetteville we took seventeen cannon, besides a large quantity of government stuff of various kinds in the arsenal and elsewhere.

This makes eighty-five cannon, — one third of which were field-pieces, — with carriages, caissons, and all complete. We captured about twenty-five thousand animals on our line of march. We gave food and transportation to about fifteen thousand colored refugees, thus depriving the Confederacy of colored soldiers and slaves. We also had about four thousand white refugees, all of whom were well cared for, and will be sent north to whatever destination they choose.

We operated over the following districts or counties: In South Carolina — Beaufort, Barnwell, Orangeburg, Lexington, Richland, Kershaw, Fairfield, Chester, Lancaster, Sumter, Darlington, Chesterfield, Malbourg; in North Carolina — Mecklenburg, Anson, Richland, Union, Robeson, Cumberland, and Moore.

We marched, on the whole, four hundred and fifty miles, our wings extending some thirty-five or forty miles. This would give an area of over fifteen thousand square miles which we operated over, all the time supporting men and animals on the country. Indeed, the loss we inflicted on the enemy is incalculable, and all at a trifling sacrifice of life.

The first boat to open communication was the tug Davidson, Captain Robert Stephenson, and Captain Ainsworth, of Wilmington. She had on board a guard of seventy-five men of the 13th Indiana, armed with seven-shooters, under command of Captain Theodore Reiple, Lieutenants Thomas C. Curley and Richard Jones. Too much praise cannot be given to the brave officers and men of this boat, who volunteered on this dangerous service.

CHAPTER XXIX.

THE BATTLES OF AVERYSBORO' AND BENTONVILLE. — NEWS OF LEE'S SURRENDER. — INTERVIEW BETWEEN SHERMAN AND JOHNSTON. — HOMEWARD BOUND.

GENERAL SHERMAN suspected that Hardee, in retreating from Fayetteville, would take up position in a narrow neck between Cape Fear and South Rivers, in hopes to check him until Johnston's army could fully concentrate. Sherman had instructed General Schofield, at Newbern, and General Terry, at Wilmington, that on Wednesday, the 15th, he would move for Goldsboro', and ordering them to march straight for the same place. Terry and Schofield at once commenced their march, the latter encountering the enemy at Kinston, and other points on the way.

General Kilpatrick had orders to move up the plank road to Averysboro'.

General Sherman moved from Fayetteville, on the morning of the 14th, for Goldsboro' and a permanent base. Johnston's army left Fayetteville on roads leading to Raleigh, up the Cape Fear River, and it was confidently expected that he would attempt to prevent our junction with Schofield by an attack on our left as we marched along the Goldsboro' road. To prepare for this, General Slocum's wing of the army was directed to move light — that is, without trains — on the left flank. Geary's division, of the 20th corps, and Baird's, of the 14th, were in charge of the trains of both corps, on an interior road, General Howard's wing moving on roads farther south and nearer the coast in the same order. Jackson's and Wood's divisions, of the 20th corps, Carlin's and Morgan's, of the 14th, with Kilpatrick's cavalry, followed Johnston up the plank road, as if moving on the capital of the state. Kilpatrick found the enemy five miles from Fayetteville, and skirmished with him, pressing his rear guard to a point on the road near Kyles's Landing, where he was brought to a stand on the night of the 15th. During the pursuit, Captain Winthrop, of Kilpatrick's scouts, had picked out Colonel Alfred Rhett, 1st South Carolina heavy artillery, from the front of his command, and established pretty conclusively the fact that a large force of rebels was in front. General Kilpatrick sent back for a brigade of infantry to support him, and Colonel Hawley, of the 1st division, 20th corps, was sent up.

On the morning of the 15th, Kilpatrick and Hawley attacked the enemy's cavalry, drove them back half a mile or more, and developed a line of works, with artillery in position. The whole of the 20th corps was brought up and put in position against this line at 9 o'clock on the forenoon of the 15th, Kilpatrick fighting on the flanks. Dustan's and Case's brigades, of Ward's division, 2d corps, carried the works at 11 o'clock, capturing three pieces of artillery. About three hundred prisoners were captured along the line. The enemy fell back to their main line of works, extending from Black River on their left to Cape Fear River on their right, covering the roads to Raleigh, Smithfield, and Goldsboro'.

On the 16th Carlin and Morgan were brought up, and an attempt made to force the rebels back and uncover the Goldsboro' road. Severe fighting took place during the day without any satisfactory results. The enemy held his position, although suffering heavy loss. His line overlapped ours on the right, and everything indicated the presence of Hardee's whole army corps. He evacuated the line during the night of the 16th, however, and fell back to Averysboro', pursued by Ward's division of the 20th corps. His dead and wounded were left on the field, and abandoned along the road. General Ward pressed up to Averysboro', holding the plank road in our front, while the balance of the command moved off to the right, across Black River, on the Goldsboro' road, now uncovered. Our loss in the fight on Black River was four hundred and forty-six in the 20th corps, one hundred and eight in the 14th, one hundred and seventeen in Kilpatrick's command. The number of rebels buried on the field and paroled wounded was three hundred and twenty-seven. This was exclusive of those they carried off and the unhurt prisoners we captured.

Nothing, save an occasional skirmish with a small body of cavalry, occurred till we reached three miles south of Bentonville, twelve from Cox's Bridge (on the Neuse), on the morning of the 20th. As at Black River, the enemy showed nothing at first but a small force of cavalry, of Dibbrell's or Talbot's command, which were easily driven back by the skirmishers of Carlin's division in advance. Coming to a point where the skirmish line could go no farther, and the enemy fired from a piece of artillery, General Carlin formed Buell's and Hobart's brigades in line to drive the troublesome cavalry away. Generals Buell and Hobart moved to the left of the road on the enemy's flank, about a mile in advance of Morgan's division, when they discovered the enemy's infantry in a strong line of works, and in great numbers. Although it seemed incredible that the rebels could be in any great force here, General Slocum made preparations for a fight. Morgan's division was formed, and word sent back for the two divisions of the 20th corps to hurry forward. The enemy's line extended far beyond Morgan's right, and Coggswell's brigade, of the 1st division, 28th corps, was put in there when it came up. Still the rebel left could not be found.

At noon the enemy left his works and advanced on Jeff C. Davis's two divisions. Buell and Hobart were overwhelmed, and pressed back through the woods more than a mile and a half. Vandeveer's, Mitchell's, Ferring's, and Coggswell's brigades, on the right, fought stubbornly and desperately, and lost but little ground. There was a temporary confusion, and a rout was imminent. Five batteries of artillery were massed at a point where a hospital had been established in the morning, the balance of Jackson's division, 20th corps, put in on the left, and a new line formed. During the day five grand charges

PREPARATIONS FOR A BATTLE. 363

were made by the enemy massed, but each was repulsed. They succeeded in capturing three guns of the 19th Indiana battery, but only two were taken off. There was desperate fighting all day, the musketry fire being as heavy as our men have heard in a long time. Although they gained considerable ground on the left during the day, the rebels retired to their main line when night fell, leaving the greater part of their dead and wounded on the field.

Without being disposed to exaggerate in the least, we figure their loss at twenty-five hundred killed and wounded. Seven hundred were captured. The 26th Tennessee regiment was captured entire, colors and all, with a large part of the 12th Louisiana. Our loss was quite severe. Nearly eight hundred cases had been treated in the hospitals. The proportion of our killed to the enemy's killed found lying on the battle-field was as one to four by actual count. During the temporary confusion caused by the furious burst on Carlin's division, we lost about two hundred and fifty prisoners.

Rebels were captured from every one of the commands known to be in the south and west. Hoke, Cheatham, Stephen D. Lee, Wade Hampton, D. H. Hill, Wheeler, Butler, Joe Johnston, Hardee, and Bragg were on the field in person, for captives assert they rode around the lines in the morning, cheered by the troops. General Johnston thought that he would destroy Slocum's column before Sherman could get up to support it with the right wing. A forced march from Smithfield enabled him to strike him with forty thousand men. The thing looked bad at one time; yet as soon as the troops saw what was required of them, affairs brightened.

This important battle, in which Johnston commanded in person, and in which the combined forces of Hoke, Hardee, and Cheatham were hurled against the left wing in six consecutive charges, was solely conducted by General Slocum, and to him General Sherman assigns the credit of so ably sustaining the unequal contest.

On the 21st of March General Schofield entered Goldsboro', and General Terry had possession of the Neuse River, at Cox's

Bridge, and pontooned the river, so that the three armies were in actual connection, and Goldsboro', Sherman's objective point, fully secured.

The different armies now lay around Goldsboro', with the intention of getting supplies.

Sherman's real intention, as soon as his army was ready to march, was to move northward, feigning on Raleigh, and striking for Burksville, and wedging in between Johnston and Lee. When he heard of the battles around Petersburg, he changed his mind, and resolved to strike right for Johnston. At this time Johnston had his army well in hand about Smithfield, commanding the Goldsboro' and Raleigh Railroad.

At daybreak, on the 10th of April, Sherman's army was again in motion. Hampton's cavalry opposed our advance, but were scarcely able to check our march.

Johnston rapidly retreated across the Neuse River, having burned the bridge at Smithfield, in his rear.

At Smithfield we learned that Lee's army had surrendered; and the joy of officers and men was unbounded, and displayed in exuberant excesses.

Sherman ordered the trains to be dropped, and pursued Johnston, and reached Raleigh on the 13th; Johnston, all the time, rapidly falling back towards Greensboro'.

A rainstorm now set in, and the infantry had to halt at Raleigh. Kilpatrick, though, dashed on with his cavalry to Durham Station. Major General Stoneman was at Slatesville, thus commanding Johnston's only line of retreat by Salesburg and Charlotte.

On the 14th General Johnston had written, under flag of truce, to General Sherman, requesting an interview about terms of surrender. Sherman agreed to meet Johnston on the 17th.

The conference was held at a Mr. Bennet's house, at Durham Station, on the North Carolina Railroad, and eighteen miles from Raleigh.

This was rather a remarkable meeting. Sherman and party arrived first, and were soon after joined by Johnston and party.

The meeting at first was courteous, but constrained; after a little friendlier feeling prevailed, and the different battles, politics, the state of the country, and other subjects, were freely discussed.

General Sherman smoked his cigar, had his hands stuffed in his pockets, as usual — on the whole, looked at ease, and perfectly master of the situation.

Johnston, on the other hand, was taciturn, and looked haggard and care-worn, but still maintained the dignity of the soldier and the gentleman, as he certainly is.

Wade Hampton looked savage enough to eat little Kil, with a grain of salt; while the latter returned his looks most defiantly.

It was evident that they would break out. At length Hampton taunted Kil about his recent surprise of his camp.

Kil replied that he had to leave faster than he came, without being able to carry off a color.

Words grew hot, — both parties expressing a desire that the issue of the war would be left between their cavalry. The affair was becoming too personal; so Sherman and Johnston had to interfere.

After this the conference went on pleasantly enough.

It is not my province here to enter into this subject, or question Sherman's policy regarding the terms he had offered Johnston. I think his own letters make his intentions evident. It is but just to state that a majority of the corps commanders approved of his policy.

He also had just learned the general satisfaction Lee's surrender had given throughout the north, and he had a Richmond paper, published by permission of the Federal authorities, in which was a proclamation of General Weitzel, as military governor of Richmond, convening the Virginia rebel legislature for the purpose of taking measures to restore the state to the Union.

He believed that a magnanimous spirit of forbearance pervaded the councils of the north.

All these things conspired to make him lenient; but if he erred, it was on mercy's side; and his military services have been too glorious for a people whom he has done so much to save from anarchy and ruin not to forgive an error of political judgment.

Homeward Bound.

Sherman's army marched through Richmond on their way home, and over the bloody battle-fields on which their brother army of the Potomac so long and so nobly contended, and concentrated around Washington and Alexandria.

On the 23d of May the grand army of the Potomac, numbering about seventy-five thousand troops, passed in review through Washington before the president and dignitaries not only of this country, but of foreign nations.

The greatest anxiety prevailed to see Sherman's army; every door, window, and house roof were crowded with eager spectators. Arches of flowers festooned the streets and windows.

About 10 o'clock, Sherman, and staff, and generals appeared at the head of the column. The air echoed with cheers and shouts as the worn veterans marched up Pennsylvania Avenue, their bands playing, and their shattered and torn banners floating on the breeze. It was a glorious sight and a noble welcome — a country rejoicing at the return of its heroes of a hundred battles.

The streets were strewn with flowers; garlands were woven around the horses' necks, and bouquets of the most exquisite kind presented to the general, officers, and even privates. As they reached the stand occupied by the president and the *élite* of other nations, and decked with the banners of their different battle-fields, all rose, and in wild and grateful acclamations welcomed our heroes home.

APPENDIX.

I.

SKETCH OF THE LIFE OF GENERAL SHERMAN.

THE following sketch of Major General WILLIAM TECUMSEH SHERMAN is taken from the New York *Herald* of December 12, 1864: —

The prominence of this officer before the country very naturally invites a desire to know something of his history. Every one remembers his conduct at Shiloh, at Vicksburg, at Chattanooga, and the abilities displayed in his great campaign in Georgia. We now merely wish to connect these and the earlier portions of his life in consecutive biography.

William Tecumseh Sherman was born in Lancaster, Ohio, on the 8th day of February, 1820. His father was the Hon. Charles R. Sherman, one of the judges of the Supreme Court of Ohio, and he is brother of the Hon. John Sherman, United States Senator from Ohio. As a child young Sherman was educated in the family of the Hon. Thomas Ewing. At the age of sixteen he entered the United States Military Academy at West Point, and graduated June 30, 1840, class rank six.

On the 1st of July, 1840, he was promoted to second lieutenant of the 3d United States artillery. He served in Florida during the winter of 1840 and 1841. November 1, 1841, he was promoted to first lieutenant. Soon after he was stationed at Fort Moultrie, near Charleston, South Carolina. In 1846 he was engaged in active service in California, and held the position of acting Assistant Adjutant General of the 10th military department until 1847. May 30, 1848, he was breveted captain "for meritorious services in California during the Mexican war."

In September, 1850, he received the staff appointment of commissary of subsistence, with the rank of captain. In 1853 he resigned his commission in the army, and took charge of the banking-house of Lucas, Turner, & Co., at San Francisco. In 1860 he was the president of the State Military Academy of Louisiana, and remained in that position until the outbreak of the present war.

He had carefully watched the development of the portentous events of the winter of 1860 and 1861, and even before the first shot on Sumter sounded the summons to arms felt confident of the impossibility of avoiding an open rupture between the two sections of the country. True to the old flag, he addressed a letter of resignation to the authorities of the institution. The letter is so characteristic of the man that we embody it in full: —

January 18, 1861.

Governor THOMAS O. MOORE, Baton Rouge, La.: —

Sir: As I occupy a *quasi* military position under this state, I deem it proper to acquaint you that I accepted such position when Louisiana was a state in the Union, and when the motto of the seminary was inserted in marble over the main door — "By the liberality of the general government of the United States — the Union. *Esto perpetua.*"

Recent events foreshadow a great change, and it becomes all men to choose. If Louisiana withdraws from the Federal Union, I prefer to maintain my allegiance to the old constitution as long as a fragment of it survives, and my longer stay here would be wrong in every sense of the word. In that event I beg you will send or appoint some authorized agent to take charge of the arms and munitions of war here belonging to the state, or direct me what disposition should be made of them.

And furthermore, as president of the Board of Supervisors, I beg you to take immediate steps to relieve me as superintendent the moment the state determines to secede; for on no earthly account will I do any act or think any thought hostile to or in defiance of the old government of the United States.

With great respect, &c.,

W. T. SHERMAN.

His resignation was accepted, and he removed to St. Louis. During that season of dreadful suspense intervening the inauguration of the new president and the bombardment of Fort Sumter, Captain Sherman was in Washington. He conversed freely with persons of all positions and views, and was surprised to see the indifference exhibited upon the great question of the day. A personal friend thus narrates the captain's views at that time: —

"He was astonished at the apparent ignorance and incredulity of the government in regard to the real condition of the Southern States. He declared that the men in authority were sleeping on a volcano, which would surely burst upon them unprepared. Filled with this idea, he addressed a letter to the secretary of war, stating that as he was educated at the expense of the United States, and owed everything to his country, he had come to tender his military services. He warned Mr. Cameron, in earnest language, that war was imminent, and that we were not prepared. He also called upon the president, and, in like manner, stated his views and tendered his services. The president jocularly replied, 'We shall not need many men like you; the whole affair will soon blow over.' He was then urged by his friends to go to Ohio, and take care of the organization of three months' regiments. This he declined, as he did not believe in such trifling expedients. He declared it would be as wise to undertake to extinguish the flames of a burning building with a squirt gun as to put down the rebellion with three months' troops. His plan was to organize for a gigantic war, to call out the whole military power of the country at once, and, by the exercise of irresistible force, to crush the rebellion in its incipiency."

On the increase of the regular army by the addition of a number of new regiments, Captain Sherman was promoted to the colonelcy of the 13th regular infantry, dated May 14, 1861. In the first battle of Bull Run, July 21, Colonel Sherman commanded the 3d brigade, 1st division, Brigadier General Daniel Tyler commanding (McDowell's army), and behaved with marked gallantry. After the battle he was appointed, at the extra session of Congress, a brigadier general of volunteers, to date from May 17, 1861, and was ordered to the department of Kentucky, and was second in command to General Robert Anderson. Soon after his arrival in the department, General Sherman was ordered to occupy Muldraugh's Hill, Kentucky, — an important point south of the Rolling Fork, or Salt River, — with seven thousand men, made up of volunteers and Kentucky home guards. Upon reaching his destination his home guards left him, and troops designed for him were detached on other expeditions. In the end he found himself with less than five thousand men arrayed against Buckner's entire rebel force of more than twenty-five thousand men. In October General Sherman succeeded General Anderson in command of the department then known as the department of the Cumberland. In November he addressed General McClellan upon the strength and perilous situation of his command, concluding with the remark, "Our forces are too small to do good, and too large to be sacrificed."

General McClellan asked, "How long could McCook keep Buckner out of Louisville, holding the railroad, with power to destroy it inch by inch?"

The unsatisfactory nature of this reply, and the circumstances of the situation, were anything but agreeable, and any one else but Sherman would have abandoned the positions held by the troops, or resigned his command. By skilfully manœuvring his troops he managed to hold his ground.

About this time an incident occurred which should be narrated. I quote the words of Lieutenant Colonel Bowman:—

"General Sherman had had an interview with Secretary Cameron, in presence of Adjutant General Thomas, at Lexington, Kentucky, and fully explained to him the situation of his command, and also of the armies opposed to him, and, on being asked what force was necessary for a successful forward movement in his department, answered, 'Two hundred thousand men.' By the 1st of November Adjutant General Thomas's official report of this conversation, in all its details, was published in most of the newspapers of the country, *giving the enemy full knowledge* of many important facts relating to General Sherman's department. He was too weak to defend our lines, and the enemy knew it. He had no hope of reënforcement, and, withal, was evidently in discredit with the war department, as being too apprehensive of the power, strength, and resources of the enemy. He therefore felt he could not successfully conduct the campaign, and asked to be relieved. He was succeeded by General Buell, who was at once reënforced, and enabled to hold his defensive position, until Grant, in the following spring, should advance down the Mississippi and up the Cumberland. General Sherman was now set down as 'crazy,' and quietly retired to the command of Benton Barracks, near St. Louis. The evidence of his insanity was his answer to the secretary of war,—that to make a successful advance against the enemy, then strongly posted at all strategic points, from Mississippi to Cumberland Gap, would require an army two hundred thousand strong. The answer was the inspiration, or the judgment, of a military genius; but to the mind of Mr. Secretary Cameron it was the prophecy of a false wizard."

In the early part of the year 1862, General Sherman was again called to the field, and assigned to the command of the district of Cairo. In February his headquarters were at Paducah, Kentucky; and the general rendered invaluable service in forwarding troops and supplies to General Grant in his operations on the Tennessee and Cumberland Rivers. After the capitulation of Fort Donelson, General Sherman was assigned to the command of the 5th division, army of the Tennessee, Major General U. S. Grant commanding. At Shiloh Sherman first displayed to the army and the country that hidden merit which before then was only exhibited to meet the ridicule of ignorant men. We will permit his fellow-officers to speak of him there. After the battle a cavalry officer remarked, —

"Having occasion to report personally to General Sherman, about noon of the first day of Shiloh, I found him dismounted, his arm in a sling, his hand bleeding, his horse dead, himself covered with dust, his face besmeared with powder and blood. He was giving directions at the moment to Major Taylor, his chief of artillery, who had just brought a battery into position. Mounted orderlies were coming and going in haste; staff officers were making anxious inquiries; everybody but himself seemed excited. The battle was raging terrifically in every direction. Just then there seemed to be universal commotion on our right, where it was observed our men were giving back. 'I was looking for that,' said Sherman; 'but I am ready for them.' His quick, sharp eye flashed, and his war-begrimed face beamed with satisfaction. The enemy's packed columns now made their appearance, and as quickly the guns which Sherman had so carefully placed in position began to speak. The deadly effect on the enemy was apparent. While Sherman was still managing the artillery, Major Sanger, a staff officer, called his attention to the fact that the enemy's cavalry were charging towards the battery. 'Order up those two companies of infantry,' was the quick reply; and the general coolly went on with his guns. The cavalry made a gallant charge, but their horses carried back many empty saddles. The enemy was evidently foiled. Our men, gaining fresh courage, rallied again, and for the first time that day the enemy was held stubbornly in check. A moment more and he fell back over the piles of his dead and wounded."

General Rousseau, a division officer of Buell's army of the Cumberland, speaks of him in the following handsome manner: —

"He gave us our first lessons in the field in the face of an enemy; and of all the men I ever saw he is the most untiring, vigilant, and patient. No man that ever lived could surpass him. His enemies say that he was surprised at Shiloh. I tell you no. He was not surprised nor whipped, for he fights by the week. Devoid of ambition, incapable of envy, he is brave, gallant, and just. At Shiloh his old legion met him just as the battle was ended; and at the sight of him, placing their hats upon their bayonets, gave him three cheers. It was a touching and fitting compliment to the gallant chieftain. I am thankful for this occasion to do justice to a brave, honest, and knightly gentleman."

Nor did he escape the attention of his commanding officer. General

Grant, in a letter to the war department, under date of July 25, 1863, said, —

"To General Sherman I was greatly indebted for his promptness in forwarding to me, during the siege of Fort Donelson, reënforcements and supplies from Paducah. At the battle of Shiloh, on the last day, he held, with raw troops, the key-point of the landing. It is no disparagement to any other officer to say, that I do not believe there was another division commander on the field who had the skill and experience to have done it. To his individual efforts I am indebted for the success of that battle."

General Halleck, in his despatch to the secretary of war, recommending General Sherman for promotion, said of him, —

"It is the unanimous opinion here that Brigadier General W. T. Sherman saved the fortunes of the day on the 6th of April, and contributed largely to the glorious victory of the 7th. He was in the thickest of the fight on both days, having three horses killed under him, and being wounded twice. I respectfully request that he be made a major general of volunteers," to date from the 6th instant.

Acting upon this recommendation, General Sherman was promoted to the rank designated, to date from May 1, 1862. He next took part in the operations against Corinth, and his troops were the first to enter the enemy's works upon the morning of May 30.

The summer of 1862 was passed in completely overrunning and subjecting that portion of Tennessee lying west of the Tennessee River. Sherman moved at the head of a column across the country towards Memphis. The city capitulated to the gunboats on the 6th of June, and Sherman occupied it, and assumed command July 22. It is not necessary to particularize upon his administration. The turbulent element of the community was soon reduced to order, and the Union people were allowed all reasonable privileges. In November the general was assigned to the command of the right wing of the army of the Tennessee, and conducted an expedition threatening the enemy's rear south of the Tallahatchie River, and enabled General Grant to occupy the position without a fight. In December, he, having returned to Memphis, was assigned to the command of the 15th army corps, still continuing, however, in the general command of the right wing of the army. In the middle of the same month he organized an expedition, composed of the 13th and 15th corps, and moved down the Mississippi on transports, with a view to an attack upon Vicksburg from the Yazoo River, near Chickasaw Bayou and Haines's Bluff. The surrender of Holly Springs, Mississippi, enabling the enemy to concentrate at the point of attack frustrated the efforts of our troops.

The terrible fighting of December 27, 28, and 29, settled the fact that the place could not be taken by storm, and the troops were withdrawn to consummate the glorious victory of Arkansas Post, in January, 1863. In this last action General Sherman was subordinate to General McClernand, having been assigned by that officer to the command of the right wing of the temporary army of the Mississippi. Upon the concentration of troops, preparatory to further movements against Vicksburg, General Sherman was stationed with his corps in the vicinity of Young's Point. In March, 1863, he conducted the expedition up Steele's Bayou, and released Admiral Porter's fleet of gunboats, which, having been cut off and invested by the enemy, was in imminent danger of being captured.

This expedition was, perhaps, one of the most severe ever undertaken by his troops. They penetrated through a country cut up by numerous and deep bayous and swamps, and overgrown by immense forests of cottonwood and cypress. Sherman, with his usual determination, was not to be thwarted, and pushed ahead and accomplished his object.

Upon the inauguration of General Grant's movement across the Peninsula to Grand Gulf and Bruinsburg, during April, 1863, General Sherman made a feint upon Haines's Bluff, on the Yazoo River. His demonstration (April 28 and 29) was intended to hold the enemy about Vicksburg while the main army was securing a foothold on the eastern shore of the Mississippi, below. Having successfully performed this duty, by means of rapid and forced marches he moved down the Louisiana side of the river, crossed at Grand Gulf, and immediately pushed forward and rejoined General Grant's main army.

Sherman, with his corps, accompanied McPherson in his movement against Jackson, the capital of Mississippi. In the battle of Jackson Sherman took no prominent part, in consequence of the rout of the enemy being effected by McPherson's corps alone. The day after the battle McPherson hurried towards Baker's Creek, while Sherman remained in Jackson some hours longer, to complete the destruction of the enemy's stores and the railroad. He then moved on a line parallel with the route of march of McPherson's column, crossed the Big Black River, and took possession of Walnut Hills, near Vicksburg, on May 18. The occupation of this important position enabled General Grant to open communication with his depots of supplies on the Mississippi River, by way of Yazoo River, from Chickasaw Bayou.

During the siege of Vicksburg Sherman's corps held the left of General Grant's lines, and coöperated in all the combined attacks of the centre and right.

During the conference between the rebel commander Pemberton and General Grant, in regard to the terms of capitulation for the garrison and city of Vicksburg, Sherman was vigorously engaged in organizing an expedition at the Big Black River. No sooner had Vicksburg surrendered than he received orders to throw his force across the river, and move out into the country.

Vicksburg surrendered, and was occupied on the morning of the 4th of July. The same afternoon troops were converging from all parts of the old lines, and Sherman's advance had already crossed the Big Black.

It is not necessary to pursue the details of this expedition. Two days' march found Sherman investing Joe Johnston in Jackson. Before the beginning of August he engaged the enemy, and, defeating him severely, was about to close in upon his rear, when the rebel commander very prudently withdrew.

For his great services in the military operations of 1863, Major General Sherman was promoted to the rank of brigadier general in the regular army, to date from July 4, 1863, and was confirmed by the United States Senate, February 29, 1864.

Upon the assignment of General Grant to the command of the military division of the Mississippi, General Sherman succeeded, by authority of the president, to the command of the department and army of the Tennessee, to date from October 27, 1863. After making some necessary changes in the disposition of the troops on the Mississippi River, Sherman concentrated portions of the 15th and 16th corps at Corinth, and in the month of November moved, by way of Tuscumbia and Decatur, Alabama, to join and participate with General Grant in his winter campaign against Chattanooga.

General Sherman's forces moved up the north side of the Tennessee River, and during the nights of the 23d and 24th of November established pontoon bridges, and effected a lodgment on the south side, between Citico Creek and the Chickamauga River.

After the development of the plans along other portions of the lines, on the 24th, Sherman carried the eastern end of Missionary Ridge up to the tunnel. On the next day the whole of Missionary Ridge, from Rossville to the Chickamauga, was carried, after a series of desperate struggles.

By the turning of the enemy's right, and forcing it back upon Ringgold and Dalton, Sherman's forces were thrown between Bragg and

Longstreet, completely severing the enemy's lines. No sooner was this end attained than Thomas and Hooker forced Bragg into Georgia, while Sherman, with his own and Granger's forces, moved off to the succor of Knoxville. Burnside, by a gallant defence of the position, held out against Longstreet, who, upon the appearance of Sherman, was obliged to raise the siege, and effected his escape by withdrawing into Virginia.

The enemy being defeated at every point, his army broken, and his plans completely disarranged, and Grant's army in winter quarters, General Sherman, personally, left for Cairo, thence for Memphis, arriving in the beginning of January.

After organizing a portion of the 16th corps for the field, he despatched it upon transports to Vicksburg. In the latter part of the month he joined it, and finished the organization of a fine body of troops, composed of portions of the 16th army corps, Major General S. A. Hurlbut commanding, and the 17th army corps, Major General James B. McPherson commanding.

On the 3d of February the expeditionary army, commanded in person by Sherman, crossed the Big Black, and after continuous skirmishing along the route, entered Meridian, Mississippi, February 14, 1864, driving Polk, with a portion of his army, towards Mobile, another portion towards Selma, and completely cutting off Lovell from the main army, pursuing him with cavalry northward towards Marion. Remaining in possession of Meridian four days, the railroads converging there were destroyed within a radius of twenty miles. The army then returned by a different route, reaching Canton, Mississippi, February 26. Turning over the command of his army to McPherson, with instructions to devastate the country, and then to continue the return march to Vicksburg, General Sherman, at 8 o'clock the next morning, escorted by the 2d Iowa cavalry, pushed through in advance of the army, riding over sixty miles in twenty-four hours, and reached Vicksburg on the morning of February 28. Remaining in the city but a few hours, he embarked on one of the boats of the Mississippi marine brigade, and left for New Orleans. At the expiration of eight days he returned to Vicksburg, having, during his absence, consulted with General Banks upon the Red River expedition, towards which he was to contribute a coöperating column. This force was immediately organized and equipped, and embarked in March for the mouth of Red River, and was commanded by Generals A. J. Smith and Thomas Kirby Smith, both veteran officers, of large experience and ability. Sherman now left for Memphis.

The promotion of General Grant to the rank of lieutenant general and commander-in-chief of the armies of the United States, opened a still higher promotion to General Sherman. By authority of the president, expressed in general orders, dated March 12, he was assigned to the command of the military division of the Mississippi. On the 14th of March he received notification of his appointment, while at Memphis. He immediately left for Nashville, and held a conference with General Grant upon the subject of the spring operations. Between the two officers there was a full and complete understanding of the policy and plans for the ensuing campaign, which was designed to embrace a vast area of country.

On the 25th General Sherman commenced a tour of inspection of the various armies of his command, visiting Athens, Decatur, Huntsville, and Larkin's Ferry, Alabama; Chattanooga, Loudon, and Knoxville, Tennessee. In the course of his visit he held interviews with Major General McPherson at Huntsville, Major General Thomas at Chattanooga, and Major General Schofield at Knoxville. With these officers he arranged in general terms the lines of communication to be guarded, the strength of the several columns and garrisons, and appointed the 1st of May as the time for everything to be in readiness. While these commanders were carrying out their instructions, General Sherman returned to Nashville, giving his personal attention to the subject of supplies, organizing a magnificent system of railroad communication by two routes from Nashville. The storehouses and depots of Chattanooga soon groaned beneath the weight of abundance. The whole of East Tennessee and Northern Alabama contributed to the general store, while the whole north-west and west poured volumes of sustenance through the avenues of communication from Louisville.

On the 27th of April the three great armies of his division were converging at Chattanooga. The 1st of May witnessed over sixty thousand troops and one hundred and thirty guns, forming the army of the Cumberland, Major General George H. Thomas commanding, encamped in the vicinity of Ringgold, Georgia.

The gallant McPherson, with a portion of Grant's old veteran and victorious battalions of the army of the Tennessee, numbering twenty-five thousand troops of all arms, and ninety-six guns, lay at Gordon's Mill, on the historic Chickamauga.

General Schofield, with over thirteen thousand troops and twenty-eight guns, constituting the army of the Ohio, lay on the Georgia line, north of Dalton.

In the aggregate these three armies formed a grand army of over ninety-eight thousand men, and two hundred and fifty-four guns, under the supreme command of General Sherman.

The enemy, superior in cavalry, and with three corps of infantry and artillery, commanded by Hardee, Hood, and Polk, and all under the general command of General Joseph E. Johnston, lay in and about Dalton. His position was covered by an inaccessible ridge known as the Rocky Face, through which ran Buzzard Roost Gap. The railroad and wagon road following this pass the enemy had strongly defended by abatis and well-constructed fortifications. Batteries commanded it in its whole length, and especially from a ridge at its farther end, like a traverse directly across its debouche. To drive the enemy from this position by the front was impossible. After well reconnoitring the vicinity, but one practicable route by which to attack Johnston was found, and that was by Snake Creek Gap, by which Resaca, a point on the enemy's railroad communication eighteen miles below Dalton, could be reached. Accordingly McPherson was instructed to move rapidly from his position at Gordon's Mill by way of Ship's Gap, Villanow, and Snake Creek Gap, directly upon Resaca. During this movement Thomas was to make a strong feint attack in front, and Schofield was to press down from the north. Thomas occupied Tunnel Hill, May 7, facing Buzzard Roost Gap, experiencing little opposition, except from cavalry. McPherson reached Snake Creek Gap May 8, surprising a brigade of the enemy while *en route* to occupy it. May 9, Schofield moved down from the north close on Dalton. The same day Newton's division of the 4th corps carried the ridge, Geary, of the 20th corps, crowding on for the summit. While this was going on at the front, the head of McPherson's column made its appearance near Resaca, and took position confronting the enemy's works. May 10, the 20th corps (Hooker) moved to join McPherson; the 14th corps (Palmer) followed; the 4th corps (Howard) commenced pounding Dalton from the front. Meanwhile Schofield also hastened to join McPherson. May 11, the whole army, with the exception of Howard's corps and some cavalry, was in motion for Snake Creek Gap. May 12, McPherson debouched from the gap on the main road, Kilpatrick, with his cavalry, in front; Thomas moved on McPherson's left, Schofield on Thomas's left; Kilpatrick drove the enemy within two miles of Resaca. Kilpatrick having been wounded, Colonel Murray took command, and, wheeling out of the road, McPherson's columns crowded impetuously by, and driving the enemy's advance within the defences of Resaca, occupied a ridge of bold hills, his right resting on the Oustenaula, two miles below the railroad bridge, and his left abreast the town. Thomas, on his left, facing Camp Creek, and Schofield, forcing his way through a dense forest, came in on the extreme left. The enemy had evacuated Dalton, and was now concentrated at Resaca. Howard occupied Dalton, and hung upon the enemy's rear. May 14, the battle of Resaca commenced. May 15, it continued. The same night the enemy was flying towards the Etowah. The whole army followed in pursuit. May 19, Sherman held all the country north of the Etowah, and several crossings of that stream. May 23, the whole army was moving upon the flank of the enemy's position in the Allatoona Mountains. May 25, Hooker whipped the enemy near New Hope Church. On May 28, McPherson killed and wounded about five thousand of the enemy near Dallas. June 6, the enemy was in hasty retreat to his next position, at Kenesaw Mountains. June 8, Blair arrived at Ackworth, with the fresh troops of the 17th corps. June 11, the sounds of Sherman's artillery reverberated among the rugged contortions of Kenesaw. July 3, the enemy was pressing for the Chattahoochee; the mountains and Marietta were occupied by our forces the same day. The enemy had a *tête de pont* and formidable works on the Chattahoochee, at the railroad crossing. Sherman advanced boldly, with a small force, on the front. July 7, Schofield had possession of one of the enemy's pontoons, and occupied the south side of the Chattahoochee. By July 9, Sherman held three crossings. Johnston abandoned his *tête de pont*, and there was no enemy north or west of the Chattahoochee, July 10. July 17, the whole army was in motion across the Chattahoochee. July 18, Atlanta was cut off from the east. Rousseau, with an expeditionary cavalry force, was operating within the enemy's lines. July 20, all the armies closed in upon Atlanta. The same afternoon, the enemy attacked Hooker, and was driven into his intrenchments. On July 22, Johnston was relieved, and Hood, in command of the enemy, suddenly attacked McPherson's extreme left with overpowering numbers. Giles A. Smith held the position first attacked, with a division of McPherson's troops. First he fought from one side of the parapet; then, being attacked in the rear, he fought from the other. McPherson's whole army soon became engaged. The battle was the most desperate of the campaign. McPherson was killed when the contest was the thickest. His last order saved the army. Logan succeeded to command. "McPherson and revenge" rang along the lines. The effect was electric, and victory closed in with the night. The battle footed up nine thousand of the enemy against four thousand of our own troops killed and wounded — a balance in our favor of five thousand dead and mangled bodies.

Sherman gradually enveloped the city. August 31, Hood again attacked the army of the Tennessee, now commanded by Howard. It took two hours to run up a list of twenty-five hundred killed and wounded of the enemy, and hurl him back within his defences. September 1, the enemy retreated south. That night, heavy explosions were heard in the direction of Atlanta. The next morning, the city was found evacuated. Pursuing the enemy for a short distance, Sherman withdrew his whole army for rest, encamping it at points near and around Atlanta. He instantly banished all the inhabitants of the place, and accumulated a large supply of stores. The wisdom of this step was soon apparent. The enemy, in October, moved around the flank of Sherman's army. Sherman encouraged him. Hood made demonstrations upon the lines of communication, but gained no success. Sherman now organized two armies. One, under Thomas, was to look after Hood; with the remainder he set out, about the middle of November, upon what promised to be one of the most brilliant campaigns of the war. With regard to this movement, Mr. Lincoln aptly remarked, "We all know where Sherman went in; it now remains to be seen where he will come out."

In all of General Sherman's career he has evinced a determination in the cause of the government, and a correctness of views, that have not failed to elicit the remark and admiration of the country. He rose amid a singular ordeal, and, while the ephemeral lights of the early war broke forth, flickered for a moment, and then expired, he applied himself quietly and usefully to the fighting of the enemy. He advanced slowly but surely, and to-day, in military skill and ability of execution, is second to no officer in the army. He also possesses a remarkable moral force. He never consults the comfort of an enemy in regard to his measures, but orders and carries out. He always has a line of duty, from which he cannot be moved. For instance, when he commenced preparations for his Georgia campaign, the depots at Chattanooga were empty. · The following was the substance of one of his first orders: —

"Provisions will no longer be issued to citizens at military posts south of Nashville. When citizens cannot procure provisions in the country, there is no alternative but to remove to the rear.

"Supplies must not be sold to any person save officers in the service of the United States, and men employed by quartermasters, or in other departments of the government, at a rate not to exceed one ration per day. It is idle to be pushing forward subsistence stores, if lavished and expended upon persons not belonging to the army."

The order was carried out.

During the same campaign, members of the Christian Commission applied for permission for its delegates to pass within his lines. He replied to their letter, —

"Certainly not; crackers and oats are more necessary for the army than any moral or religious agency, and every regiment has its chaplain."

When, afterwards, he traversed the long, single line of rickety railroad, beset by guerrillas, and upon which he was obliged to depend for supplies for his army, and now that we realize how much of the success of his campaign depended upon secret combinations and sudden movements, we can appreciate the necessity for this stringent military control over his rear communication, and approve the policy of the general who makes the material support of the army his first and constant care.

A great deal might also be said of Sherman in relation to his views upon the questions of the war, the treatment of guerrillas, the treatment of secession sympathizers, and upon the important subject of military necessities; but his letters are not yet forgotten, and their principles are now beneficially at work in many portions of the south-west.

In physical appearance, General Sherman is about an inch less than six feet in height. His frame is of good size; but a moderate development of muscle gives him an appearance of being more slender than he really is. His hair and eyes are dark, his forehead high, and so exceedingly fair, that, standing as it does in marked contrast with his hair and eyes, it is his prominent feature. His cheeks are marked with deep lines. A benevolent countenance, together with a kind and genial manner, make him look more like a minister than the stern soldier he is.

The following is a picture of Sherman, as he appeared during one of the movements around Atlanta. It is given by a correspondent.

"While I was watching to-day the endless line of troops shifting by, an officer with a modest escort rode up to the fence near which I was standing, and dismounted. He was rather tall and slender, and his quick movements denoted good muscle, added to absolute leanness — not thinness. His uniform was neither new nor old, but bordering on a hazy mellowness of gloss, while the elbows and knees were a little accented from the continuous agitation of those joints.

"The face was one I should never rest upon in a crowd, simply because, to my eye, there was nothing remarkable in it save the nose, which organ was high, thin, and planted with a curve as vehement as the curl of a Malay cutlass. The face and neck were rough, and covered with reddish hair; the eye light in color and animated, but, though restless, and bounding like a ball from one object to another, neither piercing nor brilliant; the mouth well closed, but common; the ears large; the hands and feet long and thin; the gait a little rolling, but firm and active. In dress and manner there was not the slightest trace of pretension. He spoke rapidly, and generally with an inquisitive smile. To this *ensemble* I must add a hat which was the reverse of dignified or distinguished, — a simple felt affair, with a round crown and drooping brim, — and you have as fair a description of General Sherman's externals as I can pen.

"Seating himself on a stick of cordwood, hard by the fence, he drew a bit of pencil from his pocket, and, spreading a piece of note paper on his knee, he wrote with great rapidity. Long columns of troops lined the road a few yards in his front, and beyond the road, massed in a series of spreading green fields, a whole division of infantry was waiting to take up the line of march, the blue ranks clear cut against the verdant background. Those who were near their general looked at him curiously; for in so vast an army the soldier sees his commander-in-chief but seldom. Page after page was filled by the general's nimble pencil, and despatched.

"For a half hour I watched him; and though I looked for and expected to find them, no symptoms could I detect that the mind of the great leader was taxed by the infinite cares of a terribly hazardous military *coup de main*. Apparently it did not lay upon his mind the weight of a feather. A mail arrived. He tore open the papers, and glanced over them hastily, then chatted with some general officers near him, then rode off with characteristic suddenness, but with fresh and smiling countenance, filing down the road beside many thousand men, whose lives were in his keeping."

II.

ORGANIZATION OF GENERAL SHERMAN'S STAFF AND ARMY.

I will say a few words about the chiefs of the leading departments, Sherman's personal staff, and different commanders.

Major General BARRY, a descendant of the noble house of Barrymore, of Cork, Ireland, chief of artillery, is a veteran soldier, of judgment and experience, and is also a kind, courteous gentleman, possessing a good deal of the frank, honest manner of the old school.

Of the merits of Brigadier General EASTON, chief quartermaster, I have before spoken in this work.

General C. EWING, inspector general, is brother-in-law to General Sherman; is a thorough soldier, and a kind, courteous gentleman. Efficient in the discharge of his duties, kind to the afflicted, he never turned a deaf ear to real suffering, and his charitable interference saved many a poor family from ruin.

Dr. MOORE, chief medical director of the army, has proved himself not only a skilful practitioner, but also a man of fine organizing administrative powers. The despatch with which hospitals were established, and the admirable manner in which the wounded were carried and cared for during our campaigns and marches through Georgia and the Carolinas, reflect the highest credit upon his controlling influence, and on the medical staff in general. Dr. Moore is, I think, a north of Ireland man.

Colonel BECKWITH, chief commissary, was an energetic, calculating, hard-working man, of great conception and endurance.

Personal Staff of General Sherman in the Field.

Major McCOY, A. D. C.
Captain AUDENRIED, A. D. C.
Major HITCHCOCK, A. A. G.
Captain DAYTON, A. D. C., performing the duties of adjutant general.

The following officers transacted the important duties of the Nashville bureau: —

Brigadier General WEBSTER,
Lieutenant Colonel R. M. SAWYER, A. A. G.
Captain ROCHESTER, A. A. G.
Captain WARNER, A. Q. M.
Captain COVERDALE, A. Q. M.

APPENDIX.

Captain JENNY, in charge of the engineer bureau at Nashville.

The signal corps was represented by Captain BACHTAL, who proved himself a very active and intelligent officer.

Colonel POE was chief of engineers, a man of genius and scientific knowledge.

Captain BAYLOR, chief of ordnance.

The army was divided into two wings, one under command of Major General HOWARD, comprising the 15th and 17th corps.

The other, under command of Major General SLOCUM, comprised the 14th and 20th corps.

The 15th corps was commanded by Major General JOHN A. LOGAN until its arrival in Washington, when, General Howard being transferred to the freedmen's bureau, General Logan was transferred to his command, and General HAZEN took command of the 15th corps.

Its division commanders were — 1st division, General WOOD; 2d division, General HAZEN; 4th division, General CORSE. Its 3d division has been consolidated with the others.

The 17th corps was commanded by General FRANK BLAIR. Its division commanders were — 1st division, General FORCE; 2d division, General GILES E. SMITH; 3d division, General LEGATE.

Howard's command has been called the army of the Tennessee, and Slocum's the army of Georgia.

The 14th corps was commanded by General JEFF C. DAVIS. At the opening of the campaign it was commanded by General PALMER, then by General JOHNSON.

Its division commanders were — 1st division, General CARLIN; 2d division, General J. D. MORGAN; 3d division, General BAIRD.

The 20th corps was commanded up to Atlanta by Major General HOOKER, subsequently by General WILLIAMS.

Its division commanders were — 1st division, General JACKSON; 2d division, General J. W. GEARY; 3d division, General W. T. WARD.

The cavalry corps was under the command of Major General KILPATRICK.

Badges of the different Corps.

The 20th corps, a star — 1st division, red; 2d, white; and 3d, blue.

14th corps, an acorn — red, white, and blue.

17th corps, an arrow — red, white, and blue.

15th corps, a cartridge-box — red, white, and blue, and yellow for 4th division.

There is a little story connected with this badge. An Irish soldier belonging to the 15th corps, as he trudged along, met a soldier of the 20th corps. The latter asked Pat, —

"What corps do you belong to?"

"Faix, then, John Logan's corps."

"Haven't you any badge?"

"Badge — arrah, what's that?"

"Look here," said the other, proudly pointing to his bran new star; "there is my badge?"

"An' here, by japers, is my badge; forty rounds in me cartridge-box," was the other's ready reply, as he gave a sound slap to the said cartridge-box in proof of his assertion.

General Logan was so well pleased at Paddy's reply, that he adopted the cartridge-box as the badge of the corps.

III.

THE SURRENDER AND PAROLE OF GENERAL JOHNSTON'S ARMY.

The details of the condition and surrender of General Johnston and his army to General Sherman, which we copy from the New York *Herald*, were left in the hands of Major General Schofield.

General Sherman, having made proper arrangements for the final march and disposition of his army, took his leave, with the intention of joining them at Alexandria.

Generals Howard and Slocum commanded the two columns which broke camp around Raleigh on the 29th and 30th ult.

We arrived at Greensboro' about 4 o'clock yesterday to begin the parolling of the prisoners. A large number of paroled officers and men were loitering about the depot. The women crowded out to see the Yankee troops, but the men made no display; even the bands refrained from playing.

Before night the rebels and ourselves were on the best possible terms with one another. Rebel and Federal soldiers were grouped together around the fires, trading coffee, whiskey, meat, and tobacco. Some of them were fighting their battles over again.

General Hardee had a carriage and barouche in readiness for the party, and drove them to the residence of Ex-Governor Morehead, where they took up their quarters. In the evening, Generals Schofield,

Cox, and staff paid a visit to General Johnston at his headquarters, about a mile and a half from the town.

General Johnston's camp was a very plain one, scarcely as respectable as a division general's in the Union army. The tents were old, and scattered about without much regard to regularity. The general's tent was a plain wall tent, not much better than the rest. In front of this, General Johnston and some five or six officers of his staff were sitting. On the lid of a mess-chest near them were the remains of a very plain, frugal supper. Johnston is a man of about five feet nine inches in height, rather slight, but muscularly built frame. From appearance I should take him to be about fifty. Only that his hair and beard are so gray, you would not think him so old. He is evidently a man of great reflective powers, schooled into the greatest subserviency, combined with untiring energy. His conversation is so natural, dignified, and easy that you at once feel at your ease, though, at the same time, you are conscious that he is reading your thoughts like an open book. He has much of the refined ease and elegance of a gentleman, with the penetration and firmness of a soldier. He conversed freely.

A remark was made on the hopelessness of the south contending against the north with her vast wealth and unbounded resources, both in men and means. While this war has depopulated and devastated the south, the north was never so flourishing, and never had so large a population.

"True enough; yet we did not fail so much from the want of men and means as from mismanagement. Had we your government, sir, the result might be quite different."

He thinks the mass of the people will quietly return to their homes, and conform to the new state of things. He was bitter on the murder of President Lincoln.

"Lincoln, sir," he said, "was a good man and a conservative man. His death placed in power a man of radical principles — a southern man — a man, I fear, of strong private prejudices, who will not try to heal up the wounds of the nation. The scoundrel Booth was a hot-brained man, full of a kind of tragic desire of immortality. He was no friend to the south. If, at any time, such an act could complicate the Federal government, it is not now. Even should the president's death help our cause for a season, it would be sure to bring a curse upon it; for never did a cause flourish by assassination. All good men and true soldiers detest the assassin. I hope he may be taken alive, in order to come at his accomplices."

General Johnston spoke in very flattering terms of General Sherman's military abilities, but was very bitter on Jeff Davis, in fact, attributing the whole failure to his bungling administration.

In a few days the rebel army will march to their respective states to be disbanded and paroled. It is thought that about thirty thousand will be paroled, the remainder having broken up in squads, and scattered over the country. This they did while the peace negotiations were pending. They were glad of the chance. The obloquy of desertion being removed, they bade good by to the rebel cause, and thought they would carry on a little war on their own account, which they are doing by pillaging and plundering the wretched inhabitants through the country. Johnston had close on fifty thousand men, all told, infantry, and cavalry, under him. Thirty thousand being paroled, leaves a desertion of nearly twenty thousand. The south might justly exclaim, "From our friends, O Lord deliver us!"

We have got in but very few battle-flags or horses. All of them have been either destroyed or carried off. We have about fifteen thousand stand of small arms, with about one hundred and ten or twenty pieces of artillery. One fifth of the men were allowed to retain their arms, to guard the rest and their supplies on their way home. Only the officers' paroles have been signed on the spot. The others have been given to the brigade commanders, not to be distributed until they are disbanding. This was done in order to keep them together.

Lee's and Hardee's corps were stationed at High Point, some fourteen miles from Raleigh; Stewart's corps at Hoyt's place, about five miles from town.

The number of men and officers paroled in each corps is—

In Hardee's, about eight thousand five hundred; Stewart's, close on eight thousand; S. D. Lee's, about five thousand; in the cavalry, about three thousand five hundred. To these might be added several independent commands.

Generals Debrill's and Young's divisions of cavalry, which have been operating on the confines of Georgia and South Carolina, are not likely to come in to be paroled, but will disband themselves, or become guerrillas. Wade Hampton and Wheeler have betaken themselves no one knows where. It is generally supposed that they are with the dethroned Jeff Davis.

There is no blame attached to General Johnston on account of the desertion of his troops. He had sent word to General Schofield, a few days previous, that his men were breaking up in bodies, and that he was powerless to prevent them, as they had lost all regard for order or discipline. They even stole most of the headquarters horses, leaving the general and staff to shift for themselves. They have even dismounted several of their officers, with the polite intimation that "the d—d sons of b—s rode long enough; it was their turn now, and to get off quick, or they would let the light through them." The outraged, despised scions of aristocracy would of course submit to such killing arguments.

This proves that the rebel army was not actuated by a spirit of patriotism, but coerced by military despotism or fanaticism.

The poor privates are trying to work their way home, lame, naked, and hungry, despised and loathed by the chivalry, for whose dynasty they fought. I have seen ladies, who would treat you to two mortal hours' bitter invective against the Yanks, refuse to feed poor, deluded, foot-sore rebel soldiers, while Union soldiers freely shared their hard tack and coffee with them, or Union officers handed them their lunches from their saddle-bags.

There is a bitter feeling growing in the south among the democracy against the aristocracy.

I remarked that there was nothing like the same order and neatness in the rebel camps that marked the Federals. No nicely laid out streets; no shaded pavilions for headquarters; but they looked like a bivouac, or as if there was a heavy shower of dirty tents' and there they stood, higgledy-piggledy, big and little, as they fell. About eleven o'clock next morning we left Greensboro'. General Johnston called to bid General Schofield good by, and remained a long time in conversation, in the carriage with him. The people greeted us, as we stopped at the different stations. The ladies received us with bouquets of flowers and waving handkerchiefs. At Company Shops station, there was quite a meeting of negroes, of all shades and sizes, awaiting us.

Major General Cox remains at Greensboro', where he is about establishing his headquarters; so also is Kilpatrick. A division of the 23d corps is to remain at Raleigh; another, Rogers's, at Charlotte; the remainder between Salisbury, Hillsboro', and other points. The bulk of Kilpatrick's cavalry will also garrison the same places, while the dismounted and useless portion will be sent home.

This morning General Hardee's party left Raleigh at five o'clock, and reached Durham's at half past seven. By invitation, they breakfasted with General Kilpatrick, after which they continued on to Greensboro'. I accompanied the party from Durham's. General Hardee received me in a very cordial, generous, unreserved manner. We talked freely on all subjects of interest at the present time. In speaking of the war, he made this remarkable assertion: "Sir, I accept this war as the providence of God. He intended that the slave should be free, and now he is free. Slavery was never a paying institution. I have often told my friends so. For instance, my wife owned about one hundred negroes; forty of the hundred were useless for work, yet she had to feed these forty, in order to get the work of the other sixty. The negro will be worse off for this war. Will any of your abolitionists of the north feed and clothe half a dozen little children, in order to get the work of a man and woman? Sir, our people can pay the working negroes a fair compensation for their services, and let them take care of their own families, and then have as much left at the end of the year as we had under the old system."

"General, do you think we will soon have real peace?"

"I do. I think the people of the south are anxious for it. They wanted it two years ago. I then saw that our cause could not succeed."

"Will we not have guerrilla warfare?"

"So help me God, sir, if we do, I am willing and ready to fight to put an end to it."

"Is the same sentiment entertained by the other general officers who have been in the Confederate service?"

"It is. I have not the slightest doubt but they will use every means they can command to bring quietness and security again in the land. They will in no wise support those who do not obey the laws."

"How will it be in South Carolina?"

"South Carolina is the worst whipped state in the Union."

"But will not her leading spirits control the masses?"

"They, too, are crushed. She has no leading spirits now. Let me impress it upon you that the people of the south want to live in peace with the people of the north, and you will find they will do it. They will do it cheerfully, provided your government does not resort to harsh measures. If it does resort to such measures, I cannot answer for the consequences. We staked our all on the success of our arms, and they failed us; and now we are willing to return to and live under the laws of the United States as we find them, although they may not be as we would desire to have them."

"Your officers have no money. What are they going to do?"

"They must go to work. The prospect before them is most gloomy indeed. It will be very hard on old men like me. I cannot now commence a profession."

"Do you think Jeff Davis was pleased at the assassination of President Lincoln?"

"I do not think he was. The people of the south do not like Andy Johnson. How can they, compared to Mr. Lincoln? Lincoln had been in office four years, and knew whom he could trust. He had also learned to govern. He had made a name. He could have done many things for the south that Johnson cannot. I do not believe that Lincoln was a party man — that is, that he was particularly so. Johnson is a party man. He is new, and the fear is, he will be radical. I hope he will not, for the good of the country and the welfare of the people."

"It is said that Jeff Davis went off with several millions in specie. Is it so?"

"I cannot particularly say whether it is or not. I know that General Johnston asked Mr. Davis to order some of the troops to be paid off in gold, and he replied that he had no control over the money. He said that the most of it had been taken from the Virginia banks, and that when these were again able to receive it, he would see that it was properly returned."

"Do you think that if Mr. Davis takes the money out of the confederacy, he will return it to the banks?"

"I think he will."

"Is there much cotton in the south, general?"

"O yes. And, by the way, let me say that it will oppress the people of the south very much, if the government of the United States confiscates the cotton belonging to private individuals. These people need the cotton and tobacco to commence business on. They are the only articles they have to sell. Give them a chance to sell their cotton and their tobacco, and there will be greenbacks introduced, and trade will revive. The cotton which the Confederate government owned, I believe to be the rightful property of the United States; and further, believe that the people of the south should be honest, and turn that property in to the agents authorized to receive it. One man told me he had some Confederate cotton on his plantation, and that he intended to burn it before the enemy should get possession of it. I told him he would be doing very wrong in committing such an act. On my wife's plantation in Alabama I have some cotton that belonged to the Confederate government, which I am well guarding, and will turn it over whenever the United States agents are ready to receive it."

At this juncture, a special train with United States troops, and Generals Schofield, Cox, and Kilpatrick on board, arrived close behind ours, at a station where the engine was stopped for wood and water. The second train had left Raleigh at 7 A. M., and was also bound for Greensboro'. General Hardee, and two other rebel officers, repaired to the car in which the Union generals were sitting, whereupon introductions took place, and agreeable conversation ensued.

On the line of the North Carolina Railroad, the appearance of the Union soldiers was hailed with gladness. The ladies waved their handkerchiefs, the band played, the soldiers cheered, the darkies danced, and all seemed delighted and overjoyed. A bright mulatto girl, who got in conversation with an officer, inquired if Massa Greeley was on board of the train. If so, she said she had a bouquet for him. As we passed one house, on the way up, an old lady came out, waved the dishcloth, and danced, as though the joyous character of her feelings made her limbs to work like piston-rods. All on the train noticed the old lady's movements, and marked her joy. At Company Shops, the ladies had prepared dinner for the generals, but, owing to the necessity of pushing on, the officers had to forego the pleasures of the feast prepared for them.

At Company Shops there are a large depot, and extensive works for the construction of cars, railroad iron, and engines. The buildings are all of brick. A feature of the place is the number of well-constructed brick houses, built by the company for the families of its employees.

On our arrival at Greensboro', General Hardee conducted Generals Schofield, Cox, and Kilpatrick to the headquarters of General Johnston, where the Union generals were politely received, a conference ensuing. While the same was going on, the 104th Ohio volunteer regiment was marched into the town, to do provost guard duty. As was quite natural, a very large crowd collected to see the ambassadors from Yankeedom. The streets were full of rebel soldiers, some of whom were paroled, and some not. We found two or three hotels open, doing business, and succeeded in getting rooms at one of them.

After the Union generals had conferred with General Johnston, the gentlemen of the press were formally presented and introduced to the rebel commander, who rose and received them in the most friendly manner.

During a brief period, when the general was disengaged, I had a private conversation with him, on subjects pertaining to the war, and the surrender of his army. I read to him the following: —

WAR DEPARTMENT,
WASHINGTON, April 24, 1865.

This department has information that the president's murder was organized in Canada, and approved at Richmond.   *   *   *

EDWIN M. STANTON, *Secretary of War.*

After which I inquired, "General, do you think that Mr. Davis had any thing to do with the assassination?"

"I do not," he replied. "When I told President Davis that President Lincoln had been assassinated, he was very much grieved indeed. I do not believe — in fact, am sure that President Davis did not in any way countenance the act."

"General Hampton went away without being paroled?"

"Yes; I understand he was ordered by the president to accompany him."

General Johnston admitted that one division of Wheeler's cavalry had gone off with Davis. Wheeler, it was reported to-day, had also gone with him.

General Johnston says that all the rebel forces in the States of North and South Carolina, Georgia, and Florida, are included in the surrender.

I find that the leading southern men are widely divided in sentiment among themselves. And what is more, General Sherman's course has been the source of much trouble for the north. By not demanding an immediate surrender, it enabled Jeff Davis to escape with much gold and silver, and to have it guarded by a strong rebel cavalry force. The armistice afforded an opportunity for the rebel commanders to make speeches to their commands, and they improved that opportunity to do so. One commander (General Hoke) told his men that the war was over; that they were overpowered; that he would like to have them remain with him and be paroled, but if any of them wanted to go home, they could do so.

The consequence was, that fully two thirds of his command did go home, scattering throughout the country, some carrying their arms with them, and some not. It is the same of many other rebel commanders. General Johnston says there was no absolute, immediate necessity for the surrender; that he could have got away from General Sherman. He said, —

"But I saw that we must come up somewhere. We would certainly have had to stop at the Mississippi; so I negotiated as I did with General Sherman, believing it criminal to prolong a hopeless war another day. The fate of the Confederacy was decided in Virginia. When Lee surrendered, there was an end to it. Had I marched my army away, as I could have done, it was only dragging Sherman after me. He would have foraged on the country, and I would have been compelled to do the same. The country would have been devastated, and we would have had to come to some terms at last."

Judging from General Johnston's conversation, and from what I have heard from those who were present at the conference, he would have surrendered his army at once on the terms granted to Lee.

General Johnston's headquarters are located in a pleasant grove, on a high hill, at a distance of about two miles west of Greensboro'. The members of his staff still remain with him. The whole are in tents.

The General Officers paroled.

As the following officers belonged to the headquarters department, and to the navy, I give their names, as also the number of men belonging to their respective commands surrendered: —

Rank.	No. of Men.
Admiral R. Semmes, naval brigade,	246
General P. T. G. Beauregard, and staff officers,	54
Major Smith, quartermaster commissary,	21
Flag Officer Forrest, naval brigade,	74
Captain Taylor, detachment Lee's army,	96
Lieutenant Duvall, signal corps,	36
James Sloan, major and chief of staff,	27
General Brettler, staff cavalry,	9
General Logan, staff cavalry,	6
Captain E. M. Holloway, commanding escort,	76
J. F. Caldwell, telegraph corps,	21
Captain W. Quirk, provost guard,	61
Captain West, camp of instruction,	106
Captain Brickner,	46
Isaiah Yorkeman,	1
Major Shannon,	55
Dr. Hines, post hospital,	10
J. Hammon,	13
Captain Harris, artillerists,	120
Colonel Park, invalid corps,	7
Surgeon E. W. Jolus,	13
Captain A. Cammack, acting quartermaster,	5
Captain H. P. Abell,	126
Captain J. P. Yates,	97
Captain A. A. Mosly, Palmer's battalion,	41
Major Johnson, officers engineer corps,	28
Lieutenant McGuire, mounted infantry,	36
Lieutenant Colonel Sharr, field and staff, artillery, Major Morris, brigade,	57
Brigadier General Herbert,	3
Captain Southerland, artillery,	87
Captain Badham,	68
Major Maye,	3
Captain Kelly, artillery, Colonel Stor,	100

Rank.	No. of Men.
Captain Ellis, artillery, Colonel Stor,	53
J. V. Darden, artillery, Colonel Stor,	18
Major Pregnesert, commissary department,	44
Major H. B. McClellan, cavalry headquarters,	61
Captain William Wallace, post commander,	154
Colonel E. J. Harvie, army headquarters,	170
Surgeon John Closter,	4
Lieutenant Colonel Gougates, Hardee's chief of artillery,	8
Colonel Coffer, assistant, and the provost marshal,	245
Daniel Morgan,	37
Lieutenant Colonel Clew, horse artillery,	26
Lieutenant M. L. Stevenson,	1
Surgeon O. H. Moore, hospital patients, Greensboro',	735
Lieutenant H. Hometer,	1
Lieutenant Colonel W. W. Wien,	1

Among the paroled prisoners is the notorious pirate Semmes, and Commodores Lynch and Forrest. These naval heroes, looking upon discretion as the better part of valor, gave up the sea for the secure quiet of domestic life. Another officer paroled was the notorious Major Gilchrist, who boasts that the first shot of the war was fired by him at the Star of the West, in Charleston Harbor.

General Johnston was not formally paroled. He simply pledged his verbal parole to General Sherman.

IV.

GENERAL SHERMAN'S TESTIMONY BEFORE THE COMMITTEE ON THE WAR.

MAJOR GENERAL SHERMAN being sworn and examined: —
By the Chairman.— Q. What is your rank in the army? A. I am major general in the regular army.

Q. As your negotiation with the rebel General Johnston in relation to his surrender has been the subject of much public comment, the committee desire you to state all the facts and circumstances in regard to it, or which you wish the public to know. A. On the 15th day of April last I was at Raleigh, in command of three armies: the army of the Ohio, the army of the Cumberland, and the army of the Tennessee; my enemy was General Joseph E. Johnston, of the Confederate army, who commanded fifty thousand men, retreating along the railroad from Raleigh by Hillsboro', Greensboro', Salisbury, and Charlotte; I commenced pursuit by crossing the curve of that road in the direction of Ashboro' and Charlotte; after the head of my column had crossed the Cape Fear River at Aven's Ferry, I received a communication from General Johnston, and answered it, copies of which I most promptly sent to the war department, with a letter addressed to the secretary of war, as follows: —

Headquarters Military Division of the Mississippi,
in the Field, Raleigh, N. C., April 15, 1865.

General U. S. GRANT and Secretary of War: I send copies of a correspondence to you with General Johnston, which I think will be followed by terms of capitulation. I will grant the same terms General Grant gave General Lee, and be careful not to complicate any points of civil policy. If any cavalry has retreated towards me, caution them to be prepared to find our work done. It is now raining in torrents, and I shall await General Johnston's reply here, and will prepare to meet him in person at Chapel Hill.

I have invited Governor Vance to return to Raleigh, with the civil officers of his state. I have met Ex-Governor Graham, Messrs. Badger, Moore, Holden, and others, all of whom agree that the war is over, and that the states of the south must resume their allegiance, subject to the constitution and laws of Congress, and must submit to the national arms. This great fact was admitted, and the details are of easy arrangement.

W. T. SHERMAN, *Major General.*

I met General Johnston in person at a house five miles from Durham Station, under a flag of truce. After a few preliminary remarks, he said to me, since Lee had surrendered his army at Appomattox Court-house, of which he had just been advised, he looked upon further opposition by him as the greatest possible of crimes; that he wanted to know whether I could make him any general concessions — anything by which he could maintain his hold and control of his army, and prevent its scattering; anything to satisfy the great yearning of their people; if so, he thought he could arrange terms satisfactory to both parties. He wanted to embrace the condition and fate of all the armies of the southern Confederacy to the Rio Grande, — to make one job of it, as he termed it.

I asked him what his powers were — whether he could command and control the fate of all the armies to the Rio Grande. He answered that he thought he could obtain the power, but he did not possess it at that moment; he did not know where Mr. Davis was, but he thought if I could give him the time he could find Mr. Breckinridge, whose orders would be obeyed everywhere, and he could pledge to me his personal faith that whatever he undertook to do would be done.

I had had frequent correspondence with the late president of the United States, with the secretary of war, with General Halleck, and with General Grant, and the general impression left upon my mind, that if a settlement could be made, consistent with the constitution of the United States, the laws of Congress, and the proclamation of the president, they would not only be willing, but pleased, to terminate the war by one single stroke of the pen.

I needed time to finish the railroad from the Neuse Bridge up to Raleigh, and thought I could put in four or five days of good time in making repairs to my road, even if I had to send propositions to Washington; I therefore consented to delay twenty-four hours, to enable General Johnston to procure what would satisfy me as to his authority and ability, as a military man, to do what he undertook to do; I therefore consented to meet him the next day, the 17th, at 12 noon, at the same place.

We did meet again. After a general interchange of courtesies, he remarked that he was then prepared to satisfy me that he could fulfil the terms of our conversation of the day before. He then asked me what I was willing to do; I told him, in the first place, I could not deal with anybody except men recognized by us as "belligerents," because no military man could go beyond that fact. The attorney general has since so decided, and any man of common sense so understood it before; there was no difference upon that point as to the men and officers accompanying the Confederate armies. I told him that the president of the United States, by a published proclamation, had enabled every man in the southern Confederate army, of the rank of colonel and under, to procure and obtain amnesty, by simply taking the oath of allegiance to the United States, and agreeing to go to his home and live in peace. The terms of General Grant to General Lee extended the same principles to the officers, of the rank of brigadier general and upward, including the highest officer in the Confederate army, viz., General Lee, the commander-in-chief. I was therefore willing to proceed with him upon the same principles.

Then a conversation arose as to what form of government they were to have in the south. Were the states there to be dissevered, and were the people to be denied representation in Congress? Were the people there to be, in the common language of the people of the south, slaves to the people of the north? Of course I said, "No; we desire that you shall regain your position as citizens of the United States, free and equal to us in all respects, and wish representation upon the condition of submission to the lawful authority of the United States as defined by the constitution, the United States courts, and the authorities of the United States supported by those courts." He then remarked to me that General Breckinridge, a major general in the Confederate army, was near by, and, if I had no objection, he would like to have him present. I called his attention to the fact, that I had on the day before explained to him that any negotiations between us must be confined to belligerents. He replied that he understood that perfectly. " But," said he, " Breckinridge, whom you do not know, save by public rumor, as secretary of war, is, in fact, a major general; I give you my word for that. Have you any objection to his being present as a major general?" I replied, " I have no objection to any military officer you desire being present as a part of your personal staff." I myself had my own officers near me at call.

Breckinridge came a stranger to me, whom I had never spoken to in my life, and he joined in the conversation. While that conversation was going on, a courier arrived and handed to General Johnston a package of papers; he and Breckinridge sat down and looked over them for some time, and put them away in their pockets; what they were I know not, but one of them was a slip of paper, written, as General Johnston told me, by Mr. Reagan, postmaster general of the southern Confederacy; they seemed to talk about it *sotto voce*, and finally handed it to me; I glanced over it; it was preceded by a preamble, and closed with a few general terms. I rejected it at once.

We then discussed matters; talked about slavery, talked about everything. There was a universal assent that slavery was as dead as anything could be; that it was one of the issues of the war long since determined; and even General Johnston laughed at the folly of the Confederate government in raising negro soldiers, whereby they gave us all the points of the case. I told them that slavery had been treated by us as a dead institution, first by one class of men from the initiation of the war, and then from the date of the emancipation proclamation of President Lincoln, and finally by the assent of all parties. As to the reconstruction, I told them I did not know what the views of the administration were. Mr. Lincoln, up to that time, in letters and by telegrams to me, encouraged me by all the words which could be used in general terms to believe, not only in his willingness, but in his desires, that I should make terms with civil authorities, governors, and legislatures, even as far back as 1863. It then occurred to me that I might write off some general propositions, meaning little, or meaning much, according to the construction of parties, — what I would term " glittering generalities,"— and send them to Washington, which I could do in four days. That would enable the new president to give me a clew to his policy in the important juncture which was then upon us, for the war was over; the highest military authorities of the southern Confederacy so confessed to me openly, unconcealedly, and repeatedly. I therefore drew up the memorandum (which has been published to the world), for the purpose of referring it to the proper executive authority of the United States, and enabling him to define to me what I might promise, simply to cover the pride of the southern men, who thereby became subordinate to the laws of the United States, civil and military. I made no concessions to General Johnston's army or the troops under his direction and immediate control; and if any concessions were made in those general terms, they were made because I then believed, and now believe, they would have delivered into the hands of the United States the absolute control of every Confederate officer and soldier, all their muster-rolls, and all their arms. It would save us all the incidental expense resulting from the military occupation of that country by provost marshals, provost guards, military governors, and all the machinery by which alone military power can reach the people of a civilized country. It would have surrendered to us the armies of Dick Taylor and Kirby Smith, both of them capable of doing infinite mischief to us by exhausting the resources of the whole country upon which we were to depend for the future extinguishment of our debt, forced upon us by their wrongful and rebellious conduct. I never designed to shelter a human being from any liability incurred in consequence of past acts to the civil tribunals of our country; and I do not believe a fair and manly interpretation of my terms can so construe them; for the words "United States courts," "United States authorities," "limitations of executive power," occur in every paragraph. And if they seemingly yield terms better than the public would desire to be given to the southern people, if studied closely and well it will be found that there is an absolute submission on their part to the government of the United States, either through its executive, legislative, or judicial authorities. , Every step in the programme of these negotiations was reported punctually, clearly, and fully, by the most rapid means of communication that I had. And yet I neglected not one single precaution necessary to reap the full benefits of my position in case the government amended, altered, or absolutely annulled those terms. As those matters were necessarily mingled with the military history of the period, I would like at this point to submit to the committee my official report, which has been in the hands of the proper officer, Brigadier General Rawlings, chief of staff of the army of the United States, since about the 12th instant. It was made by me at Manchester, Virginia, after I had returned from Savannah, whither I went to open up the Savannah River and reap the fruits of my negotiations with General Johnston, and to give General Wilson's force in the interior a safe and sure base from which he could draw the necessary supply of clothing and food for his command. It was only after I had fulfilled all this that I learned, for the first time, through the public press, that my conduct had been animadverted upon, not only by the secretary of war, but by General Halleck, and the press of the country at large. I did feel hurt and annoyed that Mr. Stanton coupled with the terms of my memorandum, confided to him, a copy of a telegram to General Grant which he had never sent to me. He knew, on the contrary, that, when he was at Savannah, I had negotiations with civil parties there, for he was present in my room when those parties were conferring with me, and I wrote him a letter setting forth many points of it, in which I said I aimed to make a split in Jeff Davis's dominions, by segregating Georgia from their course. Those were civil negotiations, and, far from being discouraged from making them, I was encouraged by Secretary Stanton himself to make them.

By coupling the note to General Grant with my memorandum, he gave the world fairly and clearly to infer that I was in possession of it. Now, I was not in possession of it, and I have reason to know that Mr. Stanton knew I was not in possession of it. Next met me General Halleck's telegram, indorsed by Mr. Stanton, in which they publicly avowed an act of perfidy, namely, the violation of my terms, which I had a right to make, and which, by the laws of war and by the laws of Congress, is punishable by death, and no other punishment. Next, they ordered an army to pursue my enemy, who was known to be surrendering to me, in the presence of General Grant himself, their superior officer; and, finally, they sent orders to General Wilson and to General Thomas, my subordinates, acting under me on a plan of the most magnificent scale, admirably executed, to defeat my orders, and to thwart the interests of the government of the United States. I did feel indignant; I do feel indignant. As to my honor, I can protect it. In my letter of the 15th of April I used this language: "I have invited Governor Vance to return to Raleigh, with the civil officers of his state." I did so because President Lincoln had himself encouraged me to a similar course with the governor of Georgia when I was in Atlanta. And here was the opportunity which the secretary of war should have taken to put me on my guard against making terms with civil authorities, if such were the settled policy of our government. Had President Lincoln lived, I know he would have sustained me.

The following is my report, which I desire to have incorporated into and made part of my testimony: —

Headquarters of the Military Division of the Mississippi,
in the Field, City Point, Virginia, May 9, 1865.

GENERAL: My last official report brought the history of events, as connected with the armies in the field subject to my immediate command, down to the 1st of April, when the army of the Ohio, Major General J. M. Schofield commanding, lay at Goldsboro', with detachments distributed so as to secure and cover our routes of communication and supply back to the sea at Wilmington and Morehead city; Major General A. H. Terry, with the 10th corps, being at Faison's Depot; the army of the Tennessee, Major General O. O. Howard commanding, was encamped to the right and front of Goldsboro', and the army of Georgia, Major General H. W. Slocum commanding, to its left and front; the cavalry, Brevet Major General J. Kilpatrick commanding, at Mount Olive. All were busy in repairing the wear and tear of our then recent and hard march from Savannah, and in replenishing clothing and stores necessary for a further progress.

I had previously, by letter and in person, notified the Lieutenant General commanding the armies of the United States, that the 10th of April would be the earliest possible moment at which I could hope to have all things in readiness, and we were compelled to use our railroads to the very highest possible limit in order to fulfil that promise. Owing to a mistake in the railroad department in sending locomotives and cars of the five-foot gauge, we were limited to the use of the few locomotives and cars of the four foot eight and a half inch gauge already in North Carolina, with such of the old stock as was captured by Major General Terry at Wilmington and on his way up to Goldsboro'. Yet such judicious use was made of these, and such industry displayed in the railroad management, by Generals Easton and Beckwith, and Colonel Wright and Mr. Van Dyne, that by the 10th of April our men were all reclad, the wagons reloaded, and a fair amount of forage accumulated ahead.

In the mean time, Major General George Stoneman, in command of a division of cavalry operating from East Tennessee in connection with Major General George H. Thomas, in pursuance of my orders of January 21, 1865, had reached the railroad about Greensboro', North Carolina, and had made sad havoc with it, and had pushed along it to Salisbury, destroying *en route* bridges, culverts, depots, and all kinds of rebel supplies, and had extended the break in the railroad down to the Catawba Bridge.

This was fatal to the hostile armies of Lee and Johnston, who depended on that road for supplies, and as their ultimate line of retreat. Major General J. H. Wilson, also in command of the cavalry corps organized by himself under special field orders No. —, of October 24, 1864, at Gaylesville, Alabama, had started from the neighborhood of

Decatur and Florence, Alabama, and moved straight into the heart of Alabama, on a route prescribed for General Thomas after he had defeated General Hood at Nashville, Tennessee; but the roads being too heavy for infantry, General Thomas had devolved that duty on that most energetic young cavalry officer, General Wilson, who, imbued with the proper spirit, has struck one of the best blows of the war at the waning strength of the Confederacy. His route was one never before touched by our troops, and afforded him abundance of supplies as long as he was in motion, namely, by Tuscaloosa, Selma, Montgomery, Columbus, and Macon. Though in communication with him, I have not been able to receive, as yet, his full and detailed reports, which will in due time be published and appreciated. Lieutenant General Grant, also in immediate command of the armies about Richmond, had taken the initiative in that magnificent campaign, which, in less than ten days, compelled the evacuation of Richmond, and resulted in the destruction and surrender of the entire rebel army of Virginia under command of General Lee.

The news of the battles about Petersburg reached me at Goldsboro' on the 6th of April. Up to that time my purpose was to move rapidly northward, feigning on Raleigh and striking straight for Burkesville, thereby interposing between Johnston and Lee. But the auspicious events in Virginia had changed the whole military problem, and, in the expressive language of Lieutenant General Grant, "the Confederate armies of Lee and Johnston" became the "strategic points." General Grant was fully able to take care of the former, and my task was to capture or destroy the latter. Johnston at that time, April 6, had his army well in hand about Smithfield, interposing between me and Raleigh. I estimated his infantry and artillery at thirty-five thousand, and his cavalry from six thousand to ten thousand. He was superior to me in cavalry, so that I held General Kilpatrick in reserve at Mount Olive, with orders to recruit his horses, and be ready to make a sudden and rapid march on the 10th of April.

At daybreak of the day appointed, all the heads of columns were in motion straight against the enemy,—Major General H. W. Slocum taking the two direct roads for Smithfield; Major General O. O. Howard making a circuit by the right, and feigning up the Weldon road to disconcert the enemy's cavalry; Generals Terry and Kilpatrick moving on the west side of the Neuse River, and aiming to reach the rear of the enemy between Smithfield and Raleigh. General Schofield followed General Slocum in support.

All the columns met, within six miles of Goldsboro', more or less cavalry, with the usual rail barricades, which were swept before us as chaff, and by 10 A. M. of the 11th, the 14th corps entered Smithfield, the 20th corps close at hand. Johnston had rapidly retreated across the Neuse River, and, having his railroad to lighten up his trains, could retreat faster than we could pursue. The rains had also set in, making the resort to corduroy absolutely necessary to pass even ambulances. The enemy had burned the bridge at Smithfield, and as soon as possible Major General Slocum got up his pontoons and crossed over a division of the 14th corps. We there heard of the surrender of Lee's army at Appomattox Court-house, Virginia, which was announced to the armies in orders, and created universal joy. Not an officer or soldier of my armies but expressed a pride and satisfaction that it fell to the lot of the armies of the Potomac and James so gloriously to overwhelm and capture the entire army that had held them so long in check, and their success gave new impulse to finish up our task. Without a moment's hesitation we dropped our trains and marched rapidly in pursuit to and through Raleigh, reaching that place at 7.30 A. M. of the 13th, in a heavy rain. The next day the cavalry pushed on through the rain to Durham's Station, the 15th corps following as far as Morrisville Station, and the 17th corps to Jones's Station. On the supposition that Johnston was tied to his railroad as a line of retreat by Hillsboro', Greensboro', Salisbury, Charlotte, &c., I had turned the other columns across the bend of that road towards Ashboro'. (See Special Field Orders, No. 55.) The cavalry, Brevet Major General J. Kilpatrick commanding, was ordered to keep up a show of pursuit towards the "Company's Shops," in Alamance County; Major General O. O. Howard to turn to the left by Hackney's Crossroads, Pittsboro', St. Lawrence, and Ashboro'; Major General H. W. Slocum to cross Cape Fear River at Aven's Ferry, and move rapidly by Carthage, Caledonia, and Cox's Mills; Major General J. M. Schofield was to hold Raleigh and the road back, and with his spare force to follow an intermediate route.

By the 15th, though the rains were incessant and the roads almost impracticable, Major General Slocum had the 14th corps, Brevet Major General Davis commanding, near Martha's Vineyard, with a pontoon bridge laid across Cape Fear River at Aven's Ferry, with the 20th corps, Major General Mower commanding, in support; and Major General Howard had the 15th and 17th corps stretched out on the roads towards Pittsboro', while General Kilpatrick held Durham's Station and Chapel Hill University.

Johnston's army was retreating rapidly on the roads from Hillsboro' to Greensboro', he himself at Greensboro'. Although out of place as to time, I here invite all military critics who study the problems of war to take their maps and compare the position of my army on the 15th and 16th of April with that of General Halleck about Burkesville and Petersburg, Virginia, on the 26th of April, when, according to his telegram to Secretary Stanton, he offered to relieve me of the task of "cutting off Johnston's retreat." Major General Stoneman at the time was at Statesville, and Johnston's only line of retreat was by Salisbury and Charlotte. It may be that General Halleck's troops can outmarch mine, but there is nothing in their past history to show it; or it may be that General Halleck can inspire his troops with more energy of action. I doubt that also, save and except in this single instance, when he knew the enemy was ready to surrender or disperse, as advised by my letter of April 18th, addressed to him when chief of staff at Washington city, and delivered at Washington on the 21st instant by Major Hitchcock of my staff.

Thus matters stood at the time I received General Johnston's first letter, and made my answer of April 14, copies of which were sent with all expedition to Lieutenant General Grant and the secretary of war, with my letter of April 15. I agreed to meet General Johnston in person at a point intermediate between our pickets on the 17th at noon, provided the position of the troops remained *statu quo*. I was both willing and anxious thus to consume a few days, as it would enable Colonel Wright to finish our railroad to Raleigh.

Two bridges had to be built, and twelve miles of new road made. We had no iron except by taking up that on the branch from Goldsboro' to Weldon. Instead of losing by time, I gained in every way; for every hour of delay possible was required to reconstruct the railroad to our rear and improve the condition of our wagon roads to the front, so desirable in case the negotiations failed and we be forced to make the race of near two hundred miles to head off or catch Johnston's army, then retreating towards Charlotte.

At noon of the day appointed, I met General Johnston for the first time in my life, although we had been interchanging shots constantly since May, 1863.

Our interview was frank and soldier-like, and he gave me to understand that further war on the part of the Confederate troops was folly, that *the cause* was lost, and that every life sacrificed after the surrender of Lee's army was the "highest possible crime." He admitted that the terms conceded to General Lee were magnanimous, and all he could ask; but he did want some general concessions that would enable him to allay the natural fears and anxieties of his followers, and enable him to maintain his control over them until they could be got back to the neighborhood of their homes, thereby saving the State of North Carolina the devastations inevitably to result from turning his men loose and unprovided on the spot, and our pursuit across the state.

He also wanted to embrace in the same general proposition the fate of all the Confederate armies that remained in existence. I never made any concession as to his own army, or assumed to deal finally and authoritatively in regard to any other; but it did seem to me that there was presented a chance for peace that might be deemed valuable to the government of the United States, and was at least worth the few days that would be consumed in reference.

To push an army whose commander had so frankly and honestly confessed his inability to cope with me were cowardly, and unworthy the brave men I led.

Inasmuch as General Johnston did not feel authorized to pledge his power over the armies in Texas, we adjourned to meet the next day at noon. I returned to Raleigh, and conferred freely with all my general officers, *every one* of whom urged me to conclude terms that might accomplish so complete and desirable an end. All dreaded the weary and laborious march after a fugitive and dissolving army back towards Georgia, almost over the very country where we had toiled so long.

There was but one opinion expressed; and, if contrary ones were entertained, they were withheld, or indulged in only by that class who shun the fight and the march, but are loudest, bravest, and fiercest when danger is past.

I again met General Johnston on the 18th, and we renewed the conversation. He satisfied me then of his *power* to disband the rebel armies in Alabama, Mississippi, Louisiana, and Texas, as well as those in his immediate command, namely, North Carolina, South Carolina, Florida, and Georgia.

The points on which he expressed especial solicitude were, lest their states were to be dismembered and denied representation in Congress, or any separate political existence whatever, and that the absolute disarming his men would leave the south powerless, and exposed to depredations by wicked bands of assassins and robbers.

President Lincoln's message of 1864; his amnesty proclamation; General Grant's terms to General Lee, substantially extending the benefits of that proclamation to all officers above the rank of colonel; the invitation to the Virginia legislature to reassemble in Richmond by General Weitzel, with the approval of Mr. Lincoln and General Grant, then on the spot; a firm belief that I had been fighting to re-establish the constitution of the United States; and last, and not least, the general and universal desire to close a war any longer without organized resistance, were the leading facts that induced me to pen the "memorandum" of April 18, signed by myself and General Johnston.

It was designed to be, and so expressed on its face, as a mere "basis" for reference to the president of the United States and constitutional commander-in-chief, to enable him, if he chose, at one blow to dissipate the military power of the Confederacy which had threatened the national safety for years. It admitted of modification, alteration, and change. It had no appearance of an ultimatum, and by no false reasoning can it be construed into a usurpation of power on my part. I have my opinions on the questions involved, and will stand by the memorandum; but this forms no part of a military report. Immediately on my return to Raleigh I despatched one of my staff — Major Hitchcock — to Washington, enjoining him to be most prudent and careful to avoid the spies and informers that would be sure to infest him by the way, and to say nothing to anybody, until the president could make known to me his wishes and policy in the matter.

The news of President Lincoln's assassination on the 14th of April (wrongly reported to me by telegraph as having occurred on the 11th) reached me on the 17th, and was announced to my command on the same day in Special Field Orders, No. 56. I was duly impressed with its horrible atrocity and probable effect upon the country; but when the property and interests of millions still living were involved, I saw no good reason to change my course, but thought rather to manifest real respect for his memory, by following, after his death, that policy which, if living, I feel certain he would have approved, or, at least, not rejected with disdain. Up to that hour I had never received one word of instruction, advice, or counsel as to the "plan or policy" of government, looking to a restoration of peace on the part of the rebel states of the south. Whenever asked for an opinion on the points involved, I had always evaded the subject. My letter to the mayor of

Atlanta has been published to the world, and I was not rebuked by the war department for it.

My letter to Mr. N—— W——, at Savannah, was shown by me to Mr. Stanton before its publication, and all that my memory retains of his answer is, that he said, like my letters generally, it was sufficiently "emphatic, and could not be misunderstood."

But these letters asserted my belief that, according to Mr. Lincoln's proclamations and messages, when the people of the south had laid down their arms and submitted to the lawful power of the United States, *ipso facto* the war was over as to them; and, furthermore, that if any state in rebellion would conform to the constitution of the United States, "cease war," elect senators and representatives to Congress, if admitted (of which each House of Congress alone is the judge), that state became *instanter* as much in the Union as New York or Ohio. Nor was I rebuked for this expression, though it was universally known and commented on at the time. And again, Mr. Stanton in person, at Savannah, speaking of the terrific expenses of the war, and difficulty of realizing the money necessary for the daily wants of government, impressed me most forcibly with the necessity of bringing the war to a close as soon as possible, for *financial reasons*.

On the evening of April 23, Major Hitchcock reported his return to Morehead city with despatches, of which fact General Johnston, at Hillsboro', was notified, so as to be ready in the morning for an answer. At 6 o'clock A. M. on the 24th, Major Hitchcock arrived, accompanied by General Grant and members of his staff, who had not telegraphed the fact of his coming over our exposed road for prudential reasons.

I soon learned that the memorandum was disapproved, without reasons assigned, and I was ordered to give the forty-eight hours' notice, and resume hostilities at the close of that time, governing myself by the substance of a despatch then enclosed, dated March 3, 12 noon, at Washington, District of Columbia, from Secretary Stanton to General Grant, at City Point, but not accompanied by any part of the voluminous matter so liberally lavished on the public in the New York journals of the 24th of April. That was the *first* and *only time* I ever saw that telegram, or had one word of instruction on the important matter involved in it; and it does seem strange to me that every bar-room loafer in New York can read in the morning journals "official" matter that is withheld from a general whose command extends from Kentucky to North Carolina.

Within an hour a courier was riding from Durham's Station towards Hillsboro', with notice to General Johnston of the suspension of the truce, and renewing my demand for the surrender of the armies under his immediate command (see two letters, April 24, 6 A. M.), and at 12 noon, I had the receipt of his picket officer. I therefore published my Orders, No. 62, to the troops, terminating the truce at 12 M. on the 26th, and ordered all to be in readiness to march at that hour on the routes prescribed in Special Field Order, No. 55, April 14, from the positions held April 18.

General Grant had orders from the president, through the secretary of war, to direct military movements, and I explained to him the exact position of the troops, and he approved of it most emphatically; but he did not relieve me, or express a wish to assume command. All things were in readiness, when, on the evening of the 25th, I received another letter from General Johnston, asking another interview to renew negotiations.

General Grant not only approved, but urged me to accept; and I appointed a meeting at our former place at noon of the 26th, the very hour fixed for the renewal of hostilities. General Johnston was delayed by an accident to his train, but at 2 P. M. arrived. We then consulted, concluded, and signed the final terms of capitulation.

These were taken by me back to Raleigh, submitted to General Grant, and met his immediate approval and signature. General Johnston was not even aware of the presence of General Grant at Raleigh at the time.

Thus was surrendered to us the second great army of the so-called Confederacy; and though undue importance has been given to the so-called negotiations which preceded it, and a rebuke and public disfavor cast on me wholly unwarranted by the facts, I rejoice in saying it was accomplished without farther ruin and devastation to the country, without the loss of a single life to those gallant men who had followed me from the Mississippi to the Atlantic, and without subjecting brave men to the ungracious task of pursuing a fleeing foe that did not want to fight. As for myself, I know my motives, and challenge the instance during the past four years, where an armed and defiant foe stood before me, that I did not go in for a fight; and I would blush for shame if I had ever insulted or struck a fallen foe. The instant the terms of surrender were approved by General Grant, I made my Orders, No. 65, assigning to each of my subordinate commanders his share of the work, and, with General Grant's approval, made Special Field Orders, No. 66, putting in motion my old army (no longer required in Carolina) northward for Richmond. General Grant left Raleigh at 9 A. M. of the 27th, and I glory in the fact that during his three days' stay with me, I did not detect in his language or manner one particle of abatement in the confidence, respect, and affection that have existed between us throughout all the varied events of the past war; and, though we have honestly differed in opinion, in other cases as well as this, still we respected each other's honest convictions.

I still adhere to my then opinions, that by a few general concessions, "glittering generalities," all of which in the end must and will be conceded to the organized states of the south, that this day there would not be an armed battalion opposed to us within the broad area of the dominions of the United States. Robbers and assassins must, in any event, result from the disbandment of large armies; but even these should be, and could be, taken care of by the local civil authorities, without being made a charge on the national treasury.

On the evening of the 28th, having concluded all business requiring my personal attention at Raleigh, and having conferred with every army commander, and delegated to him the authority necessary for his future action, I despatched my headquarter wagons by land, along with the 17th corps, the office in charge of General Webster, from Newbern, to Alexandria, Virginia, by sea, and in person, accompanied only by my personal staff, hastened to Savannah, to direct matters in the interior of South Carolina and Georgia. I had received across the rebel telegraph wires cipher despatches from General Wilson, at Macon, to the effect that he was in receipt of my Orders, No. 65, and would send General Upton's division to Augusta, and General McCook's division to Tallahassee, to receive the surrender of those garrisons, take charge of the public property, and execute the paroles required by the terms of surrender. He reported a sufficiency of forage for his horses in South-west Georgia, but asked me to send him a supply of clothing, sugar, coffee, &c., by way of Augusta, Georgia, whence he could get it by rail. I therefore went rapidly to Goldsboro' and Wilmington, reaching the latter city at 10 A. M. of the 29th, and the same day embarked for Hilton Head in the blockade runner "Russia," Captain A. M. Smith. I found General Q. A. Gillmore, commanding department of the south, at Hilton Head, on the evening of April 30, and ordered him to send to Augusta at once what clothing and small stores he could spare for General Wilson, and to open up a line of certain communication and supply with him at Macon. Within an hour the captured steamboats "Jeff Davis" and "Amazon," both adapted to the shallow and crooked navigation of the Savannah River, were being loaded, the one at Savannah and the other at Hilton Head. The former started up the river on the 1st of May, in charge of a very intelligent officer (whose name I cannot recall) and forty-eight men,—all the boat could carry,—with orders to occupy temporarily the United States Arsenal at Augusta, and open up communication with General Wilson at Macon, in the event that General McCook's division of cavalry was not already there. The "Amazon" followed next day, and General Gillmore had made the necessary orders for a brigade of infantry, to be commanded by General Molyneaux, to follow by a land march to Augusta as its permanent garrison. Another brigade of infantry was ordered to occupy Orangeburg, South Carolina, the point farthest in the interior that can at present be reached by rail from the sea coast (Charleston).

On the 1st of May I went on to Savannah, where General Gillmore also joined me, and the arrangements ordered for the occupation of Augusta were consummated.

At Savannah I found the city in the most admirable police, under direction of Brevet Major General Grover, and the citizens manifested the most unqualified joy to hear that, so far as they were concerned, the war was over. All classes, Union men as well as former rebels, did not conceal, however, the apprehensions naturally arising from a total ignorance of the political conditions to be attached to their future state. Anything at all would be preferable to this dread uncertainty.

On the evening of the 2d of May I returned to Hilton Head, and there, for the first time, received the New York papers of April 28, containing Secretary Stanton's despatch of 9 A. M. of the 27th of

APPENDIX. 407

April to General Dix, including General Halleck's, from Richmond, of 9 P. M. of the night before, which seems to have been rushed with extreme haste before an excited public, namely, morning of the 28th. You will observe from the dates that these despatches were running back and forth from Richmond and Washington to New York, and there published, while General Grant and I were together in Raleigh, North Carolina, adjusting, to the best of our ability, the terms of surrender of the only remaining formidable rebel army in existence at the time east of the Mississippi River. Not one word of intimation had been sent to me of the displeasure of the government with my official conduct, but only the naked disapproval of a skeleton memorandum sent properly for the action of the president of the United States.

The most objectionable features of my memorandum had already (April 24) been published to the world, in violation of official usage, and the contents of my accompanying letters to General Halleck, General Grant, and Mr. Stanton, of even date, though at hand, were suppressed.

In all these letters I had stated clearly and distinctly that Johnston's army would *not* fight, but, if pushed, would "disband" and "scatter" into small and dangerous guerrilla parties, as injurious to the interests of the United States as to the rebels themselves; that all parties admitted that the rebel cause of the south was abandoned, that the negro was free, and that the temper of all was most favorable to a lasting peace. I say all these opinions of mine were withheld from the public with a seeming purpose; and I do contend that my official experience and former services, as well as my past life and familiarity with the people and geography of the south, entitled my opinions to at least a decent respect.

Although this despatch (Mr. Stanton's of April 27) was printed "official," it had come to me only in the questionable newspaper paragraph headed, "Sherman's Truce Disregarded."

I had already done what General Wilson wanted me to do, namely, had sent him supplies of clothing and food, with clear and distinct orders and instructions how to carry out, in Western Georgia, the terms for the surrender of arms and paroling of prisoners, made by General Johnston's capitulation of April 26, and had properly and most opportunely ordered General Gillmore to occupy Orangeburg and Augusta, strategic points of great value at all times, in peace or war; but, as the secretary had taken upon himself to order my subordinate generals to disobey my "orders," I explained to General Gillmore that I would no longer confuse him or General Wilson with "orders" that might conflict with those of the secretary, which, as reported, were sent, not through me, but in open disregard of me and of my lawful authority.

It now becomes my duty to paint in justly severe character the still more offensive and dangerous matter of General Halleck's despatch of April 26 to the secretary of war, embodied in his to General Dix of April 27.

General Halleck had been chief of staff of the army at Washington, in which capacity he must have received my official letter of April 18, wherein I wrote clearly that if Johnston's army about Greensboro' were "pushed," it would "disperse"—an event I wished to prevent. About that time he seems to have been sent from Washington to Richmond to command the new military division of the James, in assuming charge of which, on the 22d, he defines the limits of his authority to be the "department of Virginia, the army of the Potomac, and such part of North Carolina *as may not be occupied by the command of Major General Sherman.*" (See his General Orders, No. 1.) Four days later, April 26, he reports to the secretary that he has ordered Generals Meade, Sheridan, and Wright to invade that part of North Carolina which *was* occupied by my command, and pay "no regard to any truce or orders of" mine. They were ordered to "*push* forward, regardless of any orders save those of Lieutenant General Grant, and cut off Johnston's retreat." He knew at the time he penned that despatch and made those orders that Johnston was not retreating, but was halted under a forty-eight hours' truce with me, and was laboring to surrender his command and prevent its dispersion into guerrilla bands, and that I had on the spot a magnificent army at my command, amply sufficient for all purposes required by the occasion.

The plan for cutting off a retreat from the direction of Burkesville and Danville is hardly worthy one of his military education and genius. When he contemplated an act so questionable as the violation of a "truce" made by competent authority within his sphere of command, he should have gone himself, and not have sent subordinates, for he knew I was bound in honor to *defend* and *maintain* my *own* truce and pledge of faith, even at the cost of many lives.

When an officer pledges the faith of his goverment, he is bound to defend it; and he is no soldier who would violate it knowingly.

As to Davis and his stolen treasure, did General Halleck, as chief of staff or commanding officer of the neighboring military division, notify me of the facts contained in his despatch to the secretary? No, he did not. If the secretary of war wanted Davis caught, why not order it, instead of, by publishing in the newspapers, putting him on his guard to hide away and escape? No orders or instructions to catch Davis or his stolen treasure ever came to me; but, on the contrary, I was led to believe that the secretary of war rather preferred he should effect an escape from the country, if made "unknown" to him. But even on this point I enclose a copy of my letter to Admiral Dahlgren, at Charleston, sent him by a fleet steamer from Wilmington on the 25th of April, two days before the bankers of Richmond had imparted to General Halleck the important secret as to Davis's movement, designed, doubtless, to stimulate his troops to march their legs off to catch *their* treasure for *their* own use.

I know now that Admiral Dahlgren did receive my letter on the 26th, and had acted on it *before* General Halleck had even thought of the matter; but I do not believe a word of the treasure story,—it is absurd on its face,—and General Halleck or anybody has my full permission to chase Jeff Davis and cabinet with their stolen treasure through any part of the country occupied by my command.

The last and most obnoxious feature of General Halleck's despatch is

APPENDIX. 409

wherein he goes out of his way, and advises that my subordinates, Generals Thomas, Stoneman, and Wilson, should be instructed not to obey "Sherman's" commands.

This is too much; and I turn from the subject with feelings too strong for words, and merely record my belief that so much mischief was never before embraced in so small a space as in the newspaper paragraph headed "Sherman's Truce Disregarded," authenticated as "official" by Mr. Secretary Stanton, and published in the New York papers of April 28.

During the night of May 2, at Hilton Head, having concluded my business in the department of the south, I began my return to meet my troops then marching towards Richmond from Raleigh. On the morning of the 3d we ran into Charleston Harbor, where I had the pleasure to meet Admiral Dahlgren, who had, in all my previous operations from Savannah northward, aided me with a courtesy and manliness that commanded my entire respect and deep affection; also General Hatch, who, from our first interview at his Tullifinney camp, had caught the spirit of the move from Pocotaligo northward, and had largely contributed to our joint success in taking Charleston and the Carolina coast. Any one who is not *satisfied* with war should go and see Charleston, and he will pray louder and deeper than ever that the country may in the long future be spared any more war. Charleston and secession being synonymous terms, the city should be left as a sample, so that centuries may pass away before that false doctrine is again preached in our Union.

We left Charleston on the evening of the 3d of May, and hastened with all possible speed back to Morehead city, which we reached at night of the 4th. I immediately communicated by telegraph with General Schofield at Raleigh, and learned from him the pleasing fact that the lieutenant general commanding the armies of the United States had reached the Chesapeake in time to countermand General Halleck's orders, and prevent his violating my truce, invading the area of my command, and driving Johnston's surrendering army into fragments. General Johnston had fulfilled his agreement to the very best of his ability; and the officers charged with issuing the paroles at Greensboro' reported about thirty thousand (30,000) already made, and that the greater part of the North Carolina troops had gone home without waiting for their papers, but that all of them would doubtless come into some one of the military posts, the commanders of which are authorized to grant them. About eight hundred (800) of the rebel cavalry had gone south, refusing to abide the terms of the surrender, and it was supposed they would make for Mexico. I would sincerely advise that they be encouraged to go and stay; they would be a nuisance to any civilized government, whether loose or in prison.

With the exception of some plundering on the part of Lee's and Johnston's disbanded men, all else in North Carolina was "quiet." When to the number of men surrendered at Greensboro' are added those at Tallahassee, Augusta, and Macon, with the scattered squads who will come in at other military posts, I have no doubt fifty thousand (50,000) armed men will be disarmed and restored to civil pursuits by the capitulation made near Durham's Station, North Carolina, on the 26th of April, and that, too, without the loss of a single life to us.

On the 5th of May I received, and here subjoin, a further despatch from General Schofield, which contains inquiries I have been unable to satisfy, similar to those made by nearly every officer in my command whose duty brings him in contact with citizens. I leave you to do what you think expedient to provide the military remedy.

By Telegraph from Raleigh, N. C., May 5, 1865.

To Major General W. T. SHERMAN, Morehead City.

When General Grant was here, as you doubtless recollect, he said the lines had been extended to embrace this and other states south. The order, it seems, has been modified so as to include only Virginia and Tennessee. I think it would be an act of wisdom to open this state to trade at once. I hope the government will make known its policy as the organ of state governments without delay. Affairs must necessarily be in a very unsettled state until that is done; the people are now in a mood to accept almost anything which promises a definite settlement.

What is to be done with the freedmen, is the question of all, and is the all-important question. It requires prompt and wise action to prevent the negro from becoming a huge elephant on our hands. If I am to govern this state, it is important for me to know it at once. If another is to be sent here, it cannot be done too soon; for he will probably undo the most that I shall have done. I shall be glad to hear from you freely when you have time to write.

I will send your message to Wilson at once.

J. M. SCHOFIELD, *Major General*.

I give this despatch entire, to demonstrate how intermingled have become civil matters with the military, and how almost impossible it has become for an officer in authority to act a pure military part.

There are no longer armed enemies in North Carolina, and a soldier can deal with no other sort. The marshals and sheriffs with their *posses* (of which the military may become a part) are the only proper officers to deal with civil criminals and marauders. But I will not be drawn out in a discussion of this subject, but instance the case to show how difficult is the task become to military officers, when men of the rank, education, experience, nerve, and good sense of General Schofield feel embarrassed by them.

General Schofield, at Raleigh, has a well-appointed and well-disciplined command, is in telegraphic communication with the controlling parts of his department, and remote ones in the direction of Georgia, as well as with Washington, and has military possession of all strategic points.

In like manner, General Gillmore is well situated in all respects, except as to rapid communication with the seat of the general government. I leave him also with every man he ever asked for, and in full and quiet possession of every strategic point in his department; and General Wilson has, in the very heart of Georgia, the strongest, best appointed, and best equipped cavalry corps that ever fell under my command; and he has now, by my recent action, opened to him a source and route of supply by way of Savannah River that simplifies his military problem, so that I think I may with a clear conscience leave them and turn my attention once more to my special command — the army with which I have been associated through some of the most eventful scenes of this or any war.

I hope and believe none of these commanders will ever have reason to reproach me for any "orders" they may have received from me; and the president of the United States may be assured that all of them are in position, ready and willing to execute to the letter and in spirit any orders he may give. I shall henceforth cease to give them any orders at all, for the occasion that made them subordinate to me is past; and I shall confine my attention to the army composed of the 15th and 17th, the 14th and 20th corps, unless the commanding general of the armies of the United States orders otherwise.

At 4 P. M. of May 9 I reached Manchester, on the James River, opposite Richmond, and found that all the four corps had arrived from Raleigh, and were engaged in replenishing their wagons for the resumption of the march towards Alexandria.

I have the honor to be your obedient servant,

W. T. SHERMAN, *Major General Commanding.*

General JOHN A. RAWLINS, Chief of Staff, Washington, D. C.

Q. Did you have, near Fortress Monroe, a conference with President Lincoln, and if so, about what time? A. I met General Grant and Mr. Lincoln on board a steamboat lying at the wharf at City Point, and during the evening of the 27th of March; I resumed my visit to the president on board the same steamer anchored in the stream on the following day, General Grant being present on both occasions.

Q. In those conferences was any arrangement made with you and General Grant, or either of you, in regard to the manner of arranging business with the Confederacy in regard to the terms of peace? A. Nothing definite; it was simply a matter of general conversation; nothing specific and definite.

Q. At what time did you learn that President Lincoln had assented to the assembling of the Virginia rebel legislature? A. I knew of it on the 18th of April, I think; but I procured a paper with the specific order of General Weitzel, also a copy of the amnesty proclamation on the 20th of April.

Q. You did not know at that time that that arrangement had been rescinded by the president? A. No, sir; I did not know that until afterwards; the moment I heard of that I notified General Johnston of it.

Q. Then at the time you entered into this arrangement with General Johnston, you knew that General Weitzel had approved of the calling together of the rebel legislature of Virginia by the assent of the president? A. I knew of it by some source unofficially; I succeeded in getting a copy of the paper containing General Weitzel's order on the 20th or 21st of April.

Q. But at the time of your arrangement you did not know that that order had been rescinded? A. No, sir; I learned that several days afterwards, and at once sent word to General Johnston.

Q. At the time of your arrangement you also knew of the surrender of Lee's army, and the terms of that surrender? A. I had that officially from General Grant; I got that at Smithfield on the 12th of April.

Q. I have what purports to be a letter from you to Johnston, which seems to imply that you intended to make the arrangement on the terms of Lee's surrender. The letter is as follows: —

> Headquarters, Division of the Mississippi, in the Field,
> Raleigh, N. C., April 14, 1865.
>
> General J. E. JOHNSTON, Commanding Confederate Army.
>
> General: I have this moment received your communication of this date. I am fully empowered to arrange with you any time for the suspension of further hostilities as between the armies commanded by myself, and will be willing to confer with you to that end. I will limit the advance of my main column to-morrow to Morristown, and the cavalry to the University, and I expect you will maintain the present position of your forces until each has notice of a failure to agree.
>
> Thus a basis of action may be had. I undertake to abide by the same terms and conditions as were made by Generals Grant and Lee at Appomattox Court-house, of the 9th instant, relative to the two armies, and, furthermore, to obtain from General Grant an order to suspend the movements of any troops from the direction of Virginia. General Stoneman is under my command, and my orders will suspend any devastation or destruction contemplated by him. I will add that I really desire to save the people of North Carolina the damage they would sustain by the march of this army through the central or western parts of the state.
>
> I am, with respect, your obedient servant,
>
> W. T. SHERMAN, *Major General.*

A. Those were the terms as to his own army, but the concessions I made him were for the purpose of embracing other armies.

Q. And the writings you signed were to include other armies? A. The armies of Kirby Smith and Dick Taylor, so that afterwards no man within the limits of the southern Confederacy could claim to belong to any Confederate army in existence.

Q. The president addressed a note to General Grant, perhaps not to you, to the effect of forbidding officers of the army from entering into anything but strictly military arrangements, leaving civil matters entirely to him? A. I never saw such a note signed by President Lincoln; Mr. Stanton made such a note or telegram, and says it was by President Lincoln's dictation; he made it to General Grant, but never to me; on the contrary, while I was in Georgia, Mr. Lincoln telegraphed to me, encouraging me to discuss matters with Governor Brown and Mr. Stephens.

Q. Then you had no notice of that order to General Grant? A. I had no knowledge of it, official or otherwise.

Q. In the published report of your agreement there is nothing about slavery, I believe? A. There was nothing said about slavery, because it did not fall within the category of military questions, and we could not make it so. It was a legal question, which the president had disposed of, overriding all our actions. We had to treat the slave as *free*, because the president, our commander-in-chief, said he was free. For me to have renewed the question when that decision was made, would have involved the absurdity of an inferior undertaking to qualify the work of his superior.

Q. That was the reason why it was not mentioned? A. Yes, sir; subsequently I wrote a note to Johnston, stating that I thought it would be well to mention it for political effect when we came to draw up the final terms with precision; that note was written pending the time my memorandum was going to Washington, and before an answer had been returned.

Q. At the time you entered into those negotiations, was Johnston in a condition to offer any effectual resistance to your army? A. He could not have resisted my army an hour if I could have got hold of him; but he could have escaped from me by breaking up into small parties, or by taking the country roads, travelling faster than any army with trains could have pursued.

Q. Then your object in negotiating was to keep his army from scattering into guerrilla bands? A. That was my chief object; I so officially notified the war department.

Q. And not because there was any doubt about the result of a battle? A. There was no question as to the result of a battle, and I knew it; every soldier knew it; Johnston said, in the first five minutes of our conversation, that any further resistance on his part would be an act of folly, and all he wanted was to keep his army from dispersing.

By Mr. Loan. — Q. In your examination by the chairman you stated that you were acting in pursuance of instructions from Mr. Lincoln, derived from his letters and telegrams at various times? A. Yes, sir.

Q. Have you any of these letters and telegrams which you can furnish to the committee? A. I can furnish you a copy of a despatch to General Halleck from Atlanta, in which I stated that I had invited Governor Brown and Vice President Stephens to meet us, and I can give you a copy of Mr. Lincoln's answer, for my despatch was referred to him, in which he said he felt much interested in my despatch, and encouraged me to allow their visit; but the letter to which I referred specifically was a longer letter, which I wrote to General Halleck from my camp on Big Black, Mississippi, at General Halleck's instigation, in September, 1863, which was received in Washington, and submitted to Mr. Lincoln, who desired to have it published, to which I would not consent; in that letter I gave my opinions fully and frankly, not only upon the military situation, but also the civil policy necessary; Mr. Lincoln expressed himself highly pleased with my views, and desired to make them public, but I preferred not to do so.

Q. And by subsequent acts he induced you to believe he approved of these views? A. I *know* he approved of them, and always encouraged me to carry out those views.

By the Chairman.—Q. The following is a letter published in the newspapers, purporting to have been addressed by you to Johnston, dated April 21, 1865:—

> Headquarters of the Military Division of the Mississippi,
> in the Field, Raleigh, N. C., April 21, 1865.

General J. E. JOHNSTON, Commanding Confederate Army.

General: I send you a letter for General Wilson, which, if sent by telegraph and courier, will check his career. He may mistrust the telegraph; therefore better send the original, for he cannot mistake my handwriting, with which he is familiar. He seems to have his blood up, and will be hard to hold. If he can buy corn, fodder, and rations down about Fort Valley, it will obviate the necessity of his going up to Rome or Dalton.

It is reported to me from Cairo that Mobile is in our possession; but it is not minute or official.

General Baker sent in to me, wanting to surrender his command, on the theory that the whole Confederate army was surrendered. I explained to him, or his staff officer, the exact truth, and left him to act as he thought proper. He seems to have disbanded his men, deposited a few arms about twenty miles from here, and himself awaits your action. I will not hold him, his men, or arms, subject to any condition other than the final one we may agree upon.

I shall look for Major Hitchcock back from Washington on Wednesday, and shall promptly notify you of the result. By the action of General Weitzel in relation to the Virginia legislature, I feel certain we will have no trouble on the score of recognizing existing state governments. It may be the lawyers will want us to define more minutely what is meant by the guaranty of rights of persons and property. It may be construed into a compact for us to undo the past as to the rights of slaves and leases of plantations on the Mississippi of vacant and abandoned plantations. I wish you would talk to the best men you have on these points, and, if possible, let us, in our final convention, make these points so clear as to leave no room for angry controversy. I believe if the south would simply and publicly declare, what we feel, that slavery is dead, that you would inaugurate an era of peace and prosperity that would soon efface the ravages of the past four years of war. Negroes would remain in the south, and afford you abundance of cheap labor, which otherwise will be driven away; and it will save the country the senseless discussions which have kept us all in hot water for fifty years.

Although, strictly, this is no subject for a military convention, yet I am honestly convinced that our simple declarations of a result will be accepted as good law everywhere. Of course, I have not a single word from Washington on this or any other point of our agreement; but I know the effect of such a step by us will be universally accepted.

I am, with great respect, your obedient servant,

W. T. SHERMAN, *Major General U. S. A.*

Q. This is the letter in which you say that it would be well to declare publicly that slavery is dead? A. Yes, sir, that is the letter.

By Mr. Loan. — Q. Will you furnish the committee a copy of the letter written by you to Mr. Stanton in January last from Savannah? A. I will do so.

Mr. Chairman. — And when the manuscript of your testimony is prepared it will be remitted to you for revision, and you can add to it any statement or papers that you may subsequently desire or consider necessary.

I have the above, and now subjoin copies of letters from my letter-book in the order of the bringing in the questions revised by this inquiry.

Headquarters Middle Department of the Mississippi, in the Field, Raleigh, N. C., April 18, 1865.

Lieutenant General U. S. GRANT, or Major General HALLECK, Washington, D. C.

General: I enclose herewith a copy of an agreement made this day between General Joseph E. Johnston and myself, which, if approved by the president of the United States, will produce peace from the Potomac to the Rio Grande. Mr. Breckinridge was present at the conference in the capacity of major general, and satisfied me of the ability of General Johnston to carry out to the full extent the terms of this agreement; and if you will get the president to simply indorse the copy and commission me to carry out the terms, I will follow them to the conclusion. You will observe that it is an absolute submission of the enemy to the lawful authorities of the United States, and disposes his army absolutely; and the point to which I attach most importance is, that the disposition and dispersement of the armies is done in such a manner as to prevent them breaking up into a guerrilla crew. On the other hand, we can retain just as much of an army as we please. I agree to the mode and manner of the surrender of armies set forth, as they give the state the means of suppressing guerrillas, which we could not expect to do if we strip them of all armies.

Both Generals Johnston and Breckinridge admitted that slavery was dead, and I could not insist in embracing it in such a paper, because it can be made with the states in detail. I know that all the men of substance in the south sincerely want peace, and I do not believe they will resort to war again during this century. I have no doubt but that they will, in the future, be perfectly subordinate to the laws of the United States. The moment my action in this matter is approved, I can spare five corps, and will ask for, and have, General Schofield here with the 10th corps, and go myself, with the 14th, 15th, 17th, 20th, and 23d corps, via Burkesville and Gordonsville, to Frederick or Hagerstown, there to be paid, and mustered out.

The question of finance is now the chief one, and every soldier and officer not needed, to go home at work. I would like to be able to begin the march north by May 1.

I urge on the part of the president speedy action, as it is important to get the Confederate armies to their homes, as well as our own.

I am, with great respect, your obedient servant,

W. T. SHERMAN, *Major General Commanding.*

Headquarters Middle Department of the Mississippi,
in the Field, Raleigh, N. C., April 18, 1865.

General H. W. HALLECK, Chief of Staff, Washington, D. C.

General: I received your despatch describing the man Clark detailed to assassinate me. He had better be in a hurry, or he will be too late. The news of Mr. Lincoln's death produced a most intense effect on our troops. At first I feared it would lead to excesses, but now it has softened down, and can easily be quieted. None evince more feeling than General Johnston, who admitted that the act was calculated to stain his cause with a dark hue, and he contended that the loss was most severe to the south, who had begun to realize that Mr. Lincoln was the best friend the south had.

I cannot believe that even Mr. Davis was privy to the diabolical plot, but think it the emanation of a lot of young men of the south, who are very devils. I want to throw upon the south the care of this class of men, who will soon be as obnoxious to their industrious class as to us.

Had I pushed Johnston's army to an extremity, it would have dispersed and done infinite mischief. Johnston informed me that General Stoneman had been at Salisbury, and was now about Statesville. I have sent him orders to come to me.

General Johnston also informed me that General Wilson was at Columbus, Georgia, and he wanted me to arrest his progress. I leave that to you. Indeed, if the president sanctions my agreement with Johnston, our interest is to cease all destruction. Please give all orders necessary according to the views the executive may take, and inform him, if possible, not to vary the terms at all, for I have considered everything, and believe that the Confederate armies are dispersed. We can adjust all else fairly and well.

I am yours, &c.,

W. T. SHERMAN, *Major General Commanding.*

Lest confusion should result to the mind of the committee by the latter part of the above letter, I state it was addressed to General Halleck as chief of staff, when he was in the proper " line of order " to the commander-in-chief. The whole case changed when, on the 26th of April, he became the commander of the separate division of the James.

As stated in my testimony, General Grant reached Raleigh on the 24th; and on the 25th, on the supposition that I would start next day to chase Johnston's army, I wrote him the following letter, delivered in person: —

Headquarters Department of the Mississippi, in the Field, }
Raleigh, N. C., April 25, 1865. }

Lieutenant General U. S. GRANT, — Present.

General: I received your letter of April 21, with enclosures, yesterday, and was well pleased that you came along, as you must have observed that I held the military control, so as to adapt it to any phase the case might assume.

It is but just that I should record the fact that I made my terms with General Johnston under the influence of the liberal terms you extended to the army of General Lee, at Appomattox Court-house, on the 9th, and the seeming policy of our government as evinced by the call of the Virginia legislature and governor back to Richmond under your and President Lincoln's very eyes. It now appears this last act was done without any consultation with you or any knowledge of Mr. Lincoln, but, rather, in opposition to a previous policy well considered.

I have not the least desire to interfere in the civil policy of our government, but would shun it as something not to my liking; but occasions arise when a prompt seizure of results is forced on military commanders not in immediate communication with the proper authority. It is possible that the terms signed by General Johnston and myself were not clear enough on the point well understood between us — that our negotiations did not apply to any parties outside the officers and men of the Confederate armies, which could easily have been remedied.

No surrender of any army not actually at the mercy of the antagonist was ever made without "terms," and those always define the military status of the surrendered. Thus you stipulated that the officers and men of Lee's army should not be molested at their homes so long as they obeyed the laws at the place of their residence. I do not wish to discuss these points involved in our recognition of the state governments in actual existence, but will merely state my conclusion, to await the solution of the future.

Such action on one point in no manner recognizes for a moment the so-called Confederate government, or makes us liable for its debts or acts. The laws and acts done by the several states during the period of rebellion are *void*, because done without the oath prescribed by our constitution of the United States, which is a condition precedent. We have a right to use any sort of machinery to produce military results, and it is the commonest thing for military commanders to use the civil government *in actual existence* as a means to an end. I do believe we could and can use the present state governments lawfully, constitutionally, and as the very best possible means to produce the object desired, viz., entire and complete submission to the lawful authority of the United States.

As to the punishment of past crimes, that is for the judiciary, and can in no manner or way be disturbed by our acts; and, so far as I can, I will use my influence that rebels shall suffer all the personal punishment provided by law, as also the civil liabilities accruing from this past act.

What we now want is the new form of law, by which common men may regain their position of industry, so long disturbed by the war.

I now apprehend that the rebel army will disperse; and, instead of dealing with six or seven states, we will have to deal with numberless bands of desperadoes, headed by such men as Mosby, Forrest, Red Jackson, and others who know not and care not for danger and its consequences.

I am, with great respect, your obedient servant,

W. T. SHERMAN, *Major General.*

On the same day I wrote and mailed to the secretary of war the following: —

Headquarters Middle Division of the Mississippi,
in the Field, Raleigh, N. C., April 25, 1865.

Hon. E. M. STANTON, Secretary of War, Washington.

Dear Sir: I have been furnished a copy of your letter of April 21, to General Grant, signifying your disapprobation of the terms on which General Johnston proposed to disarm and disperse the insurgents on condition of amnesty, &c. I admit my folly in embracing in a military convention any civil matter; but unfortunately, such is the nature of our situation that they seem inextricably united; and I understood from you at Savannah that the financial state of the country demanded military success, and would warrant a little leaning to policy.

When I had my conference with General Johnston, I had the public example before me of General Grant's terms to Lee's army, and General Weitzel's invitation to the Virginia legislature to assemble. I still believe that the general government of the United States has made a mistake; but that is none of my business. Mine is a different task, and I had flattered myself that, by four years of patient, and unremitting, and successful labor, I deserved no reminder such as is contained in the last paragraph of your letter to General Grant.

You may assure the president that I heed his suggestion.

I am truly, &c.,

W. T. SHERMAN, *Major General Commanding.*

The last sentence refers to the fact that General Grant had been sent to Raleigh to direct military movements. That was the first time in my life I had ever had a word of reproof from the government of the United States, and I was naturally sensitive. But all I said to any one was to General Meigs, who came with General Grant: "It was not kind on the part of Mr. Secretary Stanton." The fact known did not justify my military conduct. The first interview with General Johnston followed, and the terms of capitulation were agreed upon and signed, and General Grant started for Washington bearing the news.

When, on the 28th of April, I received in the New York Times the most extraordinary budget of Mr. Stanton, which for the first time startled me, I wrote to General Grant this letter: —

       Headquarters Military Division of the Mississippi,
         in the Field, April 28, 1865.

Lieutenant General U. S. GRANT, General-in-Chief, Washington, D. C.

General: Since you left me yesterday, I have seen the New York Times of the 24th instant, containing a budget of military news, authenticated by the signature of the secretary of war, which is grouped in such a way as to give very erroneous impressions. It embraces a copy of the basis of agreement between myself and General Johnston of April 18, with commentaries which it will be time enough to discuss two or three years hence, after the government has experimented a little more in the machinery by which power reaches the scattered people of the vast country known as the south. But, in the mean time, I do think that my rank (if not past services) entitled me at least to the respect of keeping secret what was known to none but the cabinet until further inquiry comes to be made, instead of giving publicity to documents I never saw, and drawing inferences wide of the truth.

I never saw, or had furnished me, a copy of Mr. Stanton's despatch to you of the 3d of March, nor did Mr. Stanton or any human being ever convey to me its substance, or anything like it; but, on the contrary, I had seen General Weitzel in relation to the Virginia legislature made in Mr. Lincoln's very person, and had failed to discover any other official hints of a plan of reconstruction, or any idea calculated to allay the fears of the people of the south after the destruction of their armies and civil authorities would leave them without any government at all.

We should not drive a people to anarchy, and it is simply impossible for one military power to waste all the masses of this unhappy country.

I confess I did not want to drive General Johnston's army into the hands of armed men going about without purpose, and capable only of indefinite mischief.

But you saw, on your arrival at Raleigh, that I had my armies so disposed that his escape was only possible in a disorganized shape; and as you did not choose to direct military operations in this quarter, I infer that you were satisfied with the military situation.

At all events, the moment I learned — what was proper enough — the disapproval of the president, I wished in such manner to compel the surrender of Johnston's whole army on the same terms you had prescribed to General Lee's army when you had it surrounded and in your absolute power.

Mr. Stanton, in stating that my order to General Stoneman was likely to result in the escape of "Mr. Davis to Mexico or Europe," is in deep error.

General Stoneman was not at Salisbury then, but had gone back to Statesville. Davis was supposed to be between us, and Stoneman was beyond him.

By turning towards me, he was approaching Davis; and had he joined me as ordered, I then would have had a mounted force needed for that and other purposes. But even now I do not know that Mr. Stanton wants Davis caught. And as my official papers, deemed sacred, are hastily published to the world, it will be imprudent for me to state what has been done in this respect.

As the editor of the Times has (it may be logically and fairly) drawn the inference from this singular document that I am insubordinate, I can only deny the intention. I have never in my life questioned or disobeyed an order, though many and many a time have I risked my life, my health, and reputation in obeying orders, or even hints, to execute plans and purposes not to my liking. It is not fair to withhold from me plans and policy (if any there be), and expect me to guess at them; for facts and events appear quite different from different standpoints. For four years I have been in camp dealing with soldiers; and I can assure you that the conclusion at which the cabinet arrived with such singular unanimity differs from mine. I conferred freely with the best officers in this army as to the points involved in this controversy; and, strange to say, they were singularly unanimous in the other conclusion; and they will learn with pain and sorrow that I am deemed insubordinate, and wanting in common sense; that I, who have labored day and night, winter and summer, for four years, and have brought an army of seventy thousand men in magnificent condition across a country deemed impassable, and placed it just where it was wanted almost on the day appointed, have brought discredit on the government.

I do not wish to boast of this; but I do say that it entitled me to the courtesy of being consulted before publishing to the world a proposition rightfully submitted to higher authority for adjudication, and then accompanied by statements which invited the press to be let loose on me.

It is true that non-combatants — men who sleep in comfort and security while we watch on the distant lines — are better able to judge than we poor soldiers, who rarely see a newspaper, hardly can hear from our families, or stop long enough to get our pay. I envy not the task of reconstruction, and am delighted that the secretary has relieved me of it.

As you did not undertake to assume the management of the affairs of this army, I infer that on personal inspection your mind arrived at a different conclusion from that of Mr. Secretary Stanton. I will therefore go on and execute your orders to the conclusion, and when done will, with intense satisfaction, leave to the civil authorities the execution of the task of which they seem to me so jealous; but as an honest man and soldier, I invite them to follow my path; for they may see some things and hear some things that may disturb their philosophy.

With sincere respect,
W. T. SHERMAN, *Major General Commanding.*

P. S. As Mr. Stanton's singular paper has been published, I demand that this also be made public; though I am in no manner responsible to the press, but to the law and my proper superiors.
W. T. SHERMAN, *Major General Commanding.*

Since my arrival at Washington I have learned from General Grant that this letter was received, but he preferred to withhold it until my arrival, as he knew I was making towards Washington with my army. Upon my arrival I did not insist on its publication till it was drawn out by this inquiry. I also append here the copy of a letter from Colonel T. S. Bowers, A. A. G., asking me to modify my report as to the point of violating my truce, with my answer.

Headquarters Armies of the United States,
Washington, May 25, 1865.

Major General W. T. SHERMAN, Commanding Middle Division of the Mississippi.

General Grant directed me to call your attention to the part of your report in which the necessity of maintaining your truce at the expense of many lives is spoken of. The general thinks that in making a truce the commander of an army can control only his own army, and that the hostile general must make his own arrangements with other armies acting against him.

While independent generals, acting against a common foe, would naturally act in concert, the general claims that each must be the judge of his own duty, and responsible for its execution.

If you should wish, the report will be returned for any change you deem best.

Very respectfully, your obedient servant,
T. S. BOWERS, *Assistant Adjutant General.*

Headquarters Military Division of the Mississippi,
Washington, D. C., May 26, 1865.

Colonel T. S. BOWERS, Assistant Adjutant General, Washington, D. C.

Colonel: I had the honor to receive your letter of May 25 last evening, and I hasten to answer. I wish to precede it by renewing the assurance of my entire confidence and respect for the president and Lieutenant General Grant, and that in all matters I will be most willing to shape my official and private conduct to suit their wishes. The past is beyond my control, and the matters embraced in the official report to which you refer are finished. It is but just the reasons that actuated me, right or wrong, should stand on record; but in all future cases, should any arise, I will respect the decisions of General Grant, though I think them wrong.

Suppose a guard has prisoners in charge, and officers of another command should aim to rescue or kill them; is it not clear the guard must defend the prisoners as a safeguard? So jealous is the military law to protect and maintain *good faith* when pledged, that the law adjudges death, and no alternative punishment, to one who violates a safeguard in foreign ports. (See Articles of War, No. 55.) For murder, arson, treason, and the highest military crimes, the punishment prescribed by law is death or some minor punishment; but for the violation of a "safeguard," death, and death alone, is the prescribed penalty. I instance this to illustrate how, in military stipulations to an enemy, our government commands and enforces "good faith." In discussing this matter I would like to refer to many writers on military law, but am willing to take Halleck as the text. (See his chapter, No. xxvii.)

In the very first article he states that *good faith* should always be observed between enemies in war, because, when our faith has been pledged to him, so far as the promise extends, he ceases to be an enemy. He then defines the meaning of *compacts* and *conventions*, and says they are made sometimes for a general or a partial suspension of hostilities, for the "surrender of an army," &c. They may be *special*, limited to particular places or to particular forces, but, of course, can only bind the armies subject to the general who makes the truce, and co-extensive only with the extent of his command. This is all I ever claimed, and it clearly covers the whole case: all of North Carolina was in my immediate command, with General Schofield, its department commander, and his army present with me. I never asked the truce to have effect beyond my own territorial command. General Halleck himself, in his Order No. 1, defines his own limits clearly enough, viz., "Such part of North Carolina as was not occupied by the command of Major General Sherman." He could not pursue and cut off Johnston's retreat towards Salisbury and Charlotte without invading my command; and so patent was his purpose to defy and violate my truce, that Mr. Stanton's publication of the fact, not even yet recalled, modified, or explained, was headed "Sherman's Truce Disregarded;" and the whole world drew but one inference,—it admits of no other. I never claimed that that truce bound Generals Halleck or Canby within the sphere of their respective commands, as defined by themselves.

It was a partial truce of very short duration, clearly within my limits and right, justified by events, and, as in the case of prisoners in my custody, or the violation of a safeguard given by me in my own territorial limits, I am bound to maintain good faith. I prefer not to change my report, but again repeat that in all future cases I am willing to be governed by the interpretation of General Grant, although I again invite his attention to the limits of my command, and those of General Halleck at the time, and the pointed phraseology of General Halleck's despatch to Mr. Stanton, wherein he reports that he had ordered his generals to pay no heed to *my orders* within the clearly defined area of my command.

I am yours,

  W. T. SHERMAN, *Major General U. S. A. Commanding.*

I now add the two letters written to Mr. Stanton at Savannah, and the despatch from Atlanta mentioned in the body of my testimony, with Mr. Lincoln's answer: —

    Headquarters Military Division of the Mississippi,
     in the Field, Savannah, January 2, 1865.

Hon. Edwin M. STANTON, Secretary of War, Washington, D. C.

Sir: I have just received from Lieutenant General Grant a copy of that part of your telegram to him of 26th December, relating to cotton, a copy of which has been immediately furnished to General Eaton, my chief quartermaster, who will be strictly governed by it.

I had already been approached by all the consuls and half the people of Savannah on this cotton question, and my invariable answer has been, that all the cotton in Savannah was prize of war, and belonged to the United States, and nobody should recover a bale of it with my consent; and that as cotton had been one of the chief causes of this war, it should help pay its expenses; that all cotton became tainted with treason from the hour the first act of hostility was committed against the United States, some time in December, 1860, and that no bill of sale subsequent to that date could convey title.

My orders were, that an officer of the quartermaster's department U. S. A. might furnish the holder, agent, or attorney a mere certificate of the fact of seizure, with description of the bales, marks, &c., the cotton then to be turned over to the agent of the treasury department, to be shipped to New York for sale; but since the receipt of your despatch I have ordered General Eaton to make the shipment himself to the quartermaster at New York, where you can dispose of it at pleasure. I do not think the treasury department ought to bother itself with the prizes or captures of war.

Mr. Barclay, former consul at New York, — representing Mr. Molyneux, former consul, but absent since a long time, — called on me in person with reference to cotton claims by English subjects. He seemed amazed when I told him I should pay no respect to consular certificates, and that in no event would I treat an English subject with more favor than one of our own deluded citizens; and that, for my part, I was unwilling to fight for cotton for the bénefit of Englishmen openly engaged in smuggling arms and munitions of war to kill us; that, on the contrary, it would afford me great satisfaction to conduct my army to Nassau, and wipe out that nest of pirates. I explained to him, however, that I was not a diplomatic agent of the general government of the United States, but that my opinion, so frankly expressed, was that of a soldier, which it would be well for him to heed. It appeared, also, that he owned a plantation on the line of investment of Savannah, which of course is destroyed, and for which he expected me to give him some certificate entitling him to indemnification, which I declined emphatically.

I have adopted, in Savannah, rules concerning property, severe, but just, founded upon the laws of nations and the practice of civilized governments, and am clearly of opinion that we should claim all the belligerent rights over conquered countries, that the people may realize the truth that war is no child's play.

I embrace in this a copy of a letter dated December 31, 1864, in answer to one from Solomon Cohen, a rich lawyer, to General Blair, his personal friend, as follows:—

"Major General F. P. BLAIR, Commanding 17th Army Corps.

"General: Your note, enclosing Mr. Cohen's of this date, I received, and I answer frankly through you his inquiries.

"1st. No one can practise law as an attorney in the United States without acknowledging the supremacy of our government. If I am not in error, an attorney is as much an officer of the court as the clerk, and it would be a novel thing in a government to have a court to administer law that denied the supremacy of the government itself.

"2d. No one will be allowed the privileges of a merchant—or, rather, to trade is a privilege which no one should seek of the government — without in like manner acknowledging its supremacy.

"3d. If Mr. Cohen remains in Savannah as a denizen, his property, real and personal, will not be disturbed, unless its temporary use be necessary for the military authorities of the city. The title to property will not be disturbed in any event, until adjudicated by the courts of the United States.

"4th. If Mr. Cohen leaves Savannah under my Special Order, No. 143, it is a public acknowledgment that he 'adheres to the enemies of the United States,' and all his property becomes forfeited to the United States. But, as a matter of favor, he will be allowed to carry with him clothing and furniture for the use of himself, family, and servants, and will be transported within the enemy's lines, but not by way of Port Royal.

"These rules will apply to all parties, and from them no exception will be made.

"I have the honor to be, general, your obedient servant,

"W. T. SHERMAN, *Major General.*"

This letter was in answer to specific inquiries. It is clear and specific, and covers all the points; and should I leave before my orders are executed, I will endeavor to impress upon my successor, General Foster, their wisdom and propriety.

I hope the course I have taken in these matters will meet your approbation, and that the president will not refund to parties claiming cotton or other property without the strongest evidence of loyalty and friendship on the part of the claimant, or unless some other positive end is to be gained.

I am, with great respect, your obedient servant,

W. T. SHERMAN, *Major General Commanding.*

Headquarters of the Military Division of the Mississippi,
in the Field, Savannah, January 19, 1865.

Hon. E. M. STANTON, Secretary of War, Washington, D. C.

Sir: When you left Savannah, a few days ago, you forgot the map which General Geary had prepared for you, showing the route by which his division entered the city of Savannah, being the first troops to occupy that city. I now send it to you. I avail myself of the opportunity also to enclose you copies of all my official orders touching trade and intercourse with the people of Georgia, as well as for the establishment of the negro settlements. Delegations of the people of Georgia continue to come, and I am satisfied that a little judicious handling, and by a little respect being paid to their prejudices, we can create a schism in Jeff Davis's dominions. All that I have conversed with realize the truth that slavery, as an institution, is defunct; and the only questions that remain are, what disposition shall be made of the negroes themselves. I confess myself unable to offer a complete solution of these questions, and prefer to leave it to the slower operations of time. We have given the initiative, and can afford to wait the working of the experiment.

As to trade matters, I also think it is to our interest to keep the people somewhat dependent on the articles of commerce to which they have been hitherto accustomed. General Grover is now here, and will, I think, be able to manage this matter judiciously, and may gradually relax, and invite cotton to come in in large quantities.

But at first we should manifest no undue anxiety on that score, for the rebels would at once make use of it as a power against us. We should assume a tone of perfect contempt for cotton and everything else in comparison with the great object of the war — the restoration of the Union, with all its rights and power. If the rebels burn cotton as a war measure, they simply play into our hands, by taking away the only product of value they now have to exchange in foreign ports for war ships and munitions. By such a course, also, they alienate the feelings of the large class of small farmers that look to their little parcels of cotton to exchange for food and clothing for their families. I hope the government will not manifest too much anxiety to obtain cotton in large quantities, and, especially, that the president will not indorse the contracts for the purchase of large quantities of cotton. Several contracts, involving from six to ten thousand bales, indorsed by Mr. Lincoln, have been shown me, but were not in such a form as to amount to an order for me to facilitate their execution.

As to the treasury trade agents, and agents to take charge of confiscated and abandoned property, whose salaries depend on their fees, I can only say that, as a general rule, they are mischievous and disturbing elements to a military government, and it is almost impossible for us to study the law and regulations so as to understand fully their powers and duties. I rather think the quartermaster's department of the army could better fulfil all their duties, and accomplish all that is aimed at by the law. Yet, on this subject, I will leave Generals Foster and Grover to do the best they can.

I am, with great respect, your obedient servant,

W. T. SHERMAN, *Major General Commanding.*

Headquarters of the Middle Division of the Mississippi,
in the Field, Atlanta, Georgia, September 15, 1864.

Major General HALLECK, Washington, D. C.

My report is done, and will be forwarded as soon as I get a few more of the subordinate reports. I am awaiting a courier from General Grant. All well, and troops in fine, healthy camps, and supplies coming forward finely. Governor Brown has disbanded his militia to gather the corn and sorghum of the state. I have reason to believe that he and Stephens want to visit me, and I have sent them a hearty invitation. I will exchange two thousand prisoners with Hood, but no more.

W. T. SHERMAN, *Major General Commanding.*

WASHINGTON, D. C., September 17, 1864 — 10 A. M.

MAJOR GENERAL SHERMAN: I feel great interest in the subjects of your despatch mentioning corn and sorghum, and contemplated a visit to you.

A. LINCOLN, *President United States.*

I have not possession here of all my official records, most of which are out west; and I have selected the above from my more recent letter-books, and offer them to show how prompt and full have been my official reports, and how unnecessary was all the clamor made touching my action and opinions at the time the basis of agreement of April 18 was submitted to the president.

All of which is most respectfully submitted.

W. T. SHERMAN, *Major General United States Army.*

V.

SPEECH OF GENERAL SHERMAN AT ST. LOUIS.

I feel to-night more than usually honored, for I am in the presence of many with whom I have been associated in years gone by in business, and in the social circle, and in public affairs. To receive the warm commendations I have just heard from the gentleman preceding me affords me the greatest pleasure; and I would I were as gifted as my friend who has just taken his seat, so that I might interest you. I would travel all over the world to find topics to suit the occasion. Gladly would I talk of Greece and Rome (but I fear they are gone by); or, better still, point to the history of our own great country, that is teeming with recollections — recollections that to me are doubly, trebly dear, from associations; to the history of the Spaniard on the lone river; or, still more, to old Colonel Bonneville, who is yet living among you, and whom I saw yesterday. But the world sweeps on, and I will not pause. And I see, by the paper before me, that you bring me before you as an actor in the scenes just passed, and classify me as one of those men who have simply wafted our country past a dangerous abyss, and placed it on a firm ground, where it may sally forth again on a new career of prosperity and glory. (Cheers.) I admit that the four past years seem even to me a dream now; I can hardly realize the part I have taken, although step by step rises up when my memory retraces them; but yet it seems as a dream that men reared under our laws — men who were enjoying the prosperity which they themselves admitted never was surpassed — should rise up in rebellion against the land and government of Washington. It seems to me an impossibility; yet it was a possibility; but it is now past, thank God. (Cheers.) We have a right, as citizens and historians, to cast our eyes and memory back, and see if, in the past events, we can learn lessons — lessons of wisdom — that will make us better men, better citizens, and better patriots in the future; and if I can trace anything in the past, calculated to effect this object, I will account myself repaid. Here, in St. Louis, probably, began the great centre movement which terminated the war; a battle-field such as never before was seen, extending from ocean to ocean almost with the right wing and the left wing; and from the centre here, I remember one evening, up in the old Planters' House, sitting with General Halleck and General Cullum, and we were talking about this, that, and the other. A map was on the table, and I was explaining the position of the troops of the enemy in Kentucky when I came to this state. General Halleck knew well the position here, and I remember well the question he asked me — the question of the school teacher to his child — "Sherman, here is the line; how will you break that line?" "Physically, by a perpendicular force." "Where is the perpendicular?" "The line of the Tennessee River." General Halleck is the author of that first beginning, and I give him credit for it with pleasure. (Cheers.) Laying down his pencil upon the map, he said, "There is the line, and we must take it."

The capture of the fort on the Tennessee River by the troops led by Grant followed. (Cheers.) These were the grand strategic features of that first movement, and it succeeded perfectly. General Halleck's plan went farther — not to stop at his first line, which ran through Columbus, Bowling Green, crossing the river at Henry and Donelson, but to push on to the second line, which ran through Memphis and Charleston; but troubles intervened at Nashville, and delays followed; opposition to the last movement was made, and I myself was brought an actor on the scene. I remember our ascent on the Tennessee River. I have seen to-night captains of steamboats who first went with us there. Storms came, and we did not reach the point we desired. At that time, General C. F. Smith was in command. He was a man indeed. All the old officers remember him as a gallant and elegant officer; and had he lived, probably some of us younger fellows would not have attained our present positions. But that is now past. We followed line — the second line — and then came the landing of forces at Pittsburg Landing. Whether it was a mistake in landing them on the west instead of the east bank, it is not necessary now to discuss. I think it was not a mistake. There was gathered the first great army of the west; commencing with only twelve thousand, then twenty, then thirty thousand; and we had about thirty-eight thousand in that battle; and all I claim for that is, that it was a contest for manhood; there was no strategy. Grant was there, and others of us, all young at that time, and unknown men; but our enemy was old; and Sidney Johnson, whom all the officers remembered as a power among the old officers, high above Grant, myself, or anybody else, led the enemy on that battle-field, and I almost wonder how we conquered. But, as I remarked, it was a contest for manhood — man to man, soldier to soldier. We fought, and we held our ground; and therefore accounted ourselves victorious. (Cheers.)

From that time forward we had with us the prestige. That battle was worth millions and millions to us by reason of the fact of the courage displayed by the brave soldiers on that occasion. And from that time to this I never heard of the first want of courage on the part of our northern soldiers. (Cheers.) It then became a game of grand war. Armies were accounted equal, and skill and generalship came into play. We gained thereby the movement on Corinth which Halleck designed here. There his command ceased, and a new shuffle of the cards of war was made. Halleck went to the east and Grant to the west; but summer overtook us with heat, and we could not march. Northern Mississippi was dry as ashes. It was impossible for men to live and march from stream to stream; and to follow the roads that lie between these, men would have perished with thirst, been overcome by heat. Therefore we delayed until fall; and late that fall I met Grant, by appointment, at Columbus; and there again we went over the map, and the next thing was to break the line on the Tallahatchie.

Many of you here remember that movement. You citizens do not understand it at all, for I have never yet seen a newspaper account of it that approximates to the truth. (Laughter.) Pemberton commanded the army of the Confederacy in our front. We had superior numbers. Our men were scattered, and we first concentrated on the Tallahatchie, below Holly Springs. Grant moved direct on Pemberton, while I moved from Memphis, and struck directly into Grenada; and the first thing that Pemberton knew, the depot of his supplies was almost in the grasp of a small cavalry force; and he fell into confusion, and gave us the Tallahatchie without a battle.

But with some people an object gained without a battle is nothing. But war means success by any and every means; it is not fighting alone. Bulls do that, and bears, and all beasts; but men attain objects by intellect, and the introduction of physical power, moved upon salient points. And so we gained the Tallahatchie, and although hardly a gun was fired, yet we gained a battle equal in its results to any other battle on earth. (Cheers.) It gave us uninterrupted possession of Northern Mississippi, and undisputed possession of the resources of that country; and that country has been in our possession ever since, in a military sense. Then came the great campaign of your river, upon which you and I and all of us were more deeply interested than in any other that can ever be developed by any war on this continent.

The possession of the Mississippi River is the possession of America (cheers); and I say that, had the southern Confederacy (call it by what name you may)—had that power represented by the southern

Confederacy held with a grip sufficiently strong the lower part of the Mississippi River, we would have been a subjugated people, and they would have dictated to us if we had given up the possession of the Lower Mississippi. It was vital to us, and we fought for it and won it. We determined to have it; but we could not go down with our frail boats past the batteries of Vicksburg. It was a physical impossibility. Therefore, what was to be done? After the Tallahatchie line was carried, Vicksburg was the next point. I went with a small and hastily collected force, and repeatedly endeavored to make a lodgment on the bluff between Vicksburg and Haines's Bluff, while General Grant moved with his main army so as to place himself on the high plateau behind Vicksburg; but "man proposes and God disposes," and we failed on that occasion. I then gathered my hastily collected force, and went down farther; and then, for the first time, I took General Blair and his brigade under my command.

On the very day I had agreed to be there I was there, and we swung our flanks around, and the present governor of Missouri fell a prisoner to the enemy on that day. We failed. I waited anxiously for a coöperating force inland and below us, but they did not come; and after I had made the assault, I learned that the depot at Holly Springs had been broken up, and that General Grant had sent me word not to attempt it. But it was too late. Nevertheless, although we were unable to carry it at first, there were other things to be done. The war covered such a vast area, there was plenty to do. I thought of that affair at Arkansas Post, although others claim it, and they may have it if they want it. We cleaned them out there, and General Grant then brought his whole army to Vicksburg; and you in St. Louis remember well that long winter, how we were on the levee, with the water rising and drowning us like muskrats; how we were seeking channels through Deer Creek and Yazoo Pass, and how we finally cut a canal across the Peninsula in front of Vicksburg.

But all that time the true movement was the original movement, and everything not approximating to it came nearer the truth. But we could not make a retrograde movement. Why? Because your people of the north were too noisy. We could not take any step backwards, and for that reason we were forced to run the batteries at Vicksburg, and make a lodgment on the ridges on some of the bluffs below Vicksburg. It is said I protested against it. It is folly. I never protested in my life — never. (Laughter.) On the contrary, General Grant rested on me probably more responsibility even than any other commander under him; for he wrote to me, "I want you to move upon Haines's Bluff, to enable me to pass the next fort below — Grand Gulf. I hate to ask you, because the fervor of the north will accuse you of being rebellious again." (Laughter.) I love Grant for his kindness. I did make the feint on Haines's Bluff, and by that means Grant ran the blockade easily to Grand Gulf, and made a lodgment down there, and got his army up on the high plateau in the rear of Vicksburg, while you people here were beguiled into the belief that Sherman was again repulsed. But we did not repose confidence in everybody. Then followed the movement on Jackson, and the 4th of July placed us in possession of that great stronghold, Vicksburg; and then, as Mr. Lincoln said, "the Mississippi went unvexed to the sea."

From that day to this, this war has been virtually and properly settled. It was a certainty then. They would have said, "We give up;" but Davis would not ratify it, and he had them under good discipline, and therefore it was necessary to fight again. Then came the affair of Chickamauga. The army of the Mississippi lying along its banks were called into a new field of action, and so one morning early I got orders to go to Chattanooga. I did not know where it was, hardly. (Laughter.) I did not know the road to go there. But I found it, and got there in time (laughter and cheers); and although my men were shoeless, and the cold and bitter frosts of winter were upon us, yet I must still go to Knoxville, thirteen miles farther, to relieve Burnside. That march we made. (A voice — And you got there in time.) Then winter forced us to lie quiet. During that winter I took a little exercise down the river; but that is of no account.

www.ingramcontent.com/pod-product-compliance
Lightning Source LLC
Chambersburg PA
CBHW020541300426
44111CB00008B/753